Modern Design

A COMPLETE
SOURCEBOOK

Mid-Century Modern Design

A COMPLETE SOURCEBOOK

DOMINIC BRADBURY

WITH OVER 1,000 ILLUSTRATIONS

TO NOAH

NOTE TO THE READER

Names that appear in CAPITAL LETTERS indicate
cross-references to main entries in the book
(pp. 26–501).

Names that appear with asterisks* indicate cross-
references to entries in the A-Z section (pp. 504-534).

PAGE 1 A selection of mid-century lighting fixtures
by Le Klint.

PAGE 2 Forest pattern gift wrap, with graphic design
by Charley Harper for Associated American Artists
of New York, 1953.

OPPOSITE Side chairs designed by Harry Bertoia
for Knoll, USA, 1952.

First published in the United Kingdom in 2014
as *Mid-Century Modern Complete* by Thames &
Hudson Ltd, 181A High Holborn, London WC1V 7QX

First published in the United States of America in 2014
as *Mid-Century Modern Complete* by Abrams

This compact paperback edition published in 2020
in the United Kingdom by Thames & Hudson Ltd,
London, and in the United States of America by
Thames & Hudson Inc., 500 Fifth Avenue, New York,
New York 10110

Reprinted 2024

Mid-Century Modern Design © 2014 and 2020
Dominic Bradbury
Design and layout © 2014 and 2020
Thames & Hudson Ltd, London

For illustration credits, see page 539

Designed by Karolina Prymaka

'Mid-Century Product Design in Germany' translated
from the German by Nicole Linhardt-Rich

British Library Cataloguing-in-Publication Data
A catalogue record for this book is available from
the British Library

Library of Congress Control Number 2020931518

ISBN 978-0-500-02347-1

Printed and bound in China by C&C Offset
Printing Co. Ltd

Be the first to know about our new releases,
exclusive content and author events by visiting
thamesandhudson.com
thamesandhudsonusa.com
thamesandhudson.com.au

CONTENTS

INTRODUCTION

The mid-century period was an age of dreams and optimism. In the post-war years, after all the chaos and crisis of a global conflict, the world began to rebuild and rethink itself. It was an era of hope, when many asserted their claims to freedom and gave voice to their ambitions, looking for new beginnings and possibilities. The 1950s and '60s were all about 'making it new', about laying claim to the future. For designers and architects, especially, it was an extraordinary time to be at work, and the opportunities for creativity and originality were widespread and welcome.

The twin fuels of rapid growth, particularly in the West, were the vast reconstruction effort underway in Europe – underwritten by the American Marshall Plan – and the vast spending power of the American people. These gave rise to an unprecedented consumer age; a sustained era of golden growth that spurred demand for a whole new spectrum of goods, products and services, which the world of design was happy to provide. In many respects, the patterns and expectations of American and Western consumers in the mid-century period laid down the template for modern living itself and formed a foundation for our own lifestyles in the 21st century.

In Europe, countries such as Britain, France, Germany and Russia had paid a terrible price during the war years in every respect. The post-war years saw the unravelling of the European colonial support network, as dependent countries sought their independence, and large swathes of many European cities – from Coventry to Caen to Cologne – had suffered appalling damage, not to mention the human cost. It would take many years for these countries to emerge from austerity, and in Britain the rationing of some foods and materials continued right up until 1954. But after the horrors and upheaval of the war years, the sense of relief in 1945 cannot be underestimated.

Reconstruction, in itself, offered a chance for a fresh start and a significant spur to European economies, as well as to their designers and architects. The efficient wartime production lines of Europe and America could now be adapted to make cars and bicycles, tractors and trains, toasters and kettles. The gradual rebuilding of London, Berlin and other towns and cities was an enormous undertaking and brought work and employment to thousands. Coventry Cathedral – famously devastated in a 1940 firestorm and rebuilt from 1956 to 1962 – became a post-war symbol of regeneration within a design by architect BASIL SPENCE that preserved the ruins of the original building while creating a bold, new structure that rose out of the ashes.

The revitalization of the German and Japanese economies in the post-war period was, in particular, an extraordinary success story. Having learnt the lessons of a humiliating German surrender and its ultimate consequences back in 1918, and wanting to boost Germany and Japan as stable bulwarks against the might of the USSR as the Cold War got underway, the Allies – especially the Americans – were eager to rebuild the two countries as effectively as they could. Aid and support programmes helped jump-start the design and manufacturing industries in both countries, to the point that German car manufacturing soon became hugely successful, while the Japanese economy was growing at just over 10% a year by the 1960s and by the early 1970s was the third largest economy in the world.

It was in America, however, that the consumer revolution really gathered pace in the post-war years. America had also paid a heavy price during the war years, but – for the most part – the war had not been fought on American soil. Its manufacturing base was not just intact but finely tuned after its wartime footing of maximum capacity. The US design and manufacturing industry was ready to take advantage of all kinds of innovations developed or perfected during the war years, from plywood through to jet engines.

Most importantly, the American consumer had never had it so good. They had money in their pockets, even after the war years, and those pockets began to bulge in the boom times of the 1950s and '60s, when America was busily exporting its products and expertise

BELOW Coventry Cathedral under reconstruction, to a design by Basil Spence, 1962.

ABOVE Screenprint from an advertisement of 1955, showing a Pan American Airways pilot greeting a mother and her three children as they board an international flight.

around the globe. With the Americans, more than any of the other Allies, it really was a case of 'to the victor the spoils', as the American public unleashed an almost insatiable demand for everything from dinnerware to international travel.

The American consumer offered the catalyst for a massive expansion in the world of design. This not only took the form of houses, interiors, textiles and home products but also 'big ticket' items like refrigerators and automobiles. Designers and manufacturers eagerly answered the call of the consumer to 'make it new'. The car industry famously developed the notion of the 'annual upgrade' – adding new styling and trims to what was often, essentially, the very same car so as to encourage another trade-in purchase.

A whole new sector of design really came into its own in the 1950s, working alongside some key partners. This was graphic design, which began producing the logos, branding and advertising posters for a fast-growing corporate culture. The first Burger King opened in 1954, and McDonald's a year later. They – and their counterparts in fields such as the hotel sector or airline industry – needed instantly recognizable logos and a strong corporate identity. The graphics departments worked with the advertising gurus and the marketing men ... and women. The whole world of marketing took off, along with consumer culture, the throw-away society, big business and global corporations. Issues of image, identity

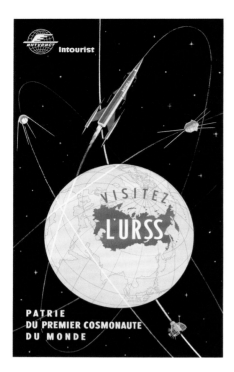

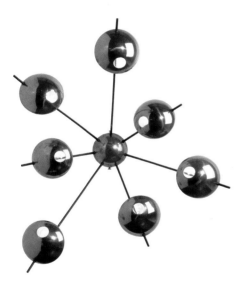

TOP A colour litho poster advertising travel to the USSR, Russian School, c. 1955.

ABOVE A wall light in brass and enamelled metal by Stilnovo, Italy, c. 1950.

and styling had never been so crucial. A corporate logo was not just a badge on the front of a car, a piece of clothing or the outside of a hotel building. It was a symbol, and full of symbolic meaning. And, above all, it needed to be modern.

The very idea of modernity was transformed in the mid-century period. Notions of the contemporary and visions of the future helped shape design throughout the 1950s and '60s. It is true, of course, that modernism had established itself back in the 1920s and '30s when pioneers such as Le Corbusier*, Auguste Perret, Rudolph Schindler, Frank Lloyd Wright* and others laid the foundation stones of the modern movement.

The war years introduced the world – dramatically and frighteningly – to atomic energy and jet engines, as well as other innovations such as radar. By the 1940s, then, we had entered the atomic age. By the early 1950s, the first commercial jet airliner – the De Havilland Comet – had been introduced and the F-100, the first supersonic fighter jet, made its appearance in 1953, the same year that Edmund Hillary conquered Everest. The first commercial computers, nuclear-powered submarines and pocket transistor radios were all introduced in the early 1950s, along with polio vaccines and the four-minute mile, courtesy of Roger Bannister.

If that wasn't enough to take in, during 1957 the USA and the USSR test-fired their first intercontinental ballistic missiles, and the space race began in earnest as the Russians launched Sputnik 1. Four years later Yuri Gagarin was the first man in space, on board Vostok 1, and in 1969 Apollo 11 made the first landing on the moon – an achievement that still seems almost magical from today's perspective.

It was an age of ages – the atomic age, the space age, the jet age, the computer age, with the first commercially produced computers introduced in 1951 and IBM pioneering the first computer data storage discs in 1956, while the microchip followed a year later. There were nuclear power stations, hovercraft, electric watches, transatlantic television pictures, miniskirts, the Pill, James Bond films and the inaugural Super Bowl. The pace of change was dazzling, even by today's standards.

For designers, fast-developing technologies and manufacturing methods meant adapting quickly and making the most of new opportunities to create a whole new generation of products. Designers such as CHARLES & RAY EAMES and ARNE JACOBSEN made the most of fresh materials such as plywood in their furniture, while VERNER PANTON, Olivier Mourgue* and PIERRE PAULIN explored plastics. DIETER RAMS at Braun* was one of the leading product designers to respond to the electronic age, designing calculators, hi-fi systems and radios that were sleek, compact, functional and logical. Philips* in the Netherlands and Sony* in Japan also pioneered products and appliances that were more alluring than ever but also portable. By the end of the 1950s Sony had even launched a portable television. The future had arrived.

Many of these new technological developments were mirrored by another key trend of the mid-century period – the move towards internationalism, or, as Marshall McLuhan put it, the rise of the 'global village'. The spread of television, film, music and information technology to a global level helped spur the invention and design of a new fleet of products to help bring all of this content into our homes and offices. At the same time, multinational companies – from Hilton to Honda, from Pan Am to Piaggio – were spreading their wings around the planet.

In 1959, Boeing introduced the first 707 airliner and transatlantic flight times were cut down to eight hours, and by 1960 passengers were clocking up a collective 74 billion air miles. Car, scooter and motorbike ownership also shot up, vastly increasing personal mobility. By 1970 transatlantic fibre-optic cables opened the way for direct dial calls across the ocean. People and ideas, then, were travelling faster than ever, and products – from furniture to freezers – were being shipped overseas like never before. It was easier

than ever to transmit ideas, designs and products from one place to another, opening up an even greater world of opportunity for designers, who began to become brand names in themselves.

RAYMOND LOEWY, EERO SAARINEN, DAVID HICKS and Arne Jacobsen became figureheads of design, jumping on board the new breed of jumbo jets and taking their work overseas. Others, such as RUSSEL WRIGHT, JOE COLOMBO, ROBIN & LUCIENNE DAY and Charles & Ray Eames actively used the media and marketing tools to present an image of themselves to the world, becoming well-known faces in design magazines and newspapers.

Out there in the global village, ideas spread like viruses. We are now used to the notion of an idea or an image going 'viral', but the new media, technology and products of the mid-century period made the concept a reality for the first time. Around the world, people fought for their rights and freedoms, helped by national and international movements with multiple contacts and connections.

Independence movements in European colonial territories exploded into activity and newly independent states were often used as proxies by the sparring Cold War superpowers. But this was also a busy time for civil rights activists, feminists and idealists of all kinds. Everywhere, people were seeing their chance and seizing their moment and were able to spread their message more effectively than ever. Multiple conflicts rose and raged around the world, but none could be as destructive as the world war that had ended in 1945. This was still an age of optimism and liberation.

Liberation expressed itself in many different ways, of course. There was political liberation, but also social and sexual liberation. New cultural movements echoed social change, from rock 'n' roll to flower power to Pop Art. This was also the age of festivals and expos that celebrated modernity in their different ways, from the Festival of Britain* in 1951 to Woodstock in 1969. In some ways, at least, the world had never had it so good.

Along with cultural revolution came design revolution. America had received a particular gift in the form of some of the greatest and most inventive minds of a generation, who had fled to the States in the run-up to World War II or emigrated some years before. They included many scientists and academics, but also a whole host of architects and designers, such as Walter Gropius*, MARCEL BREUER, LUDWIG MIES VAN DER ROHE, JENS RISOM and RICHARD NEUTRA. All had been born and largely educated in Europe, but were now working and teaching in America. Eliel Saarinen* co-founded the Cranbrook Academy of Art*, which became a leading centre for modern design. Breuer and Gropius taught at Harvard University, as well as practising architecture and design.

These pioneering thinkers and creative personalities also collaborated – in many instances – with progressive furniture companies like Knoll* and Herman Miller*. Such companies also encouraged innovation and research with new materials. Jens Risom used army stock webbing for his first line of chairs for Knoll, while HARRY BERTOIA's experiments with latticed steel rod furniture – also with Knoll – were highly successful.

America, in the 1950s, seemed like the country of the future and the concept of the American Dream still held great sway. Architects such as JOHN LAUTNER, CRAIG ELLWOOD and PHILIP JOHNSON helped develop a new kind of home that was fluid and free, with open-plan living spaces and a constant sense of connection to the great outdoors. These were dream homes that were to prove highly influential and were captured in evocative images by the likes of Julius Shulman*, which made them seem all the more glamorous and seductive. The furniture, too, was modern and fresh. It was as though the world we lived in was being reinvented.

While America was a natural centre point in the design world in the 1950s and '60s, there was – of course – plenty going on in other parts of the world. Regional modernist architects and designers were also establishing international reputations, including OSCAR

NIEMEYER in Brazil, Luis Barragán* in Mexico and HARRY SEIDLER in Australia. The French and Italian design scenes remained strong, and product and industrial design in Germany and Japan were developing fast.

Scandinavia was also a focal point for what some might call 'soft modernism'. Here the emphasis was on craftsmanship, detailing and organic materials, whether in architecture and interiors by ALVAR AALTO or Arne Jacobsen, or exquisitely designed and made furniture by HANS WEGNER or Børge Mogensen*. The craft tradition still held out in places, even if the spotlight was gradually shifting to new materials – especially plastics – and methods of mass production.

ABOVE Roulette wool carpet designed by Verner Panton and produced by Unika Vaev, Denmark, c. 1965.

RIGHT PK0 chair in lacquered plywood, designed by Poul Kjærholm for Fritz Hansen, 1952.

LEFT Wishbone armchair, designed by Hans Wegner in lacquered wood and rope for Carl Hansen, 1950.

ABOVE Tongue chair by Pierre Paulin, stretch jersey over tubular steel, produced by Artifort, 1967.

By the 1960s, space age futurism had infused the design world. Shapes were rounded, streamlined and sensual, while the colours were bold and even garish. Furnishings by EERO AARNIO, Pierre Paulin, Verner Panton and Luigi Colani* had the look of abstract Pop Art sculptures. Houses by CHARLES DEATON, John Lautner and others also had something of a space-ship, sci-fi look, and Deaton's Sculptured House in Colorado featured in Woody Allen's futuristic comedy, *Sleeper*, in 1973. Patterns were vibrant and warm, with MARIMEKKO's in particular helping to define the period.

The world of mid-century design both mirrored the rapid changes in 1950s and '60s society and helped in making them possible, as it worked to give shape and identity to a new kind of lifestyle and a new wave of consumer products. For many, the interiors, architecture and furniture of the period still feel fresh, modern and inspirational. Owning a Hans Wegner or Eames chair remains a symbol of enlightened patronage from someone who appreciates modern design. Countless pieces of furniture from the period have attained iconic status and become 20th-century classics, with the originals much in demand for collectors and many now back in production. Mid-century glass and ceramics also enjoy a powerful reputation.

More than anything, the spirit of mid-century design can be characterized as pioneering. It was a time in which so much of the way we live now – and the products we use – was really shaped, from inside/outside living to open plans, modular furniture, plastic products and gadget miniaturization. It is hard to imagine Apple's iPods and other products without the innovative work of Dieter Rams and Sony. It is hard to imagine contemporary architecture without the lessons of Mies van der Rohe and his contemporaries. The world of today, you might say, was born in the 1950s and '60s.

MEDIA
AND
MASTERS

FURNITURE

THE REALITY OF THE CLOSE BOND BETWEEN FURNITURE DESIGN AND ART IS SUGGESTED BY THE NUMBER OF DESIGNERS WHO WORKED ACROSS THE TWO SPHERES

Among the key characteristics of mid-century modern furniture, one of the most fascinating is the close synergy to be found between the worlds of art and design. It is a relationship with a long history, yet during the post-war period furniture design became increasingly sculptural in quality, infused with a sense of artistic ambition and drawing inspiration from the art world. Later, in the 1960s, during an era of abstraction, furniture also became more abstract in nature and more surreal, while borrowing many of the vibrant, playful colours seen in the Pop Art movement.

The reality of the close bond between furniture design and art is suggested by the number of designers who worked across the two spheres. American designer Paul McCobb* trained as a fine artist, while Erwine and Estelle Laverne* were both painters. Wharton Esherick* was a sculptor, craftsman and furniture maker, and ISAMU NOGUCHI (see under 'Lighting') was a highly respected sculptor, as well as a furniture and lighting designer, who studied sculpture and worked for a time as an assistant to Constantin Brancusi. JOAQUIM TENREIRO, in Brazil, was also a much-lauded sculptor and painter as well as a designer. In addition, there was HARRY BERTOIA, who invented one of the great classics of 20th-century design, the Diamond chair, the success of which helped fund his move towards concentrating directly on sculpture and art, often in ambitious, experimental and abstract forms.

By the 1950s, the character of mid-century furniture in general was increasingly sinuous and fluid, with tapered legs, smooth finishes and crafted forms. CARLO MOLLINO, GIO PONTI and others explored organic, sensual shapes and biomorphic creations. Chairs, armchairs and loungers became more ergonomic than ever and more inviting, but also exhibited the curves, craftsmanship and artistry of a gallery exhibit.

For some, including Esherick, their work was closely related to craft as well as art. A number of key mid-century designers came out of a craft and cabinet-making tradition, and spliced this with a deep understanding of contemporary aesthetics, as well as inspiration – in some cases – from other craft traditions, particularly in Japan and China.

In Denmark, HANS WEGNER emerged from a well-established cabinet-making culture and secured a global reputation with timber furniture that was not only beautifully designed but also expertly crafted and detailed. Wegner and POUL KJÆRHOLM were key figures in the evolution of soft modernism, with a Scandinavian sensibility. In America, Japanese-American designer GEORGE NAKASHIMA appropriated a dual craft heritage from East and West, and created some of the most original and highly organic furniture of the period, mostly made in his own workshops. Nakashima always preferred to call himself a 'woodworker' rather than a designer.

Along with art and craft, the other great influence on mid-century furniture design was architecture. Many of the most respected furniture designers of the 1950s and '60s were either also working as architects or had studied architecture, including ALVAR AALTO (see under 'Houses and Interiors'), ARNE JACOBSEN, EERO SAARINEN, CHARLES EAMES, Carlo Mollino, Gio Ponti and others.

For some, such as Aalto, Jacobsen, Ponti and Mollino, many of their furniture designs actually evolved out of specific architectural and interiors projects, where the remit extended into a total design concept, down to the seating and even the door handles. But all of these architect-designers brought a particular sensibility to their furniture – not only an understanding of how it might work within an architectural and spatial context, but also a special appreciation of materials, engineering and form. Furniture was one facet of a broader fascination with design in its widest sense, which perhaps helps to explain why so many of these architect-designed pieces have a natural synergy with modernist living spaces.

LEFT Model 5569 Coconut chairs, designed by George Nelson for Knoll, 1955, with steel and aluminium frames and upholstered seats.

THE USE OF NEW MATERIALS AND NEW MANUFACTURING METHODS CLEARLY SET MID-CENTURY FURNITURE WELL APART FROM ITS PRE-WAR COUSINS

Architects, especially, were easily tempted by the possibilities offered by many of the new materials being developed in the post-war period, which also played a pivotal role in shaping the identity of mid-century furniture design. Eames, Jacobsen, Kjærholm, Mollino and others explored in full the opportunities presented by plywood, which was pliable enough to be sculpted into ergonomic and sculptural forms but strong enough to be robust and long-lasting.

Charles and Ray Eames, working with Bertoia, began exploring plywood during the years of World War II, famously developing a plywood leg splint that was lightweight, strong and stackable, and could be put to good use by the American military. They also pioneered the use of fibreglass, employing it for a fresh and innovative range of chairs that are still much in demand today.

The use of new materials and new manufacturing methods clearly set mid-century furniture well apart from its pre-war cousins. The 1940s in Europe was still an age of austerity and utility, in which many designers had to use any available materials in the best way possible. ERNEST RACE developed his BA chair with recycled scrap aluminium; in the States, JENS RISOM used army surplus webbing for the seat of his iconic WSP chair.

By the 1950s, however, materials were more widely available and new mass-manufacturing techniques developed rapidly, while a forward-thinking generation of furniture companies – Knoll*, Herman Miller*, Fritz Hansen*, Vitra*, Cassina*, etc. – were busily commissioning unique new designs.

BELOW A feature on the giants of mid-century furniture design: George Nelson, Edward Wormley, Eero Saarinen, Harry Bertoia, Charles Eames and Jens Risom, photographed by Martin Koner for the July 1961 edition of *Playboy* magazine.

GEORGE NELSON
serving cart

EDWARD WORMLEY
"a" chair

EERO SAARINEN
womb chair

HARRY BERTOIA
diamond chair

CHARLES EAMES
eames chair

JENS RISOM
open armchair

decor BY JOHN ANDERSON

PHOTOGRAPHED ESPECIALLY FOR PLAYBOY BY MARVIN KONER AND DANIEL RUBIN

DESIGNS FOR LIVING
unfettered by dogma, the creators of contemporary american furniture
have a flair for combining functionalism with esthetic enjoyment

Bertoia, WARREN PLATNER and others worked with lattices of woven steel wire to create a new class of light, flexible and super-strong furniture that – unlike ply – had the added advantage of allowing light to pass through it and assumed a gentle, modest presence in a space. In Scandinavia, Kjærholm also experimented with metals and took them in a new direction, giving his steel chair frames a precise, crafted and delicate quality, often teamed with natural materials, such as leather.

But a more profound revolution was coming fast in the shape of plastics, which really came into their own in the 1960s and largely defined the identity of that decade's furniture design, as well as turning the entire world of product design and packaging upside down. Fibreglass – or glass-reinforced plastic, using polyester or epoxy – was only one aspect of the plastics revolution. Injection-moulding techniques using thermoplastics made possible ROBIN DAY's infamous Polyprop chair, which could be mass-produced at low cost and was light, durable and stackable. VERNER PANTON, working with Vitra, developed the Panton chair in the late 1960s – an injection-moulded plastic chair in one single piece, forming a sculpted S-shape, available in bright Pop colours. EERO AARNIO's Ball and Bubble chairs of the 1960s were like rooms within a room – delightful plastic cocoons.

Other contemporaries, including PIERRE PAULIN and JOE COLOMBO, used the new plastics to develop ambitious seating systems, experimenting with foam and upholstered finishes to create designs that were increasingly abstract and futuristic. This was the design of the Space Age, expressed in the most radical of materials.

The design also remained highly sculptural. During the late 1960s and early 1970s, furniture by Paulin, Olivier Mourgue*, Gaetano Pesce*, Luigi Colani* and others stopped resembling seating in any traditional sense and became moulded artworks, exuberant sculptures and exotic playthings.

It is hard to overplay the importance of mid-century furniture design and its lasting legacy. So many of the chairs, seats and tables of the period still feel contemporary and fresh, continuing to sell in vast numbers. For many, pieces by Saarinen, Wegner and others still sum up a vision of sophisticated modernity. The prototypes and early issues of the pioneering figures of the 1950s and '60s, meanwhile, are fiercely sought after by collectors. These pieces have now assumed the iconic status of artworks in themselves.

TOP LEFT An advertising poster for Knoll furniture, designed by Herbert Matter, featuring a Model 72 chair by Eero Saarinen.

ABOVE LEFT Eero Saarinen's Tulip chair for Knoll, 1956, made with fibreglass and enamelled aluminium.

LEFT Model 42 low-back cantilevered armchair, designed by Alvar Aalto in birch and beech, c. 1932.

RIGHT Rudder dining table, Model IN-20, by Isamu Noguchi for Herman Miller, 1944, in lacquered birch and steel.

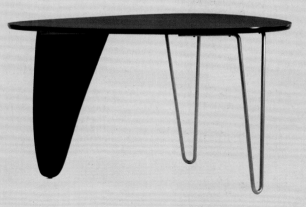

COLLECTING MID-CENTURY DESIGN
RICHARD WRIGHT

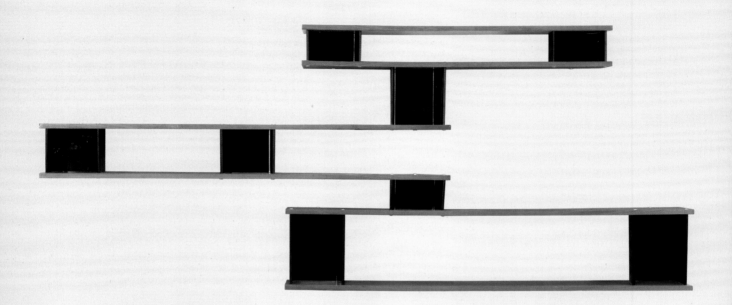

Design at mid-century represents a Golden Age. It marks a beginning where the possibilities of design go beyond the utopian dreams of earlier periods to become a mass movement encompassing optimism and opportunities for the future. Mid-century marks the start of the broad dissemination of design – a process still actively playing out today as design touches every facet of our lives. Mid-century design is a great field for collecting, as it is historically important, well documented and still widely accessible. First-rate examples of iconic designs are still being introduced to the market and new discoveries within the field are still being made.

When collecting mid-century design, it is important to buy what you love. Great collections exhibit the passion of their collectors. There is no reason to buy things you do not love (even if they are by an important designer). Furthermore, by buying items you are passionate about you can ensure satisfaction with your purchases. Make educated acquisitions by learning before you buy. This is my best advice: 'The more I know, the more I see.' When you educate your eye, you really do see things differently and appreciate the work more. So study the period and the materials. This will guide you in making better choices and will add to the overall experience of collecting. Finally, buy the best that you can afford. While quirky, unsung oddities from the past may appeal, the bulk of any collection should be focused on the best quality examples that you can find. I try to collect only in areas where I can afford to buy the best. For me this means collecting works by CHARLES & RAY EAMES and not JEAN PROUVÉ, but there are many levels in between.

Begin by working with the top professionals in the field of design. Auction houses, dealers, museums and artist foundations are all resources that can help you make informed

OPPOSITE Nuage
Bibliothèque, designed by
Charlotte Perriand, c. 1956,
made by Ateliers Jean Prouvé
for Galerie Steph Simon,
in ash, enamelled steel and
aluminium.

BELOW LEFT A 1957 Marcoule
banquette from the Centre
de Réadaptation Fonctionnelle,
Nancy, by Jean Prouvé, in
enamelled steel and leather.

BELOW RIGHT Frenchman's
Cove table by George
Nakashima, c. 1968, in Persian
walnut and rosewood.

decisions. Remember to ask questions – seemingly basic advice but too often ignored, as new collectors may not wish to appear to be novices, or some collectors may think they already know the answers.

Auction houses are an under-utilized resource. They have handled thousands of items and are familiar with the nuances of many designs as well as the variations within a designer's body of work. In addition, the top auction houses sell works with a guarantee: they have market specialists and researchers who vet the items on offer and ensure their authenticity. Often auction houses have specific information to share and more details than they publish in their catalogues. It is well worth asking about aspects including condition, provenance and the auctioneer's estimation of a work before you bid at auction.

Dealers are the backbone of the design industry, and working with the top dealers in the field is a great place to start a collection. These experts tend to have a more focused interest in designers and genres, and their business relies on sharing their knowledge and experience. Working with the best dealers will not only provide you with information but can also save you money, as costly mistakes can be prevented. Dealers make it their business to know where to find outstanding, fresh pieces. Again, ask lots of questions: it is always the best way to learn.

Museums are the gatekeepers of culture and often decide what will become the defining pieces of an era. They have the responsibility of choosing well and preserving the evolving history of design. Visit museums, attend exhibitions and reference publications to get a better picture of the period in which you are collecting. Understanding the context for the works you choose to collect can help you understand the processes and materials used.

Refer to artist foundations and archives whenever possible. These are dedicated to the works of specific designers and often have primary resource materials, such as sketches, invoices or notes from the designer at their disposal. You may find that an organization, such as the Isamu Noguchi Foundation, has access to a catalogue raisonné. If you contact its researchers regarding a specific work, they can probably tell you about related works and may also be able to provide exhibition history or additional provenance details. Some organizations, such as the George Nakashima Foundation, also keep original hand-written order cards for commissioned designs, which can help determine the date or collection from which a work comes. Not all foundations or archives are free of charge, but their fees are a small price to pay for the information and assurance they can provide.

There is also a wealth of information available on the internet, and more and more museums and catalogue raisonnés are publishing their collections and information online. Unfortunately it can be difficult to verify all online resources, so it is important to pay attention to the source and to refer to primary materials and scholarly books whenever possible. Well-regarded publications are valuable assets and provide a wealth of knowledge.

Albert Sack's *Fine Points of Furniture: Early American, Good, Better, Best*, written in 1950 (before many of the pieces I handle were even designed), outlines criteria for collecting based on the quality of the design, the quality of the manufacturing and the materials used in construction. Sack's criteria can and should be applied to mid-century design as well. The quality of a design is quantifiable within a designer's body of work and within the field in general (sometimes these are different). Material considerations are also important. Most mid-century pieces were made with variations, some more successful than others. An Eames Storage Unit is better in primary colours than in the neutral variation, as the former echoes the Eames's famous house. An ARNE JACOBSEN Egg chair is quite special in original natural leather, but less so in orange fabric.

Luxurious materials and excessive craftsmanship were not the goals of modernism; instead modernism aimed to bring good design to the masses, thus most mid-century designs were mass-produced instead of hand-crafted. There are wonderful designs made from moulded plywood, which, despite the inexpensive and simple materials, are valued highly within the field. As a result, quality in mid-century furnishings necessarily involves the condition. Condition is the single most under-appreciated aspect of good collecting. It is always best to buy items in good condition: the best pieces have been cared for over time but still show their age. A great collector will consider a masterpiece even with a condition issue (or restoration), but a connoisseur understands the extra premium and pride when paying for a work in its original state. Fortunately, the field is still young enough that you can be choosy and find works in fine original condition. Remember, patina is a good thing – it is the evidence and stuff of life!

Collecting mid-century not only means living with history in terms of an item's condition but also in terms of its provenance. I like to know the history of ownership before I buy something. I like it when a piece has been with the original owner or family for a very long time. I also like it when works are 'fresh' to the market, to use a term from the auction industry. Items fresh to the market and from a single owner are more valued than an item traded repeatedly. It should be noted, however, that while provenance can add to an item's value, 'star' provenance should be viewed with caution. A prized possession owned by a famous person may be a bit more special, but a beat-up Eames chair that happened to belong to Andy Warhol is, in my view, simply not all that interesting. In general, I would never add more than a 10% increase to an item's value based on star provenance.

Rarity is, broadly speaking, a plus when collecting mid-century, but it should not be the goal of a collection in and of itself. In collecting design, prototypes sometimes come to market. Their desirability can vary. Collectors should be aware that the word 'prototype' can be used as a marketing term for a piece that should be more accurately described as an early production or custom example. True prototypes are actually working models of a design and they can provide interesting insight into the design process, but ultimately the final version was arrived at for a reason. Variations can be rare but they aren't necessarily desirable. I once handled a double-width Marshmallow sofa that was custom-ordered from Herman Miller*. Twice as long as the original, it is little more than an elongated version of the classic and it is unlikely that GEORGE NELSON ever dreamed of this variation. When collecting, it is better to go for a dead original example of the standard model. This same collecting rule applies to works by obscure designers. While the history of modernism is still evolving and it may be appealing to learn the story of a new or obscure designer,

it is not something I would emphasize in a collection: obscure works make great footnotes and accents but not the core. Regardless, I will confess that I have always wanted to handle a Charles & Ray Eames three-leg DCM – a real working prototype and clearly inferior to the final famous chair. However, as a link to one of the best chairs of the century (and the quirky path creativity takes), I find this prototypical example to be desirable.

There is always a bit of mystery as to why some pieces achieve high prices and others more modest values. The mechanics of the market broadly follow supply and demand: when the supply is very low and demand high, prices rise, while it is harder to maintain consistently strong prices when supply is high. Auction houses have become the major outlet for serious design material in the past decade. Auctions thrive on competition, yet just two determined bidders can set up price spikes that reverberate throughout the market. For example, at Christie's in June 2005 a dining table by CARLO MOLLINO, conservatively estimated at $100,000–150,000, attracted bids by several parties of up to around $500,000 (a more accurate market estimate for that time); from there two bidders, both with agents in the room on cell phones, continued head to head until finally there was a winner at $3,824,000! The Mollino dining table was a rare item and a fine example, but it was not a true masterpiece by the architect and this extraordinary result is still talked about within the industry. The high price had the effect of not only raising prices in the Mollino market but also setting the bar much higher for unique works within the field.

Well-capitalized dealers are another factor in a strong market. Dealers provide stability by buying when prices are low and re-selling for a profit. The market for French material is particularly strong for a number of reasons, including a culture of committed dealers in France. A dedicated, top-end core compete at high-level prices for rare works by Jean Prouvé, Charlotte Perriand* and Le Corbusier* before a retail client even steps in. I believe there is an evolution that occurs with great dealers over time: all dealers want to get items at a good price (a deal, after all), but ultimately the best dealers also want to be recognized as handling the best and rarest pieces. And often great dealers are collectors themselves. This blend of business and passion only further increases market values.

Finally, you need to be aware that there are fakes on the market. Until you are a seasoned collector, buy from the experts, top dealers and auction houses. Many mid-century designs have been reproduced and there are both authorized and unauthorized reproductions. Authorized reproductions often come from the original manufacturers, but, while they are legitimate, they are not the domain of the collector because almost always there are subtle (and not so subtle) differences in manufacturing over time. Experts can guide you on the specifics. Then there are knock-offs, or unauthorized reproductions. These are usually easy to spot for they are often made of inferior materials and with unusual details. Obviously these should be avoided.

Experts are constantly on alert and vetting their offerings to ensure authenticity. It is helpful when pieces are signed (though signatures can be faked, too). You can also protect yourself by looking for signs of authentic age and patina and by asking questions about the history or provenance of works. There are very few segments of the market that still have reliable authentication processes; hopefully this will change but currently in the art world it is moving in the opposite direction. Yet, as noted, there are a number of resources available to help you make educated decisions.

The history of design has added so much to the lives of so many. We are part of a material culture, living with and sometimes defined by the acquired world that surrounds us. This is one of the qualities that make us human. Collecting mid-century design and exploring this world has led me to wonderful discoveries, friends and experiences. I hope you, too, will enjoy the journey.

SCANDINAVIAN FURNITURE: MID-CENTURY PHENOMENON
JUDITH GURA

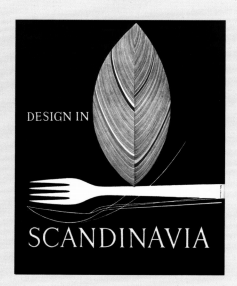

ABOVE Cover design for
*Design in Scandinavia: An
Exhibition of Objects for the
Home*, edited by A. Remlov
and published by Kirstes
Boktrykkeri, Oslo, 1954.

'Scandinavian Style' may be the most misleading designation in design history. There is really no such thing, any more than there is a single Scandinavian language, or a country called Scandinavia. In the literal and geographical sense, Scandinavia consists of the peninsula of Norway and Sweden and the adjacent island nation of Denmark, but Finland and Iceland are almost always included in the group as well – five countries with some shared history and many things in common, but each with its own language and national characteristics, in design as well as everything else.

The fact that these five countries came to be perceived as one in terms of design was partly their own doing. In the mid-20th century, when Swedish modern and then Danish modern furniture became highly fashionable, it was simply easier for the other nations to allow themselves to benefit by association. All the countries (except Iceland) collaborated on an international exhibition and on government-sponsored promotional activities using the term 'Scandinavia', and consumers abroad, particularly those in affluent post-World War II America, were quick to embrace both the term and its pleasant connotations.

For the next two decades, Scandinavian furniture enjoyed international renown for its warm and accessible style of modernism – an alternative to the steel-and-glass severity of Bauhaus* design. It evoked an aesthetic that embraced the heritage of tradition, revered hand-craft, favoured natural materials and drew inspiration from nature. Although that positive image helped to create a large potential market for Scandinavian design, it did have drawbacks. Not all of the countries had production facilities, or products that were easily marketable abroad. And more significantly, the composite image tended to blur the very real differences between the nations.

The image of Scandinavians in popular culture tends to sameness – flags with similar patterns but different colours, names that (except for Finns) sound alike, and a popular image of fresh-faced blondness. What is unquestionably true is an almost universal love of nature, sea and summer that comes naturally to countries largely surrounded by water and far enough north to value sunlight. Ahead of most of the Western world in social welfare, Scandinavians are famously unpretentious and socially liberal, ready to accept new ideas but unwilling to abandon worthy old ones. How does this affect design? Aversion to showiness, reluctance to introduce new pieces when the existing ones function well, and a belief that good design is not elitist, which dates back to the words 'beautiful things for everyday use' proposed by Swedish writer Gregor Paulsson in 1919.

As for the differences between the countries, they can be attributed at least in part to their interlocking though varied histories. The links between the Nordic nations (the accurate designation for the group) were forged across water rather than land. As early as the 12th century, Denmark was a powerful seafaring nation, even controlling part of Sweden until the 18th century, when Sweden, too, became powerful. Norway remained dependent on Denmark until 1814, and was then ruled by Swedish kings until 1905. Finland, the easternmost of the group, was actually part of Sweden until 1809, when it was traded to

Russia, finally declaring its independence in 1917. Only Iceland, an island halfway between Europe and America, was not a trophy to be traded in war, though it was essentially under Danish rule. It was the last to become independent, which happened only in 1944. The individual design traditions, or lack of them, can be seen as reflecting either the self-assurance of long sovereignty (for those who were independent early) or the need to assert national identity (for those who struggled to throw off outside influence).

Geographically separated from the European mainland, the Nordic nations retained many of their folk and vernacular craft traditions, occasionally melding them into 'imported' styles. Sweden's countrified interpretation of the Neoclassical wave that swept most of Europe in the 19th century was a charming and enduring example of this. Its Nordic neighbours flirted with their own versions of Art Nouveau, translated from Germany's *Jugendstil*. Modernism, however, was a late arrival, and when Denmark and Finland presented their wares in Paris at the 1925 'Exposition des Arts Décoratifs et Industriels Modernes', it was hand-blown Swedish glass (from Orrefors) that drew international attention. The complimentary phrase 'Swedish Grace' was coined by a journalist to describe the country's design as a whole. Looking to Europe, the Stockholm Fair of 1930 showcased Functionalism, though it was not widely embraced by a nation still clinging to its traditions.

The real beginning of international celebrity for any Scandinavian furniture design or designer came at the 1939 New York World's Fair, when the Finnish Pavilion by ALVAR AALTO (see under 'Houses and Interiors') featured an interior display with an undulating wall of Finnish birch and photographs of wooded landscape, evoking an ambience rather than only showing products. It was the first step in what became a concerted effort to woo world markets, using design as a marketing tool to create national identity.

Except for German-occupied Norway, the Scandinavian countries were largely spared the destruction wrought on most of Europe by World War II, and so its furniture producers were well positioned to meet newly revived post-war demand for consumer goods. Finland, Denmark and Sweden participated in the Triennale di Milano IX in 1951, the first post-war event of this major international showcase of design, and Norway joined in 1954. Garnering medals and attention for their individual design achievements, the four

ABOVE Nanna and Jørgen Ditzel, Egg chair for Pierantonio Bonacina, Italy, wicker and steel with seat cushion, 1957.

BELOW Bruno Mathsson, Pernilla chaise in laminated steam-bent beech and canvas, 1936.

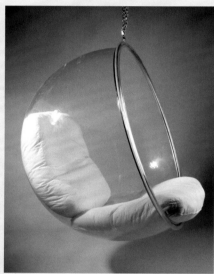

countries sponsored 'Design in Scandinavia', an exhibition that travelled around the United States and Canada from 1954 to 1957, and was enormously successful in raising Western consciousness of the appeal of the Nordic nations and their designs. From 1950 to 1955, when the Museum of Modern Art in New York staged annual exhibitions of 'Good Design', Scandinavian furniture and designers were among the star attractions. Both the museum shows and an influential Scandinavian promotion in Bloomingdale's department store in 1958 showed goods from all the participating nations, but it was Danish furniture that took the lead ... and 'Scandinavian Modern' became, for most of the world, 'Danish Modern'.

Of all the countries, Denmark had the longest heritage of furniture-making, dating back to the publicly funded Royal Furniture Emporium founded by Christian VII in 1777, which established an enduring tradition of quality and fine craftsmanship. When Danish design moved to modernism – in furniture as well as virtually every other product category – it combined functionalism with an appealing humanism. This was an approach initiated by Kaare Klint, who was appointed director of the influential Department of Furniture and Interior Decoration at the Copenhagen Academy of Fine Arts in 1924. Klint studied ergonomics and developed a system of measurements based on human proportions similar to Le Corbusier's* Modulor. Klint taught that furniture must be both well designed and comfortable, standards that influenced his students HANS WEGNER and Jacob Kjær* as well as two generations of furniture designers. The sculptural furniture of Finn Juhl*, and even ARNE JACOBSEN's moulded plastic forms, are among the inheritors of Klint's tradition. Then from 1929, the Danish Cabinetmakers Guild staged annual exhibitions that paired designers with master craftsmen to make individually crafted pieces – a collaboration that encouraged originality and produced iconic works by designers including Finn Juhl, Børge Mogensen* and Grete Jalk*. The works of POUL KJÆRHOLM and VERNER PANTON departed from the usual Danish modernism, focusing not on wood but on metal or plastics. The 1954 MGM film *Hans Christian Andersen* also helped to create an image of warmth and approachability that accrued favourably to all things Danish.

Sweden, after making its mark with glassware, moved into prominence in furniture design with Svenskt Tenn, the company that hired JOSEF FRANK (see under 'Textiles'), once a member of the Wiener Werkstätte, to design for the Swedish market after he relocated to Stockholm. As well as furniture, Frank designed fresh and colourful textiles – mostly stylized florals – that have come to be thought of as distinctively Swedish. At about the same time as Aalto, the Swede Bruno Mathsson* began designing his distinctive, curving, laminated wood seating, and other Swedish designers marketed clean-lined, blond wood furniture that characterized 'Swedish Modern'. None of it was as widely admired as Danish furniture, which, in addition to its other attractions, had the benefit of a larger furniture industry (Danish factories, though small, produced more moderately priced versions of the hand-crafted pieces shown at the Cabinetmakers' exhibitions, and were the force that drove the engine marketing Danish design and Scandinavia along with it). It would be left to Saab and later IKEA to give Sweden an independent design identity.

Finland – after Alvar Aalto, who was responsible for the most celebrated Finnish furniture designs, still in production today and among the most successful Scandinavian designs ever made – came late to furniture-design fame, leaving MARIMEKKO fabrics (see under 'Textiles'), Iittala* glassware and Arabia* dinnerware to carry the country's flag to gain attention abroad. Somewhat separated from its neighbours, Finnish design followed its own direction, and was quicker to accept new materials and modern techniques ... as with EERO AARNIO's whimsical designs, far ahead of their time, and Yrjö Kukkapuro's* fibreglass-shell lounge. But it was not until the 1980s that Finland would make an aggressive effort to create a separate identity for its furniture, which tended to be more lighthearted in approach and ultimately more original than that of its neighbours.

Norway's longest design tradition was in silver and folklore-based 'Dragon Style'. With a very small furniture industry and more attention paid to fishing, and, once it was discovered, oil, design was a relatively low priority. Most designs were influenced by those from Denmark, and only Arne Norell and later Peter Opsvik became internationally known.

As for Iceland, far removed from all but Danish influence (its few designers trained in Denmark, and there were no furniture producers in Iceland itself), the economy was based on industries such as fishing and wool. Although fine crafts were produced, they were primarily for local consumption.

So it was that almost every piece of famous 'Scandinavian Modern' furniture was actually 'Danish Modern'. Along with the spare designs of earlier Bauhaus*-trained modernists and those of emerging first-generation Americans such as CHARLES & RAY EAMES and GEORGE NELSON, they constituted the most important and influential furniture designs of the mid-20th century. But their time in the spotlight was limited. The fault was largely the designers' own. In part, their success led to complacency, and in part their practical and humanistic view saw good design as timeless. There seemed no reason to discard a worthy product in favour of something new and different, but they failed to consider the fickleness of the marketplace and the idiosyncrasies of fashion.

When post-war Italy, its factories decimated by war, began to rebuild its industries and develop furniture for export, adventurous designers and supportive small manufacturers were eager to explore new vistas with plastics and inexpensive materials. Their designs were unconventional, provocative, witty, and – best of all – new. In contrast, the classic Scandinavian designs seemed less exciting, and the media, always searching for new things to report, turned its attention elsewhere. Consumers followed, and Scandinavian furniture fell out of favour.

As a new century dawned, however, Scandinavian furniture, along with other mid-century designs, began to take on the status of classics. Seen from the perspective of distance, their combination of comfort and visual appeal, and the emphasis on natural materials and quality construction that enabled them to stand up to decades of use as they acquired the attractive patina of age, have proved that their designers were right in believing that good design could be timeless. At private dealers and the major auction houses, and in vintage stores and the pages of design magazines – mixing comfortably with other modern pieces and today's cutting-edge art-furniture – Scandinavian furniture is again in the limelight ... and deservedly so.

EERO AARNIO
BORN 1932

FINNISH DESIGNER NOTED FOR
SCULPTING HIGHLY ORIGINAL
FORMS THAT HELPED DEFINE
1960S DESIGN

The work of Finnish designer Eero Aarnio was infused with the futuristic spirit of the Space Age as well as a Pop culture sense of playfulness and exuberance.

His most enticing and groundbreaking design was the acrylic Bubble chair of 1968 (see p. 24), which challenged almost every traditional assumption of what a chair should be. It had no legs, but was suspended from the ceiling by a heavy-duty chain, and it was almost completely transparent, apart from a cushion and back support placed within the sphere. The impression was of an other-worldly object, hanging in space. Being so original, it was bound to become an instant focal point. But more than this it was fun, it was pleasurable and quietly subverted any sense of pretension or ostentation in a room.

The Bubble was one of a sequence of striking pieces designed by Aarnio that made the most of the possibilities presented by the new plastics. Like VERNER PANTON, Aarnio allowed his imagination free rein and sculpted forms that helped define 1960s design.

Originally Aarnio began to train as an architect, but then decided instead to study design at the Institute of Industrial Arts in Helsinki. Graduating in 1957, he opened his own studio five years later. Initially, he began

experimenting – like many of his Scandinavian contemporaries – with natural materials but was soon drawn towards new mediums. 'Plastic gives designers total freedom in terms of form and colour,' he once said, 'which allows them to produce items that strike a middle ground between being functional and playful.'

In 1965 Aarnio created an equally famous forerunner of the Bubble chair, known as the Ball, or Globe, chair. This, too, used a spherical shape, sliced to one side, but sat on a neat circular aluminium base. The chair was made with moulded fibreglass – most commonly in a gleaming white, but also in red, black and orange – and the inside was fully coated in a foam upholstery with a bright fabric finish, creating an enticing womb-like effect. Two years later Asko released Aarnio's fibreglass Armchair, with the appearance of a sleek egg cup, cut away to one side.

Aarnio also used fibreglass in the design of his Pastille chair of 1968 (sometimes known as the Gyro chair), which had the look of an indented sweet, with a rounded bottom and no legs, almost like a Space Age bean bag with a static shell. The design was pioneering, but had a child-like appeal and came in a range of bright Pop colours: reds, orange and apple green. It could be used either indoors or out and echoed the shape of the Garden Egg by Peter Ghyczy*, which came out around the same time, again using moulded fibreglass.

Later designs became increasingly abstract on the one hand and zoomorphic on the other. The bright red fibreglass Tomato chair of 1971 resembled two shiny plastic tomatoes welded together; the Pony (or Mustang) chair also released in the early 1970s took the form of an abstract animal. New Aarnio designs were released in the 1990s and many earlier pieces were also reissued.

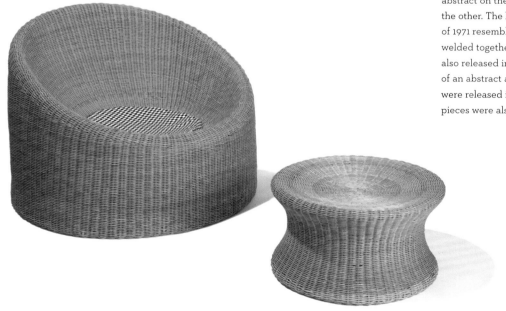

LEFT Wicker lounge chair and ottoman, c. 1965, produced by Asko.

RIGHT Pony chair, manufactured by Adelta, Germany, 1973, with stretch jersey fabric over a foam structure.

BELOW Gel-coated fibreglass and reinforced polyester Kantarelli table, made by Asko, 1965.

BELOW AND OPPOSITE Ball
chairs, made with gel-coated
fibreglass and upholstery on
an aluminium base, produced
by Asko, 1965.

HARRY BERTOIA
1915–1978

ITALIAN-AMERICAN POLYMATH,
WHOSE DESIGNS INCLUDE
THE CLASSIC DIAMOND CHAIR

Throughout the 1950s and '60s, the relationship between the worlds of art and design was often intimate, with cross-fertilization between the two in a complex process of exchange. One of the most striking examples of the polymath artist and designer is the sculptor, furniture designer, graphic artist, jewelry maker and composer Harry Bertoia.

Bertoia is best known in design circles for creating the Diamond chair (Model 421LU) for Knoll* in 1952. This is one of the most distinctive and sculptural pieces of the mid-century period, made of a shimmering lattice of steel mesh perched upon a lightweight but hard-wearing tubular steel frame. The shape of the seat was indeed a diamond, but one that was moulded to the contours of the body and resembled an extraordinary steel flower. It was perfect for relaxed lounging. 'If you look at the chairs,' he said, 'they are mainly made of air, like sculpture. Space goes right through them.'[1]

The Diamond chair was an almost instant success. Knoll happily acknowledged Bertoia's talent and rewarded him with enough money to buy his Pennsylvania farmhouse and his studio workshop, as well as funding a move towards sculpture.

Arieto – or Ari – Bertoia was born in a small Italian village around fifty miles north of Venice. He studied at school in Italy until he was 15, when he went to visit his older brother in America. Ari became Harry after he decided to stay on to study at the Cass Technical High School in Michigan. He was then awarded a scholarship to the Detroit Society of Arts & Crafts (he became an American citizen in 1946).

In 1937 Bertoia won another scholarship to the Cranbrook Academy of Art*, co-founded by Eliel Saarinen*, to study painting and drawing. Here he met CHARLES & RAY EAMES, along with Florence Knoll. Saarinen spotted Bertoia's talents and asked him to head the school of metalworking, concentrating mostly on jewelry design; Bertoia later designed wedding rings for the Eameses. At the same time he was producing art prints, which also earned significant respect.

Bertoia moved to California in 1943 to work with the Eameses on the development of new techniques for moulding plywood. But he soon decided that he wanted to pursue his own ideas and took up an offer from Hans and Florence Knoll to design furniture for

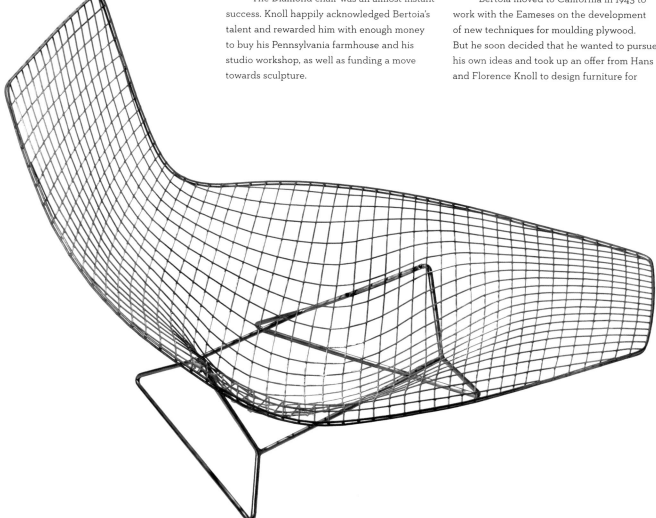

their company and moved, together with his family, to Pennsylvania.

Here, the Knolls gave him creative freedom and Bertoia produced a small but hugely popular series of lattice steel furniture, including the Diamond chair. These were hand-made with bent and welded steel rods, while loose upholstery or cushions were often added to the frame; the Diamond chair was often seen dressed in a vibrant red seat cover. Other designs included the Bird chair and ottoman (423LU) and the Model 420C dining or office chair (all 1952).

Bertoia's Knoll collection gave him the freedom to begin developing his sculptural work almost immediately. Commissions came in for public works on a large scale, but he was best known for his series of sounding sculptures. These were assemblies of interwoven rods springing upwards and sometimes capped with metal droplets like flowerheads, with one series inspired by the form of dandelions. These sculptures produced mesmerizing metallic sounds, like wind chimes, which formed the basis for eleven albums of recordings.

Multi-talented and always prolific, Bertoia found great success in almost every medium within which he worked. He was the ultimate mid-century Renaissance man but his work reached the widest of audiences through a sculpted diamond that travelled the world.

BELOW A set of children's wire chairs, produced by Knoll, c. 1965, in enamelled steel.

OPPOSITE Prototype lounge chair, c. 1952, in welded steel wire. Knoll exhibited this piece in their Park Avenue store in 1953, and it remained in the Bertoia family for many years.

RIGHT AND BELOW
Bird chairs and ottomans,
manufactured by Knoll,
1952, in enamelled steel
with upholstered seat pads.

BELOW Diamond chair
and ottoman, 1952, produced
by Knoll, in plastic-coated
steel wire with upholstered
seat pads.

LEFT 'Multi-Plane Construction' sculpture, 1956, in brass and brass melt-coated copper, acquired from Bertoia by Edward Durell Stone.

BELOW 'Sonambient' sculpture, c. 1970, in beryllium copper and brass.

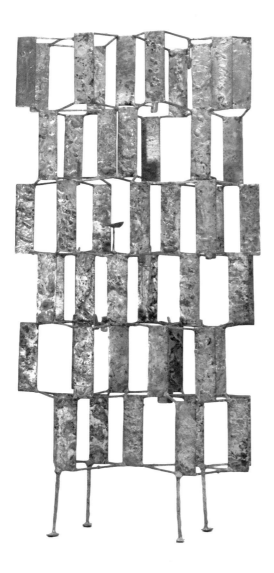

OPPOSITE 'Willow' sculpture, c. 1970, in stainless steel and steel wire, made by the Bertoia Studio.

JOE COLOMBO
1930–1971

ITALIAN DESIGNER WHO
DEVELOPED CONCEPTS FOR
MULTI-FUNCTIONAL FURNITURE
WITH INTEGRATED STORAGE
AND HOME TECHNOLOGY

Italian designer Joe Colombo packed an entire career into a single but extraordinary decade. He embraced design relatively late and died tragically young, of heart failure, but within just a short space of time he had established himself as one of the great innovators of the mid-century period.

He put his name to a whole range of furniture, lighting and other products but also took a wider view of the role of design in people's lives and living spaces. He also embraced the possibilities offered by new materials – particularly plastics – and by mass production.

Cesare 'Joe' Colombo initially studied painting and then architecture in Milan, before working as a painter and sculptor. But after his father fell ill in 1958, he and his brother, Gianni, took over the family factory, which made electrical conductors. Colombo gave up his career as an artist and began working as a designer while looking into new manufacturing techniques and plastic technology at the factory.

In 1962 Colombo opened his own design studio in Milan, where he balanced a wide portfolio of work, including architectural and interiors commissions, as well as furniture, lighting and product design. A charismatic playboy dandy and a brilliant self-publicist, he published his own apartments in magazines in order to promote his designs.

His most famous furniture design was the Elda armchair of 1963. This large, easy lounge chair resembled a vast baseball glove sitting on a rigid base and back. As with so much of Colombo's work, it was full of innovative thinking, being one of the first large armchairs to include a structural fibreglass frame, while the base rotated, creating the kind of ergonomic flexibility that fascinated Colombo.

A number of his early chair designs – such as the LEM armchair for Bieffeplast and the highly sculptural 4801 chair for Kartell* (both 1964) – originally used plywood in their construction. But Colombo was intrigued by plastics and developed one of the first injection-moulded chairs in the form of the Universale 4860/4867, also for Kartell. This stackable chair had detachable legs in two different heights and echoed VERNER PANTON's Panton chair. Other innovative Colombo designs included the modular Tube chair of 1969, which consisted of a series of

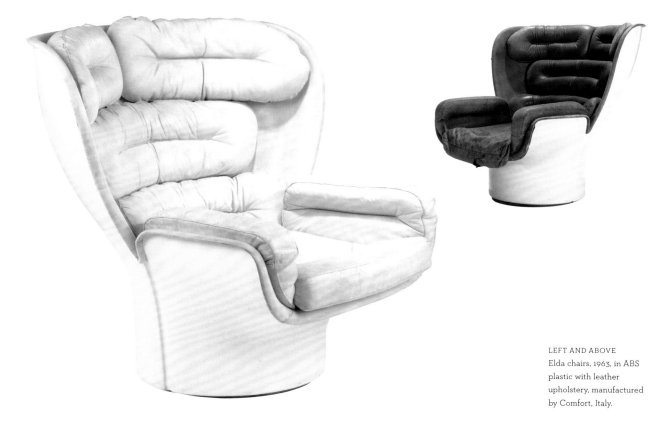

LEFT AND ABOVE
Elda chairs, 1963, in ABS
plastic with leather
upholstery, manufactured
by Comfort, Italy.

interlocking, upholstered tubes that could be arranged in a variety of combinations.

Colombo was also a pioneering lighting designer and one of his earliest lights, designed with his brother Gianni, was the Acrilica of 1962, made by Oluce. This wave-shaped desk and table lamp was made with transparent Plexiglas, an acrylic resin. The bulb was concealed in the metal base of the lamp, allowing the light to be diffused by the illuminated Plexiglas. Other key lighting designs include the Spider lamp of 1965 and the Coupé table and floor lamps of 1967. Colombo's series of swivelling tubular table lights for Kartell (1965) featured a translucent inner cylinder and a colourful outer layer with single or multiple geometric openings cut into them, presaging VICO MAGISTRETTI's rotating Eclisse – or 'Eclipse' – light of 1967 (see under 'Lighting').

Colombo also concerned himself with more ambitious solutions to home living that combined furniture, lighting, storage and other aspects of domestic technology. These included his Rotoliving multi-functional room divider of 1969, which featured an integrated

television, stereo system, lighting and dual-level swivelling table that rotated outwards to the front or back of the system. Colombo's Cabriolet bed from the same year also included integrated elements such as a radio, ashtray and fold-down canopy. Both designs were featured in Colombo's own apartment on the Via Argelati in Milan.

Other storage systems include the Boby trolley (1970), featuring trays and compartments within a mobile unit on gliding castors for mobility. Just before his death, Colombo designed his Total Furnishing Unit (1972), which included seating, a kitchenette, entertainment systems and fold-down beds. This compact multi-faceted Space Age design was a forerunner of concepts applied to many prefabricated houses and apartments, as well as modular hotel rooms and mobile homes.

By 1971, when Colombo died, he had also designed car radios, cutlery, tableware, fans, clocks and watches. His playful and all-encompassing approach paved the way for later exponents of the multi-disciplinary approach, such as Philippe Starck and Karim Rashid.

BELOW Tube chair in Arcipiuma plastic with foam upholstery, manufactured by Flexform, Italy, 1969.

BOTTOM Set of three Boby trolleys – or *taborets* – made in ABS plastic by Bieffeplast, 1970.

BELOW Additional-System
seating (a series of cushions
that can be arranged
in different patterns with
connecting pins), made by
Sormani, Italy, 1967.

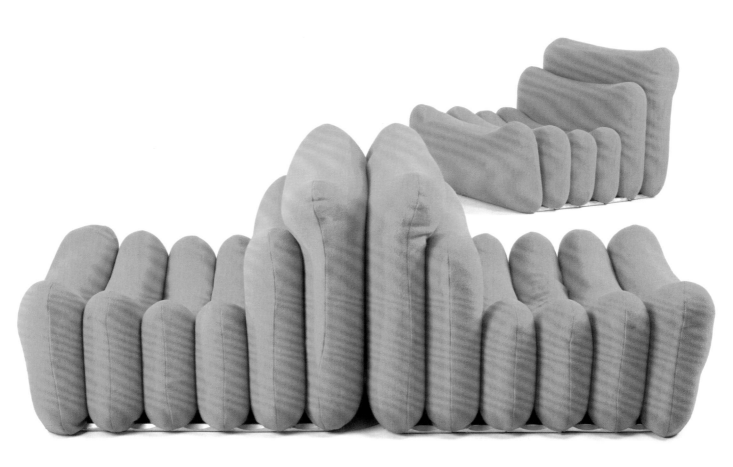

ROBIN DAY
1915–2010

ONE OF BRITAIN'S MOST
CELEBRATED AND
RECOGNIZABLE
MID-CENTURY DESIGNERS

Few chairs have achieved the kind of ubiquitous familiarity of Robin Day's Polyprop, a stackable staple of countless village halls, hospitals and council meetings. Some estimates suggest that over 50 million of the chairs have been sold worldwide. Famously, Day even came across legless Polyprop seats bolted on to dug-out canoes in Botswana's Okavango Delta.

Day's ambition was to make good design available to a wide market in the form of affordable, reliable and ergonomic furniture. Although too modest and affable to boast about his achievements, it was an ambition that he more than met. In the mid-1950s, such was his fame that – together with his wife, textile designer LUCIENNE DAY (see under 'Textiles') – he even appeared in an advert for Smirnoff Vodka, surrounded by his own designs.

The son of a police constable, Day was born in High Wycombe, where he won a scholarship to the School of Art. He was offered a job by Lucian Ercolani, founder of the furniture maker Ercol*, but chose instead to study at the Royal College of Art. Here, he met Lucienne Conradi, who he married in 1942. He went on to teach at the Beckenham School of Art, and in 1948 won a design competition for low-cost furniture – with fellow tutor Clive Latimer – organized by New York's Museum of Modern Art.

Robin and Lucienne Day's star ascended rapidly in the years that followed, as they became an English equivalent of CHARLES & RAY EAMES, who Day greatly admired. But while the Eameses collaborated together regularly, Day and his wife worked back to back in the same studio but seldom came together directly over commissions or projects.

One notable exception was the 1951 Festival of Britain*, where Day designed a number of interiors for the Homes & Garden pavilion, filled with his furniture designs, and asked Lucienne to create complementary textiles (he was also asked to design seating for the Royal Festival Hall). By the time the Festival was over, the Days were stars in the world of design.

Day's relationship with the manufacturer S. Hille & Co. (later known as Hille International) began in 1949. The London-based company was family-owned and -run at the time and Day collaborated with the Hilles for over 20 years as a consultant designer, also becoming involved in the brand identity and marketing of the firm, as well as the interiors of Hille's showroom.

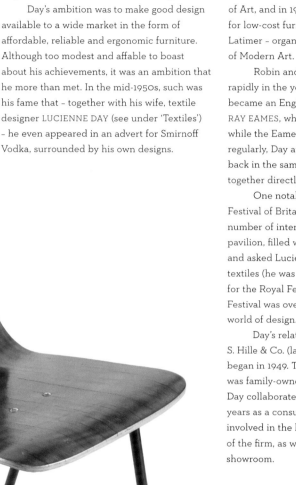

LEFT Q Stak chair in laminated wood, veneered with cherrywood, with tubular steel legs, manufactured by S. Hille & Co., 1953.

BELOW Polyprop chairs, manufactured by S. Hille & Co., with seats made of injection-moulded polypropylene plastic and lightweight tubular steel legs, 1963.

Their first great success was the Hillestak plywood chair released in 1950, originally made with a beech frame and a moulded walnut seat and backrest. Beautifully designed and made, yet easily affordable, available and stackable, it was the perfect chair for a country just emerging from an age of austerity.

The Polyprop followed in the early 1960s. Polypropylene had been invented in 1954 and Day saw the material's potential for creating mass-produced furniture. It was lightweight and hard-wearing, but also inexpensive and highly malleable, suited to an injection-moulding process where an all-in-one seat could be factory-produced in large numbers. Most commonly, the seat was fitted to standard steel chair legs but it could also be used in other ways, such as for stadium seating or barstools.

Always quick with a marketing idea, Day arranged for six hundred architects, journalists and tastemakers to receive a free Polyprop. Before long, the chair was being produced under licence all over the world and smaller versions were being made for children.

Other furniture designs included shelving units and sofas, such as the Forum sofa from 1964. Day also designed televisions for Pye, acted as a consultant for John Lewis department stores, and created interiors and seating for institutions as diverse as the Barbican Centre and Gatwick Airport.

Day was endlessly energetic and active, indulging a love of mountaineering and skiing when he was not at work. In the 1990s, his work was reissued by Habitat and others, while new pieces were produced for SCP and Magis. Day continued working into his nineties.

RIGHT Dining set made by S. Hille & Co., 1949, in walnut, mahogany and maple, with upholstered chair seats.

ABOVE LEFT Seventeen-inch-screen television with wood and steel stand, manufactured by Pye, UK, 1957.

ABOVE Large, moulded walnut ply chair, with leather upholstery, produced by S. Hille & Co., c. 1951.

CHARLES EAMES
1907–1978
& RAY EAMES
1912–1988

AMERICAN DESIGNER DUO
RESPONSIBLE FOR MANY OF
THE MOST FAMOUS CLASSICS
OF 20TH-CENTURY DESIGN

It is hard to think of anyone who shaped the face of mid-century modern design quite as much as Charles and Ray Eames. Their work spanned many different mediums, always to great effect. They took a democratic approach, seeking to 'bring the most of the best to the greatest number of people for the least', and they pioneered the use of new materials.

For many, their furniture – in particular – is still a symbol of modernity and remains in high demand. It feels fresh and enticing, moulded to a certain kind of lifestyle as much as to the curves of our bodies. The sequence of classic chairs that the Eameses developed in the 1950s and '60s began with the ply 'Lounge Chair Wood' (LCW) of 1945 – one of a series of plywood pieces developed just after the war with a revolutionary sense of ingenuity and vibrant aesthetic charm.

Later, the pair began experimenting with another new material, fibreglass, developed by the US military. Their sumptuous La Chaise of 1948 featured the sensuous curves of a reclining body or pouting lips. A wave of fibreglass models followed, produced by Herman Miller* in the late 1940s and early 1950s: the 'Rocking Armchair Rod' (RAR),

the 'Dining Armchair Rod' (DAR) and the 'Dining Side Rod' (DSR).

There were experiments with wire chairs, each design starting off with a sculpted, ergonomic seat. And, of course, there was the iconic Model No. 670 lounge chair and ottoman. Based on a 1940 prototype, the chair was finally released in 1956 and has become a must-have piece for a generation or more. This was just a fraction of the Eames output, which also included aluminium office chairs that helped define the progressive mid-century office and airport seating first developed for Washington's Dulles Airport and Chicago's O'Hare.

Charles Eames was born in St Louis and his potential was clear from an early age, although the premature death of his father meant that his childhood studies were usually balanced with part-time jobs. He won an architecture scholarship to Washington University in St Louis, where he met his first wife. He practised architecture in the 1930s until Eliel Saarinen* offered him a fellowship at Cranbrook Academy of Art*. Here, he formed a close friendship with EERO SAARINEN – with whom he collaborated on a number of projects – and he also met Ray Kaiser.

LEFT AND ABOVE DCW chair
in birch plywood and black
LCW chair in aniline-dyed
ash plywood, both Herman
Miller, 1945.

BELOW Calf skin and ash
plywood LCW chair, Herman
Miller, 1945.

Ray was a gifted artist, who had studied at the Art Students League and with painter Hans Hofmann before moving to Cranbrook. She married Charles in 1941 and they moved together to Los Angeles, where Charles began working in Cedric Gibbons's art department at MGM and Ray designed magazine covers for John Entenza's *Arts & Architecture* magazine.

At the same time, the couple began experimenting with plywood and developed a ply leg splint that was taken up by the US Navy. War effort projects gave the Eameses access to materials and encouraged them to open their own design office. In the late 1940s their reputation soared and the head of design at Herman Miller, GEORGE NELSON, began to put their designs into production.

The Eameses were also intimately involved in Entenza's Case Study Program*, which aimed to publicize a new generation of contemporary homes that would be relatively affordable and make good use of new materials and manufacturing methods. Charles Eames collaborated with Eero Saarinen on the design of two houses in Pacific Palisades – one for Entenza and one for the Eameses themselves.

The design of the two-storey Eames House (or Case Study #8) was significantly reconfigured late in the day by Charles, but used the same prefabricated steel frame, which went up in just a day and a half. The project incorporated the Eames's home and a separate studio building, the two divided by a courtyard. It was one of the most influential Californian houses of the period and a showcase for a mid-century modern way of living.

Following the great success of the Eames's furniture designs for Herman Miller in the 1950s – as well as ongoing architectural commissions – the designers became increasingly interested in film-making and exhibition design. When Charles died in 1978, Ray worked to complete projects that were already underway but did not seek out any new commissions.

OPPOSITE PAW chairs,
produced by Herman Miller,
1950, with a fibreglass shell
and birch and steel legs.

RIGHT RAR rocking chair,
Herman Miller, 1950, in
moulded fibreglass with steel
and birch legs/rockers.

BELOW RKR chair,
manufactured by Herman
Miller, 1950, in enamelled
steel, birch and upholstery.

RIGHT ESU 220-N storage
cabinet, produced by Herman
Miller, 1950, in birch plywood,
laminate, lacquered Masonite
and chrome-plated steel.

BELOW Model 670 lounge
chair with matching 671
ottoman, Herman Miller,
1956, in rosewood plywood,
enamelled aluminium and
leather upholstery.

BELOW Rear view of an ESU
400 storage cabinet/shelving
unit, Herman Miller, 1952,
made with birch plywood,
enamelled Masonite, fibreglass
and chrome-plated steel.

LEFT A set of ten DSR chairs, Herman Miller, 1950, with fibreglass seats and enamelled steel legs.

BELOW ETR table, produced by Herman Miller, 1951, with a laminate-over-plywood table top and enamelled steel legs.

ARNE JACOBSEN
1902–1971

PRE-EMINENT DANISH
MODERNIST, WHO BUILT
ON HIS ARCHITECTURAL
COMMISSIONS TO CREATE
SOME OF THE MOST ICONIC
MID-CENTURY DESIGNS

BELOW Swan settee, Model
3321, produced by Fritz
Hansen, 1958, with upholstery
over an aluminium frame.

Danish architect and designer Arne Jacobsen recognized the close synergy between different fields of design. He liked to involve himself in every aspect of his architectural projects, which took him deep into the realms of interior and furniture design. Rather like his Finnish contemporary ALVAR AALTO, he found no detail too small for his attention, and his work as an architect blended with the creation of chairs, tables, lamps, textiles and cutlery.

Many of his most famous pieces had their origins in specific architectural commissions. His iconic plywood Ant chair of 1952 was initially designed for a canteen building for Novo Nordisk, a pharmaceutical company. The highly sculptural, fluid forms of the Swan and Egg chairs (both 1958) evolved from his work on the architecture and interiors of the SAS Royal Hotel in Copenhagen. His classic Oxford office and desk chair of 1965 – an upholstered plywood seat on a swivelling base with castors – was created for St Catherine's College, Oxford, where once again an architectural commission led through to a complete *Gesamtkunstwerk*.

Born in Copenhagen, Jacobsen showed a promising artistic talent as a child and had ambitions to be a painter, but his father helped to steer him towards architecture. He travelled in Germany and Italy during his twenties and served an apprenticeship as a bricklayer before studying architecture at the Royal Danish Academy of Fine Arts.

As a student he won a prize for a chair design at the 'Exposition Internationale des Arts Décoratifs' in 1925 and won a gold medal for his graduation project. A few years later, together with Flemming Lassen, he designed a 'House of the Future' for an exhibition in Copenhagen: the house included wind-down windows, a helicopter pad, a boathouse and a garage complete with a Dodge Coupé.

After establishing his own architectural office, Jacobsen designed a number of significant private houses in the 1930s. He also worked on the development of a resort at Klampenborg, where his Bellevue Sea Bath of 1932 included everything from watch towers for the lifeguards to the design of the entry tickets. Coming from a Jewish family, Jacobsen was

forced to flee to Sweden with his wife Jonna
during the German occupation of Denmark, but
he continued working throughout the war and
re-established his practice in Copenhagen soon
afterwards, with a wide range of commissions
from town halls to housing to schools.

In the early 1950s, Jacobsen became
interested in the possibilities for plywood
furniture after noting the pioneering work of
CHARLES & RAY EAMES. His Ant chair for Novo
Nordisk came in just two pieces: the moulded
plywood seat – with its distinctive ant-like
shape, including an indented tuck between
seat and back – and a tubular steel base,
originally with just three legs. Fritz Hansen*
began manufacturing the chair in 1952, adding
a four-legged version, then Jacobsen produced

a variation that was to become one of the
most successful designs of the 20th century.
This was the iconic Series 7 plywood chair,
first produced in 1955, with a fluid form and
V-shaped back (see p. 21). Another ply piece,
Model 3130 of 1955, was dubbed the 'Grand
Prix' after scooping a prize at the Milan XI
Triennale in 1957.

'I based my work on a need,' Jacobsen
said of his plywood designs, which could be
easily manufactured and stacked. 'I found
that people needed a new type of chair for
the small kitchen dinettes that are found in
most new buildings today – a little, light and
inexpensive chair.'[2]

The SAS Royal Copenhagen hotel
commission, completed in 1960, also spurred

a range of new designs that were to become
known throughout the world. These included
the AJ task light, the Swan chair and sofa,
and the luxurious Egg chair, whose rounded
form had the sculptural presence of a
modernist piece of art.

Jacobsen's building for St Catherine's
College, finished in 1963, is regarded as one
of his finest architectural achievements. Again,
nothing escaped his attention. It is said that
he even specified the species of fish that
should inhabit the pond in the college grounds.

BELOW Ox lounge chair, 1966, in leather and aluminium, manufactured by Fritz Hansen.

LEFT A pair of Pot chairs, 1959, produced by Fritz Hansen, with a chrome-plated steel frame and vinyl-coated upholstery.

BELOW Custom Ant table, with three rotating, fold-out surfaces stored under the main table top, Fritz Hansen, c. 1965, in teak and chrome-plated steel.

BOTTOM Model 3302 settee in leather and chrome-plated steel, manufactured by Fritz Hansen, 1956.

RIGHT AND BELOW Egg chairs in brown and black leather over a plastic shell and sitting on an aluminium base, Fritz Hansen, 1958.

OPPOSITE ABOVE Matching table and chairs made by Asko, 1971, using lacquered birch with suede seats.

OPPOSITE BELOW LEFT Seagull chair, Fritz Hansen, 1969; lacquered wood, upholstery and chrome-plated steel.

OPPOSITE BELOW CENTRE Grand Prix chair, Fritz Hansen, 1957; leather and chrome-plated steel.

OPPOSITE BELOW RIGHT Drop chair from the SAS Royal Hotel, Copenhagen, made by Fritz Hansen, 1958; leather and bronze-coated steel.

POUL KJÆRHOLM
1929–1980

INNOVATIVE DANISH DESIGNER
WHO EXPERIMENTED WITH
STEEL FRAMES TO CREATE
LIGHTWEIGHT, FUNCTIONAL
SCULPTURES

BELOW PK22 lounge
chair, produced by E. Kold
Christensen, Denmark, 1956,
in matt chrome-plated steel
and leather.

The work of Danish furniture designer
Poul Kjærholm was defined by a sense
of sophisticated elegance. Considered and
refined, it showed significant influence from
pioneering modernist and International Style
designers – particularly LUDWIG MIES VAN
DER ROHE (see under 'Houses and Interiors') –
rather than Scandinavian contemporaries.

In contrast with his Danish contemporary
HANS WEGNER, with whom he is sometimes
compared, Kjærholm was not so interested in
working with timber but was more concerned
with pioneering experiments using lightweight
steel frames to create chairs and tables that
were light and functional but also exquisitely
made and sculpturally enticing. 'I consider
steel a material with the same artistic merit
as wood and leather,' he once said.[3]

Kjærholm's most famous design was
perhaps the PK22 – simply named, like all his
furniture, with an initial and model number.
The slim leather seat and back – which also
came in woven cane – gave the chair an organic
quality and established a neat contrast with
the more industrial nature of the metalwork.
The PK22 has often been compared with Mies
van der Rohe's iconic Barcelona chair (Model
MR90, 1929, reissued by Knoll*), but it is much
lighter, even delicate in appearance.

Kjærholm, born in northern Jutland,
studied furniture design at the Danish School
of Arts & Crafts in Copenhagen from 1949
to 1951 after serving an apprenticeship as
a carpenter. He married Hanne Dam, an
architect, in 1953. Kjærholm himself combined
an almost architectural approach to space

and interiors with the precision of an engineer
and the artistic touch of a sculptor. He would
experiment with materials and production
methods to achieve pure forms made with
a minimal number of components.

A number of Kjærholm's earliest pieces
were manufactured by Fritz Hansen*, who
employed him for a period in the early 1950s.
These pieces include the PK25 chair of 1951,
a forerunner of the PK22, with a seat and back
made of flag halyard rope woven like guitar
strings onto a flat steel frame (flag halyard was
a material also explored by Wegner). There
was also the extraordinary three-legged PK0
chair, made of just two pieces combined in one
fluid form with the rounded curves and sleek
finish of an airplane fin or shining, shell-like,
racing-car hubs (see p. 10).

In the mid-1950s Kjærholm began
a long collaboration with furniture producer
and friend Ejvind Kold Christensen – a working
relationship that was to continue until Kjærholm's
death. The PK22 was an early success. In the
1960s, Kjærholm created the PK20 chair,
its legs bent backwards like the ski runners
of an old-fashioned sledge. There was also the
inviting, ergonomically curved PK24 Hammock
chair – a reinterpretation of a deck lounger,
but again defined by a sculptural elegance
and lightness of touch.

After Kjærholm's death, Fritz Hansen
took over production of many of the Kold
Christensen pieces, including the PK22 and the
PK24 Hammock. Kjærholm Productions, run by
the designer's son, Thomas, also manufactures
a series of coffee tables.

OPPOSITE ABOVE
PK9 chairs in matt chrome-
plated steel and leather,
manufactured by E. Kold
Christensen, 1960.

OPPOSITE CENTRE
PK31/3 sofa in chrome-
plated steel and leather,
E. Kold Christensen, 1958.

OPPOSITE BELOW
PK80 daybed, produced by
E. Kold Christensen, 1957, in
chrome-plated steel, leather
and lacquered plywood.

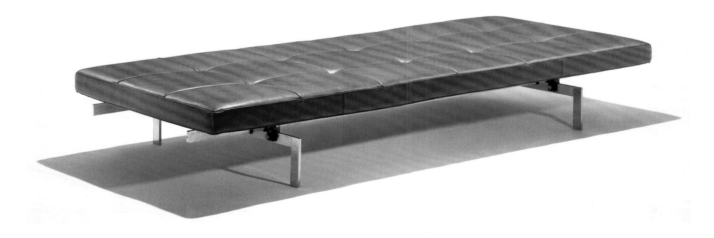

OPPOSITE ABOVE A pair of PK22 lounge chairs in matt chrome-plated steel with a wicker seat and back, E. Kold Christensen, 1956.

OPPOSITE BELOW PK24 chaise longue for Fritz Hansen, 1965, in stainless steel and cane.

LEFT PK20 lounge chair, E. Kold Christensen, 1968, in matt chrome-plated steel and leather.

BELOW PK1 chairs, produced by PP Møbler, Denmark, 1956, in matt chrome-plated steel and cane.

CARLO MOLLINO
1905–1973

FLAMBOYANT ITALIAN DESIGNER
WHOSE UNUSUAL, OFTEN
LIMITED-EDITION WORKS HAVE
BECOME HIGHLY COLLECTABLE

There are few characters in the world of mid-century design as flamboyant and as fascinating as Carlo Mollino. Although a dandy and a showman, he was an extraordinary polymath – an architect and interior designer, who became one of the most revered furniture designers of the period. Also a passionate skier, a pilot with a love of stunt acrobatics and a racing-car driver, he even invented the car that he took to Le Mans in 1955 – an aerodynamic red rocket called the Bisiluro. Added to this, he was a photographer, with a penchant for erotic Polaroids, and he had an interest in the occult.

Much of Mollino's furniture was designed for use in particular buildings and interiors of his own design, such as the indulgent red armchairs he designed for the RAI Auditorium in Turin. The limited production runs and hand-crafted quality of many of these pieces have made them rare and much sought-after, although a small number of designs were put into wider production by Zanotta*, such as the chair that Mollino originally designed for the Faculty of Architecture in Turin and later reissued as the 211 Fenis.

Mollino drew his influences and inspiration from a wide range of sources, including the work of Scandinavian designers such as ALVAR AALTO (see under 'Houses and Interiors') but also the more expressive and sinuous Art Nouveau of Antoni Gaudí. To think of Mollino's furniture is to picture tables and chairs with biomorphic qualities and touches of the surreal; crafted timber takes on the look of horns and hooves, yet woven into forms that are modern and even futuristic. Mollino's Model 1114 coffee table, for example, uses a maple base shaped like antlers to cradle a glass tabletop and secondary level below for books or magazines. Similarly sinuous, Mollino's Arabesque tables were made with sculpted sections of plywood – a favourite material for Mollino.

The chair that he designed for Lisa and GIO PONTI in 1940, with a brass frame and upholstered seat, featured a segmented seat and a cloven back, like a raised hoof. The idea of a split back in two distinct parts was explored in later designs, such as the oak Casa del Sole (or Pavia) chairs, where each of the rear legs splays as it rises, forming a divided back held together by brass screws.

Born in Turin, Mollino studied at the School of Architecture at the University of Turin, and was the son of engineer and architect Eugenio Mollino. He began work with his father's practice but soon established his own reputation for a 'Turinese Baroque' style, exquisite detailing, and a cohesive approach to combining architecture and interiors. By 1937, he had established his own studio. He designed homes for himself and others, including the Miller House (1936), the Casa Devalle (1940), and the Ada and Cesare Minola House (1944), all in Turin. There were also a number of dynamic mountain buildings that reinterpreted the idea of the Alpine chalet in a unique modernist style, such as Villa K2 from 1953, situated near Lake Maggiore.

RIGHT A chair from the Casa del Sole dining room in Cervinia, Italy, c. 1951, made by Ettore Canali, in oak and brass.

OPPOSITE A Model 1114 coffee table in maple, Securit glass and brass, produced by Apelli & Varesio, Italy, c. 1950.

RIGHT A desk from the
offices of Reale Mutua di
Assicurazioni in Turin,
made by Apelli & Varesio,
1946, in oak and brass.

BELOW A pair of theatre
chairs from the RAI
Auditorium in Turin,
in velvet and brass, 1951.

From early on, Mollino began designing pieces of furniture specifically for his clients and their buildings. For the Minola House, he designed a sumptuous armchair with a timber frame, velvet upholstery and a tall back that transformed into a pair of soft horns, reminiscent of HANS WEGNER's Ox chair. Later armchairs – such as the Acotto lounge chair of 1952 – also used deep, rich upholstery, giving a luxurious, indulgent quality.

Mollino seemed able to turn his hand to almost anything, including beds, cabinets and console tables. His oak desks for the Società Reale Mutua di Assicurazioni combine functionality with a sculptural quality. His Gaudí chair for the Orengo House of 1949 is a more explicit homage to the Catalan designer. Although a number of Mollino's buildings and interiors were destroyed after his death, his reputation is now more than secure.

ABOVE A cabinet designed for the Ferruccio Ferro residence in Turin, made by Apelli & Varesio, c. 1952, in maple, skai and brass.

LEFT A pair of armchairs from Lutrario Hall, Turin, produced by Doro, Italy, 1959, in enamelled steel, Italian walnut and vinyl-coated upholstery.

GEORGE NAKASHIMA
1905–1990

JAPANESE-AMERICAN SELF-DESCRIBED 'WOODWORKER', WHOSE DIVERSE INFLUENCES AND REVERENCE FOR CRAFT MADE HIS WORK FAMOUS

For good reason, we tend to think of the post-war period as a time when mass production became dominant. Encouraged by fierce competition to produce all kinds of machines and products to feed the war effort, by the 1950s grand production lines and mass-assembly plants had become familiar. Yet there was an alternative to factory-produced furniture. One thinks of the careful, considered hand-made furniture of HANS WEGNER and other Scandinavian contemporaries, for whom craft was a vital ingredient. Another name that comes to mind is that of George Nakashima.

Nakashima's passion was for the texture, grain and character of timber and for his own response – as a master craftsman – to materials of natural integrity. His influences were numerous. There was the Shaker and Arts & Crafts heritage of North America, where he grew up, and then there was also a Japanese woodworking tradition in which he immersed himself. The combination of all these elements with a fertile imagination – open to modern influences, but on his own terms – created a unique aesthetic.

The son of a Japanese newspaper man who had settled in America, Nakashima was born in Spokane, Washington. He studied architecture at the University of Washington, followed by a masters at the Massachusetts Institute of Technology. After completing his studies, he travelled to Europe, North Africa and then Japan, where he met a fellow American who was to prove a mentor and key

OPPOSITE King-size bed in
oak burl, American black
walnut and laurel, 1971.

RIGHT Minguren II coffee
table, c. 1960, in English
walnut, American black
walnut and rosewood.

BELOW RIGHT Special order
cross-legged desk, 1976,
in American black walnut,
hickory and rosewood.

influence – architect Antonin Raymond, who
helped Frank Lloyd Wright* with his Imperial
Hotel project in Japan and stayed on.

Nakashima worked at Raymond's
Tokyo practice, then – in the late 1930s
– was commissioned to build a dormitory in
Pondicherry, India. When he returned to
America, he initially founded his own furniture
workshop in Seattle, but along with many
others of Japanese descent was confined
to an Idaho internment camp during the war
years. Fortunately his time in the camp was
not wasted, as he met a master craftsman
– Gentaro Hikogawa – who tutored him in
traditional woodworking methods.

In 1943, Raymond managed to sponsor
Nakashima's release from Camp Minidoka
and encouraged him to come to his own
farm at New Hope, Pennsylvania. Here
Nakashima and his family settled, and here
he ultimately established a compound of
buildings, many to his own design, including
a studio and workshop.

Many of Nakashima's pieces were made
by hand at New Hope, with much of the
furniture made to commission. His work
– such as his famous spindle-backed chairs
or his Host rocker – clearly drew on traditional
ideas and familiar forms, but the pieces were
always reinterpreted and made with a passion
for detail and character. Powerful slices of
timber were reinvented as coffee tables, great
slabs of walnut became desk tops and a floral
segment of oak burl might become a striking
headboard. Nakashima embraced the unique
qualities of his woods, allowing them to express
themselves and using the natural shapes and
outlines of the cut timber as part of the overall
composition of much of his furniture.

Certain pieces – such as the Conoid
dining chairs – were made in some quantity
by Nakashima's studio. He was seldom tempted
to release his designs to others for production,
preferring to control quality at New Hope.
One exception was Knoll*, after Raymond
introduced Nakashima to Hans and Florence

Knoll. Nakashima's studio began producing
a spindle-backed chair – known as the Straight
chair – for Knoll in the 1940s but then passed
production to the company direct, along
with a small range of other pieces, including
the N10 coffee table (or Splay-Leg table) and
the N12 dining table. Widdicomb-Mueller also
produced a number of Nakashima designs,
including the Origins dining chair (Model
206-W, 1958).

Larger Nakashima commissions included
two hundred pieces of furniture for Nelson
Rockefeller's home at Pocantico Hills, and
Altars for Peace installed at the Cathedral of
St John the Divine in New York City and other
places of worship around the world. Nakashima
was one of the few mid-century designers to
establish an international reputation while
remaining very much within the American craft
and art furniture movement.

FAR LEFT Turned-Leg Table, 1955, in American black walnut and rosewood.

LEFT Round Turned-Leg Table, c. 1960, made with American black walnut.

BELOW A Nakashima long chair, 1951, in American black walnut with a webbed canvas seat.

GEORGE NELSON
1908–1986

AMERICAN MODERNIST
AND CREATIVE POLYMATH
RENOWNED FOR HIS
COLOURFUL, PLAYFUL DESIGNS

George Nelson was a creative polymath who helped give shape to the mid-century modern world through his writings, ideas and collaborations with others as much as through his own furniture designs. He is credited with concepts as varied as the modern shopping mall, built-in storage wall, family room and modular furniture system.

As director of design at Herman Miller* from 1945 through to 1972, he became a midwife to designers such as CHARLES EAMES, ALEXANDER GIRARD (see under 'Textiles') and ISAMU NOGUCHI (see under 'Lighting'). But Herman Miller also became the producers of some of Nelson's own most famous designs, including the Coconut chair of 1955, with a sculpted seat in the shape of a coconut segment made from an upholstered steel shell resting on a triptych of steel legs (see pp. 14–15), and the Marshmallow sofa of 1956, originally produced in a hand-made edition of just two hundred. These were pieces of startling geometrical purity, but at the same time they were visually appealing and playful.

Born in Hartford, Connecticut, Nelson studied architecture at Yale before periods in Washington and Rome. While in Europe,

he began interviewing pioneering architects and designers, and submitted his pieces to a magazine called *Pencil Points*. In 1935 he became an editor at *Architectural Forum* magazine and formed working relationships with many key American innovators, a number of whom – such as Buckminster Fuller* and Isamu Noguchi – became good friends.

Through his writings and books, Nelson's ideas began to circulate, and in 1945 D. J. DePree, Herman Miller's chairman, invited him to be director of design at the company. It was an arrangement that allowed Nelson a great deal of creative freedom, both to commission and design for Herman Miller and also to pursue outside interests. The security of his contract gave him the opportunity to launch his own design studio two years later, which became George Nelson Associates, Inc.

Among Nelson's earliest Herman Miller designs was the MAA chair of 1958, which used an innovative ball and socket design with moulded fibreglass to create an office chair with an adjustable back – a highly influential design that helped to shape the evolution of the modern office chair. There was also his Modular seating system of 1956, with a range

RIGHT A George Nelson & Associates DAF chair, 1958, produced by Herman Miller, in fibreglass, chrome-plated steel and aluminium.

LEFT AND BELOW
Model 5670 Marshmallow
sofas in white and yellow,
1956, manufactured by
Herman Miller, with a
framework of enamelled
and chrome-plated steel
and with upholstery pads
coated in naugahyde.

of steel-framed upholstered seating in a sleek, modern style. The line still looks distinctly contemporary today and created a precedent for modular furniture systems that are now in wide use. Another key design was the Sling sofa of 1964, using a webbed rubber sling on a tubular steel frame to support leather-finished cushions, and partly inspired by car seats.

As well as furniture, there were other, more playful products. Nelson designed a whole range of distinctive clocks for Howard Miller – a company founded by Herman Miller's son. These included the Sunflower clock and the famous Ball clock – a series of colourful balls perched on metal spokes, like the abstract face of a flower. The design of the Ball clock apparently emerged from a lively evening of conversation and doodling spent with Noguchi, Fuller, and Irving Harper, who worked in the Nelson design studio.

Harper later suggested that the credit for a number of key Nelson pieces – including the Marshmallow sofa – did not lie with George Nelson alone. However, this is not to undermine the wide-ranging achievements of a man who undoubtedly helped lend character, thought and intelligence to mid-century American design.

BELOW Model 5215 miniature chest for Herman Miller, 1952, in walnut, laminate and aluminium.

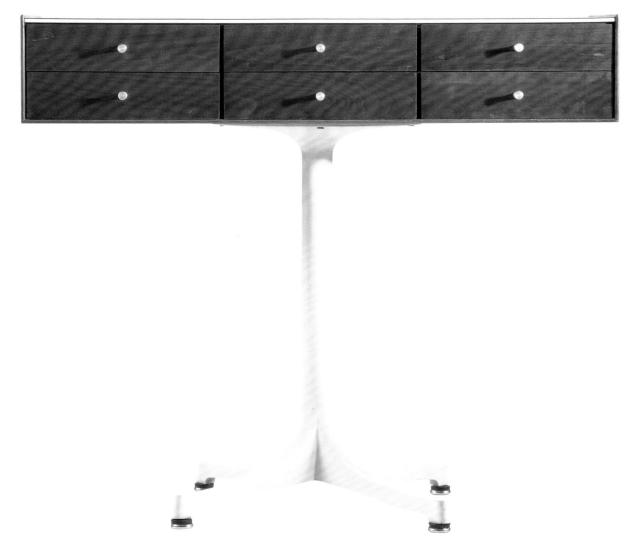

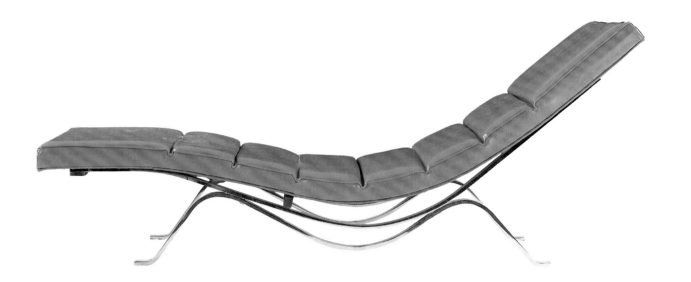

ABOVE George Nelson &
Associates prototype chaise
longue for Herman Miller,
1954, in chrome-plated steel
and vinyl; presented as
a gift from Nelson to artist
Richard Lippold.

RIGHT Custom Thin Edge
cabinet, c. 1960, produced
by Herman Miller, made
with teak, chrome-plated
steel and porcelain handles.

BELOW Model 4743 stereo
cabinet in combed oak,
lacquered wood, glass
and aluminium, with a linen
circular speaker outlet,
Herman Miller, 1946.

RIGHT Model 5259 Soft
Edge Curved dining table,
1952, manufactured by
Herman Miller, made with
walnut, lacquered wood
and enamelled steel.

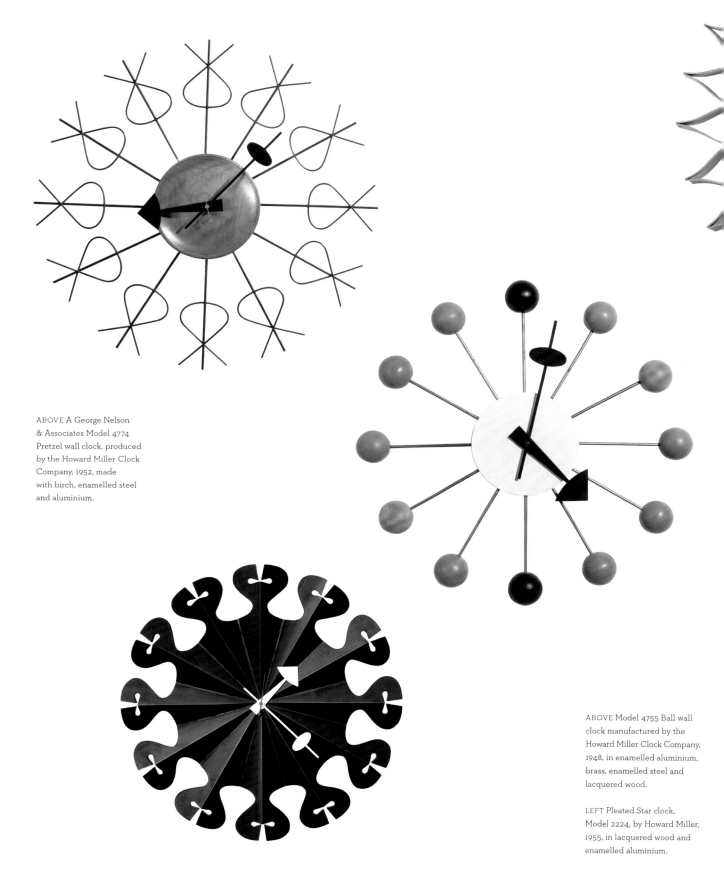

ABOVE A George Nelson & Associates Model 4774 Pretzel wall clock, produced by the Howard Miller Clock Company, 1952, made with birch, enamelled steel and aluminium.

ABOVE Model 4755 Ball wall clock manufactured by the Howard Miller Clock Company, 1948, in enamelled aluminium, brass, enamelled steel and lacquered wood.

LEFT Pleated Star clock, Model 2224, by Howard Miller, 1955, in lacquered wood and enamelled aluminium.

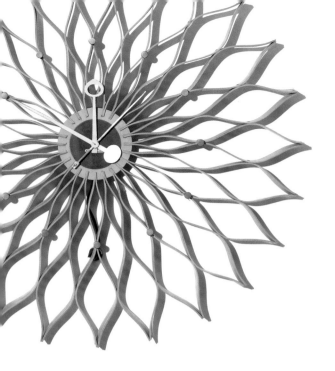

LEFT Sunflower wall clock, Model 2261, produced by the Howard Miller Clock Company, 1958, in lacquered plywood, laminated ash plywood and brass.

BELOW Model 4658 Home Office desk, 1946, produced by Herman Miller, in walnut, steel and leather.

VERNER PANTON
1926–1998

DANISH ICONOCLAST, WHOSE
PIONEERING EXPERIMENTS WITH
PLASTICS BECAME SYNONYMOUS
WITH THE PROGRESSIVE SPIRIT
OF THE 1960S

Verner Panton's work was theatrical, playful, colourful, optimistic, futuristic and innovative. More than anyone, he summed up the iconoclastic spirit of the 1960s, creating furniture, interiors and lighting threaded through with new thinking and fresh ideas. An inventor and showman, he made an extraordinary impact upon the world of design and his work is still very much in demand.

Born in a small village on the island of Fünen, Denmark, to a family of innkeepers, Panton studied at the technical college at Odense and then joined the Danish resistance movement towards the end of the war. In 1947 he moved to Copenhagen to study architecture at the Royal Academy of Art. There he met the designer POUL HENNINGSEN, who became a mentor, So too was ARNE JACOBSEN, who Panton assisted from 1950 to 1952, helping to develop Jacobsen's famous Ant chair among other projects.

It soon became clear, however, that Panton was not a designer in the familiar mould of many of the great Scandinavian modernists, who placed a particular emphasis on organic, carefully crafted forms. By the mid-1950s, Panton was already looking further afield and took himself off on road trips across Europe, in a Volkswagen camper van, meeting designers and talking to manufacturers.

His first furniture designs were produced by Fritz Hansen* in 1955 but it was the Cone chair of 1958, produced by Danish company Plus-Linje, that really caught a wider audience. Like a futuristic padded flower or paper water cup, sitting on a supporting steel cross, this was a chair like no other and challenged all preconceptions of what furniture should look like and how it should be made. The chair was originally designed for his parents' new restaurant but was soon on sale in Europe and New York, establishing Panton as a new and highly imaginative voice.

Pieces that followed were similarly avant-garde, with the Wire Cone and Adjustable Peacock chairs of 1960 created using bent steel lattices. But Panton was also fascinated by the potential of plastics and started working on designs for a single-piece chair in 1957. A Danish manufacturer produced a prototype in 1960 using Polysteron plastic, but it proved unsuitable for mass production. Then came a move to Basel, where Panton worked together with Willi Fehlbaum, the founder of the Vitra* furniture manufacturing company, developing a refined design of the chair and trialling a number of plastics that would suit industrial manufacturing. The S-shaped, stackable Panton chair – the first to be made with a single piece of injection-moulded plastic – was finally launched at the Cologne Furniture Fair in 1968. It was an instant success and – unwittingly – helped to pave the way for the millions of mass-produced plastic monobloc chairs that now circle the globe.

Other chairs included the S chair in bent ply for Thonet* (1966), which echoed the shape of the Panton, and there were also futuristic furniture systems, such as the Pantower – or Living Tower – lounger of 1969, made with upholstered polyurethane foam and resembling a sci-fi climbing frame.

ABOVE S-Stuhis Model 276 chair in laminated and bent plywood, made by A. Sommer for Thonet, 1956.

OPPOSITE A set of ten Panton chairs in injection-moulded plastic, 1958, manufactured by Vitra.

BELOW Model K2 wire cone
chairs, produced by Plus-Linje,
1959, in galvanized and
chrome-plated steel with
an upholstered pad seat.

Panton was also an interior designer, creating sculpted, Space Age restaurants and room installations: the interiors of his own home in Basel in the 1970s had the surreal flavour of a Pop Art statement. Then there was lighting design, at which Panton also excelled. His Moon, Onion and VP Globe pendant lights have the dream-like, hi-tech beauty of sculpted flying objects. Panton's Panthella table and floor lamps of 1970, for Louis Poulsen*, with

tulip bases and dome-like heads, are another constant classic. In the late 1960s Panton also designed a range of textiles that explored some of the vibrant shapes, colours and patterns seen in his other work (see p. 10). The sense of theatre and showmanship in Panton's work was always backed up with a real sense of substance. His forms and curves have created a lasting design legacy, and a substantial portion of his portfolio is still in production.

RIGHT AND BELOW Heart
Cone chairs in red and
orange, made by Plus-Linje,
1958, with a steel frame
and base and upholstery.

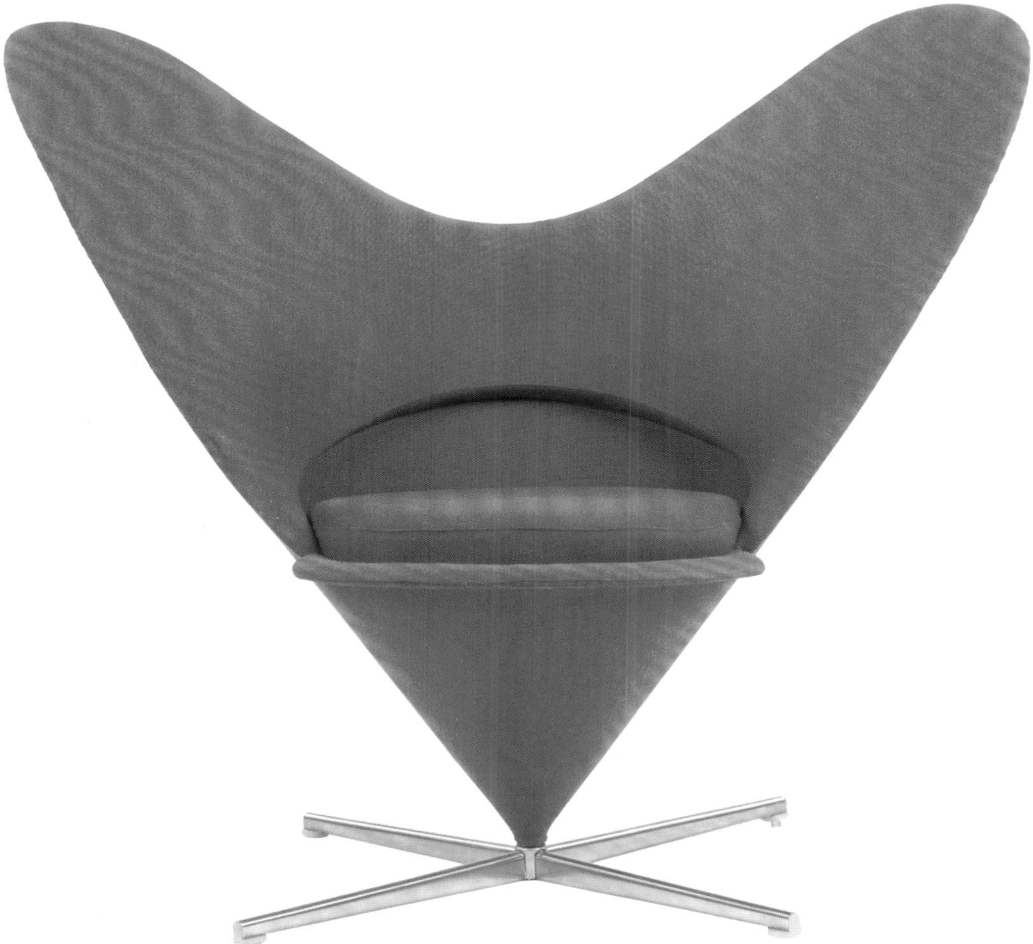

RIGHT Model 423P occasional table, produced by x-design, Denmark, c. 1971, in laminated wood and enamelled steel.

BELOW A pair of Pantonova Model 113T chairs in chrome-plated steel, with upholstered seats, produced by Fritz Hansen, 1971.

OPPOSITE Model E 1-2-3 System lounge chairs, 1973, produced by Fritz Hansen, made with aluminium, chrome-plated steel and leather.

PIERRE PAULIN
1927–2009

INNOVATIVE FRENCH DESIGNER,
WHOSE BRIGHT, FUTURISTIC
WORK WAS ALSO NOTED FOR
ITS SOFT, SENSUOUS QUALITIES

Conjuring a picture of 1950s furniture and design might involve a wealth of warm, natural textures and fluid, sculpted forms in timber, ply and also steel, woven into new forms. With 1960s furniture, the shapes and sinews became even more sculptural and abstract, while colour became all-important and new materials, such as plastics and polyurethane foam, were combined with a Pop Art sensibility. If 1950s design was rather hard-edged and sometimes a little serious, then the 1960s were more about making design soft, sensuous and playful.

These three adjectives serve well to describe the work of Pierre Paulin. His furniture came in high-impact and occasionally lurid Pop colours, and was sometimes even psychedelic and wrapped in vibrant patterns. One of his most famous chairs was dubbed 'the Tongue' and certainly resembled a languid, disembodied wolf's lick (see p. 10). The Ribbon chair of 1966 was also an extraordinary work of art – one of the most sculptural and visually seductive pieces of the 1960s, yet very comfortable as well. Paulin had an artist's eye, but never forgot about the practicalities and ergonomics of the pieces that he designed.

Paulin was born in Paris, but grew up in the Picardie area of northern France. One of his childhood heroes was his uncle, George Paulin, who was a car designer for Bentley, Peugeot and others (as well as a Resistance fighter in the war). Pierre hoped to become a sculptor and trained as a stone-carver but gave up on this dream after injuring his arm. Instead he went to study design at the famous École Camondo in Paris.

Paulin's first pieces began appearing in the 1950s when he started working with Thonet*, but he was also studying the work of Scandinavian and American furniture makers and manufacturers, as well as being influenced by Japanese design. It was the 1960s when he really began to make an impact, using polyurethane foam and fibreglass to create powerfully expressive shapes and sensuous forms, largely in collaboration with Dutch manufacturers Artifort*.

'I considered the manufacture of chairs to be rather primitive and I was trying to think up new processes,' he said. 'At Artifort, I started using new foam and rubber from Italy and a light metallic frame combined with stretch material. Those new, rounder, more comfortable shapes were such a success.... I have always considered design to be a mix of invention and industrial innovation.'[4]

Paulin began working with Artifort in the late 1950s. His Orange Slice (Model 437) chair looked like two smiling, brightly coloured segments spliced together to form seat and back. By the early 1960s his work was becoming more abstract and he introduced the Mushroom chair – or Model 560 – made with latex foam stretched over a tubular steel frame and coated with bright upholstery. It was a move towards a lower, more informal style of lounge seating that came to define the period.

The design of the Tongue chair (Model 577) was apparently met with some suspicion by the head of Artifort, but when he saw how his son and his friends took to the seat – made again with upholstered foam over a fluid

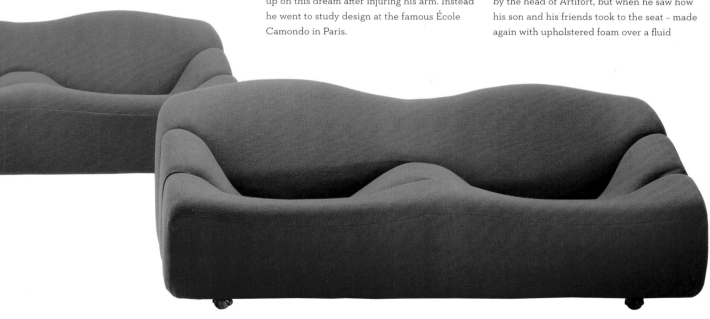

OPPOSITE A pair of ABCD
sofas, 1968, produced by
Artifort, in chrome-plated
steel, rubber and upholstery.

BELOW Ribbon armchair,
1966, in lacquered wood
and upholstery, manufactured
by Artifort.

BOTTOM Model 560
Mushroom chairs, 1960,
manufactured by Artifort
with stretch jersey over foam
and steel.

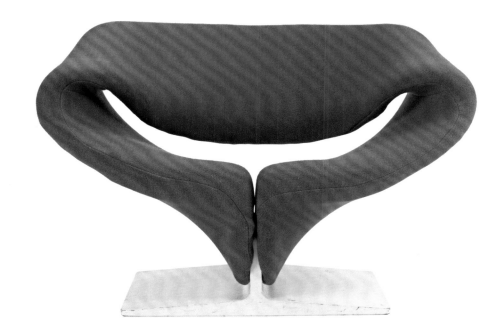

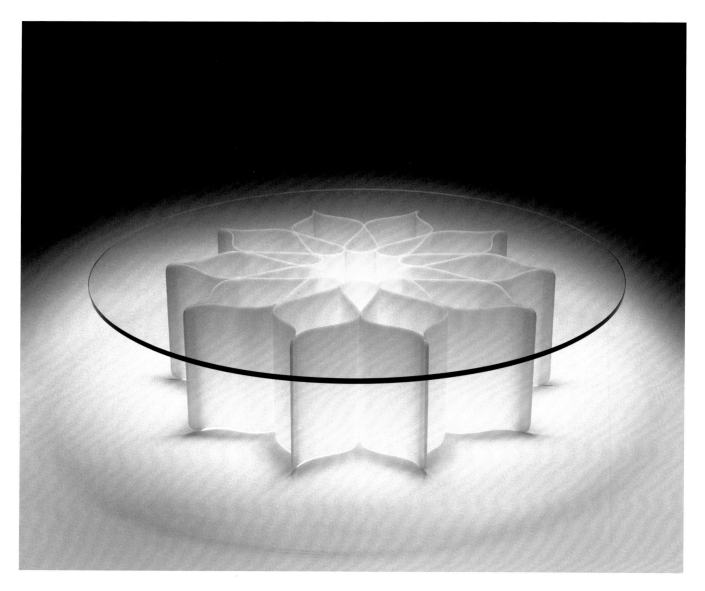

tubular steel frame – he began to realize its potential for a younger audience who wanted something casual, modern and iconoclastic.

The ABCD seating system of 1968 used polyurethane foam over fibreglass shells and could be manipulated to form individual chairs or combined in a triptych to create a sofa. The Model F598 chair (1973) seemed like an evolution of ideas seen in the Ribbon chair (Model 582) but in a wider, more familiar form, using a stretch fabric over a slim tubular steel frame. In the late 1970s, Paulin also designed a bestselling plastic monobloc garden chair, known as the Dangari, for Allibert.

In 1971, Paulin was chosen to design four rooms for President Georges Pompidou and later, in 1984, he was asked to furnish President François Mitterrand's office. Many of his pieces have been reissued in recent years. His work sits alongside pieces by contemporaries such as Olivier Mourgue*, who also explored the use of colourful, sculpted forms in a series of low-slung, Space Age designs.

ABOVE Élysée light table, produced by Alpha Internationale, France, 1971, in acrylic and glass. Fewer than fifteen examples were produced for the Palais de l'Élysée in Paris.

BELOW Model 687 Arachnoid armchair, 1965, manufactured by Artifort with lacquered wood, rope and leather.

BOTTOM LEFT Model F444 lounge chair, in stainless steel and black leather, made by Artifort, 1963.

BOTTOM RIGHT Model 675 Butterfly chair, in chrome-plated steel and leather, Artifort, 1963.

WARREN PLATNER
1919–2006

AMERICAN MODERNIST NOTED
FOR HIS SOPHISTICATED,
THEATRICAL DESIGNS,
INCLUDING INTERIORS AND
ARCHITECTURE AS WELL
AS FURNITURE

Warren Platner was not afraid of colour, texture or even opulence. A sense of delight threaded through his designs, interiors and architecture that made them stand apart from the work of other modernists, who may have demanded a greater sense of purity and restraint.

Platner worked within many different mediums, but it was his furniture collection designed for Knoll* that made the greatest impact. First designed in 1966, the Lounge Collection of tables, armchairs and stools has been in production ever since. The designer saw a gap for a range of furniture that was distinctly modern, yet also gentle and graceful, combining an ornamental aspect with practicality and function.

He began to experiment with steel wire and came up with an ergonomic collection that used a series of welded rods, coated in nickel or bronze, in a vertical wheatsheaf formation to create table bases and armchairs. Used together, these rods created a strong support, like a semi-transparent drum or upturned basket, which did away with the need for more traditional legs and struts. The simple, lightweight lattice was revolutionary and ingenious, but it was also unique and pleasing, with a sensuous, crafted shape.

Platner had wanted to design a classic and here it was, with glass used for tabletops and colourful upholstery pads for stools and chairs. 'A classic is something you look at often and always accept as it is,' Platner once said. 'You can see no way of improving it.'[5]

Born in Baltimore, Maryland, Platner studied architecture at Cornell University. From 1945 to 1950 he worked in the office of industrial designer RAYMOND LOEWY (see under 'Product and Industrial Design'), then spent fifteen years in the office of architect and designer EERO SAARINEN, where he was involved in the design of Dulles International Airport in Washington, D.C., and the Vivian Beaumont Repertory Theater at Lincoln Center for the Performing Arts, New York. He also collaborated with Irish-American architect Kevin Roche on the design of the Ford Foundation in Manhattan.

In 1967 Platner established his own design practice in New Haven, Connecticut. Early projects included a New York showroom for the Danish silverware company Georg Jensen* (1968). Freestanding buildings included the Kent Memorial Library in Suffield, Connecticut (from 1972). His interior scheme for the American Restaurant (1974) in Kansas City was lifted by vibrant pink banquettes, illuminated by fitted brass lamps leaning over the tables like eager eavesdroppers.

One of his most high-profile interiors commissions was for the Windows on the World restaurant at the top of the former World Trade

LEFT Lounge chairs,
manufactured by Knoll, 1966,
in chrome-plated steel with
upholstered seats.

Center North Tower in Manhattan, finished in 1976. Perhaps most striking was the reception area, which included a number of Platner's own lounge chairs and a console-like reception desk within a futuristic, almost sci fi-inspired room.

Platner's own home in Guildford, Connecticut (1970), included a vast, high-ceilinged living room arranged around a square fur-covered sofa, forming a conversation pit. His Knoll lounge chairs are again much in evidence. Other innovations included internal windows and integrated window seats.

Platner designed many other pieces of furniture – desks and ottomans, chairs, side tables and office furniture – but the Lounge Collection continues to define his career and endures to this day as a symbol of sophisticated, sensuous modernism.

BELOW A set of dining chairs in chrome-plated steel and upholstery, produced by Knoll, c. 1966.

BOTTOM A dining set with a dining table in bronze-plated steel and glass, and matching upholstered chairs, produced by Knoll, c. 1965.

ABOVE Executive desk,
c. 1970, produced by Lehigh
Leopold, USA, made with
teak, granite, bronze and
leather.

LEFT Sofa, c. 1970, in
chrome-plated steel, walnut
and leather, manufactured
by Lehigh Leopold.

BELOW Credenza in walnut,
chrome-plated steel and
granite, made by Lehigh
Leopold, c. 1970.

OPPOSITE A Lehigh
Leopold-produced lounge
chair in brass-plated steel,
walnut and leather, c. 1970.

GIO PONTI
1891–1979

GIFTED AND PROLIFIC
POLYMATH, DUBBED THE
GODFATHER OF MODERN
ITALIAN DESIGN

The sheer breadth of Gio Ponti's achievements is quite startling. Famously, he would pack an extraordinary amount of work into a single day, rising early and working again after dinner and well into the evening. His career was long and he embraced countless opportunities in many different mediums of design, as well as being a teacher, writer and magazine editor. He was generous and passionate, revelling in the vitality and power of good design and opening himself up to a vast diaspora of architectural and design influences, as well as to a cornucopia of materials and colours. 'Love architecture, be it ancient or modern,' he said, with typical missionary zeal. 'Love it for its fantastic, adventurous and solemn creations.'[6]

As a furniture designer, Ponti was prolific. Many pieces were designed for specific projects, such as the Hotel Parco dei Principi in Rome (1964), or residential commissions including the Villa Arreaza (1954) and Villa Planchart (1957), both in Caracas, Venezuela, the latter remaining one of Ponti's best preserved architectural and interiors commissions.

Famously, Ponti also collaborated with Piero Fornasetti* on a number of furniture designs, with Fornasetti adding his flamboyant embellishments to Ponti's secretaires, desks and cabinets. One can also see occasional common traits between Ponti's furniture and that of another colleague and friend, CARLO MOLLINO, with a shared interest in tapered legs and biomorphic and organic influences, as well as a weakness for richly upholstered armchairs.

But Ponti also delighted in designing furniture and products for commercial manufacture. A number of these pieces were reinterpretations of familiar classics, such as his modern retelling of the Murano glass chandelier from the mid-1940s. In particular, there was the reinvention of the classic Chiavari chair, named after the Italian coastal town where this ubiquitous dining chair with a light and simple wooden frame was invented in the early 19th century. In 1950 Ponti produced a modern, lightweight chair for Cassina*, called the Leggera, available in walnut with a cellulose seat or ash with leather. This design was refined further over the years to become the strong, elegant and streamlined Superleggera (1957) in ash and woven rush, one of Ponti's most famous designs and so light that it could be lifted with a single finger.

Giovanni Ponti was born in Milan, the city that would be his base throughout his lifetime. His studies in architecture at the Polytechnic of Milan were interrupted by military service during World War I, but he graduated in 1921. In the 1920s he combined architectural commissions with a position

OPPOSITE Chair in Italian
walnut with an upholstered
seat, c. 1936, made by Casa
e Giardino, Italy. A number
of variations on the design
were produced, including
a 1949 edition by Cassina.

BELOW Model 589 armchair
in walnut and upholstery,
manufactured by Cassina,
1955.

as art director for ceramics manufacturer Richard Ginori, for whom he designed a wide range of pieces. In 1928, he launched and edited the widely influential architectural and design journal *Domus*, which he contributed to for many years (apart from a brief sojourn in the 1940s, when he founded another magazine called *Stile*).

The pace of Ponti's architectural commissions accelerated in the 1950s and beyond, with a series of houses and hotels – including the celebrated Parco dei Principi Hotel in Sorrento (1962), sister to the Rome hotel of the same name – as well as a number of larger projects. Chief among them was the Pirelli Tower in Milan (1958), followed by a number of churches and the Cathedral of Taranto in 1970, and the Denver Art Museum in 1971.

Key product designs included the La Pavoni coffee machine of 1947, a shining chrome creation that looked like a racing-car engine split into two and came to define the sophisticated coffee shops of post-war Europe. Furniture designs for Cassina included the Distex upholstered lounge chair and the Diamond lounge chairs and sofa, all released in 1953.

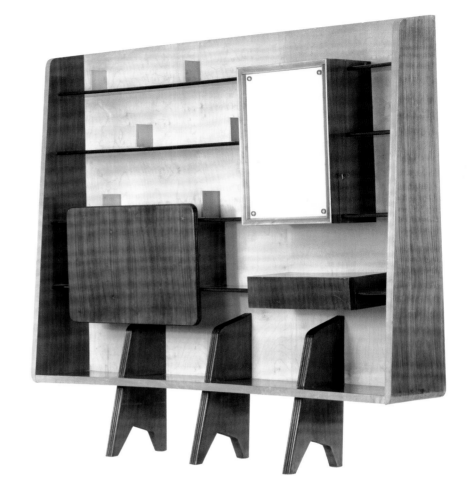

ABOVE Bookcase produced by Arturo Colombo, Italy, 1945, in Italian walnut, maple, glass and brass.

LEFT Armchair in Italian walnut and upholstery, made by Reguitti, Italy, 1954.

OPPOSITE A set of Leggera chairs in walnut and cane, produced by Cassina, Italy, 1950.

TOP A pair of Diamond
lounge chairs from the Villa
Goldschmidt in Buenos Aires,
Argentina, 1953, produced
by Cassina in skai, enamelled
aluminium and upholstery.

ABOVE Diamond sofa
manufactured by Cassina,
1953, in leather, brass and
upholstery.

BELOW Lounge chairs, 1952, produced by Cassina, in leather, mohair and walnut.

BOTTOM A pair of lounge chairs from the Hotel Parco dei Principi in Rome, 1964, produced by Cassina, made with skai, lacquered wood and upholstery.

JEAN PROUVÉ
1901–1984

RADICAL FRENCH INNOVATOR
WHO SOUGHT TO USE GOOD,
AFFORDABLE DESIGN TO
IMPROVE THE QUALITY OF LIFE
FOR ALL

Finding a neat pigeonhole for Jean Prouvé is no easy thing. He was an architectural innovator as much as a furniture designer, but he was also an engineer. He delighted in seeking out new ideas and radical solutions and turning his discoveries into reality on the floor of his workshops. There was an uncompromising, avant-garde edge to his designs, which retained a semi-industrial aesthetic even when destined for the home. Never precious or refined, his work was sophisticated, intelligent and often raw.

Prouvé's furniture has a revolutionary, experimental quality threaded through it. Some of his earliest pieces, from the late 1920s, used 'tube aplati' – or flattened, extra-strong sections of tubular steel – to great effect. One piece was the Chaise Inclinable en Tôle d'Acier of 1930 – a folding and stacking chair with nickel-plated metalwork and an upholstered seat. The Chaise Standard Demontable (1931/1934) was another rugged, utilitarian design in steel, tubular steel and plywood that could again be produced in large numbers and stacked. In 1931, Prouvé also designed a range of furniture for the Cité Universitaire in Nancy; his elegant, curvaceous,

steel-framed Cité armchair in particular went on to establish itself as a design icon.

Jean Prouvé was the son of the artist and painter Victor Prouvé, a pivotal figure in the development of French Art Nouveau in Nancy. In 1916, Jean was apprenticed to a metalworker and retained a fascination with experimental metal construction and furniture throughout his life. He opened his first workshop in Nancy in 1923 and began producing doors and railings before developing his earliest, self-designed pieces of furniture. By the early 1930s, he was able to expand his business and produced many pieces – such as desks, chairs and tables – for schoolrooms and institutional use.

During the same period, he began to collaborate with architects and other designers on a number of innovative and progressive buildings. By 1939 he was developing a range of prefabricated buildings, including demountable barracks for the French army. During the war, Prouvé was involved in the French Resistance and after the liberation of France he was elected mayor of Nancy. He was also commissioned to develop his ideas about prefabricated buildings even further with his Maisons à Portiques – factory-made housing for war refugees. In the years that followed, these experiments led on to the Maisons Tropicales – a small series of lightweight prefab houses dispatched to Niger and the Congo – as well as Prouvé's own house in Nancy (1954), which made use of a number of prefabricated components, or 'leftovers'.

By 1950, Les Ateliers Jean Prouvé was a large operation, with around 250 workers, and Prouvé was awarded the Légion d'Honneur. But three years later he lost control of his factory to his backers and was forced to begin again, opening a new design studio in Paris in 1954 and beginning a fresh series of projects and collaborations.

Furniture designs from the 1950s are just as sought-after as some of the earlier designs. The brightly coloured bookcase unit

LEFT Model 356 Antony chair, 1954, made by Ateliers Jean Prouvé, in ash plywood and enamelled steel.

LEFT Model 300 demountable Caféteria chair, c. 1952, manufactured by Ateliers Jean Prouvé, in enamelled steel and ash.

BELOW Model 305 Standard chair, from the Maritime Exchange in Paris, 1950, produced by Ateliers Jean Prouvé, in enamelled steel and stained ash plywood.

TOP Curved Compass desk
and Standard chair, 1953,
in enamelled steel, laminate
and beech plywood, with
aluminium and vinyl
upholstery for the chair;
made by Ateliers Jean Prouvé.

ABOVE Ateliers Jean Prouvé
Grande Compass table, 1953,
in enamelled steel with
laminate top.

designed with Charlotte Perriand* and Sonia Delaunay in 1952 for the library at Paris's Cité Universitaire's Maison du Mexique is highly collectable. Other pieces from the period include the Guéridon series table, with its triangular legs connected by a star-shaped steel bolt, most commonly seen as a café-style table with a circular timber or metal top. There was also the Compass table and desk, first produced in 1953, and the Antony chair, first designed in the early 1950s for a competition for seating for the Cité Universitaire in Antony.

As has sometimes been remarked, there is a curious irony in the fact that Prouvé concerned himself, above all, with creating affordable, practical and progressive designs but that his work has now become so

eminently collectable, with original designs and prototypes earning large sums at auction. This can be seen as a mark of the respect with which Prouvé's work is now regarded and his extraordinary reputation as an inventor and innovator. Many Prouvé designs have also been reissued in recent years.

BELOW Guéridon table in bent and enamelled steel and aluminium with rectangular laminate top, produced by Ateliers Jean Prouvé, 1950.

BOTTOM Ateliers Jean Prouvé school desk in bent and enamelled steel and oak, 1946.

ERNEST RACE
1913–1964

CREATOR OF SLIM, CLEAN,
STREAMLINED DESIGNS THAT
SUGGESTED A NEW AND MODERN
DIRECTION FOR BRITISH DESIGN

While America enjoyed a consumer boom and rapid economic and consumer growth in the years after World War II, Britain struggled. She had paid a terrible price for victory and would never again assume the same prominence and importance in the world as she had before 1939. Not only had bomb damage weakened the country's manufacturing base and caused immense destruction in many British cities, but the war effort itself had hoovered up raw materials at a frightening rate.

This was the context in which designer Ernest Race was working when he started looking at creating new lines of furniture immediately after the war's end. This was the age of 'Utility furniture'*, a government-led scheme to make the most of rare reserves of timber, with a list of approved manufacturers and designs, carefully rationed right up to 1952.

Working with engineer J. W. Noel Jordan, Race looked for ways around the timber rationing, turning instead towards materials that were easier to obtain, including leftovers from the war effort. Race designed a new line of cast-aluminium furniture that was first shown at the Victoria & Albert Museum's 'Britain Can Make It' exhibition in 1946.

The BA chair and matching armchair featured recast wartime scrap metal. Around 250,000 of the chairs were sold, both for commercial and private use. Race's chairs and tables also graced the interiors of troop ships bringing back weary servicemen and women, and the showrooms of Heal & Sons*.

Race was born in Newcastle and studied interior design at the Bartlett School of Architecture in London. He worked as a draughtsman for the lighting company Troughton & Young before opening a shop in Knightsbridge, selling his own textile and carpet designs along with a line of lacquered plywood furniture brought in from suppliers. During the late 1930s he met many émigré designers and architects who were spending time in the UK before moving to the States, including Walter Gropius*. During the war itself Race served as a fireman in London.

His partnership with Jordan began after the engineer placed a newspaper advert calling for a designer to help develop a range of mass-produced furniture. Their BA chair was manufactured by Ernest Race Ltd – which later became Race Furniture – right through to the 1960s and won a gold medal at the Milan Triennale in 1954.

The Festival of Britain* exhibition in 1951 brought another key moment in Race's career, as he launched his Antelope chair and sofa. These were very different from the BA chair in character and feel, with a design that was modern, playful and colourful. The frame formed a flayed lattice back with curving arm supports, echoing the traditional Windsor chair. Lightweight with ball feet, it looked like an abstract line drawing of an animal. It came in blue, red, yellow or grey, and Race also designed a matching bench. The chairs were used as seating for the outdoor terraces around the Royal Festival Hall during the exhibition.

Race also designed the Springbok stacking chair (1951) and the Neptune folding deckchair in laminated beech for the P&O

LEFT Antelope chair, with frame of bent steel rods and ply seat, designed for the Festival of Britain, 1951.

shipping line (1953). Other key pieces included the Heron armchair of 1955, another classic of the period.

In 1962, Race resigned from his company – which continues on today – to work as a freelance designer. Among his projects was the redesign of the famous Isokon* Donkey bookcase in 1963. Perhaps the most striking elements of Race's career were his ingenuity and originality. His work feels quite unique and non-derivative, and it helped to pave the way for a new generation of forward-thinking British designers.

RIGHT BA3 chair, aluminium and upholstery, manufactured by Ernest Race Ltd, 1945.

BELOW Penguin Donkey Mark 2 bookcase, produced by Isokon, with legs in cherry wood, 1963.

RIGHT Neptune chair, 1953, produced by Ernest Race Ltd in beech and birch plywood, with upholstered seat cushions.

JENS RISOM
BORN 1916

DANISH DESIGNER KEY IN
ESTABLISHING MODERN DESIGN
WITH SCANDINAVIAN VALUES
IN POST-WAR AMERICA

'The most interesting piece to design is a chair,' said Jens Risom. 'It's also the hardest thing to design – there's no doubt about it. A chair has to fit everybody – high, low, small. But there's so much that you can do in such a small framework. If you take a look at all the chairs designed in the last three or four hundred years, it's incredible.'[7]

Risom's career took off with a chair – the No. 666 WSP side chair for Knoll*, designed in 1941, and making use of heavy-duty army surplus parachute straps to create a distinctive woven lattice. It was one of fifteen pieces that Risom created for Hans Knoll – also including stools, lounge chairs and tables – to launch the Knoll furniture company. A number of these pieces are still available from the firm today.

Risom grew up in Copenhagen, where his father, Sven Risom, worked as an architect. Sven was a key influence, but Jens also noted how his father's career had waned as his enthusiasm for his craft had faltered. From an early age, Jens resolved to be dedicated and ambitious, and to carry his work forward with passion and pragmatism.

He studied at the Copenhagen School of Industrial Arts & Design, where HANS WEGNER was a classmate, before attending business college and then working with Ernst Kuhn's architectural practice as an interior designer. In 1939, after a period in Stockholm, Risom decided to move to America.

On arrival there he found that opportunities to study or practise design seemed limited, but he eventually found freelance work with designer Dan Cooper, and then a few years later he met Hans Knoll. Their impressive collaboration was, however, cut short by the war. Risom began designing camouflage jackets for Sherman tanks that could be zipped and unzipped in moments, but – because he spoke German – he found himself serving as a translator with General Patton.

After the war was over, Hans and Florence Knoll expected Risom to return to their fold, but he had other plans. Unenthused by the Bauhaus*-inspired look that Florence Knoll was now pushing for, he was more interested in an organic approach. Risom's pieces – created for his own company, Jens Risom Design, founded in 1946 – mixed natural materials, playful colours and sensuous, ergonomic curves. 'Wood is really my favourite material,' he said. 'I like walnut very much – it has a richness and a grain characteristic that lends itself to all kinds of things.'[8]

RIGHT Walnut magazine table, manufactured by Jens Risom Design, c. 1949.

OPPOSITE ABOVE Model 654L side chairs in birch and webbed canvas seating, c. 1949, produced by Knoll.

OPPOSITE BELOW Coffee table produced by Jens Risom Design, c. 1950, in walnut, iron and copper.

The Jens Risom Design company grew fast, and Risom and his family settled in New Canaan, Connecticut, within easy striking distance of both the Manhattan showroom and a dedicated furniture factory. Before long, JRD was established as an international brand, with offices in Europe and South America. But in 1970 Risom sold the company and it was shut down a few years later by its new owners, to the designer's disappointment.

He continued to produce freelance designs and in the early years of the 21st century his work experienced a renaissance, with companies such as Design Within Reach commissioning new pieces and others, including Knoll, reissuing classic mid-century Risom designs.

SERGIO RODRIGUES
BORN 1927

CRAFTSMAN WHO GAVE A
VOICE TO BRAZILIAN FURNITURE
DESIGN, INSTILLING AN
EMPHASIS ON SOLID FRAMES
AND LUXURIOUS UPHOLSTERY

BELOW Sheriff lounge chairs,
in rosewood and leather,
produced by Atelier Sergio
Rodrigues, 1961.

The work of Sergio Rodrigues has a uniquely Brazilian quality. Rodrigues used native materials such as wood, cane and leather within furniture designs that have a real sense of presence. These are pieces that are substantial and solidly built, with a clear sense of craftsmanship but also a degree of informality and an emphasis on comfort.

His most famous design is the Mole armchair of 1957 – also marketed under the name 'Sheriff'. Its broad wooden frame is layered with a soft coat of fluid leather cushions that form the seat and back but also drape over the armrests. The chair won a prize at the Concorso Internazionale del Mobile in Italy in 1961. The Moleca armchair of 1963 was very similar in feel, while the Tonico sofa of the same year also used generous leather cushions, with fat bolsters to support the back.

Rodrigues was born in Rio de Janeiro to a father who was a painter and illustrator but died young. Rodrigues studied architecture at the University of Brazil and started working as an architect. He soon recognized, however, that while Brazilian architecture had already forged a strong identity, furniture and interior design lagged some way behind. He began to experiment, particularly in wood, and in 1955

opened his own store and gallery in Rio, which he christened Oca, after the word for indigenous Indian cabins. He also designed the interiors of the store, whose stock included fabrics and lighting.

Rodrigues was particularly concerned with establishing a home-made range, and by 1956 Oca was selling his first creations (the Mole designs evolved from a request for a comfortable studio couch from photographer Otto Stupakoff). Within a few years Rodrigues was also being commissioned to design furniture for some of the buildings that were appearing from nowhere in the new capital of Brasilia under the guidance of its chief architect, OSCAR NIEMEYER (see under 'Houses and Interiors'). These included the Leve Beto armchair for the Palácio do Planalto and seats for the auditorium at the new University of Brasilia. In 1960 he was asked to furnish the Brazilian embassy in Rome and he also designed furniture for Niemeyer's Bloch Publishing building in Rio.

In the mid-1960s Rodrigues established a large factory in Jacareí, near São Paulo, which manufactured his furniture for a number of years, and he opened a second store focusing on affordable furniture. In 1973 he launched the Sergio Rodrigues Architecture practice in Rio but continued to design furniture for hotels and other projects.

A number of pieces – such as the Oscar and Lúcio Costa chairs (both 1956) – used a light profile and cane mesh seats and backs. But Rodrigues's work is largely characterized

by a luxurious level of upholstery, substantial frames and a bold silhouette. Armchairs – such as the Gio of 1958 and the Parati of 1963 – splice modernity with comfort. Rodrigues always took the ergonomics and the needs of the user into account rather than simply creating aesthetically pleasing sculptures.

His benches, sideboards, tables and cabinets use woods of great character with a deep, warm finish, including peroba and tauari. With their rounded corners and sinuous styling, it almost feels as though these pieces have emerged from the rich Brazilian earth. Rodrigues, one of the country's most prolific designers, now finds his work much in demand internationally.

BELOW Stella dining table, 1956, in rosewood and lacquered wood.

BELOW LEFT Lounge chair in rosewood with an upholstered seat, c. 1954.

RIGHT Navona armchair, 1960, in rosewood and upholstery, from the Brazilian embassy in Rome.

EERO SAARINEN
1910–1961

SINGULAR FINNISH-AMERICAN
INNOVATOR WHO MADE AN
EXTRAORDINARY IMPRESSION
ON MANY ASPECTS OF THE
DESIGN WORLD

Eero Saarinen's work came to define the progressive, ambitious spirit of mid-century America, allied to many key developments in the culture of the times. As an architect, his designs for the aerodynamic form of the TWA Terminal at Idlewild (now known as John F. Kennedy International Airport), New York, and his work on Washington's Dulles International Airport, helped give a powerful identity to Jet Age travel, in sympathy with the fresh, fluid forms of the airplanes themselves.

His work for the rapidly expanding giants of American corporate culture – IBM, General Motors, Bell, John Deere – reinforced the link between architecture and the outward identity and image of large companies. Along the way Saarinen also pioneered the idea of the campus office – a whole collection of buildings suited to different uses on one dedicated site.

As a furniture designer he was also to have a profound impact on 1950s and '60s America. He sought to experiment with both form and materials here, too, and produced a range for Knoll* that in many ways summed up the futuristic nature of mid-century style. This was the Tulip range – more properly called the Pedestal Group – and it was white, simple, sculptural, unified and delightful.

'The undercarriage of chairs and tables in a typical interior makes an ugly, confusing, unrestful world,' said Saarinen. 'I wanted to clear up the slum of legs. I wanted to make the chair all one thing again.'[9]

The range included chairs, stools and tables, all emerging from their distinctive single stem. A Knoll advert shows a Space Age young woman with wraparound mirrored sunglasses and metallic miniskirt posing with Saarinen's Model 150 armchair, suggesting that this is the future. Today, the Pedestal range has to be one of the most iconic and widely counterfeited furniture collections in the world.

Saarinen was the son of Finnish architect Eliel Saarinen* and textile designer Loja. The family moved to the States in 1923. There, Eliel Saarinen helped establish and create the campus of the Cranbrook Academy of Art* in Michigan, which became a focal point for a modern approach to the study and craft of design. In the early 1930s Eero studied briefly in Paris and then went to Yale University, followed by a fellowship that helped fund a lengthy trip to Europe and beyond. Upon his return, he began working with his father's architectural practice but also taught at Cranbrook, where he met CHARLES & RAY EAMES, as well as Florence Knoll and HARRY BERTOIA.

In the 1940s, Saarinen and Charles Eames collaborated on the design of the Case Study House #9 for John Entenza* in Los Angeles, next door to the Eames's own home. They also co-designed a range of eight pieces of organic furniture that won first prize in a competition curated by Eliot Noyes* for the Museum of Modern Art in New York.

BELOW LEFT A pair of Tulip stools, c. 1960, in enamelled cast aluminium with a vinyl-coated seat, produced by Knoll.

BELOW RIGHT Tulip dining table, 1957, in enamelled aluminium, manufactured by Knoll.

OPPOSITE A set of ten Model 150 Tulip chairs, 1956, manufactured by Knoll, in lacquered fibreglass and enamelled cast aluminium with a vinyl-coated cushion (the orange colour was a custom finish).

RIGHT, BELOW AND BOTTOM
Womb sofa, chairs and
ottoman, produced by Knoll,
1948, with tubular chrome-
plated steel legs and
upholstered fibreglass seats
and cushions.

In 1947, Saarinen designed his first chair for Knoll – the Grasshopper Model 61. This was soon followed by the Womb chair, Model 71, and matching ottoman (1948). The Womb chair – comfortable, ergonomic and enveloping – was a great success and was accompanied by a two-seater sofa in the same style. The Womb range is still in production, as is the Tulip collection.

In 1950, with the death of his father, Saarinen assumed control of their architectural practice, changing its name to Eero Saarinen and Associates. Over the next ten years his design output – always innovative, original and bespoke – was prolific and groundbreaking. Among the many commercial and corporate projects, there was also the Irwin Miller House in Columbus, Indiana (1957) – a single-storey pavilion, open to the landscape, and including a sunken conversation pit at its heart.

Saarinen died just a day after his 51st birthday, with a number of his major projects awaiting completion. Among them were the TWA Terminal and the Jefferson National Expansion Memorial arch (1968), which were finished after his death by his partners John Dinkeloo and Kevin Roche.

BELOW Grasshopper chair, manufactured by Knoll, made in birch and covered in cowhide, 1947.

JOAQUIM TENREIRO
1906–1992

OFTEN CALLED THE FATHER OF
MODERN BRAZILIAN FURNITURE
DESIGN, A CREATOR OF REFINED,
ORGANIC AND BEAUTIFULLY
CRAFTED PIECES

Like his American contemporary, HARRY
BERTOIA, the pioneering Brazilian designer
Joaquim Tenreiro saw himself primarily as a
sculptor and artist. Tenreiro, too, turned his
back on furniture-making just at the point
of his greatest success in the field and looked
instead – from the late 1960s onwards – to
pursuing his ambitions within the world of fine
art. Yet his legacy was powerful and original.

Though known as one of Brazilian
design's most famous figures, Tenreiro was
actually a settler in his adopted country (as was
another of Brazil's figureheads, LINA BO BARDI;
see under 'Houses and Interiors'). Tenreiro
spent his early years in Portugal and was
the son of a family of furniture-makers and
woodworkers, from whom he learnt his craft.
He also studied both painting and design
in Portugal before settling in Brazil in 1928.

He based himself in Rio de Janeiro
and found work in the interior design studios
of the German firm Laubisch & Hirth and
the furniture and tapestry house Leandro
Martins & Co. But he soon became frustrated
by these firms' reliance upon reproductions
of traditional European furniture designs
and became anxious to develop a more
contemporary line with a modernist influence.

An opportunity finally presented itself
when OSCAR NIEMEYER (see under 'Houses
and Interiors') approached Tenreiro to design
furniture for a house he had designed for the
industrialist and art collector Francisco Inácio
Peixoto in Cataguases, completed in 1943.
Tenreiro's pieces pleased Peixoto and
impressed Niemeyer – who collaborated
with Tenreiro on later projects – and Laubisch
& Hirth were prompted to put them into

production. These early pieces used native
timbers such as rosewood and imbuia, and
had a pleasing sinuous, tactile quality to them.
Some of the early dining chairs – such as the
Varetas chair of 1948 – had a lightness of touch
and a sophisticated elegance comparable
to some of GIO PONTI's pieces, including the
Leggera and Superleggera chairs of the 1950s.

Certainly, Tenreiro's work had – for
the most part – a modern sense of delicacy
that was very different from the more robust
designs of that other great pioneer of Brazilian
furniture design, SERGIO RODRIGUES. Many
of Tenreiro's dining chairs, sofas and armchairs
used cane seats and backs to great effect, but
in designs that were clearly contemporary.
They include the elegant Curve chair of 1949,
with its delicate tapered back and thin frame.
Another key piece was the Leve armchair of
1942, which again aimed for a lightness of
touch but within a substantial upholstered
chair distinguished by its subtle shape and
thin, rounded, ergonomic armrests.

In 1943, Tenreiro co-founded a new
company in Rio de Janeiro producing modern
furniture. Langenbach & Tenreiro opened its
first store in 1947, complete with room sets
and exhibitions by invited artists. By the early
1950s, Tenreiro had opened a second shop
in São Paulo – Tenreiro Furniture & Décor
– and expanded his workshops.

In 1968, he shut his stores and workshop.
He exhibited his sculptures and paintings
in the 1970s and '80s, but remains best known
for a unique line of furniture with a sense of
grace spliced with a considered understanding
of modernity and a deep respect for natural
materials and craftsmanship.

BELOW Monumental
cabinet, c. 1950, in rosewood,
embossed leather, reverse-
painted glass and brass.

BELOW Leve armchair in
satinwood, with wool-coated
upholstery, 1942.

RIGHT Cadeira Recurva
de Espaldar Alto chairs in
rosewood with cane seats
and backs, 1949.

BELOW RIGHT A pair of
nightstands, c. 1955, made
with rosewood.

HANS WEGNER
1914–2007

REVERED MASTER CRAFTSMAN
WHO INSISTED THAT HIS
FURNITURE SHOULD BE MADE
IN DENMARK BY DANISH
MANUFACTURERS

Hans Wegner earned the admiration and respect of his contemporaries to the point that he was dubbed 'the designers' designer'. This reverence was only enhanced by Wegner's resistance to invitations to move to America or to compromise his craft in any way. Instead, he preferred to remain focused on his design studio in Copenhagen and his work with Danish manufacturers.

The highlight of Wegner's long career was undoubtedly the JH 501 Round chair of 1949. With its sculpted wooden frame and woven cane seat, the piece has a timeless appeal and became known as 'The Classic Chair', or simply 'The Chair'. When CBS televised the presidential debate between John F. Kennedy and Richard Nixon in 1961, they famously chose the JH 501 for their sparse set.

Wegner was born in Tønder in southern Jutland, the son of a cobbler. As a child he spent many hours in his father's workshop and at the age of 13 was apprenticed to a local cabinetmaker, H. F. Stahlberg. Wegner developed a love and instinctive understanding of wood – always his favourite material – and remained with Stahlberg until his military service. Afterwards, he studied at the Copenhagen School of Arts & Crafts under furniture designer Orla Mølgaard-Nielsen.

In 1938, Wegner began working for architects Erik Møller and Flemming Lassen in Aarhus, followed by a position with

Møller and ARNE JACOBSEN, where Wegner designed furniture for the Aarhus Town Hall project. In 1943 he opened his own design studio in Aarhus and collaborated with Børge Mogensen* on a range of affordable furniture. In 1946 he moved to Copenhagen.

His early designs included the Chinese chair of 1943, a reinterpretation of a classic Asian design using a gently enfolding bentwood back support in cherry. This became a prototype that was redesigned and refined again and again in sculpted stretches of sinuous timber that became the Round chair and the Y chair/Wishbone chair (or Model CH 24) of 1950 (see p. 10). The Peacock chair (JH 550) from 1947 was another reinvention of a classic period design, with its elongated fan-like back reminiscent of the traditional 19th-century English Windsor seat. Such designs established Wegner not only as a brilliant craftsman but also as a 'form giver'.

Other early pieces showed great ingenuity, although still in timber. There was a three-legged stacking chair made by Fritz Hansen* (FH 4103; 1952) and a folding chair, complete with integrated wooden handles and a cane seat and back (PP 512, 1949). The Valet seat had a coat-hanger-like back for hanging a jacket, while the seat folded upwards to support a pair of trousers neatly.

All of these pieces were designed and made with great attention to detail,

RIGHT Model JH 501 Round chair in oak and cane, 1949, produced by Johannes Hansen, Denmark.

FAR RIGHT Model PP 505 Cow Horn chair in teak and cane, 1952, produced by Johannes Hansen.

BELOW Swivel chair
manufactured by Johannes
Hansen, 1955, in teak, leather
and chrome-plated steel.

craftsmanship and artistry. Yet there was also a playful quality at work. Wegner's Cow Horn chair of 1952 (PP 505) was another step on from the rounded chairs of the 1940s, with a cane seat and a sculpted mahogany back that was finished with two rounded, projecting horns at either side. It was a theme that was revisited later on with the Ox chair (EJ 100) from 1960 – a very different kind of horned beast with leather upholstery over a plywood

seat resting on steel legs. The Papa Bear chair (PP 19, 1951) is another favourite, so-called for the paw-like arms that project out, as though inviting a teddy-bear-style embrace.

Wegner's softer, sensuous and more organic pieces have become the essential icons, but there were many other, more experimental designs among the five hundred or so chairs that he designed, including the Flag Halyard armchair (GE 225, 1950) with

its taut, threaded lattice of flagline forming the seat and back. There were also occasional experiments with plywood, including the Three-Legged Shell chair from 1963.

Wegner worked with a number of different Danish manufacturers, and in recent years many of his early designs have been reissued by PP Møbler. Few other designers have created furniture that so invites one's touch, as well as flatters the eye.

OPPOSITE ABOVE LEFT
Folding chair in oak, cane and
brass, produced by Johannes
Hansen, 1949.

OPPOSITE ABOVE RIGHT
Model JH 550 Peacock chair,
1947, in ash, teak and paper
cord, made by Johannes
Hansen.

ABOVE Model EJ 100 Ox
chair, 1960, produced by A.P.
Stolen, Denmark, in chrome-
plated steel and leather.

RIGHT Model PP 19 Papa
Bear chair, in teak and
upholstery, manufactured
by A.P. Stolen, 1951.

OPPOSITE CENTRE LEFT
A Johannes Hansen-produced
Valet chair, 1953, in mahogany
and brass.

OPPOSITE CENTRE RIGHT
Fruit bowl in mahogany and
enamelled brass, 1959, made
by Johannes Hansen.

OPPOSITE BELOW LEFT Shell
lounge chair, 1948, produced
by Fritz Hansen, in teak
plywood and stained beech.

OPPOSITE BELOW RIGHT
Shell settee, 1948, in teak
plywood and beech, produced
by Fritz Hansen.

OPPOSITE A Model AT 304 drop-leaf dining table, c. 1960, produced by Andreas Tuck, Denmark, in teak and brass.

BELOW Hammock chaise longue in oak, flagline cord, leather and chrome-plated brass, 1960, manufactured by Getama, Denmark.

BOTTOM Flag Halyard lounge chair, c. 1950, in steel, flagline cord and upholstery, produced by Getama.

EDWARD WORMLEY
1907–1995

AMERICAN DESIGNER WHO
BELIEVED THAT DESIGN SHOULD
NOT BE DOGMATIC OR ELITIST,
BUT SHOULD FOCUS ON CHOICE
AND THE TASTES OF THE
CONSUMER

Edward Wormley was never afraid of the past, nor the future. He saw freedom in modernism – 'freedom to mix, to choose, to change, to embrace the new but to hold fast to what is good'.[10] He was not afraid to draw inspiration from the past or from different corners of the world, as he mixed designs that were original and fresh with others that sought to update or reinterpret existing pieces.

He designed block cabinets in rosewood and walnut with a Japanese or Chinese inspiration. His occasional tables and coffee tables incorporated GERTRUD & OTTO NATZLER (see under 'Glass and Ceramics') patterned tiles and tiles of Murano glass. His famous Riemerschmid chair of 1946, in mahogany with an upholstered seat, was a streamlined reworking of a late 19th-century design by German architect Richard Riemerschmid. The Arts & Crafts furniture and interiors of Greene & Greene were another point of inspiration.

Some constant themes also threaded through Wormley's wide-ranging output. There was a focus on craftsmanship, with most of Wormley's designs being hand-made rather than assembled on factory production lines.

Connected to this was a passion for timber, which, Wormley said, 'cannot fail to spark the imagination of the artist in ways in which impersonal metal or dead clay cannot do'.

Certainly Wormley's most striking designs use wood in compelling forms. His Model 4765 magazine trees for Dunbar (1947) are playful but beautifully conceived; his Tambour (Model 912) desks from the 1950s are highly accomplished, with twin tambour compartments at either end; his Model 5666 Woven-Front cabinet is fronted by sliding mahogany doors in a woven lattice pattern.

Wormley was born in Rochelle, Illinois, and grew up in a farming community. After a number of interior design correspondence courses he studied at the Art Institute of Chicago, but had to cut short his studies when his funds ran out. He found a job as an interior designer for the Marshall Fields department store in Chicago, then in 1930 travelled to Paris, where he met Emile-Jacques Ruhlmann.

In 1931 he began a long and fruitful relationship with the Dunbar furniture company, based in Berne, Indiana. Wormley soon became Dunbar's director of design and began to develop lines of furniture that were either modern or traditional in spirit. It soon became clear that his modernist designs – partly shaped by the soft, organic quality of mid-century Scandinavian design – were getting the best response, so Dunbar focused its efforts on the contemporary collection.

By the mid-1940s Wormley was concentrating on building up an extensive modern line that eventually included sofas, chairs, recliners, tables of all kinds, sideboards and cabinets. In 1946, he established his own design studio in New York.

Wormley's work has attracted less attention than the designs of certain other mid-century designers. This is partly a question of the profusion of Wormley pieces in the marketplace, but it also serves to make his work available to a wider audience looking to acquire more affordable vintage furniture with a strong aesthetic and sense of craftsmanship.

LEFT Model 4765 magazine
tree for Dunbar, USA,
in walnut and birch, 1947.

BELOW Model 5313 magazine table in lacquered wood, 1953, manufactured by Dunbar.

BOTTOM Model 5719 La Gondola sofa, 1957, manufactured by Dunbar, in lacquered mahogany and upholstery.

RIGHT A pair of Model 5633 Janus occasional side tables in lacquered mahogany with Murano glass tiles, 1956, produced by Dunbar.

RIGHT Model 912 Tambour desk, produced by Dunbar, c. 1957, in mahogany, rosewood and brass.

BELOW Model 4873 Listen-To-Me chaise, 1948, made by Dunbar, in laminated maple, cherry, upholstery and brass-plated steel.

BOTTOM Model 5666 Woven-Front cabinet in bleached mahogany and aluminium, Dunbar, 1956.

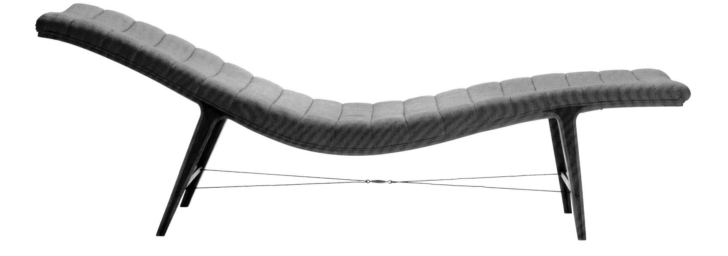

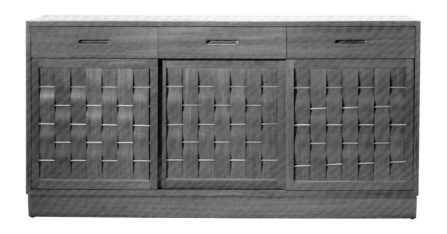

TOP Model 5580 dining chairs, 1955, in lacquered mahogany with upholstered cushions, made by Dunbar.

ABOVE A pair of Recamier sofas, c. 1967, in turned walnut and upholstery, produced by Dunbar.

RIGHT Model 5481 chairs in laminated and stained mahogany and brass with an upholstered seat, Dunbar, 1954.

LIGHTING

THE MID-CENTURY MODERN LIGHTING AESTHETIC HAS BECOME IDENTIFIED WITH PRECISION, FUNCTIONALITY AND A SCI FI-INFLUENCED GEOMETRY

The world of lighting design has always invited a uniquely dynamic level of experimentation. It is still astonishing to think that the first incandescent electric bulbs were only invented at the end of the 1870s, yet within just a few decades designers and artisans had not only adapted to electric light but had applied an extraordinary level of artistry and creativity to the first wave of lamps, chandeliers and ceiling lights. Art Nouveau embraced the electric light with open arms, fashioning sophisticated organic forms with sinuous metalwork and highly crafted glass shades. Tiffany Studios and others created lights full of colour with exotic patterns fashioned in stained glass, while Mariano Fortuny created exquisitely refined pieces in the early years of the 20th century that seem decades ahead of their time.

By the 1920s, Art Deco lighting offered a more streamlined and Machine Age approach, and early modernist pioneers such as Gerrit Rietveld, Willem Hendrik Gispen, Marianne Brandt, Christian Dell and Wilhelm Wagenfeld* were already developing a new generation of lighting designs with a clear emphasis on functionality and precision. The pace of change was startling. POUL HENNINGSEN – one of the iconic figures of post-war lighting design – developed his first designs in the closing years of the 1920s, applying a rigorous scientific analysis to the distribution, reflection and quality of light, while producing designs that were avant-garde and futuristic.

In the 1950s and '60s the speed and vigour of innovation and experimentation accelerated even further. The more ornate and decorative nature of Art Nouveau and some Art Deco lighting was largely abandoned in favour of a pared-down, geometric approach that promoted practicality and the clarity of the design itself. This was combined with a highly sculptural aesthetic that drew upon abstract modern art, with a number of mid-century lighting designers – notably ISAMU NOGUCHI and SERGE MOUILLE – also working as sculptors and applying an artist's eye to their designs.

The geometrical precision of mid-century lighting was expressed in the shape of crisp tubes and cylinders, cups and domes. But this was also the era of the space race and sci-fi fantasy, with many designers embracing futuristic, Space Age spheres, satellites and flying saucers, which were perfectly suited to lighting design. There was a profusion of lights with names such as 'Eclipse', 'Moon', 'Astral', 'Saturne' and 'Skyrocket'. Henningsen's lights, in particular, had the feel of sculpted satellites and abstract flying machines.

One of the most famous designs produced by mid-century masters ACHILLE & PIER GIACOMO CASTIGLIONI was the Arco floor lamp of 1962. This had partly evolved from the need for lighting that could be more flexible and adaptable than fixed ceiling or wall lights. The Arco could be positioned over a table or chair, wherever it might be needed, and the Castiglionis were part of a fresh generation of designers who embraced the challenge of creating lights that could be easily adjustable rather than purely static. Mid-century lighting was partially characterized by this new flexibility, with lighting that featured tilting shades and reflectors, directional lamps and spotlights that could slide along tracks or poles.

The Castiglionis were also key figures within a resurgent Italian design scene that embraced lighting design more than any other medium. A large number of Italian lighting companies (Arredoluce, Artemide*, Oluce, Stilnovo, etc.) were launched or expanded rapidly in the 1950s and '60s, ready to draw upon existing craft expertise, while embracing the talents of young designers and architects eager to express themselves and make the most of every opportunity. They became part of what is sometimes called the 'Italian Miracle', with the economic rehabilitation of the country fuelled – in part – by the renaissance within Italian design and engineering. Key figures included VICO MAGISTRETTI and GINO SARFATTI, who founded his own lighting company, Arteluce*, and reinvented

OPPOSITE Dalia Model 1563A chandelier designed by Max Ingrand and produced by Fontana Arte, Italy, 1954, in crystal and brass.

the chandelier, in particular, within a modern idiom while injecting a strong sense of exuberance and vitality into his work.

Sarfatti, Mouille and others enjoyed the challenge of giving new form to ceiling and wall lights, creating exotic multi-headed hydras. Others – including the Castiglionis and Ingo Maurer* – played with the idea of reduction and deconstruction, paring down the light until it was little more than an accentuated bare bulb. Abstraction was also taken into the realms of the surreal, with ironic lights that didn't look like lighting at all, such as Livio Castiglioni* and Gianfranco Frattini's Boalum light resembling a coiled PVC vacuum cleaner tube, Archizoom's Sanremo floor light of 1968 imitating a palm tree, and Cesare Casati and Emanuele Ponzio's Pillola light (1968) looking like a giant medicinal pill.

Lighting design was transformed all over again by the arrival of plastics, which invited another wave of innovation, particularly in the 1960s. The Castiglionis in Italy and GEORGE NELSON (see under 'Furniture') in the States experimented with a spray-on polymer applied to a light wire frame, creating translucent cocoon shades in organic forms that echoed, in some respects, the paper lanterns developed by Isamu Noguchi and LE KLINT in Denmark, which also began using plastic sheets as an alternative to paper.

ABOVE Acrylica table lamp by Joe Colombo, manufactured by Oluce, Italy, 1966, in Perspex and enamelled steel.

RIGHT Woman posing with a 'flying saucer' lamp, produced in Bonn, Germany, in brass and Plexiglas, c. 1950s.

OPPOSITE LEFT Chimera floor lamp in plastic and enamelled metal, designed by Vico Magistretti for Artemide, Italy, 1969.

OPPOSITE CENTRE A Verner Panton VP Globe light in acrylic with enamelled and chrome-plated steel reflectors, produced by Louis Poulsen, Denmark, 1969.

OPPOSITE RIGHT Model 9 Cylinder table lamp by Isamu Noguchi in cherry wood and fibreglass-reinforced polyvinyl, Knoll, USA, 1947.

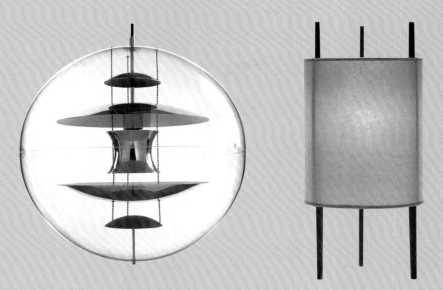

In the hands of designers including Magistretti, JOE COLOMBO and VERNER PANTON (see under 'Furniture'), plastics were used to very different effect to create lights that were dynamic and expressed in bright Pop colours. Panton's lights included the exuberant Kugel-Lampe Typ F (1969), featuring a dense array of plastic spheres, and the SP2 Spiral-Lampe (1969), with its mass of twisting plastic spirals, both forming exotic Pop chandeliers. His VP Globe light had, like Henningsen's lights, the look of a sculpted Space Age satellite.

Panton and Colombo were examples of designers who may have been best known for their furniture – pioneering the use of plastics for seating – but also produced striking lighting designs. Many other designers and architects of the period were not dedicated lighting specialists – like Henningsen or Sarfatti – but still produced highly significant and influential mid-century lighting. JEAN PROUVÉ, GIO PONTI and ARNE JACOBSEN (see under 'Furniture') all created key designs during the 1950s and '60s, while glassware designer Tapio Wirkkala* produced highly evocative and atmospheric glass shades for Iittala* in the early 1960s. With smoky and metallic colours and crisp outlines, these lights – along with so many others from the period – still feel very current.

Arne Jacobsen lighting designs include the AJ series of wall, table and standing lights first developed for the SAS Royal Hotel in Copenhagen in 1957 and manufactured by Louis Poulsen*. Fellow architect ALVAR AALTO (see under 'Houses and Interiors') also produced many lighting fixtures for his architectural projects, some of which were later put into production by Artek*, the furniture and lighting company founded by Aalto and his partners. The A805 floor light, for instance, was developed for Aalto's Villa Mairea, along with a number of other bespoke lighting pieces.

The spirit of experimentalism threaded through mid-century lighting also included designs that featured neon, halogen and fluorescent tubes. But at the heart of the vast majority of lighting there still lay an incandescent electric bulb that was much the same as those invented by Joseph Swan and Thomas Edison. It was the breadth and variety of the many sculptural forms created around this bulb that was the truly startling aspect and the artistry, innovation and creativity that went into the lamps and shades. The geometric sculptures of the 1950s and the colourful, vibrant Pop lighting of the 1960s retain a powerful allure, and many remain common staples within contemporary interiors.

LIGHTING DESIGN IN ITALY
ALBERTO BASSI

The origins of Italian industrial design have their roots in the 1920s and '30s, with the onset of the cultural, social and economic conditions that would usher in rapid success in the decades following World War II. It was during this pre-war period that the foundations of the Italian approach to design were formed: designers with an architectural background meeting a business culture – a combination that was highly entrepreneurial and new, rooted within a tradition of historical 'know-how' based on hand-craft expertise and an intuitive understanding of the importance of communication (graphic design, exhibitions, advertising, the construction of corporate identity and the use of the media).

These characteristics were supported by the evolution of two forms of production, which would remain typical of Italy: the first was large-scale manufacture, particularly in the steel and mechanical industries (generally for production of transportation vehicles or heavy and precision machinery); the second was medium-to-small artisanal workshops or mechanized craft industries, often connected at the regional scale in a system of clusters. Both of these groups began to collaborate with designers to develop their products.

In the field of industry, for example, Giuseppe Pagano designed the aerodynamic and innovative ETR 200 high-speed train (1936), while Columbus, the metal pipe manufacturer, produced Bauhaus* furniture under an agreement with Swiss manufacturer Wohnbedarf and furniture by Italian architects such as Giuseppe Terragni, whose steel chair of 1936 was used in the Casa del Fascio in Como. An entire sector developed to produce means of transportation, from ships, trains and airplanes to motorcycles and automobiles, with companies such as Alfa Romeo and Lancia collaborating to make custom vehicles with body-shops such as those headed by Carlo Felice Bianchi Anderloni at Touring or Battista 'Pinin' Farina*, both of whom would later become internationally famous car designers.

Among the smaller manufacturing companies, GIO PONTI (see under 'Furniture') worked for Ceramica Richard-Ginori, Guido Andlovitz for Ceramica Laveno and Carlo Scarpa* for VENINI (see under 'Glass and Ceramics'). In addition, many furniture and lighting companies were founded, such as Fontana Arte*, established in 1932.

The necessary relationship between manufacturing companies and designers was the subject of a cultural debate that occupied the pages of magazines such as *Domus* and *Casabella* (both established in 1928), the former founded and directed by Gio Ponti and the latter acquiring international standing under the direction of Giuseppe Pagano in the 1930s.

An important contribution to the diffusion of the industrial design culture was made by the international exhibitions of decorative and industrial arts that were held in Monza starting in 1923 and later moved to the Palazzo dell'Arte in Milan. The 1933, 1936 and 1940 exhibitions, in particular, presented the best of Italian and foreign architecture and industrial design. In 1940, the VII Triennale inaugurated the 'Mostra per la produzione in serie', the first exposition on mass-produced design in Italy, curated by Giuseppe Pagano.

The post-war period fulfilled the promises laid down between the two wars concerning the role and practice of industrial design in Italy. In the 1950s design achieved

full theoretical and practical maturity, establishing a standard of excellence and growing quantitatively to become a widespread practice.

Society and the economy grew progressively stronger. New markets opened up to industry, which was inspired to review existing product typologies or to design brand-new ones. It therefore turned to architects, who dedicated themselves primarily to the design of functional objects and furniture. They sought in their products to 'illustrate' a modern conception of society and culture, driven by a powerful ethical and democratic ethos.

Historically, this was a period of reconstruction, followed by an economic boom. It was a period that witnessed the progressive expansion of the market and the introduction of new forms of visual communication and organization of distribution, as well as new research into materials and technology and the foundation and consolidation of manufacturing companies oriented towards mechanized mass production. A determining factor, concurrently, was the dialogue between the design culture – stemming from architecture – and the new cultural and entrepreneurial reality of the country, which thrived in havens of research and experimentation, such as the Triennale di Milano (the IX and X in 1951 and 1954 were particularly important for design) and on the pages of specialist publications, especially *Stile Industria* after 1954. Equally important after 1954 was the cultural and promotional contribution of the Compasso d'Oro award, given to innovative design projects, and, after 1956, of ADI, the Association for Industrial Design.

The field of lighting, which reflects this context in its important manufacturing companies and products designed for mass diffusion, presents a number of distinguishing features: for example, production methods that combine, within a single object, an industrial approach with hand-crafted solutions, made possible by the adaptability and flexibility of the production structure and the close relationship between product, process innovation and the design culture.

Lighting design in Italy cannot be confined to a single unitary trend; rather it branches out in many directions, led by both designers and manufacturers. In the 1950s the main point of reference for the entire field was the work of GINO SARFATTI and Arteluce*, the company he founded in 1939. Over a thirty-year period, Sarfatti designed and produced hundreds of lamps; each one offers an original solution to a problem, responding to a specific need or to the stimulus of a technical innovation. The formal development of his lamps appears surprisingly inventive and is enhanced by the lamps' extreme simplicity

ABOVE Globo Tissurato lamp
designed by Ugo La Pietra:
Zama Elettronica, 1966, in
etched and clear acrylic and
enamelled metal.

– the result of a mastery of technical and functional solutions, but also an ambition to
reduce the number of parts and simplify construction. This sensibility is typical of an
industrial designer, not just an entrepreneur.

One of Sarfatti's fundamental themes – which also include modularity and design
based on the characteristics of light sources and experimentation with materials – is the
study of the movement of light in space. This interest is evident in, for example, the 1050
floor lamp (1950), with its large canopy that reflects the light directed by the two arms
fastened to the stem; or the 524 table lamp (1952), which has a moveable joint at the
centre of gravity, making it extremely simple to position the stem. Around the mid-1950s,
with the adoption of new materials such as plastic but also in consideration of production
requirements that forced his company to increase its output, Sarfatti developed a design
system that took into account methods of mass production. One example is the 1055
floor lamp (1955), winner of a Compasso d'Oro: the seven simple elements of which it
is composed may be combined into nine different configurations.

Arteluce's innovative approach more or less explicitly inspired the other lighting
companies working at the same time, from Stilnovo to Angelo Lelli's Arredoluce and
Giuseppe Ostuni's Oluce. A watershed moment in this development came with the Arco,
Toio and Taccia lamps by ACHILLE & PIER GIACOMO CASTIGLIONI, which were put into
production in 1962 by Flos*, the company founded by Dino Gavina and Cesare Cassina*.
These lamps, like most of the projects by the Castiglioni brothers, were first and foremost
a response to functional, lighting and living needs, and to the necessities of production,
which led to a simplification and reduction in the number of components. The Castiglionis
frequently mined tradition for existing solutions in various fields of technical construction,
which they then borrowed to respond to specific necessities. One particular constant in
the field of lighting was attention to the light source and to lighting effects, as these often
determined the final form and function.

The Arco – inspired, among other things, by street lamps – is a floor lamp that
imagines a different way of casting light on a plane, relying on its configuration and the
variation in light conditions. The other Castiglioni floor lamp for indirect lighting, the Toio,
was inspired by the theme of 'ready-mades', a characteristic interest of these designers,
who created products inspired by or making use of everyday objects from the most
disparate of fields. The project began by taking a special 300W automobile headlight,
which featured a silver-coated body and pressed-glass lens, and combining it with other
industrial components existing on the market, such as a universal transformer required
to compensate for the difference in voltage and installed in plain view, or the hexagonal
chrome-plated steel section that constitutes the bearing metal structure, also shaped into
a handle to carry the lamp and equipped with fishing rod guides to channel the exterior
electrical wiring. The Taccia, finally, is an elegant table lamp based on pure geometric forms,
such as the blown glass half-sphere or the cylinder, combined in a harmonious composition.
Every solution the brothers adopted, as the result of specific research as well as intuition,
led to a coherent and apparently 'natural' formal result.

The desire for innovation in the second half of the 1960s – triggered by social,
economic and cultural transformations – had a powerful impact on the design culture.
The central elements of this phase appear to be, on the one hand, the coexistence of a craft
or mechanized craft industry side by side with large industry, which benefited from up-to-
date technology and production processes and a different commercial organization and
distribution. On the other hand, there was widespread collaboration between designers
and manufacturers, which became increasingly focused upon an integral relationship.

As in other fields of design, lighting witnessed a tendency towards experimentation
with new typological and formal possibilities, questioning established notions of design

ABOVE Passiflora lamp by Superstudio for Poltronova, 1966, in yellow and opalescent methacrylate.

BELOW Asteroide lamp by Ettore Sottsass, produced by Poltronova, 1968, in enamelled aluminium, plastic and chrome-plated brass.

and production, with the idea of establishing a new relationship between object and user; of emphasizing a clearly symbolic approach. This experimentation would lead to the conception and production of many lamps with characteristics that differed sharply from the lamps manufactured up to that point. The same phenomenon was in fact taking place in furniture design as well; a case in point are the three chairs Blow (DDL, Zanotta*, 1968), Joe (DDL, Poltronova*, 1971) and Sacco (Gatti, Paolini, Teodoro; Zanotta, 1968), the first in clear inflatable plastic, the second shaped like a giant baseball glove, and the third a shapeless sack filled with polystyrene beads.

It is typical of Italian design that this challenge to culture, design and production – also sustained by experimentation with hand-crafted pieces and limited editions – was accepted and furthered by industry, which adopted different methods more focused on aspects of mass production but conducted its research with an analogous spirit of innovation. A fundamental contribution came from new materials and production technologies, starting with one of the first lamps moulded in plastic, the Nesso (1963), designed by the Gruppo Architetti Urbanisti Città Nuova. It was made out of fibreglass-reinforced polyester by Artemide*, a company founded in 1960, which laid the groundwork with this model for a fully industrialized structure in terms of production, organization and distribution.

Such directions in the structural development of manufacturing companies and the role of design were supported by experimentation with expressive languages. The most exemplary and symbolic lighting fixtures are perhaps those designed with a streak of irony or Pop culture. ETTORE SOTTSASS (see under 'Product and Industrial Design') designed lamps and lighting accessories for Poltronova, which had a strong impact and influence on the contemporary design culture: Asteroide (1968), and Cometa and Ultrafragola (1970), among others, combine colourful transparent plastic with fluorescent light sources.

The Superstudio group from Florence also experimented with light, producing a series of models for Poltronova, such as Gherpe (1967) and Olook (1968), which looked mechanical and featured moving parts, as well as Onda and Passiflora (1966-68), which were inspired by nature. The same theme inspired, among others, lamps by Gino Marotta, such as Dalia (Poltronova, 1968); the silvery Pistillo (Valenti, 1969), a table lamp by Studio Tetrarch; Sanremo (Poltronova, 1968), a phitomorphic floor lamp with indirect lighting by Archizoom; and Cespuglio (Guzzini, 1970) by Ennio Lucini, made with coloured methacrylate panels.

During those same years, Ugo La Pietra* began his experimentations, focusing on the role and enhanced image of technology, on the system of signs, and on the behaviour of man and his relationship with the environment. La Pietra's Globo Tissurato lamp (Zama Elettronica, 1966), for example, switched on with a clap of the hands, and his lamp made of horizontal cylinders (Zama Elettronica, 1966-70) was turned on by a sound. One of the most significant results of this intense period is unquestionably the Boalum by Livio Castiglioni* and Gianfranco Frattini (Artemide, 1969) – a chain of specially designed light bulbs sheathed in a clear plastic casing, so that it appears as an articulated strip of lighting that can be configured in a wide variety of shapes and lengths.

Testifying to the evolution of lighting design along experimental lines and in other strongly industrial directions at the same time, in 1969 Achille Castiglioni borrowed an idea from Pio Manzù to design the Parentesi for Flos, a completely new typology of lamp 'that did not exist before', and that proved extremely successful and long-lasting. A thin steel wire stretched between the ceiling and the floor carries a metal tube bent into the shape of a 'parenthesis': the tube supports a swivelling rubber joint carrying a light socket that can be oriented into an infinite number of positions.

The 1960s may well be considered the decade that best expresses what critic and historian Sergio Polano identified as the distinctive character of Italian design: the 'original synthesis between experimental subversion and design rationale'.

ACHILLE CASTIGLIONI
1918–2002
& PIER GIACOMO CASTIGLIONI
1913–1968

ITALIAN DUO WHO CREATED
AN EXTRAORDINARY AND
HIGHLY INFLUENTIAL PORTFOLIO
OF WORK THAT WAS BOTH
PIONEERING AND PLAYFUL

RIGHT Arco floor lamp, 1962,
produced by Flos, with an
aluminium lightshade,
telescopic steel stem
and Carrara marble base.

OPPOSITE B9 Luminator
floor lamp, 1955, produced
by Gilardi y Barzaghi in spun
aluminium and enamelled
metal.

The Milanese designers Achille and Pier
Giacomo Castiglioni embraced many aspects
of design, but they are best remembered today
for their achievements in the field of lighting,
with many of their designs still in production.
Most famous of all is their Arco floor lamp
of 1962, one of the first products released by
Flos*, which was founded that same year.

Flos was one of a new breed of
innovative Italian lighting and design houses
that were ready to take risks and invest in
young designers, including a number of
architects struggling to find building
commissions and turning instead to product
design. The company began working with the
Castiglioni brothers from the beginning, with
the designers also creating the interiors of the
first Flos store, which opened in Milan in 1968.

The design of the Arco lamp evolved
from a desire for a flexible ceiling light. The
Castiglionis had noticed that many ceiling
and suspended lights were wrongly positioned
in the home to illuminate dining tables or
reading chairs, but of course the lights were
fixed and could not easily be moved. The Arco
lamp offered the effect of a ceiling light without
being fixed in position. To allow the heavy
lamp to be moved from place to place, the
Castiglionis thoughtfully drilled a hole in its
marble plinth to allow a broom handle to be
passed through, so providing carrying handles.

The Arco formed a striking centrepiece
to a space, with the polished aluminium
bowl of its reflector like a flying satellite
floating within an interior. Yet the base was
made of a highly traditional Italian material,

art world and also acted as a forerunner of the melting pot approach to design and architectural styles seen in the post-modern movement to come.

The Toio uplighter of 1962, for example, used a car head-lamp connected to a steel stem set in an enamelled metal base and was also one of the Castiglionis' most industrial pieces in terms of its aesthetic. In some ways it echoed one of their earliest lights, the B9 Luminator of 1955, which was a floor light reduced down to its simplest elements – little more than a bulb placed on a metal stick. Such pieces helped inspire later designers, who also played with the form and candour of a bare bulb.

The Castiglionis' open attitude to experimentation and new materials also led to some highly sculptural lighting designs in the early 1960s. They embraced a spray-on, liquid polymer 'cocoon' developed in the post-war years, also used to great effect in the States by GEORGE NELSON (see under 'Furniture') and others. The Castiglionis, working with Flos, were the first European designers to experiment with the plastic cocoon approach, developing the Taraxacum, Viscontea and Gatto lights. Compared to other Castiglioni designs, the cocoon range was surprisingly organic in feel, reminiscent of translucent sea creatures found in the ocean depths.

Another striking design – very different in feel again – was the Splügen Bräu hanging light of 1961. This was originally commissioned for a bar and restaurant in Milan and took the form of a polished, ribbed, aluminium half-globe, like a metallic setting sun; Flos put the lamp into production in 1964. There was also the Taccia table light of 1962, again for Flos. This had the look of a spotlight, while its rotating glass bowl gave the lamp – like many Castiglioni designs – a welcome degree of flexibility. Another iconic design was the Snoopy table or desk light of 1967 with a marble base and protruding enamelled shade – usually in black – inspired by the cartoon-strip canine.

radically refashioned for a new purpose. The combination of old and new, past and future, was typical of the intelligence threaded through the Castiglionis' work.

Achille Castiglioni, like his two older siblings before him, studied architecture at the Politecnico di Milano and then joined his brothers' design studio in 1944. Livio Castiglioni* left the partnership in 1952 to work independently, but Achille and Pier Giacomo went on to collaborate closely on a wide range of projects, including lighting, furniture and product design.

Some of the Castiglionis' work focused on ready-made or found elements, including the Sella stool of 1957, which used a bicycle seat, and the Mezzadro stool of the same year, which used a tractor seat. Some of their lighting designs, too, had a sense of wit, using unexpected elements in an avant-garde way that echoed the work of the Dadaists in the

After Pier Giacomo's early death in 1968, Achille Castiglioni continued working as a designer, producing lighting and many other products within a long and prolific career. He was also an inspirational lecturer and teacher and helped energise a new generation of Italian and European designers with his magical combination of playfulness, sculptural forms and functionality.

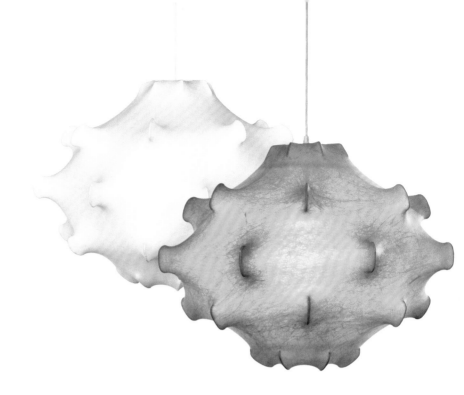

ABOVE Taraxacum pendant lights made with sprayed fibreglass over a metal frame, produced by Flos, 1960.

LEFT Taccia lamp in glass, enamelled aluminium and steel, manufactured by Flos, 1962.

OPPOSITE Snoopy table lamp, with a marble base and enamelled metal and glass hood, Flos, 1967.

POUL HENNINGSEN
1894–1967

EXPERIMENTAL DANISH
DESIGNER, WHOSE COMPLEX
GEOMETRICAL WORKS
INCLUDE THE WORLD-FAMOUS
'ARTICHOKE'

BELOW Egg lamp, produced
by Louis Poulsen, Denmark,
in enamelled metal, 1967.

Danish designer Poul Henningsen grew up in a home lit by oil lamps that cast a welcoming glow around a room. He was unsettled by the intensity of incandescent electric light bulbs and the way they seemed to dominate interiors. He described this as 'wallowing in light' and devoted a significant portion of his life to creating lighting that disguised the glare of the bulb and created a soft light echoing the qualities of the lamps of his childhood.

Henningsen's approach was, in some respects, scientific. He studied the impact of a shade's size and shape upon glare and upon the distribution of light in a space, as well as the use of different kinds and colours of materials in reflecting and affecting the intensity and warmth of the light produced.

His solutions were in addition highly creative, ingenious and full of artistry and imagination.

Perhaps his most famous light was the PH Artichoke hanging light of 1958, produced by his longstanding patron, Louis Poulsen*. The light was originally commissioned by architects Eva and Nils Koppel for their Langelinie Pavilion restaurant in Copenhagen and consisted of 72 metal or glass leaves, or fins, connected to a steel frame at varying angles and within a staggered sequence of rings running from top to bottom. The artichoke or pine cone effect was highly sculptural, but it also disguised the bulb within and offered an enticing, diffuse lighting effect. It remains one of the most mesmerizing lighting designs of the 1950s, and still – like so many designs of the period – feels relevant and progressive.

Henningsen was born in Ordrup, the son of two writers. He studied architecture in Copenhagen but declared that 'from the age of eighteen I began to experiment with light', adding, 'I have been searching for harmony in lighting'.[1] He worked as a journalist, editor and critic and also wrote poetry and film scripts, as well as producing a documentary film.

In the early 1920s he began working with Louis Poulsen – first established in 1892 in Copenhagen as an electrical supplies and tool company – to create designs for the Expositions Internationales des Arts Décoratifs et Industriels Modernes, from which the Art Deco movement took its name. Henningsen's Paris light won a gold medal and from 1926 onwards Louis Poulsen began marketing lighting fixtures, including Henningsen's designs.

His early PH table and ceiling lights used a triptych of layered metal or glass discs in three different diameters, stacked one on top of another, supposedly inspired by the look of an inverted plate, saucer and cup. By 1928, Henningsen's designs were highly sophisticated and futuristic in feel, with his PH Septima light consisting of seven circular diffusers in sandblasted glass mounted on a brass frame,

OPPOSITE ABOVE
Henningsen Plate lamp in
copper and chrome-plated
steel, Louis Poulsen, 1958.

OPPOSITE BELOW A Louis
Poulsen-produced Artichoke
lamp, in enamelled aluminium
and steel, 1958.

creating a layered effect, rather like the unfolding petals of a streamlined, inverted glass flower. The advanced nature of the design is striking and the piece feels far ahead of its time.

Using the layered petal principle, Henningsen continued to develop his PH lighting range for Louis Poulsen throughout the 1930s, including chandeliers and wall-mounted lights. During the war years – before leaving Denmark for Sweden as a political exile during the Nazi occupation – he also designed a special blackout shroud for the lamps of Copenhagen's Tivoli Gardens, allowing the park to stay open into the evening.

The 1950s saw Henningsen's experiments with light reach their peak. A number of his PH lights – such as the PH Louvre light (1957) and the Artichoke – were originally commissioned by architects for specific buildings and Henningsen has remained a particular favourite among the design and architectural communities. By now the petals of his lights had multiplied and the geometrical arrangement of his concentric shades had become far more complex; the Louvre used thirteen circular metal discs and bowls, while the PH Snowball (1958) used eight.

Henningsen went on to produce a total of around one hundred PH designs, including the Spiral hanging light of 1964, originally developed for the University of Aarhus. Many of his designs are still in production and manufactured by Louis Poulsen.

OPPOSITE PH 5 pendant lamp in enamelled aluminium and steel, Louis Poulsen, 1958.

RIGHT PH 4/3 table lamp, produced by Louis Poulsen, 1933, in enamelled steel, frosted glass, brass and Bakelite.

FAR RIGHT Reading floor lamp, Louis Poulsen, 1957, in enamelled steel and aluminium, brass and frosted glass.

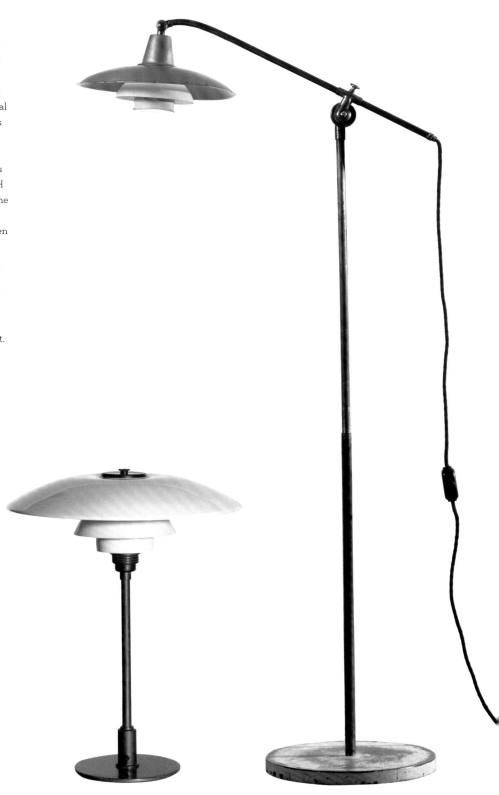

LE KLINT
FOUNDED 1943

CELEBRATED LIGHTING
COMPANY, WHOSE PLEATED
AND CURVED LAMPSHADES
TAKE THEIR ORIGINS
FROM TRADITIONAL DANISH
CRAFTSMANSHIP

The Klint family began experimenting with pleated paper lampshades in the early 20th century, but it was Tage Klint who founded the Le Klint company in Odense, Denmark, in 1943 and perfected the first hand-made designs. A surveyor and entrepreneur, Tage Klint invented a collar to hold the paper pleats of the first lampshades in place, lending them the stability needed to function effectively. These first designs are still in production.

In the 1950s and '60s Le Klint began to broaden its range of designs and introduced a series of models – both in paper and in plastic – that took the company in a fresh direction. A number of these designs were by Tage Klint's brother, architect and furniture designer Kaare Klint, who was a professor of architecture at the Royal Academy of Arts in Copenhagen (among his most famous buildings is the Bethlehem Church in Copenhagen, 1937).

Inspired by the traditional techniques developed by the family, Kaare Klint created a pleated paper globe, known as the Fruit lamp, Model No. 101. The design was organic and ephemeral – a glowing paper satellite. The Fruit lamp led directly to the evolution of a number of other iconic Le Klint designs, including the Le Klint 47 light (1949) designed by Kaare Klint's son, Esben Klint, which was a simplified version of his father's design, with the pleated globe clipped at top and base, allowing light to spill from the open bottom of the truncated sphere. Esben Klint was also

OPPOSITE A pair of Le Klint 105 pendant lampshades, designed in 1945 by Mogens Koch.

FAR LEFT A 324 Sax Lamp wall light with extending bracket, designed in 1952 by Erik Hansen.

LEFT A Vilhelm Wohlert-designed 325 reading and floor lamp, 1957.

an architect and in addition collaborated with Børge Mogensen* on furniture designs.

Other Le Klint designers included Andreas Hansen, Peter Hvidt* and Orla Mølgaard-Nielsen, who developed the sculpted forms of Le Klint pendant lights even further, creating more complex geometries, though the lights were still hand-made by the company's craftsmen.

The Le Klint range was enriched again by architect and designer Poul Christiansen, who began designing for the company in the late 1960s. Christiansen's designs began to move away from the regular pleats of earlier Le Klint shades and adopted a more abstract, sculptural approach using curved sheets of nipped and tucked PVC plastic. The first of these was the Model No. 167 light (1967) – an irregular globe with a dynamic sense of movement. But the most famous Christiansen design was the 172 Sinus lamp of 1971, which took its name from the Latin word for 'curve'. The undulations of the globe give it an extraordinary topographical surface of regulated valleys and peaks.

Le Klint's highly sculptural, translucent white shades are an extraordinary fusion of architectural thinking, traditional hand-craft techniques and imaginative artistry. In many ways they echo the range of Akari paper lights developed by ISAMU NOGUCHI, which were also inspired by traditional craft techniques and formed the basis for a new collection of mid-century designs.

At the same time Le Klint's paper and plastic lanterns bring to mind the organic cocoon designs developed by Flos* and the CASTIGLIONI brothers in Italy, which used a spray-on plastic coating supported by a wire frame to create ethereal shades – a technique also explored by GEORGE NELSON (see under 'Furniture') with his famous bubble lights in the States. In each case, the material seems perfectly wedded to its role and function, illuminating spaces in a way that is both seductive and effective.

OPPOSITE TOP LEFT
153 pendant lamp, also known
as 'The Pine Cone', designed
by Andreas Hansen, 1964.

OPPOSITE TOP CENTRE
163 pendant lamp, designed
by Esben Klint, 1967.

OPPOSITE TOP RIGHT
47 pendant light, designed
by Esben Klint, 1949.

OPPOSITE CENTRE LEFT
178 pendant lamp, designed
by Poul Christiansen, 1975.

OPPOSITE CENTRE RIGHT
172 pendant light, designed
by Poul Christiansen, 1971.

OPPOSITE CENTRE
152 pendant light, designed
by Peter Hvidt and Orla
Mølgaard-Nielsen, 1962.

OPPOSITE BELOW LEFT
167 pendant lamp, designed
by Poul Christiansen, 1967.

OPPOSITE BELOW CENTRE
101A pendant lamp, known
as 'The Lantern', designed
by Kaare Klint, 1944.

OPPOSITE BELOW RIGHT
168 pendant lamp designed
by Poul Christiansen, 1969.

ABOVE 171 pendant
lamp, designed by Poul
Christiansen, 1971.

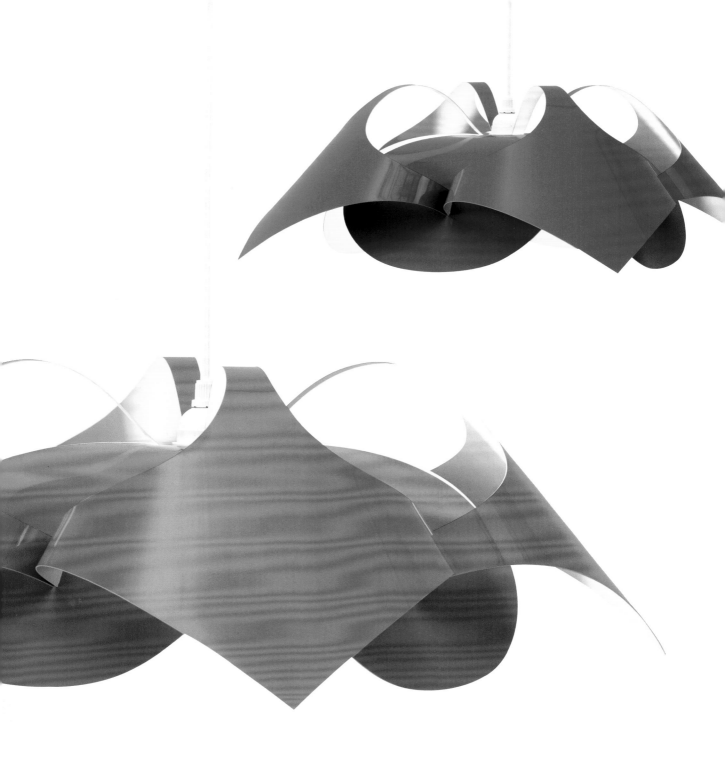

OPPOSITE, ABOVE AND RIGHT
140 pendant lamps, known
as 'The Joker', designed by
Christian Raeder, 1970.

VICO MAGISTRETTI
1920–2006

ITALIAN DESIGNER WHO
PRODUCED GROUNDBREAKING
LIGHTS IN SINUOUS, FUTURISTIC
FORMS WITH A SENSE OF
RESTRAINED SIMPLICITY

Like many polymath designers of the mid-century period, Vico Magistretti trained and worked as an architect. But along with figureheads such as GIO PONTI and ARNE JACOBSEN (see under 'Furniture') or ALVAR AALTO (see under 'Houses and Interiors'), Magistretti never allowed himself to be compartmentalized and applied himself also to lighting and furniture design. His lighting designs of the 1960s were often infused with a futuristic, Space Age quality that has been compared to the work of VERNER PANTON (see under 'Furniture').

Born in Milan, the son of an architect, Magistretti himself studied architecture during the war years and graduated from the Politecnico di Milan in 1945. He began working as an architect in Milan, but was soon tempted into other arenas by associations and friendships with entrepreneurial figures who were building a vibrant new design and manufacturing scene in post-war Italy. Cassina*, for instance, put Magistretti's Carimate 892 chair into production in 1963 – a piece originally designed for the dining room of Magistretti's Carimate Golf Club building.

Early lighting designs include the Claritas floor and table lights developed with Mario Tedeschi in 1946, featuring a metal hood or cowl over the bulb that could be adjusted with a small protruding handle. Like his Milanese contemporaries, ACHILLE & PIER GIACOMO CASTIGLIONI, Magistretti was interested in designs that allowed the user to control and vary the amount and direction of light produced.

Magistretti explored this principle further with his Eclisse – or 'eclipse' – bedside lamp of 1967, produced by Artemide*. A pivoting reflective hemisphere sits within a second, slightly larger sphere, with these interactive twins sitting upon a rounded base. By simply turning the inner sphere within the outer shell the user controls the amount of light produced, creating the effect of a partial eclipse or open beam, like a miniature lighthouse lantern blinking in its casing. The idea was simple, the form sculptural and the elements involved minimal, but the piece also had a playful, childlike quality. With a bright red finish, in particular, the light had the intrinsic appeal of a child's toy, or an orrery, offering an open invitation to play or interact. Who could resist producing their own eclipse?

Around the same time, Magistretti was experimenting with plastics. His Dalù table and bedside lamp of 1965 – also for Artemide – reduced the design of the light itself, not including the bulb and flex, down to one single element. Originally using ABS plastic (acrylonitrile butadiene styrene), Magistretti created the effect of a sphere that had been partially cut and twisted, with one part of the sphere forming the base and the remaining section forming a hood for the bulb. The pure form of the light had intense visual appeal, particularly in red with a high-gloss lipstick finish. Three years later Magistretti designed the Telegono table lamp for Artemide, again in plastic, with two intersecting elements arranged in the simple but powerful form of a futuristic helmet.

RIGHT AND OPPOSITE Dalú
table lights in ABS plastic,
produced by Artemide, 1965.

LEFT AND BELOW RIGHT
Atollo table lights, with
enamelled metal base and
reflector, produced by Oluce,
Italy, 1977.

BELOW LEFT Vico
Magistretti's design sketches
for the Atollo light.

OPPOSITE ABOVE LEFT
AND BELOW Eclisse bedside
and table lamps, with
enamelled aluminium base
and shade, manufactured
by Artemide, 1967.

OPPOSITE ABOVE RIGHT
Vico Magistretti's design
sketches for the Eclisse lamp.

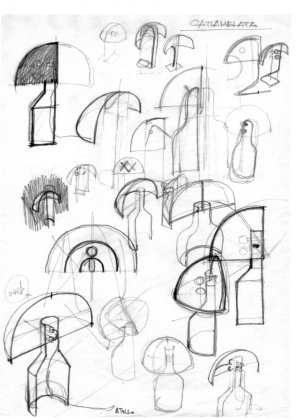

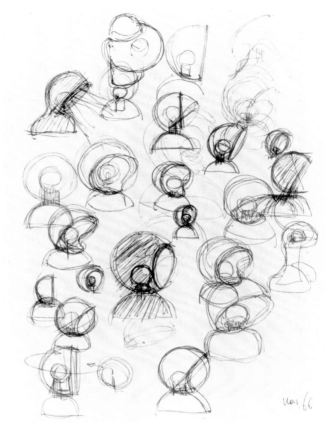

Another iconic piece followed soon after. This was the Chimera floor or standing light in the form of a rippled vertical tube (see p. 127). The creamy, translucent polymethyl methacrylate plastic used has the look of glass, giving the piece an ephemeral and sophisticated quality. A smaller version was also produced as a table/desk lamp.

One of Magistretti's most accomplished and recognizable designs of the 1970s was the Atollo table light for Oluce. Whether crisp white or jet black, the lamp was an exploration of pure geometrical form, with a cylindrical base topped by a matching cone connecting the base to a neat hemispherical shade.

Other Magistretti products included sofas, bookcases and a series of streamlined monobloc plastic chairs for Artemide (including the Selene stacking chair of 1969 and Gaudi armchair of 1970). He also taught in Milan and London. It was, however, the futuristic forms of his lights – and his pioneering use of the new plastics, which in his hands assumed a sense of value and artistry – that made him one of the key figures of 1960s and '70s Space Age design.

SERGE MOUILLE
1922–1988

FRENCH DESIGNER, RENOWNED
FOR HIS ORGANIC, TACTILE
LIGHTS IN LIMITED EDITIONS,
WITH THEIR DISTINCTIVE
BLACK FINISH

LEFT AND BELOW A pair
of Cachan sconces produced
by Ateliers Serge Mouille,
1957, in enamelled aluminium
and steel.

During the 1950s and '60s lighting design was dominated by an experimental spirit, with Italian designers and producers, in particular, playing with new forms, themes and materials. This new wave of lighting was suited to mass production and export, and by the 1960s was increasingly playful and colourful in nature. But French designer Serge Mouille took a very different approach. Reacting to what he saw as the over-complexity of the Italians, he concentrated on small editions of hand-made designs, produced in his own studio.

His designs were sculptural works of art rather than mass-produced objects, characterized by distinctive black, enamelled metal shades that took inspiration from shells, eyes and other organic forms. One of the most familiar Mouille forms was the *tétine*, or teat-shaped shade.

Mouille trained as a sculptor and silversmith in the studio of Gilbert LaCroix in the late 1930s, before attending the École des Arts Appliqués in Paris. He founded his own studio in 1945, while teaching at his old school. In 1953 architect Jacques Adnet asked him to design his first collection. This included Lampadaire a une Lampe, an enamelled steel and aluminium standing lamp, with a slender support sitting on a delicate tripod, and the head of the lamp taking the distinctive *tétine* shape and hiding the bulb and cabling from view. These *tétine* shells were also employed for a three-armed floor light and for wall lights.

Mouille exhibited his early designs at the Musée des Arts Décoratifs in 1953 and a few years later began selling his lights at the Steph Simon Gallery in Paris, which also presented work by JEAN PROUVÉ (see under 'Furniture') and others. There were also collaborations with furniture and interior designer Louis Sognot.

Over the following years, Mouille's work became more adventurous, with forms such as the spiral swirl of the Escargot light (1955), or the Coquille sconce of 1958. Mouille also explored multi-headed wall lights with spindly metal arms, reinforcing the zoomorphic quality of his work, which sometimes had the feel of exotic insects, with delicate legs and shining shells. The Trepied lamp of 1954, in particular, looked as though it might just scuttle across the table when you weren't looking.

The most linear of Mouille's designs was the tubular spotlight form of his Tuyau lamps (1953). These were an early precedent for a range of lights known as the Totem collection (1962). As the name suggests, these were vertical floor lights, with a fluorescent lighting tube revealed through a series of openings cut into the circular outline of the piece.

Mouille suffered from tuberculosis and was forced to curtail his work in the late 1950s. He ceased production in 1964, concentrating instead on his teaching and sculpture. Due to the limited production of his designs (as few as a handful of some are known to have been made), they have become much sought after. After Mouille's death, however, his family did allow a small number of his designs to be reissued.

Despite the small numbers, Mouille's lights have had a significant impact. They were emblematic of the sculptural approach within mid-century lighting, but more than that their zoomorphic quality – including the idea of the lightshade as a crafted, organic carapace – has inspired many imitations.

Mouille also designed a few furniture pieces, including the striking Table Vrillée – or Spiral Table – of 1962, its twisted steel legs like metallic antlers. The table was also produced in a small edition, of around 10 pieces.

TOP Trepied table lamp in enamelled aluminium and steel, with brass detailing, 1954, Ateliers Serge Mouille.

RIGHT A pair of Coquille sconce lights in enamelled steel and aluminium, with brass detailing, 1958.

FAR RIGHT A triptych of Tuyau sconces, 1953, in enamelled aluminium and steel, with brass detailing.

RIGHT Applique à Murale
Cinq Bras Fixes in enamelled
aluminium and brass, 1953,
Ateliers Serge Mouille.

LEFT Escargot ceiling light, 1955, in enamelled steel and aluminium, originally designed for the Cité Universitaire in Antony, France.

BELOW LEFT Lampadaire standing light, 1953, in enamelled aluminium and steel with brass detailing.

BELOW A pair of Oeil sconces, 1956, in enamelled aluminium and steel with brass detailing, Ateliers Serge Mouille.

ISAMU NOGUCHI
1904–1988

JAPANESE-AMERICAN ARTIST
WHO FUSED LIGHTING AND
SCULPTURE TO CREATE HUGELY
INFLUENTIAL AND WIDELY
IMITATED PAPER LANTERNS

In the early 1950s, during one of his many sojourns in Japan, the Japanese-American sculptor and designer Isamu Noguchi visited the city of Gifu in the centre of the country. Gifu was well known for making beautifully crafted lanterns and other traditional paper products, and Noguchi was invited by the mayor to design a new lantern that might help reinvigorate manufacturing in a country that was looking to rebuild its industry and exports following World War II. Famously, Noguchi began sketching his first ideas that same day, sparking a range of Akari lanterns (the word translates as 'light' or 'illumination') that would grow over the years to a collection of around a hundred different designs.

Noguchi's hand-made Akari lights used traditional papers made from the inner bark of mulberry trees, wrapped around supporting bamboo ribs. The lamps were lightweight and easily collapsible, making them well suited for export. But rather than focus on candle lanterns, Noguchi created contemporary designs – with eyecatching sculptural and organic forms – that were suited to electric bulbs, while also adding a metal wire support system. 'All that you require to start a home,' he said, 'are a room, a tatami and Akari.'[2]

Exported to America and internationally, the lights – made by Ozeki & Co. – were affordable and highly successful. Noguchi expanded the range throughout the 1950s and '60s, with standing lamps, table lights and ceiling lanterns exploring a rich variety of shapes and themes. The lights are still in production but have also been widely imitated.

In a sense, the Akari lights were a perfect medium for someone immersed in the worlds of both sculpture and design. They combined art and craft within a cornucopia of spheres, cylinders and ox-bows, while also having an ephemeral quality that added a new dimension to a room, often scene-stealing from more expensive or elaborate furniture and art.

Yet to call Isamu Noguchi a lighting designer alone would be a mistake. Like many of his contemporaries, Noguchi was involved in many different aspects of design, and – like HARRY BERTOIA and JOAQUIM TENREIRO (see under 'Furniture') – he saw himself primarily as a sculptor and artist.

Noguchi's personal history was complicated and throughout his life there was an ongoing story of restlessness and travelling, spurred by his peripatetic and unconventional childhood. His father was the Japanese poet Yonejiró Noguchi, who met his mother – Leonie Gilmour – in California. By the time Isamu was born, the relationship between the two was already floundering and his father had returned to Japan. Leonie Gilmour settled in Japan and Noguchi was raised there until the age of 14, yet father and son remained estranged.

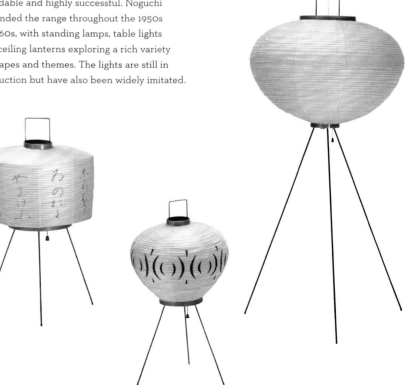

RIGHT Table and floor lamps
from the 1950s in steel,
bamboo and paper, made
by Ozeki & Co. in Japan.

Noguchi finished high school in America and began studying medicine at Columbia University but ultimately abandoned the subject to concentrate on sculpture. He won a scholarship to travel to Europe, where he assisted the sculptor Constantin Brancusi. There followed a substantial period of time during which Noguchi travelled widely and sought to balance his artwork with work as a stage-set designer. During World War II he campaigned for the rights of Japanese-American citizens in the US but was held in an internment camp for a number of months.

It was towards the end of the war and afterwards that Noguchi began to experience a degree of success, both as an artist and designer. He made a number of furniture pieces for Herman Miller*, including the iconic glass and birch IN-50 coffee table (1950) and the Rudder dining table (IN-20, 1944). He designed the Rocking stool and matching Cyclone tables of 1954 for Knoll*, and there was also the aluminium Prismatic table of 1957. Noguchi's furniture, like his lighting designs, explored fluid, rounded, organic forms inspired by the natural world.

His first forays into lighting were also developed in association with Knoll in the 1940s. In 1944 Knoll released Noguchi's first commercially produced table light after a number of experiments with 'lunar' designs. The Cylinder table light (see p. 127) featured three slim legs supporting a translucent plastic shell, which looked rather like paper and became a key forerunner of the Akari lights.

Later, Noguchi added garden design to his portfolio, and his sculpture was increasingly praised and respected. In the years before his death he oversaw the development and design of the Noguchi Museum in Long Island City, New York, which houses his own collection of works.

RIGHT Model UF4-L10 Akari floor lamp in paper over a steel frame, c. 1975.

LEFT A pair of 1950s Akari floor lamps in bamboo, iron and brass, made in Japan.

BELOW Table lamp in rice
paper and enamelled wire,
made by Ozeki & Co., 1950s.

JEAN ROYÈRE
1902–1981

FRENCH DESIGNER WITH A
HIGHLY ORIGINAL AESTHETIC
THAT COMBINED JOYFUL
PLAYFULNESS WITH REFINED
SOPHISTICATION

Looking over the highly individual and often whimsical work of French designer Jean Royère, you soon reach the conclusion that he was afraid of straight lines. His work was distinctly modern and of the mid-century period, in that there was a degree of restraint and simplicity in the palette of materials explored within an individual piece, combined with a sense of artistry and functionality. Yet his designs expressed an enduring love of ornament, decoration and geometric complexity.

Royère may have loved curves and theatrical flourishes, but these were not the sinuous, organic outlines seen in the work of CARLO MOLLINO (see under 'Furniture') or even OSCAR NIEMEYER (see under 'Houses and Interiors'). There was always a sense of playful wit within Royère's work, and he revelled in updating and reinterpreting traditional craft techniques and drawing upon some of the flavours and motifs of Art Nouveau. Today his highly respected work commands significant prices at mid-century auctions.

Perhaps most striking of all are the lighting designs that Royère developed over the course of his career. These were threaded through with originality and exoticism, while very different in character from the futuristic aesthetic being developed within Italian lighting, or the push towards innovation in form, functionality and adaptability seen in other lighting design of the period.

Rather than experiment with new materials, Royère was content to breathe new life into more familiar crafts and manufacturing techniques. Much of his lighting used metalwork of one kind or another, bent and twisted into increasingly imaginative and dramatic forms. A Royère chandelier might take the form of a vibrant collection of slender, curving, outstretched enamelled copper arms topped by paper shades. His Persane wall sconces of the early 1950s used a whole array of brass tentacles topped with white cones. His highly sought-after Liane series of 1959 was especially

flamboyant, using twisted, overlapping metal to create floor lights that resembled fantastical trees with tubular paper lanterns hanging from their branches.

Royère began his career in design in his late twenties, after working in banking and the import-export business. He worked for Pierre Gouffé in Paris and also secured a commission to design a brasserie on the Champs-Élysées. In the early 1940s he set up his own design office in Paris and quickly established a reputation as a leading interior designer, as well as creating lighting and furniture. By the 1960s his work was much in demand internationally and he designed the interior of the ocean liner *France* (1962) as well as residences for King Farouk of Egypt, the Shah of Iran and King Hussein of Jordan.

Early lighting designs of the late 1930s and the 1940s seem relatively restrained compared to the more exuberant work that followed, yet they were still infused with that whimsical Royère quality. His Geniale floor lamp (1936) was little more than a parchment cone sitting upon a slim metal stand, while the Ski standing lamp of 1941 was a simple metal pole on a round base, its curved top finished with a silk lantern.

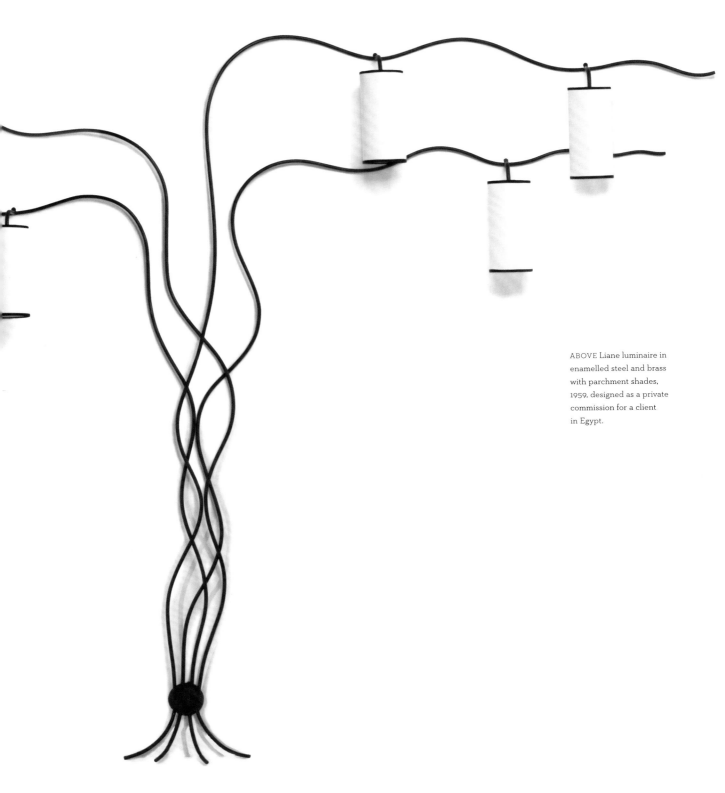

ABOVE Liane luminaire in
enamelled steel and brass
with parchment shades,
1959, designed as a private
commission for a client
in Egypt.

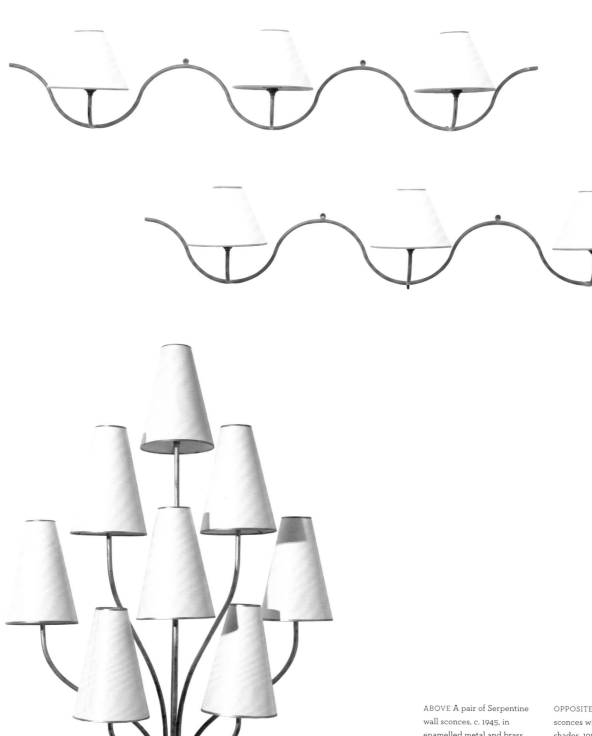

ABOVE A pair of Serpentine
wall sconces, c. 1945, in
enamelled metal and brass
with parchment shades.

LEFT Persane eight-armed
sconce light, c. 1950, in brass
and parchment.

OPPOSITE LEFT Gilt brass
sconces with parchment
shades, 1955.

OPPOSITE RIGHT Ski floor
lamp in enamelled steel
with a silk shade, 1941.

Soon lanterns multiplied, while the design became more effusive and theatrical. The Serpentine wall sconce of c. 1945 featured an undulating ocean wave of metalwork supporting a triptych of parchment shades. The Jeu d'Eau sconce (c. 1950) took the idea of wave-like motion further, introducing three lanterns perched upon gilt tentacles.

Much of Royère's lighting and furniture played with ideas of motion, provided by curving forms or scallop edging and motifs. Sometimes the distinction between lighting and furniture design was blurred, as with his wrought-iron room divider of 1949, which also included three lanterns on its framework.

Royère retired in 1970 and sold his own collection of furniture at auction in Paris ten years later, before moving to America. Rather like Piero Fornasetti* or Tony Duquette*, he was a designer whose work stepped outside the mainstream and brought a fresh sense of vitality and exuberance to interiors, furniture and lighting design.

GINO SARFATTI
1912–1984

MASTER LIGHTING DESIGNER,
EMBLEMATIC OF MID-CENTURY
ITALIAN SUPREMACY
WITHIN THE FIELD, AND
ASSOCIATED IN PARTICULAR
WITH THE REINVENTION OF
THE CHANDELIER

In Italy during the 1950s, after the chaos and destruction of the war years, a large number of design houses and studios began to establish themselves, eager to embrace new ideas, materials and aesthetics, while making the most of young, enthusiastic and energetic design talent. At the same time, the Italians were building on the foundations of a long craft, design and manufacturing tradition, as well as upon engineering expertise.

Gino Sarfatti became emblematic of the fresh, entrepreneurial spirit within post-war Italian design. He created his own company, Arteluce*, while establishing himself not only as its lead designer but as a maestro of mid-century Italian lighting design.

In particular, Sarfatti reinvented that most flamboyant and seductive of lighting forms – the chandelier. His most famous design, the 2097, which is still in production by Flos*, rebuilt the chandelier in a contemporary, stripped-down form. At the heart of the light was a steel tube that carried the mother cable and supported a series of brass or chromium-plated arms. At the end of each arm was a simple, exposed fitting and bulb, while the feeder flexes that supplied these fittings formed a series of gentle waves both contrasting with and softening the form of the chandelier. Like so many of the best ideas, it was simple but beautiful and also modern.

Sarfatti, born in Venice, began studying aeronautical engineering at the University of Genoa, but he was forced to abandon his studies due to the poor state of his family's finances. Instead he took a job in a factory manufacturing

lampshades. He soon became fascinated by lighting design and began to experiment with his own creations. Having founded Arteluce in 1939, with little more than a workshop, he opened his first store in Milan in 1951, designed by MARCO ZANUSO (see 'Product and Industrial Design'). It soon became a focal point for designers and architects.

Sarfatti designed much of Arteluce's range himself – as many as four hundred designs. A distinction is often made between the exuberant vibrancy of his early work and the purer, more functional approach to many of the later designs. Among the Sarfatti pieces of the early 1950s there were a number of striking chandeliers and hanging lights, using brass spirals planted with metallic floral cones or a circular frame with a series of protruding glass and brass cups. These were sculptural and playful, yet also elegant and sophisticated, speaking of modernity and a fresh start.

His Model No. 534 table light took the form of an exotic metallic plant, with a central stem surrounded by a series of multicoloured, enamelled, circular flowers. These discs could be adjusted and tilted to vary the direction and quality of light. Another of Sarfatti's most

RIGHT Model No. 534 table lamp in enamelled metal and brass, produced by Arteluce, 1951.

FAR RIGHT Tripod floor lamp, c. 1950, manufactured by Arredoluce, Italy, in enamelled metal and brass.

endearing pieces, the 2072 Lollipop chandelier, used plastic disc shades in an array of bold colours suspended from a simple brass mount, the flying saucers holding echoes of the mobile sculptures of Alexander Calder*.

Another arm of Sarfatti's work was more 'mechanistic' or 'essentialist' and involved a paring down of the structure and form of the light to a small number of basic yet carefully conceived elements. A wall light could be as simple as a single coloured disc protruding from a slim metal frond. The Model No. 566 table/desk light was essentially a tubular metal bulb-holder supported by a stem of steel attached to a base. Yet the head of the lamp could be lowered or raised on the stem, offering a degree of flexibility seen in a significant proportion of Italian mid-century lighting design.

ABOVE Model No. 2072 Lollipop chandelier in plastic, enamelled aluminium and brass, 1953, produced by Arteluce.

Sarfatti was certainly eager to innovate and experiment. His 1063 floor light was one of the first designs to incorporate a fluorescent lighting tube, forming little more than an exclamation mark of light and similar in ethos to the B9 Luminator floor light developed by ACHILLE & PIER GIACOMO CASTIGLIONI. In the 1960s, Sarfatti also designed a Space Age table lamp and hanging light called the Moon '69, with a futuristic, translucent plastic dome encasing a series of small bulbs, which looked like flares shining on the moon's surface seen through an atmospheric corona.

Sarfatti sold Arteluce to Flos in 1973, but many of his designs are still in production, and original pieces from the 1950s have become highly collectable.

FAR LEFT Model No. 1094 floor lamp, in enamelled steel, aluminium and frosted glass, manufactured by Arteluce, 1966.

LEFT Model No. 566 table lamp, made by Arteluce, c. 1956, in enamelled steel and polished aluminium.

LEFT An Arteluce chandelier
in brass and enamelled
aluminium, c. 1945.

BELOW Model No. 2097
chandelier in brass, produced
by Arteluce, 1958.

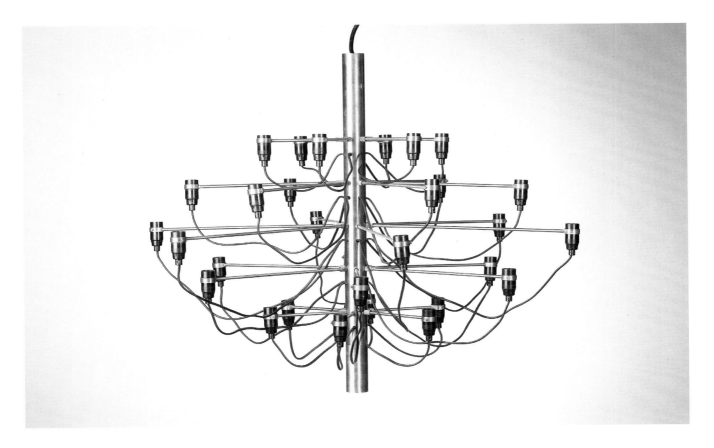

GLASS
AND
CERAMICS

FROM ACROSS THE SOCIAL SPECTRUM THE POST-WAR YEARS SAW A GROWING NEED FOR PRODUCTS THAT WERE WELL DESIGNED, AESTHETICALLY PLEASING AND AFFORDABLE

One of the key themes of mid-century design is democracy. While political democracy was being hard fought for around the globe, the post-war years also saw a spirit of social democracy pervading many aspects of Western culture. Design, in particular, began to respond to the new demand for social equality, a breaking down of class barriers, the rise of a more informal way of living and a growing need from across the social spectrum for products that were well designed, aesthetically pleasing and affordable. In part, this need was fuelled by growing prosperity in the 1950s and '60s and the growth of consumer spending and consumer power. But there was also a rising awareness of good design and an understanding that design could make life more rewarding and more enjoyable.

The multi-faceted designer RUSSEL WRIGHT summed it all up with his philosophy of 'easier living' – a way of life that was more relaxed and more informal than during the pre-war years, but also made so much better by a whole new generation of products that looked appealing and fresh but were also functional and hard-wearing. Wright's own American Modern range of dinnerware, first released in 1939 but at the height of its popularity in the late 1940s and early 1950s, was all of these things and more. The collection was beautifully conceived, with its organic shapes and bright colours, but it was also affordable and durable, and pieces could be purchased according to budget and colour preference. The line was simple, unadorned and sculptural and sold in the millions, making it one of the most democratic pieces of design of the mid-century period.

American Modern also pointed to a number of other key developments within the world of mid-century ceramics. The pieces turned away from excess and decoration in favour of lines and forms that were simple and sculptural. The colours were organic and inspired by nature – always a key source of inspiration for Wright. But the pieces were also mass-produced and mass-marketed within a close alliance between a progressive product designer and a forward-thinking pottery.

Wright's work with American Modern was echoed by other designers of the period who also looked at mass production and making their work more widely available than ever. In the States, Hungarian émigré Eva Zeisel* began designing tableware with her 1942 collection for New York's Museum of Modern Art before going on to design as many as 100,000 different pieces of tableware over the course of her long career. Indeed, she bought a house on the proceeds of her Tomorrow's Classic range of 1952.

In Scandinavia, which became a powerful focal point for mid-century ceramics and glass, KAJ FRANCK held similar views to Wright about making good design available to all. Franck's Kilta range of earthenware for Arabia of 1952 was another pioneering mix-and-match collection that was hard-wearing, stackable and affordable. It offered a fresh alternative to the more ornate and formal dinner services that had predominated for so long.

Scandinavia was also a centre of innovation in ceramics. Some of the most engaging pieces of the period were produced by designers such as AXEL SALTO, who developed a range of extraordinary forms and shapes, again taking particular inspiration from the natural world. These were highly sculptural pieces, and many Scandinavian designers and ceramicists passed between the worlds of factory production and studio pottery. Chief among them were Wilhelm Kåge and Stig Lindberg of the famous GUSTAVSBERG POTTERY in Sweden, which established a dedicated art ceramic studio as well as focusing on commercial collections.

Other ceramicists, such as LUCIE RIE and HANS COPER, both exiles who settled in London just before the war, made commercial tableware in the early parts of their careers but went on to become highly respected, influential and collectable ceramic artists,

OPPOSITE A Kartio glass pitcher, designed by Kaj Franck in 1958 for Iittala.

although they still preferred to be called 'potters'. Certainly, the connections between ceramics, studio pottery and art constantly blurred during the mid-century period, with many internationally renowned artists – from Pablo Picasso to Georges Braque and Joan Miró – working post-war in ceramics as well as in the field of painting.

Certain designers also crossed over between ceramics and glass production. They included Franck, as well as VICKE LINDSTRAND and TIMO SARPANEVA. Both Lindstrand and Sarpaneva were key figures within the revitalized Scandinavian glass-making industry, with Lindstrand intimately associated with Orrefors* and Kosta*, while Sarpaneva worked with Iittala*.

The world of glass, as with ceramics, was re-energized by a vital alliance of designers and artisans combining new ideas with long-standing skills and traditions. This was true of Scandinavia, Italy and Czechoslovakia (as it was then known) – the three great centres of mid-century glass-making. Designers such as Sarpaneva became intricately involved not just in designing new collections but also in instigating production processes, such as the burnt wood mould technique that Sarpaneva helped develop for his Finlandia range of 1964, where the burning timber would mottle the hot glass with a rugged, ice-like texture.

In Italy, the Venetian island of Murano – the famous heartland of Italian glass-making – was well positioned to take advantage of long-established glass-blowing expertise across a range of small factories. Barovier & Toso and Seguso Vetri d'Arte were two of the pre-eminent Murano factories of the period, known for their innovative forms, intense colours and pioneering production techniques. The maestro of mid-century Murano glass-making was PAOLO VENINI,

THE WORLDS OF GLASS AND CERAMICS WERE ENERGIZED BY A VITAL ALLIANCE OF DESIGNERS AND ARTISANS COMBINING FRESH IDEAS WITH LONG-STANDING SKILLS

RIGHT American Modern dinnerware by Russel Wright in use during Thanksgiving at home in the 1950s.

who collaborated with many leading designers as well as designing himself and developing new methods of glass-making. Mid-century glass was characterized by this powerful spirit of experimentation, with extraordinary forms, evocative colours and colour combinations, and pattern, layering and mosaics all explored to great effect.

Metalware, too, was full of vitality during the period. Scandinavia, once again, excelled in this arena, with landmark pieces such as Herbert Krenchel's* famous steel Krenit bowls (1953) with their brightly colour-enamelled interior surfaces. Henning Koppel* became one of the leading figures in the field with his work for the Danish company Georg Jensen*, which also benefited from designs by ARNE JACOBSEN (see under 'Furniture'). In Britain, DAVID MELLOR (see under 'Product and Industrial Design') and Robert Welch came to the fore after studying at the Royal College of Art and – in a process that somewhat mirrored creative alliances seen in ceramics and glass in other parts of the world – were able to draw on British steel-making know-how while introducing a new aesthetic approach.

GLASS DESIGN: POST-1945 TRANSATLANTIC AESTHETICS

JOY McCALL

Taken together, Scandinavian glass and the American studio glass movement of the 1950s and '60s have provided the most significant influence on global glass design. The only other comparable influence has come from Italian glass design from the same era. In regard to Scandinavian glass, its importance is demonstrated by the number of mid-20th-century designs that are still in production; indeed, the Scandinavian influence has been largely assimilated into everyday domestic glass design. In the case of the American studio glass movement, its ongoing effect is indicated by the innumerable art glass studios that have sprung up throughout the country and by the fact that key exponents of the movement, such as Dale Chihuly, have become international household names. Generally, however, the greatest volume of internationally acclaimed glasswork in this period comes from northern Europe, and it is here that interest at auction is especially focused.

Mid-century Scandinavian glass design, emerging from the austerity of the late 1940s, presented a modern aesthetic drawn from the traditions, cultures and ideologies of the Nordic nations and was hugely appealing to an international audience. It was an embodiment of a utopia, removed from a world struggling with the aftermath of the war. This, together with its status as a measure of 'good design', ensured its global significance.

The Milan Triennale of 1951 is regarded as the seminal moment when the initial impact of Scandinavia's status at the forefront of post-war international design was most evidently felt. The Scandinavian display garnered widespread critical acclaim and the Nordic designers were awarded numerous prizes. The Triennales that followed in 1954 and 1957 further reinforced Scandinavia's position on the world stage, as did major exhibitions held at museums in Britain and the US. Glass was at the vanguard in the rise of Scandinavian design primarily in Finland and Sweden.

The new aesthetic that the Nordic nations offered post-war looked to nature for inspiration, in contrast to pre-war modernism with its inclination to celebrate the Machine Age and technological advancement. While previously glass had been a material deemed particularly appropriate to modernists, it was now regarded as a natural medium alongside wood, pottery and wool. The Scandinavian countries offered a new and alternative concept of living; a form of escapism. Tapio Wirkkala* displayed glass against a backdrop of photographic images of the natural landscape, further reinforcing the romantic concept of an idyllic 'other world'.

Unlike Art Nouveau glass, however, Scandinavian glass was not absorbed by a flamboyant or detailed decorative representation of nature – as can be seen, for example, in much of the work of Émile Gallé. Rather, it was concerned with the essence of form, and displayed a refinement that was both restrained and modern. The organic, asymmetric forms had clean, flowing lines and were elegantly proportioned. Heavy, clear glass was favoured and on the occasions when colour was introduced it appeared in a restricted palette or in a highly controlled manner, in contrast to Italian glass of the period with its dramatic colours. Both air inclusions and casings were frequently employed as decorative

TOP Timo Sarpaneva, Lancet III art object in stick-blown glass, Iittala, 1955.

ABOVE Tapio Wirkkala, Jaapala vase (Ice Block), Model 3825, in still-mould blown crystal, for Iittala, 1951.

devices. Although the design was characterized by an apparent simplicity, it was, in fact, deceptively sophisticated and executed to the highest standards. Traditional craftsmanship was valued but now combined with technical innovation. The 1960s, in particular, heralded years of experimentation, with an increasing enthusiasm for texture and abstraction.

During the mid-century decades the glass industry thrived, providing luxury merchandise for the newly affluent middle classes. The glass produced was a vital component of the aesthetic known as 'Scandinavian design'. The ethos in which the glass was created and marketed was in complete harmony with the furniture, ceramics and textiles that it paralleled. It marked a departure from the heavy cut glass and industrial pressed glass that preceded it.

Mid-century glass has now become highly collectable. In the mid-1990s, specialist modern design auctions began to focus on sales of Scandinavian – and sometimes specifically Finnish – design. Prices achieved at auction have steadily risen since then, demonstrating an increased appreciation and desire to acquire such works. Just as Finland and Sweden led glass production in post-war years, so works by designers from these countries are most sought-after at auction. In Finland the dominant factories were Nuutajärvi, Iittala* and Riihmaki; in Sweden they were Orrefors* and Boda. These factories employed key glass designers, whose works appear regularly at auction and fetch higher prices than their contemporaries; specific pieces by them are particularly collectable.

Scandinavian glass of the mid-20th century would of course never have taken on such importance had it not been for the unique talent and vision of key individuals, chief among these being Tapio Wirkkala and TIMO SARPANEVA of Finland. The former was the first to be employed at Iittala in 1946 (he was joined four years later by Sarpaneva). Wirkkala was inspired by natural forms. His extraordinary Kantarelli (Chanterelle) vases – designed in 1946 and executed as two series, each of fifty vases – take their name from a variety of mushroom and are undoubtedly his most widely recognized contribution to the history of design during this period. When exhibited at the Milan Triennale in 1951, they were a resounding success and won a Grand Prix. They were subsequently produced in non-numbered versions, and at auction are frequently offered in groups. Wirkkala's mould-blown Jaapala (Ice Block) vases – designed in 1950 and in production from 1952 to 1969 – also won a Grand Prix at the Triennale. Equally desirable are Wirkkala's art objects – clear glass monoliths, such as the Marshal's Baton and Tokyo vases, which utilize suspended voids as the primary decorative feature. Wirkkala introduced colour into his bottle vase designs; the colour is divided horizontally in a manner that resembles the weight-separation of liquids of varying densities. These bottle vases differ in form.

Arguably the most memorable designs by Timo Sarpaneva are his Lansetti (Lancet) art objects and Orkidea (Orchid) vases. These pieces are not functional vessels but rather sculptural forms. The Lansetti were designed in three series produced by Iittala with opaque glass cased in clear; the asymmetry found in the first two series contrasted with the symmetrical nature of the third. The Orkidea vases, designed in 1954 for Iittala, are decorative in character. They were shown at the Milan Triennale of 1954, where they won a Grand Prix. As with many coveted forms, this design has been produced in later editions (unauthorized reproductions, intended to deceive collectors, are also known to exist). However, it is the early examples that are the most desirable. In his Finlandia series begun in 1963, Sarpaneva experimented with combining mould-blown and casting techniques. The moulds were formed of carved alder wood, which, having been used, would then be re-fired in order to ensure that no two items were identical.

While Wirkkala and Sarpaneva moved towards sculptural forms, KAJ FRANCK remained primarily concerned with the aesthetic appeal of utility wares. However, the top prices his designs have achieved at auction are not for functional wares but for decorative pieces, such as Morning in Athens. Designed in the mid-1950s, these pendant suites usually comprise between six and thirteen elements. Franck's Kremlin Bells, a series of double decanters, while not being organic in style, have a purity of form arising from the simplicity of conjoined, coloured, geometric forms. Franck also designed complementary beakers.

Franck employed Oiva Toikka as art director at Nuutajärvi from 1963. Toikka's work from the 1960s is rarely seen, but he did produce a series of vases with banded colour resembling bamboo stems. His Lollipop glass sculpture, meanwhile, is purely decorative with no practical function. Toikka's work is more colourful and in this regard distinguishes itself from the work of other designers. Nanny Still*, like Franck, concentrated her attention on designing functional objects. Her work rarely appears on the open market. Her bottles with beak-like rims were designed in a variety of forms and colours and are usually offered for sale in groups. Saara Hopea is most renowned for her Panther vases designed in 1954 and produced by Nuutajärvi. These are of thick, clear glass enclosing spots of green or purple and air inclusions, and were executed in a variety of sizes.

In Sweden, the main figures at Orrefors were Nils Landberg*, Ingeborg Lundin* and Sven Palmqvist*. Each of the three can be specifically associated with a type of object that appeals to auction buyers. In the case of Nils Landberg, it is his Tulpanglas (Tulip Glass), designed in 1957, that is collectable and frequently presented in group lots. There is some variety in the form of the glasses, but they all resemble the profile of a flower supported on a delicate stem with a broad foot, and appear in a limited range of colours. The decanter is bulbous with a tall, slender neck and an everted rim, raised on a slim stem and spreading foot. Ingeborg Lundin's Apple vase, designed in the mid-1950s, was blown with fresh green glass and surmounted by a narrow neck resembling a stalk. Sven Palmqvist's most commercial works are his Ravenna series of bowls. Executed from the 1950s to the 1970s in a variety of forms, they are distinguished by their mosaic of bold colours. Another designer, VICKE LINDSTRAND, initially worked at Orrefors but later also at Kosta*. With an interest in figurative designs, he balanced simple organic forms with engraved or encased colour decoration, in works such as the Trees in the Mist vases and his extraordinary and rare Safari vase of 1955–56.

Meanwhile, across the Atlantic, a new craft movement was also in full swing. Factory glass was hugely successful in the mid-century, with the likes of Blenko, Corning, Fenton, Anchor, Hocking, Fostoria, Libbey and Steuben producing glass to satisfy the rising consumerism, but in contrast a studio glass movement was also fully active, characterized by a growing fascination in experimenting with hot blown glass. Initially works were 'bubble blobs', but later, as techniques were mastered, there was a concentration on content aimed at imbuing the glass with meaning. Like the Scandinavians, American studio glass-makers concerned themselves with producing organic forms but, in contrast, they employed more colour in their works.

The craft revival that occurred in the US can be seen as a reaction to International Modernism, so popular in the pre-war decades and celebrating industrialization and the Machine Age. The new movement constituted a counter-culture in which the artist was also the maker, and the design process was thus humanized. The individual's freedom of expression was the central ethos. These developments may be seen as paralleling what was happening in the world of painting, with the rise of abstract art.

The studio glass movement in America was hugely important because it represented a shift from the mass production of glassware in factories to a contemporary art form in which individuals could find a means of personal creative expression. The turning point that made this possible was Harvey Littleton and Dominick Labino's discovery of a method for lowering the melting-point temperature of glass and developing small furnaces. Their experiments had arisen as a result of the 1959 American Craft Council Conference at Lake

BELOW Dale Chihuly, Navajo Blanket Cylinder, 1975.

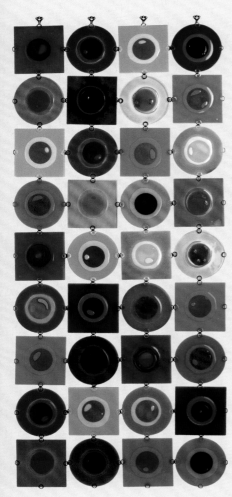

ABOVE Frances and Michael
Higgins, Rondelay Screen,
fused glass and brass, Higgins
Studio, USA, c. 1950.

George, in Colorado, where the delegates considered whether glass was a medium suitable for an artist (Littleton went on to organize a series of workshops at the Toledo Museum of Art in 1962). The pair's discovery freed individuals to work independently of the constraints of large commercial glass factories.

However, while the new studio glass movement initially appeared to be an anti-establishment statement concerned with individuals' freedom of expression, centred around the artist's ability to work independently, the movement's existence actually owed much to vital support received from established institutions. It was nurtured by universities and colleges and promoted by museums. Teaching institutions acted as a means of dissemination, enabling the next generation to be trained, and thus allowing the movement to be self-perpetuating. Harvey Littleton taught at the University of Wisconsin, and his early students included Marvin Lipofsky and Dale Chihuly. Forerunners working in glass in the late 1940s and 1950s, such as Edris Eckhardt, John Burton, Earl McCutchen, and Frances and Michael Higgins, did not receive the recognition afforded to the glass artists who gathered around Littleton. They did not have the infrastructure to pass on their learning, nor the ability to raise a second generation of exponents. Their work was not shown at international exhibitions and they were therefore little known.

As regards the leading US glass factories of the mid-century, there is currently little international following, with the exception of Steuben glass. Consequently, factory works tend not to be offered for sale in international auctions but rather at fairs and through online retailers in the US. Studio glass remains affordable, and interestingly it is work from the 1980s and onwards that appears most frequently at auction.

Harvey Littleton's work has increasingly appeared since the 1990s. A common theme in his work involves two looping elements, organic in form, which he continued to rework in later pieces. Marvin Lipofsky worked predominantly in the 1960s and '70s, producing abstract, organic, vessel-like forms with spouts, appendages and nipples. Dale Chihuly's prolific work has realized the highest prices. He epitomizes the spirit of American post-1945 glass production, and he also embodies its creative fulfilment. Notably, some of his inspiration came from studies in Venice during the 1960s. Over succeeding years, he personified key elements of the American studio glass movement. He was personally involved in the production of each piece, and his employees worked as a small, integrated team, eschewing 'mass production'. Yet Chihuly was also a canny business entrepreneur: by 2004, it was estimated that sales of his work had totalled $29m. At auction, his Blanket series of cylinders and basket bowls continues to sell well.

Both American and Scandinavian glass design in the mid-20th century demonstrated a new dynamic, partly in response to the traumatic experience of World War II. In Scandinavia, glass expressed a yearning for purity and simplicity, looking back nostalgically to an earlier lifestyle. In America, also deeply affected by involvement in the war, glass reflected an interest in an 'arts and crafts' dynamic, akin to that which had so powerfully touched British culture in the late 19th century.

In different ways, therefore, both Scandinavian and American glass design in the 1950s and '60s romantically hankered after a past that could never be regained. Yet, out of the effort expended on the search for a 'paradise lost' on both sides of the Atlantic, there developed a creative dynamic that propelled glass design into the 21st century. The differing mid-20th-century expressions of Scandinavian and American glass design still, in the early 21st century, continue to exert a significant global influence.

MID-CENTURY CERAMICS
ALUN GRAVES

In 1942, while much of Europe was at war, the ceramics manufacturer GUSTAVSBERG in neutral Sweden launched a new range of pottery at the exhibition 'Fajanser Målade I Vår' ('Faience Painted This Spring'). Featuring the designs of its art director Wilhelm Kåge and rising star Stig Lindberg, the range offered a freshness and sense of informality, and the stirrings of a feeling of optimism more usually associated with post-war design. Painted into a soft white tin glaze, Lindberg's colourful patterns of leaves, flowers and abstract motifs covered the surfaces of unfussy forms and, as he extended the range in subsequent years, softly curving, 'organic' shapes. This combination of vibrant all-over pattern with organically inspired form would emerge as one of the key tendencies in ceramics during the 1950s.

The origins of the organic, biomorphic shapes that epitomize 1950s ceramic design can be found in the earlier work of Kåge and, more particularly, in designs emerging from the USA in the late 1930s and early 1940s. RUSSEL WRIGHT's best-selling American Modern tableware for Steubenville, launched in 1939, combined streamlining with softened contours to create shapes that appeared animated. Offered in a range of vibrant glazes, American Modern also championed a new concept in tableware, the mixing and matching of colour.

Conversely, Eva Zeisel's* Museum service – a seminal piece of organic design in tableware – became the USA's first porcelain service to be offered in undecorated white. While the arrival of curvilinear, biomorphic shapes had been marked in 1940 by the New York Museum of Modern Art's competition and exhibition 'Organic Design in Home Furnishings', it was the very absence of ceramics from the show that prompted the Castleton China Company to seek the museum's advice in identifying a designer to create a modern tableware range.[1] Zeisel was approached and the sophisticated service she created gained the museum's imprimatur. Launched in 1946, it demonstrated Zeisel's belief in the expressive potential of form, and consciously sought to reflect qualities such as 'dignified' and 'uplifted' derived from Emily Post's popular writings on American manners.[2] Zeisel went on to design some of the most quintessential tableware of organic modernism, including the playfully biomorphic Town and Country (1946) for Red Wing Pottery and the more cleanly abstract Tomorrow's Classic (1952) for Hall China.

Nowhere was the impact of Zeisel and Wright's designs more profoundly felt than at the British firm of W. R. Midwinter in Staffordshire. Roy Midwinter, who had joined the family business after the war, encountered their work on a sales trip to the USA in 1952. Returning full of enthusiasm, he began designing tableware in comparable style. The flowing, curvilinear forms of his Fashion shape (1954) were entirely novel in the context of British ceramics, and incorporated, as their American predecessors had done, coupe plates with an uninterrupted upper surface. These shapes were perfect vehicles for the vibrant patterns commissioned by Roy Midwinter from freelance designers, or produced in-house by Jessie Tait, and would launch British tableware in a new contemporary direction.

Much of the most sophisticated organic modernism of the later 1940s and 1950s nevertheless emerged from Scandinavia. Here, the interdependence of studio pottery

BELOW LEFT A slip-cast and glazed porcelain bowl designed by Aune Siimes for Arabia, Finland, 1957.

BELOW RIGHT Cuban Fantasy designed by Jessie Tait, manufactured by W. R. Midwinter, 1957.

BOTTOM Terence Conran's Chequers tableware, 1957, produced by W. R. Midwinter.

and industry allowed a designer like Stig Lindberg to create subtly organic studio-style stoneware bowls and vases for small-scale production, alongside stylish mass-produced tablewares. In the art department of the Arabia* factory in Finland, artists were encouraged to work exclusively on studio wares. Vases of breathtaking elegance were produced there by Aune Siimes and Toini Muona, their daringly attenuated, asymmetric forms suggestive of grasses, reeds or flowers. Rather more visceral though similarly organic in inspiration were the wares of Danish designer AXEL SALTO, whose richly glazed vegetal forms seemed bursting with life.

The exaggeration of form that often characterizes mid-century ceramics was not limited to organic abstraction. Excessively narrow necks, or forms that flared dramatically from a narrow base, were common in wares that represented a more classical rendering of modernism, such as those of LUCIE RIE in England, GERTRUD & OTTO NATZLER in the USA, or Kyllikki Salmenhaara in Finland.

Another popular design was the waisted form, echoing the hourglass shape popularized by Dior's New Look in fashion. In tableware, the look is elegantly exemplified by the 2000 service (1954), designed by RAYMOND LOEWY (see under 'Product and Industrial Design') and Richard Latham for German porcelain manufacturer Rosenthal*. The service's flaring cups and sugar bowl are complemented by a high-waisted coffee pot, reputedly the result of Loewy flipping the original top-heavy design model over and declaring the result perfect.[3] The most adventurous of a number of sophisticated tableware

ABOVE The 2000 tableware service, designed by Raymond Loewy and Richard Latham for Rosenthal, 1954.

BELOW Lucie Rie, Oval vase, in stoneware, with pale limestone glaze inlaid with manganese, and sgraffito leaf decoration on either side, London, UK, 1960s.

designs produced by Loewy's studio, 2000 has a name that echoes its futuristic spirit and ambition. Such confidence was not misplaced: the design had lasting appeal, remaining in production until 1978.

By contrast, the popularity of organic modernism was short-lived. By the early 1960s, simple cylindrical forms were finding favour, though sometimes exaggerated to extraordinary heights, as in the coffee pots of Gillian Pemberton's Arabesque range for Denby (1963) and Susan Williams-Ellis's Totem for Portmeirion (1963).

If shape afforded new possibilities for mid-century ceramics, then pattern offered something equally fresh. The continuous, uninterrupted surfaces of the new organic forms invited seamless coverage with pattern or colour. This approach to decoration produced designs that responded to contemporary abstract painting and shared characteristics with interior furnishings such as Formica, wallpapers and most particularly fabrics. On occasion, a design would migrate from one medium to another: Terence Conran's Chequers, a pattern conceived for furnishing fabric, appeared on Midwinter tableware in 1957. Such relationships helped to cement a place for ceramics within fashionable interior schemes.

The association between ceramics and stylish contemporary living was further enhanced by the imagery used in the decoration of tableware. Chic furniture was famously depicted in Enid Seeney's Homemaker for Ridgway (1958). Similarly domestic in spirit are the stylized motifs of fruit and vegetables prepared for kitchen or table, such as appear in Marianne Westman's Picknick for Swedish manufacturer Rörstrand (1956). The suggestion of travel and foreign locations also held appeal. Scenes of Paris and the Côte d'Azur became popular following Hugh Casson's* Riviera designs for Midwinter (1954). Among the most lively patterns were those that purported to address African and Latin American themes. The stylized zebra stripes of Jessie Tait's Zambesi (1956) present a loosely interpreted exoticism, while other vibrant Midwinter patterns with evocative titles such as 'Cuban Fantasy' (1957) appear entirely abstract.

A similarly playful eclecticism began to emerge in studio pottery. Dora Billington wrote in 1955 that 'English studio pottery is at last acquiring a "New Look", more in tune with current ideas in house decoration and design generally'. It was 'gay, amusing, colourful ... an exciting mixture of sculpture, painting and potting'.[4] Her focus was the work of William Newland, Margaret Hine and Nicholas Vergette, three potters who shared a London studio and made stylized figures and decorative earthenware. As Billington observed, 'Their outlook is eclectic; travel abroad, museums, and contemporary art of all kinds have had their influence.' Yet behind all this was the influence of the Mediterranean: an influence that extended from Minoan pottery to the work of Pablo Picasso.

Picasso had himself begun to experiment with ceramics in 1946 at Vallauris in France. Working at the artisanal Madoura Pottery, he decorated the dishes and jars they produced, and began freely manipulating and assembling thrown forms to create playful sculptural pots, often of zoomorphic or anthropomorphic character. The same uninhibited spirit of experiment and casual interplay between the fields of art and design was apparent in Italy in the 1950s, where the prevalence of small-scale workshops allowed for considerable diversity and individualism. Working with confidence and ambition, potters such as Guido Gambone and Marcello Fantoni produced bold, outlandish and colourful ceramic forms that followed Picasso's lead in blending painting and sculpture.

In its freedom and eclecticism, such practice was at odds with the studio pottery movement that had emerged in Britain during the inter-war years under the growing dominance of Bernard Leach*. His aesthetic views, shaped while living in Japan, were based around a particular canon of pre-industrial East Asian and English wares that he held as appropriate models for the studio potter to follow. This was set out in his seminal A Potter's Book, a practical and aesthetic handbook published in 1940.

BELOW Totem coffee pot,
1963, designed by Susan
Williams-Ellis for Portmeirion,
Wales.

Around the same time, Leach, together with his son David, set about designing a range of Standard Ware – robust stonewares for domestic use – to be batch-produced by hand at the Leach Pottery in St Ives. Retailed by high-end stores like Heal's* and through mail-order catalogues issued from 1946, these helped fill a gap in the market at a time when Britain's pottery industry faced wartime restrictions. The model for production that Standard Ware provided, together with Leach's proselytization for the life and art of the potter in *A Potter's Book*, had considerable influence after the war, both in Britain and as far afield as New Zealand and North America. Many took up the call, establishing small-scale production potteries that met an increasing consumer demand for hand-made stoneware. By the 1960s, such wares were part of a counter-cultural movement, their very earthiness holding connotations of environmentalism and self-sufficiency. At David Canter's pioneering vegetarian restaurant Cranks, opened in London in 1961, their use was entirely apt.[5]

The increasing popularity of studio pottery for use on the table prompted a wider fashion for robust, brown stonewares. Factories quickly embraced the look, producing ranges from the late 1950s onwards. Intensely durable, stoneware was perfectly suited to the more casual approaches to dining that were emerging, and in particular the phenomenon of oven-to-table ware. Stylish cookware was now designed to be brought directly to the table, and formed part of ranges such as Stig Lindberg's Terma for Gustavsberg (1955) and Ulla Procopé's Ruska for Arabia (1960). In Britain, Gillian Pemberton's designs for Denby led the way, her Chevron range (1962) also exemplifying the growing fashion for surface-relief decoration in ceramics of the 1960s.

The tendency towards roughness of surface was a widespread phenomenon of post-war art, and this emphasis on texture and relief had a significant impact on the look of studio pottery from the late 1950s onwards. In Britain, potters associated with the Central School of Art, such as Ruth Duckworth, Gillian Lowndes and Ian Auld, produced increasingly sculptural works in stoneware, with roughly textured surfaces and muted colours. With no interest in functional pottery, they eschewed throwing on the wheel in favour of a range of handbuilding techniques that allowed almost limitless diversity of form. In contrast, HANS COPER, perhaps the most significant sculptor-potter to emerge in the period, remained committed to the wheel, assembling sculptural pots from separately thrown elements and forming his surfaces from layers of abraded slips and dry matt pigments.

Coper's work has a close association with that of fellow émigré Lucie Rie, whose London studio he shared from 1946 to 1958. Initially an assistant, Coper collaborated in the production of Rie's tableware, but was soon to develop his own output. Like that of Rie, this was underpinned by rigorous investigation focused on a limited range of shapes, resulting in pots that showed discipline and an ever-present dialogue between the modern and the archaic. Rie's sources were eclectic; her bottles echoed those of Classical Greece while her characteristic incised decoration derived from Neolithic and Bronze Age pottery. Coper's work, though usually without direct precedent, appeared ancient and totemic and reflected an interest in Cretan and pre-dynastic Egyptian pottery and Cycladic sculpture.

Yet the work of both was also informed by European modernism, had a contemporary, even metropolitan spirit, and was at home in modern interiors. Such duality was not contradictory. Rather, it gave contemporary relevance to a sense of cultural beginnings. But the resulting 'timelessness' with which their work is often credited is perhaps illusory. Many such pots, though of lasting importance, now look very much 'of their time'.

HANS COPER
1920–1981

LARGELY SELF-TAUGHT STUDIO
POTTER, WHOSE UNIQUE
SCULPTURAL, ROUGHLY
TEXTURED, ORGANIC FORMS
HAVE BECOME INSTANTLY
RECOGNIZABLE

Placing Hans Coper within any distinct design or artistic movement is not an easy task. In so many respects he was a true original and, growing up outside any particular tradition of ceramic art, his sources of inspiration were wide and disparate. As a young émigré in post-war London he often visited the British Museum, and its collections of Cycladic and Egyptian art, African tribal ceramics and primitive or folk pottery were an influence. But so were sculpture and art in the wider sense; Coper was particularly interested in the work of Jean Arp and Constantin Brancusi.

Clearly Coper's own work – with its emphasis on fluid, organic shapes alongside combinations or juxtapositions of different forms within a single piece – has a strong sculptural quality. Yet Coper never called his work 'sculpture' and resisted the label. He saw himself as a maker, a studio potter, and liked to ensure that his work had a functional aspect to it, even if – by the time of his death – his work was so collectable that it seemed unlikely that any of his pots would actually be used.

He worked with a 'T' material clay, sourced from Pontypridd in South Wales, for his white pots, along with an adapted version for his black pots. He tended to start work on the wheel, but would then sculpt his pots into more abstract shapes, often fusing clay structures together to create a new form.

Rather than experimenting with different glaze colours, Coper used only slips and subtle colourants, which were applied in layers to his leathery pots before firing and created a range of textures that were both raw and intriguing, like the surfaces of distant planets. This was combined with a sgraffito technique, whereby patterns, markings and slight incisions were scratched into the layers of slip before firing; Coper would also scour his pots in places after firing to create the finishes he wanted.

Throughout his career Coper repeatedly revisited certain forms, many drawn in one way or another from the natural world, including

shapes dubbed 'spade', 'bud', 'cup' and 'egg'. His work also embraced more complex structures, from thistle shapes to hourglass forms, and amalgams where, for instance, a disc might separate a bowl-like upper section from a conical base.

Coper was born into a prosperous family in Chemnitz, Germany. But by the mid-1930s his Jewish father had begun to suffer under the Nazi regime and eventually lost his job as manager of a textile mill. The family moved a number of times before his father committed suicide. Coper spent a short period studying at technical school in Dresden before the family was split up and Coper emigrated to London, just before the outbreak of war.

Treated with suspicion because of his German background, he was interned in a camp in Lancashire in 1940 before being sent to a second camp in Canada. A year later he volunteered for the Pioneer Corps and returned to England, working mostly on construction and engineering projects.

After the war, Coper found work making ceramic buttons in a small pottery in London owned by LUCIE RIE. Their relationship was to be profoundly important and enduring, yet Rie modestly rejected the claim that Coper was her protégé or apprentice. She saw in him the makings of an artist and encouraged his talents. Coper progressed rapidly, helped by classes at the local art school. In just a few years he was developing his own work, supported by Rie and gallery owners such as Henry Rothschild and William Ohly.

Both Rie and Coper exhibited work at the Festival of Britain* in 1951, with Coper's ceramics also shown at the Milan Triennale that same year. By the time he began living and working at Digswell House in Hertfordshire in 1958 – at the invitation of the Digswell Arts Trust – he was receiving wide recognition for the inventiveness and maturity of his work, which was increasingly abstract in nature.

Other kinds of projects drew upon Coper's ongoing fascination with engineering and architecture. In the early 1960s he developed a range of clay cladding tiles for architectural use, as well as a collection of acoustic bricks. He was also commissioned to design and make a series of candlesticks for the new Coventry Cathedral (1962), designed by BASIL SPENCE (see under 'Houses and Interiors').

In 1967, Coper bought a derelict farm in Frome, Somerset, where he lived and worked until the end of his life. He also taught at the Camberwell School of Art and the Royal College of Art. Just before his death, one of his early thistle pots had raised a record figure at auction for work by a living studio potter and his ceramics were being collected by many admirers, including Robert and Lisa Sainsbury, who donated a substantial body of Coper's work to the Sainsbury Centre at the University of East Anglia in Norwich, Norfolk.

OPPOSITE LEFT Glazed stoneware vase, c. 1960, made in London, UK.

OPPOSITE RIGHT Glazed stoneware vase, c. 1965.

LEFT Glazed stoneware vase, c. 1965.

KAJ FRANCK
1911–1989

THE SO-CALLED 'CONSCIENCE OF FINNISH DESIGN', RENOWNED FOR THE PARED-DOWN, UTILITARIAN AESTHETIC EXEMPLIFIED IN HIS BESTSELLING TABLEWARE AND GLASSWARE

There was a distinctly democratic aspect to Kaj Franck's work. Like many of his contemporaries in the mid-century period, such as ROBIN DAY (see under 'Furniture') or RUSSEL WRIGHT, Franck was passionate about the idea of making good design available to all. The Finnish designer put his ideas into practice most effectively with his Kilta range of affordable earthenware – a mix-and-match dinner service with a vivid sense of geometrical simplicity – launched in 1952 by Arabia*, the ceramics company where Franck had become artistic director a few years earlier.

Franck was concerned about the traditional and outmoded approach to tableware that was prevalent across Scandinavia, even in the post-war years. He saw that most families still relied upon highly decorated dinner services sold as elaborate sets and often inspired by period English or French decorative patterns and designs. It was either this or rustic serving bowls, with little in between.

Working at Arabia, Franck invented an alternative, with a range of plates, platters, cups and bowls that were designed with an innate sense of simplicity. They used a limited palette of unadorned geometric shapes in a single glaze, with a choice of five original colours, including white. The earthenware was mass-produced to keep costs down and pieces could be bought individually, allowing mixing and matching without the substantial investment needed in a complete dinner service. Added to this, the plates and bowls

were both easily stackable and hard-wearing, giving them a strong degree of functionality and practicality. Today, such characteristics are standard, but back in 1952 the Kilta range had an impact comparable to that of Russel Wright's American Modern tableware in the States. The range was updated in the 1980s, using stoneware with an expanded choice of colours, and renamed Teema. More than 25 million pieces of the combined lines are said to have been sold.

Franck, who came from a German-Swedish family, began his education in design at the Central School of Applied Arts in Helsinki, Finland. After graduating he worked in a number of different aspects of design, including furniture and textiles, and including a short period designing for Artek*. After the war he joined Arabia, becoming fascinated by mass-production techniques, while also designing a number of pieces of glassware for the Finnish company Iittala*.

In the 1950s Arabia's parent company also acquired the Nuutajärvi-Notsjö glass factory, where Franck took up work as design director. Once again, he involved himself closely in the production and technical processes of the factory, as well as developing design ideas. Some of these designs were signed or limited-edition pieces, such as sculptural decanters or his beautifully conceived Prisma vase of 1962. But at the same time Franck's ideas also took him once again towards a mass-produced, more accessible and versatile line of glassware.

Throughout the 1950s Franck – who also became an influential design professor and theorist – developed a number of drinking glasses and pitchers which became the Kartio range. Again, the designs were simple and seductive with a strong sense of geometric purity; the pitchers featured a tucked waist within a more angular version of the hourglass form. A smoky range of colours – such as grey and sea blue – lend the range, which is now produced by Iittala, a particular sense of character.

ABOVE Teema mugs in terracotta and white, and coffee cups in blue and black; made by Iittala, original designs dating from 1952.

OPPOSITE Teema mini serving set in turquoise, pearl grey and terracotta, produced by Iittala, originally designed 1952.

RIGHT Teema dishes
and a Kartio glass tumbler,
manufactured by Iittala.

BELOW LEFT Kartio glass
pitcher, designed in 1958
and produced by Iittala.

BELOW CENTRE Decanter
in mould-blown glass, 1955,
produced by Nuutajärvi-Notsjö.

BELOW RIGHT Kremlin Bells
double decanter, 1962, in
glass with cork, manufactured
by Nuutajärvi-Notsjö.

GUSTAVSBERG POTTERY

WILHELM KÅGE
1889–1960
STIG LINDBERG
1916–1982
BERNDT FRIBERG
1899–1981

DYNAMIC SWEDISH POTTERY STUDIO PRODUCING A WIDE RANGE OF COLLECTABLE CERAMICS

The Gustavsberg pottery in Sweden positioned itself right at the vanguard of a revolution in post-war taste and style. It was emblematic of the energy, dynamism and fresh thinking that infused Scandinavian glass and ceramics in the mid-century era, with an emphasis upon organic forms, shapes and colours on the one hand and a more playful, folk art influence on the other. Indeed, it was partly the breadth and depth of output that raised Gustavsberg to prominence, embracing the talents of three of the most respected Swedish designers and ceramic artists of the period: Wilhelm Kåge, Stig Lindberg and Berndt Friberg.

Wilhelm Kåge was originally a painter, but became art director of Gustavsberg in 1917. He balanced the pottery's commercial production with the more sophisticated output of the Gustavsberg Studio, which produced signature pieces by Kåge himself and others. In the 1930s Kåge designed a new collection

of tableware called Praktika – an earthenware range in white with green rims that could be easily stacked and stored. Kåge designed other ranges for everyday use but he also created many pieces in the studio, including his Argenta line of vases, which fused Classical influences and Art Deco elements.

Kåge's work in the post-war period was noticeably different in character, with his Farsta series of glazed stoneware having a more rustic, rugged and hand-crafted appearance and earthy glaze colours. These pieces stood

RIGHT A Stig Lindberg vase in glazed stoneware from 1966.

FAR RIGHT A Farsta vessel by Wilhelm Kåge, made with glazed earthenware, dating from the 1950s.

in contrast to the Surrea series of around the same period – a more experimental collection of white glazed stoneware with a suitably surreal quality, each vase or bowl having the appearance of being sliced in two and then reassembled but with a distinct degree of separation between the twins.

Kåge's protégé, who was to take his place as artistic director at Gustavsberg, was Stig Lindberg. After studying art and design in Stockholm, Denmark and Paris, Lindberg designed glassware and textiles, as well as working as a book illustrator. He also worked under Kåge at Gustavsberg in the late 1930s. When in 1949 he was appointed the new artistic head of the pottery, he brought with him a broad range of ideas and a lighter touch, weaving folk art references and more playful patterns and motifs into his work.

Lindberg's crisp white Veckla vessels of the early 1950s had some elements in common with Kåge's Surrea designs – highly sculptural, abstract pieces like writing paper folded into shell-like shapes and indented cones. Vessels of the 1960s were very different in nature, although still sculptural. Some pieces resembled exotic towers, combining and contrasting different shapes, with a nipped waist dividing the elements. Other stoneware vases were more rugged and organic, with earthy glazes and purposefully primitive patterns reminiscent of tribal ceramics.

BELOW LEFT A Stig Lindberg glazed stoneware vase, 1966.

BELOW CENTRE A glazed stoneware vase from 1968, designed by Berndt Friberg.

BELOW RIGHT A wheel-thrown and glazed stoneware vase from 1960, designed by Berndt Friberg.

ABOVE Farsta bowl in glazed
stoneware, designed by
Wilhelm Kåge, 1956.

Lindberg's work possessed warmth and imagination. Lighter pieces included leaf-shaped dishes with naïve folk art-inspired patterns in bright colours, while conch-shaped bowls and ceramic platters were decorated in playful hand-painted patterns. Most striking perhaps is the sheer breadth of Lindberg's designs, ranging from family-friendly ceramic horses to highly collectable studio pieces.

It is testament to the nurturing spirit of Gustavsberg that a third major figure emerged from the pottery in the mid-century period. This was Berndt Friberg, a master of the potter's wheel and the pioneer of a whole recipe book of distinctive matt glazes, from emerald greens and sky blues to field colours such as earthy browns and tree wood tones.

Friberg came from a family of potters and was employed as a thrower by Kåge and Lindberg. Within the Gustavsberg Studio he developed his own style and was given the freedom to curate and create an independent collection. The glazes and some of the forms he produced have an Eastern influence, yet his work led him in very new directions, with highly crafted egg-shaped vessels and long-necked vases like elongated ceramic gourds forming just part of his repertoire.

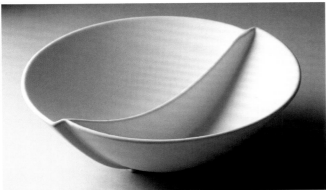

ABOVE Argenta vase by
Wilhelm Kåge, in glazed
and gilt stoneware, c. 1930.

LEFT Stig Lindberg vases in glazed stoneware, 1967 and 1970.

BELOW A grouping of Stig Lindberg glazed stoneware vessels, 1962–66.

OPPOSITE A collection of Stig Lindberg Veckla vessels in glazed stoneware, c. 1950.

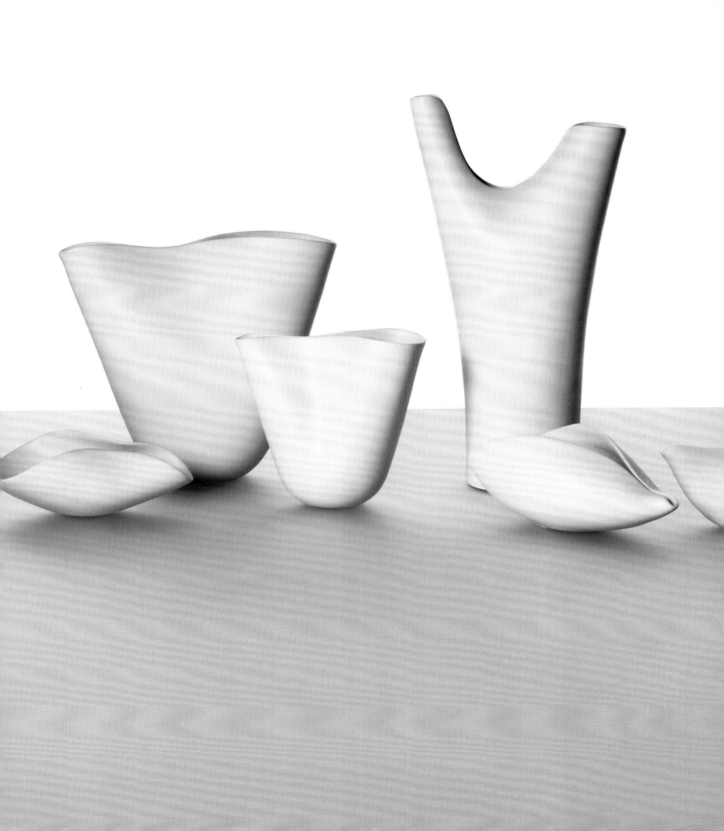

OPPOSITE ABOVE
Wheel-thrown and glazed
stoneware vessels and vases
by Berndt Friberg, c. 1960.

OPPOSITE BELOW
A collection of wheel-thrown
and glazed stoneware vases
by Berndt Friberg, 1964.

LEFT Wheel-thrown and
glazed stoneware vase by
Berndt Friberg, 1967.

BELOW A collection of
miniature vessels by Berndt
Friberg, wheel-thrown in
glazed stoneware, c. 1963.

VICKE LINDSTRAND
1904–1983

PRE-EMINENT STUDIO DESIGNER
WHOSE WORK FOR KOSTA,
ORREFORS AND OTHERS MADE
HIM A PIONEER OF SWEDISH
ART GLASS

The two leading Swedish glass-making companies of the post-war era were Kosta* and Orrefors*. Kosta's origins dated back to the 1740s, while Orrefors was founded in 1898. Both were pre-eminent in the 1950s, when Scandinavian glass and ceramics gained international importance, and both were lifted by their association with the pioneering Swedish designer Vicke Lindstrand.

Born Victor Emanuel Lindstrand, he studied at the School of Arts & Crafts in Gothenburg and worked initially in commercial art and illustration. He arrived at Orrefors in 1928 and worked alongside designers Edward Hald and Simon Gate. Their pre-war work was dominated by engraved glass with Art Deco (or Moderne) influences, a style embraced by Lindstrand in the 1930s with a series of vases – including his Pearl Fishers of 1931 – featuring Deco-inspired designs either engraved or painted onto the glass.

Lindstrand came to the fore at the company during the late 1930s, when, in addition to designing, he helped to develop new production techniques, such as the Ariel system of 1937, which allowed fluid, colourful patterns to be captured between layers of glass.

During the war years, Lindstrand moved in a different direction, joining the Swedish ceramics producer Upsala Ekeby, where he contributed a number of designs and became creative director. Founded in the 1880s, Upsala Ekeby was also at the height of its powers in the 1950s, contributing to the excitement surrounding Scandinavian design.

In the early 1950s Lindstrand returned to glass and formed a new association with Kosta, the company most intimately connected with the designer's post-war creativity. By this time his work was mature and highly original, and he soon began to steer Kosta in a new direction as chief designer and art director, working with the company right through to the early 1970s.

Lindstrand created pieces of etched glass for Kosta, such as the Cathedral vase of 1954, but the forms that he developed were more fluid and abstract than any of his work for Orrefors. The natural world was a powerful source of inspiration for his evocative Trees in the Mist vases of the 1950s, which featured curling black branches enveloping a misted glass vase. Similar designs played with three-dimensional effects and optical tricks, which gave the work an unusual sense of depth and dynamism.

There were also designs for tableware – including the Gracile and Melody collections of 1958 – but Lindstrand's innovative studio pieces capture most attention. Coloured streaks and abstract patterns were sealed within the teardrop glass shapes of his vases, such as the Zebra and Colora series, creating a powerful sense of optical and kinetic excitement. The colours themselves were often vivid and intense – ox blood reds or striking combinations of aqua greens and blues. In their abstract beauty, such pieces of blown glass resembled both seductive sculptures and exotic crystals that had somehow been born in the earth, like volcanic droplets of obsidian.

Lindstrand also developed a series of glass sculptures, worked as a painter and designed textiles. But he continued working with Kosta (later Kosta Boda) for just over twenty years, until his retirement in 1973.

BELOW A pair of glass Orchid vases, made by Orrefors, 1957.

ABOVE Trees in the Mist glass
vase, produced by Kosta, 1959.

ABOVE RIGHT Glass vase,
c. 1959, made by Kosta.

ABOVE A set of three vases produced by Kosta, 1955.

OPPOSITE ABOVE AND BELOW A Kosta vase in red, c. 1959, and a Colora vase in pale blue, 1973, produced by Kosta.

GERTRUD NATZLER
1908–1971
& OTTO NATZLER
1908–2007

AUSTRIAN POTTER AND GLAZER
PARTNERSHIP, WORKING IN
CLOSE SYNERGY TO CREATE
HARMONIOUS, WIDELY ADMIRED
CERAMICS

The revered ceramicists Gertrud and Otto Natzler always followed their instincts and set their own direction. Their work was not influenced by fashion, artistic movements or the philosophies of others, but stood alone and independent. They remained focused, limiting their social circle and perfecting their work within a prolific output.

Gertrud Natzler was the potter, creating vases, bowls and plates on the potter's wheel. Her work fell into two distinct camps: paper-thin constructions characterized by their great sense of delicacy and more 'monumental' pieces, including vases on a larger scale with a more solid appearance. Her husband, Otto, was a glaze master, developing around 2,000 recipes and experimenting with firing techniques. His approach was scientific, but he was not afraid to fail through trial and error.

One of Otto Natzler's fascinations was with reduction firing, whereby organic materials such as wood shavings and leaves are added to the kiln so that as they burn they reduce the amount of oxygen available, affecting the glaze colours while sometimes marking and scarring the pots themselves. Natzler recorded the results in great detail and kept records for around 25,000 different pieces. There were many variations of colour and texture, but Natzler is best known for surfaces with a rugged, volcanic quality – finishes that are pitted and worn, battered and uneven, rather than polished and crisp, as well as variegated glaze patterns full of depth.

Otto Natzler was born in Vienna, where his father was a dentist. He studied textile design at a young age and then worked in a necktie company, developing colour schemes, but lost his job when the Jewish-owned firm was boycotted by German retailers. In 1933 he met Gertrud Amon and divorced his first wife the following year. Gertrud was working as a secretary, but was already interested in art and ceramics. They established a studio together and Otto soon recognized his partner's talents, abandoning his own work as a sculptor to begin his experiments in glazing. Both were largely self-taught, with Otto's initial attempts at firing ending in disaster.

Yet the Natzlers' work evolved quickly and by 1937 they had won a silver medal at the Austrian Pavilion at the Paris International Exhibition. That same day, the German army moved into Austria. The couple packed up their possessions – including their potter's wheel, kiln and early pots – and moved to Los Angeles. In America, their work evolved significantly. Just two years after arriving, they mounted their first solo exhibition and began earning praise from commentators.

RIGHT Wheel-thrown,
glazed earthenware footed
vase by Gertrud & Otto
Natzler, 1942.

FAR RIGHT Closed-form vase
in wheel-thrown and glazed
earthenware, c. 1940, by
Gertrud & Otto Natzler.

OPPOSITE Split disc
composition, solo work
by Otto Natzler in glazed
stoneware, 1981.

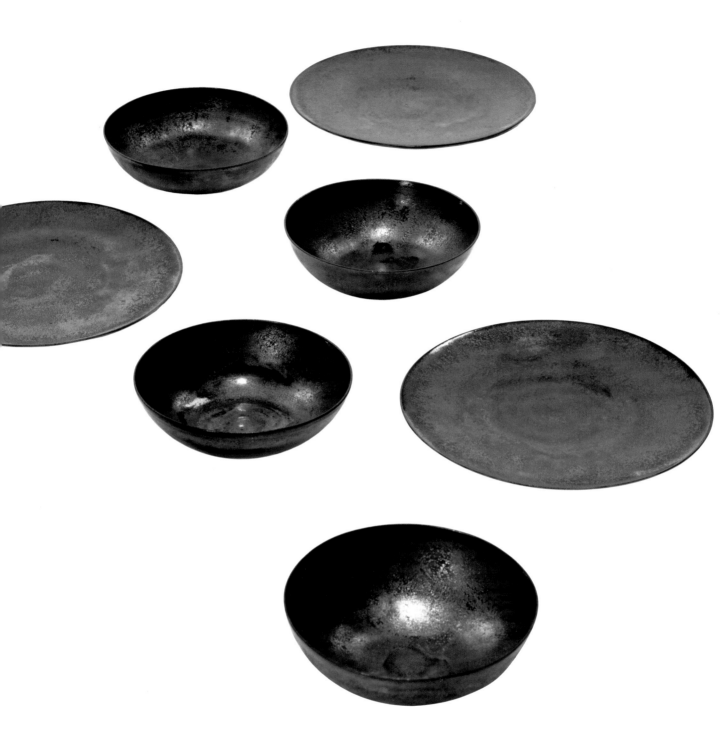

The Natzlers also developed a series of bespoke ceramic tiles, which were used as table-tops by EDWARD WORMLEY (see under 'Furniture'). Here, Otto Natzler's glazes, without the sculptural forms of his wife's pots, became the real focal point.

After Gertrud Natzler died in 1971, Otto developed his own series of pots using slab construction techniques. His wife had left behind around two hundred completed but unglazed pots, but it was many years before Otto could be persuaded to complete them. In some respects, their work could be compared with that of LUCIE RIE and HANS COPER, individualists who followed a distinct and highly creative path as studio potters.

ABOVE A collection of glazed earthenware bowls and plates by Gertrud & Otto Natzler, c. 1945.

RIGHT Wheel-thrown and
glazed earthenware vase
by Gertrud & Otto Natzler,
1962.

BELOW Gertrud & Otto
Natzler glazed earthenware
bowl, 1957.

LUCIE RIE
1902–1995

REVERED AUSTRIAN-BORN
STUDIO POTTER, WHOSE WIDE
RANGE OF WORKS EXHIBIT
BOTH A DELICATE MODERNISM
AND A RUGGED PRIMITIVISM

A fascinating paradox lies at the heart of Lucie Rie's work. On the one hand her work is grounded in modernism and an interest in design and architecture dating back to her early years of study in Vienna; yet on the other her most personal work has a depth of character and texture, as well as a powerful simplicity of form and deliberately evocative, primitive quality, that is reminiscent of the ceramic treasures unearthed in an archaeological dig.

In the late 1940s Rie apparently visited the museum at Avebury in Wiltshire and was much taken by the displays of Neolithic and Bronze Age pottery, as well as the basic tools – made with bird bones – that were used to make patterns on the clay. Certainly her work was very different in character from the model championed by the likes of Bernard Leach*, who, along with many followers, was far more influenced by Japanese and Asian ceramic traditions. Rie – rather like GERTRUD & OTTO NATZLER and her dear friend and colleague HANS COPER (all émigrés from Austria and Germany) – was more concerned with finding an individual voice, outside the mainstream.

Born Lucie Gomperz in Vienna in 1902, Rie was the youngest child of a prosperous Jewish doctor, who designed his waiting room and surgery in a modernist style. She studied at the Vienna School of Arts and Crafts under Michael Powolny and was also influenced by the modernist architect and designer, Josef Hoffmann. Her early work was characterized by a sense of austerity and purity of form.

She married Hans Rie in 1926 (the marriage was dissolved in 1940) and began exhibiting her work in the late 1930s. Her apartment in Vienna was designed by the architect Ernst Plischke in the modernist style. But in 1938, just after the Anschluss and in the face of growing anti-Semitism, Rie moved to England, taking her work and as many pieces from her apartment as she could.

She settled in London and established a studio in Albion Mews near Paddington. During the war years she worked in an optical factory. To make ends meet she then began designing and making ceramic buttons for Bimini, as well as jewelry. In 1946 Coper joined her at the pottery, later helping her develop a range of functional table and kitchen ware.

RIGHT A glazed stoneware
vase, c. 1965.

At the same time Rie was evolving her personal work and developing individual pieces in stoneware and porcelain. She and Coper provided one another with mutual encouragement and support. Certain characteristics and common interests connected their work – which was often exhibited together over the years – but Rie focused upon a more limited range of shapes and forms, particular bowls, urns and vases, within a modest output that was highly accomplished and increasingly sought after.

Coper restricted his finishes to a concentrated palette of slips and firing techniques, but Rie was intrigued by her ongoing experiments with glazes and the chemistry of ceramic textures. In this respect she had more in common with Otto Natzler, and a number of her footed bowls, bottles and vases reveal a similar interest in highly textured surfaces that are pitted and pocked, with melting colours and rugged hues.

Rie's pots have a weathered quality – as though worn down and scarred by exposure to the elements over hundreds of years. This was especially true of her work of the 1960s and beyond – using layers of slips mixed with metal oxides – while the 1950s pieces tended to have a more familiar decorative element, with sgraffito markings and simple but evocative abstract patterns. Rie's work always sat well with the interiors and architecture of the time, offering a striking focal point.

Hard-working, ordered, precise and direct, Rie began to receive considerable acclaim by the late 1960s. She taught part-time at the Camberwell School of Art but always remained highly focused on her work, calling herself, simply, a potter. 'Through her training as a potter in Vienna to her exile in London, and to her creation of a style of making that had no counterpoint in the earthy functionalism of British pottery,' wrote ceramicist and author Edmund de Waal in his assessment of Rie, 'she projected a force-field of separation from the expectations of those around her.'[6]

BELOW A stoneware vase with porcelain slip and dolomite glaze, c. 1970.

RIGHT Stoneware open bowl, c. 1965, with a yellow glaze and manganese feathered lip.

BELOW A porcelain blue and white bowl, 1956, with sgraffito markings.

BOTTOM Porcelain bowl, c. 1970, with a manganese and copper glaze on the interior and crimson pigment for incised lines on the exterior.

OPPOSITE Glazed stoneware teapot with bamboo handle, c. 1960.

AXEL SALTO
1889–1961

DANISH CERAMICIST – ONE OF THE MOST EXPERIMENTAL OF THE AGE – WHOSE EXPRESSIVE, NATURE-INSPIRED DESIGNS ARE HIGHLY COLLECTABLE TODAY

In the 1950s the endless variety and richness of the natural world was a key source of inspiration, with artists across all aspects of design – textiles, furniture, ceramics and glass – looking to natural forms, shapes and colours. Mother Nature certainly led Axel Salto, the masterful Danish ceramicist and designer, in the most extraordinary of directions.

Never afraid to venture off into territory that must often have seemed extreme and avant-garde, Salto created many designs that feel as though they are part of nature itself: exotic seed pods unearthed from the forest floor, or curious, sculptural eggs waiting to burst into life. His most richly textured vases are enriched with buds and sinuous growths, which in abstract form feel both organic and otherworldly. Within these decidedly modern creations there is, at times, perhaps also a thread of Art Nouveau elegance, or at least a shared love of winding, creeping tendrils.

Salto trained at the Copenhagen Academy of Art and his first love was painting, a passion that he continued to explore throughout his life. In 1916 he travelled to Paris, where he met Picasso and Matisse, and upon his return he founded an art journal called *Klingen* ('The Blade'). He also co-founded a loosely aligned group of Danish artists known as De Fire ('The Four'), which based itself partly in France during the 1920s.

Salto's career as a ceramicist began in the mid-1920s, when he started designing his first pieces of stoneware for the venerable Danish firm of Bing & Grøndahl. But his name is inextricably linked with Royal Copenhagen*, which produced the majority of his ceramics.

Early designs took inspiration from the Classical world, with the mythical figure of Acteon – a Theban hunter who was turned into a stag – a particular source of inspiration. Acteon appears repeatedly in Salto's work of the 1940s, in the form of ceramic plaques, sculptures and deer's head figurines.

His work for Royal Copenhagen in the 1950s became progressively more abstract, intense and surreal, as though his own imagination was being overgrown. His work of the period is often sub-divided into three categories: budding, sprouting and fluted. The budded pieces were mottled with protrusions, like sea urchins or exotic fruits. The sprouting pieces took this idea a step further, with vigorous growths emerging from the surface of the clay, as though searching for sunlight. Then there were the fluted pieces, characterized by a primitive, furrowed, zig-zag pattern, while the Living Stone collection offered a more accessible, functional range with relief patterns applied to more conventional forms. At the same time Salto developed his own glazes, ranging from celadon and Asian-inspired colours through to thick, rich finishes – like the lava-like 'solfatara' – for his more abstract pieces.

Salto also designed textiles and illustrated books of poetry. Yet his ceramics remain his most captivating and enduring legacy, full of vitality and originality.

RIGHT Budding Gourd vase in glazed stoneware, produced by Royal Copenhagen, c. 1940.

FAR RIGHT A glazed stoneware Sprouting vase, c. 1940, produced by Royal Copenhagen.

LEFT A glazed stoneware vase, made by Royal Copenhagen, c. 1940.

BELOW An abstract vessel in cast stoneware with a solfatara glaze, c. 1940, Royal Copenhagen.

BELOW A Royal Copenhagen
glazed stoneware vase, c. 1940.

BELOW RIGHT Budding
vase in glazed stoneware,
c. 1950, produced by Royal
Copenhagen.

BELOW A lidded vessel in cast
stoneware with a solfatara glaze,
c. 1945, Royal Copenhagen.

RIGHT A Royal Copenhagen
vase in glazed stoneware,
c. 1940.

TIMO SARPANEVA
1926–2006

INFLUENTIAL FINNISH DESIGNER
WHO EXPLORED NEW
PRODUCTION TECHNIQUES
AND DEVELOPED INNOVATIVE
ART GLASS COLLECTIONS

'Glass is very mysterious,' Timo Sarpaneva once said. 'It's changing all the time. That's what makes it magical.' Despite also designing textiles, ceramics and ironware, the celebrated Finnish designer was most preoccupied by the mysterious qualities of glass, and it is the material with which he is most associated. For him, glass opened up an extra dimension in design and was full of possibilities.

In some respects, Sarpaneva's approach to glass was romantic and even nostalgic. There were constant echoes of ice in his work and frozen forms, particularly in his rugged, mottled Finlandia vases (1964) and his Festivo candlesticks (1966). He spoke of the moment when, as a young child, he held a piece of ice in his hands and allowed the warmth of his fingers to shape and pierce it. The echoes of the metaphor are easy to see, particularly within Sarpaneva art pieces, their abstract clear glass forms indented with sticks while still hot and malleable.

Sarpaneva often emphasized the fact that he was the product of a Scandinavian art and craft heritage. His grandfather was a blacksmith and Sarpaneva liked to equate his memories of molten metal with his approach to glass-working. He also worked in metal itself, producing steel tableware and in 1960 a famous reinterpretation of a traditional classic in the form of a black cast-iron oven-to-table pot, with a white-enamelled interior and a detachable wooden handle to carry the pot and lift the lid, originally produced by Rosenlew and later reissued by Iittala*.

Sarpaneva trained as a draughtsman and graphic designer at the Institute of Industrial Arts in Helsinki, graduating in 1948. Soon afterwards he began working in glass and in 1951 began a long association with Iittala. In the 1930s the company worked with ALVAR AALTO (see under 'Houses and Interiors') and his wife Aino Aalto* on a range of tableware and bowls, which are still in production, but it was best known for a traditional approach to glass-making.

In the post-war years, with the input of Sarpaneva and his close contemporary Tapio Wirkkala*, Iittala began to change direction, becoming more adventurous and placing a far greater emphasis upon innovative design. Sarpaneva designed tableware for the company, including his elegant, streamlined i-glass range of tinted glass (1956), and he also designed the company logo. In addition, he began to explore new production techniques and to develop art glass collections. Most famously there was his Finlandia range, which used burnt wood moulds. From the 1950s onwards, Sarpaneva also used wet sticks to create bubble-like openings in sculptural glass forms. One of his stick-blown pieces – Lancet II – was awarded the Grand Prix at the Milan Triennial of 1954, a prize that Sarpaneva won a number of times.

Art pieces of the 1960s – such as Shadows, which resembled a melting block of ice – were even more abstract and extreme in character. Later, in the 1970s and '80s, Sarpaneva returned to more functional forms, including his Claritas vases, featuring smooth teardrop shapes with bubbles of air floating within the thick glass walls.

In addition to glass-making, Sarpaneva taught textile design and himself designed textiles, working as the artistic director of the Porin Puuvilla cotton mill in the mid-1950s. There were also tableware designs in porcelain for Rosenthal*, most notably the Suomi service of 1976. Sarpaneva also designed glass pieces for PAOLO VENINI and created large-scale glass sculptures, most notably his Ahtojää ('Pack Ice') artwork for the Finnish Pavilion of the Montreal Expo of 1967.

OPPOSITE A set of hand-blown glass Sun balls, produced by Iittala, 1960.

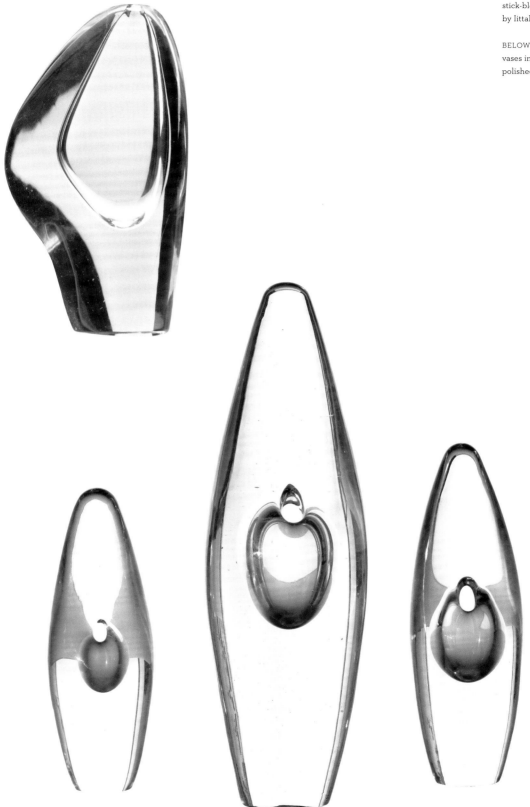

LEFT Lancet II art object in stick-blown glass, produced by Iittala from 1955.

BELOW A set of three Orchid vases in stick-blown, cut and polished glass, Iittala, 1954.

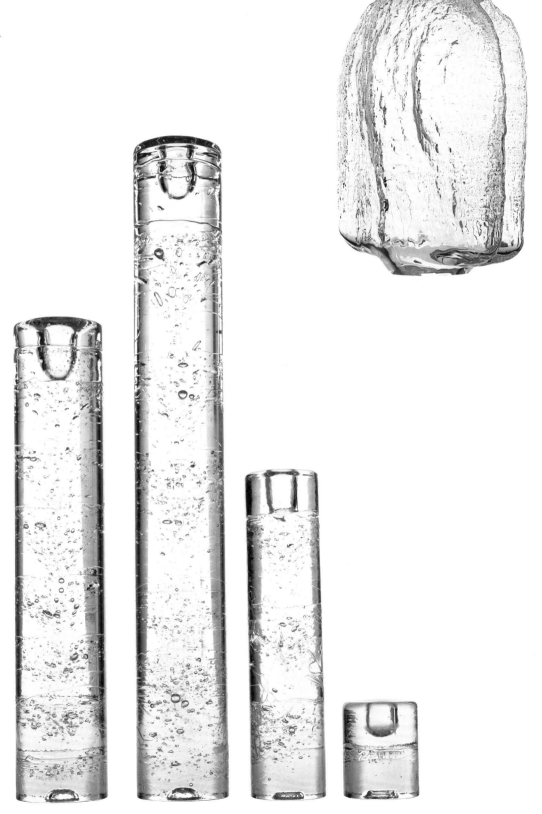

RIGHT Shadows art piece in mould-blown glass, Iittala, 1964.

BELOW Four Archipelago sculptures in mould-blown glass, produced by Iittala, 1978.

PAOLO VENINI

1895–1959

LEADING FIGURE IN THE
PRODUCTION OF MURANO
GLASS, DESIGNING AS WELL
AS MANUFACTURING HIGHLY
SUCCESSFUL ART PIECES

In the post-war period, Italian glass-making was reinvigorated and reinvented. Rather like the lighting industry during this golden age of Italian design, glass-making was revived and energized by a combination of factors, including a willingness to innovate and experiment, as well as an eagerness to embrace new talent and forge lasting collaborations with designers, architects and like-minded pioneers. Both industries were also able to draw upon an established network of modestly scaled workshops and factories, as well as a skilled workforce of artisans. One of the most successful and internationally renowned glass-making companies was the firm founded by Paolo Venini in 1921 in Murano, Venice, the long-established hub of Italian glass-making.

Venini had studied law in Milan but came from a family that had been involved in glass-making in Lake Como. He indulged his twin passions for glass and Venice by co-founding his own company with partners at the former Rioda glassworks. By the late 1920s, Venini's partners had left for other ventures and the company was renamed simply Venini & C.

An entrepreneurial and forward-thinking figure, Paolo Venini saw the importance of employing and nurturing gifted glass-makers and developing pieces of the highest quality. More than this, he recognized the need to promote the company and its work, not only in Italy but internationally. He also saw the benefits of establishing creative collaborations and working alliances with key figures in the world of design, both in Italy and beyond. He began working with Carlo Scarpa* in the early 1930s; in the 1950s, Scarpa's son Tobia* also worked with the company. In the 1940s Venini

worked with GIO PONTI (see under 'Furniture'). Other designers associated with the factory included Tyra Lundgren, Tapio Wirkkala*, Massimo Vignelli* and Fulvio Bianconi*.

Venini also involved himself very directly in production and design processes, and was a major creative force: many highly collectable Venini pieces from the late 1940s and 1950s were designed by the founder himself. He also collaborated with Bianconi on the design of the iconic Fazzoletto ('Handkerchief') vase of 1949. Variations on the original design were added in the years that followed, but the most famous design was always the lace-like white version.

Sometimes Venini would collaborate on designs or adapt existing pieces. But he also developed original glasswork and new production techniques. His Inciso range (1956) of stoppered vessels and bottles combined sculptural shapes with smoky colours, such as apple green and dusty amber, their surfaces subtly worn by abrasive wheels. Other pieces included the two-tone Murrina series (c. 1952/53) and the mosaic-effect vases of the Zanfirico and Tessuto lines (c. 1954). Venini was also instrumental in developing a mosaic-style method whereby coloured tesserae were applied to a clear base layer of glass.

From the mid-1950s, he created a range of mesmerizing glass Clessidres – or hourglasses – which combined two different colours for the top and base of each sand timer (the two-tone theme was explored further in later designs by Wirkkala and others). At the same time, Venini developed lighting collections with glass shades in sculptural shapes reminiscent of urns and amphoras, using internal patterns within the blown glass. In later years the lighting division of the company would become increasingly important.

After Venini's death the company continued – and thrived – under the guidance of his son-in-law, Ludovico Diaz de Santillana, and his widow, Ginette Gignous. It remained under family control until the mid-1980s.

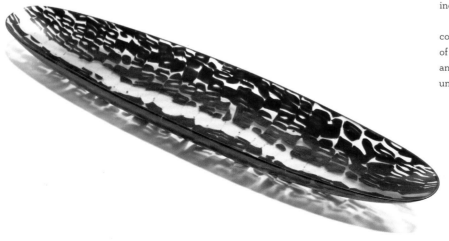

LEFT A Murrina vase, c. 1953.

OPPOSITE Model 4883 Canoa platter in fused murrina with a wheel-carved surface, 1955.

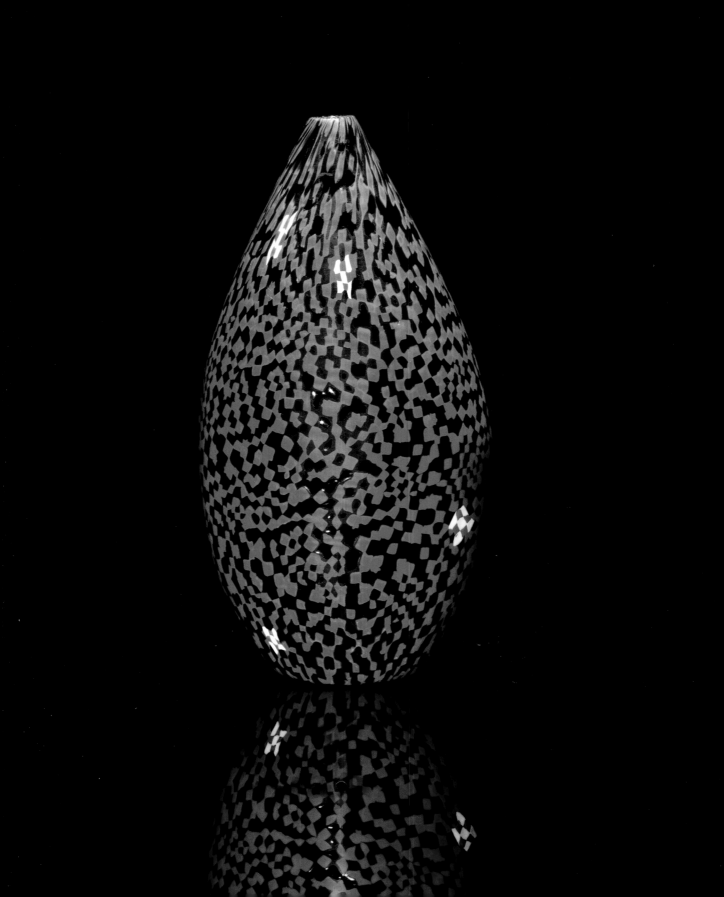

BELOW Model 3887 Mosaico
Tessuto vase, c. 1954, with
multicoloured mosaic tiles
over a clear glass body.

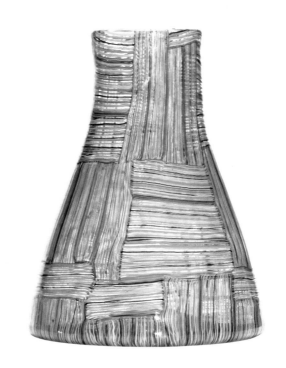

OPPOSITE Zanfirico vase,
c. 1954, with internally
decorated glass.

OPPOSITE A collection of
Inciso bottles and stoppers
in *sommerso* glass with a
wheel-carved surface, c. 1956.

BELOW A set of four glass
Clessidre sand timers, c. 1965.

RUSSEL WRIGHT
1904–1976

AMERICAN EXPONENT OF
'EASIER LIVING', FAMOUS FOR
HIS BESTSELLING RANGE OF
DEMOCRATIC DINNERWARE

The concept of 'easier living' developed by designer Russel Wright in the early 1950s had two aspects to it. Firstly, Wright was laying out the idea of a more informal way of living in the modern American home, which was being radically reinvented in every respect as pre-war conventions were challenged and cast aside. Secondly, the products that Wright and others designed in the 1940s and '50s helped introduce a new generation of goods that were functional, well designed, durable and affordable. From dinnerware through to furniture, Wright's designs made life easier.

The greatest example of his democratic view – 'good design is for everyone' – came with his American Modern range of dinnerware (see also p. 168), which sold as many as 250 million pieces between 1939, when it was first produced, and 1959, when it was finally discontinued. American Modern crockery combined Wright's great talents as an industrial designer with an interest in mass-production techniques and the creative eye of an artist.

'I thought that since most foods are amorphous in shape the dinnerware should be of simple geometric form yet without sharp angles which would attract more attention than the food,' said Wright. 'And I found that there should be no decoration on the surface...'[7]

The range was utilitarian and inexpensive, yet had a sinuous fluidity that was a key part of its appeal, combined with a range of alluring and organic colours, including chartreuse, coral, cedar green and sea foam. The water pitcher, in particular, had a powerful sculptural form and spoke of quality through both design and manufacture, despite its modest price. The range became the default service of choice for the American consumer in the 1940s and '50s, and Wright even reported that its arrival in stores caused near riots. As with so much of his work, the design felt ahead of its time and was perfectly placed to feed the growing appetite for fresh and engaging homeware in the post-war years.

Born in Ohio, Wright was fascinated with the world of art and design from an early age. Even while at Princeton University studying law, he continued to pursue a passion for art and sculpture. After finishing his studies he became a theatre-set designer in New York, then in 1927 he launched his own design studio and also married Mary Small Einstein, a sculptor who was to become his business manager, publicist and co-author of the best-selling lifestyle manual, *Guide to Easier Living*, published in 1950.

Wright began designing home accessories and pieces such as sculptural bookends in pewter. By the early 1930s there were aluminium cocktail sets and kitchen utensils, as well as cutlery and the first pieces of furniture. Wright launched a full American Modern line of furniture in 1935, made by Conant-Ball, followed by the American Modern dinnerware, produced by Steubenville.

He also developed a range of art pottery for the Bauer Pottery (which in recent years has reissued the American Modern range of ceramics). In the 1950s there were designs for lighting, textiles and the Easier Living furniture range. By this time, with his wife's help, Wright had become a design and lifestyle brand, comparable to CHARLES & RAY EAMES (see

LEFT AND OPPOSITE
American Modern tableware,
designed in 1937 and first
put into production by
Steubenville in 1939.

ABOVE A cocktail set in spun
aluminium and cork, from
Russel Wright, Inc., 1930.

under 'Furniture') or ROBIN & LUCIENNE DAY
(see under 'Furniture' and 'Textiles') – all highly
accomplished pioneers of a new way of thinking
about and marketing design within a cohesive,
personality-driven branding programme.

Wright was always interested in working
with new materials and developing new
production techniques. Just after the war,
the American Cyanamid company asked
him to design a new range of dinnerware for
mass production using melamine. From 1949
onwards, millions of pieces of Wright melamine
were sold. Again, the price was low, the
pieces hard-wearing, the forms fluid and the
colours bright, so Wright was able to persuade
American consumers that plastics had a place
in their homes.

In 1952, at the height of his success, Mary
died, leaving Wright with a young daughter
and a 75-acre estate known as Manitoga, near
Garrison in New York state. Wright decided
to push on with an ambitious naturalistic
landscaping project as well as the design of
a house and studio, which became a laboratory
for him, as he played with new ideas and
materials. Manitoga, too, seemed way ahead
of its time, with its highly contextual design,
Japanese influences and emphasis on
sustainability, and with many 'green' elements,
including a grass roof on top of Wright's studio.

ABOVE A floor vase, vase and candleholder bowl from Bauer, c. 1946, in glazed stoneware.

LEFT A set of three vases in glazed stoneware, produced by Bauer, c. 1955.

TEXTILES

THE POST-WAR ERA OF OPTIMISM, REINVENTION, FRESH STARTS AND CONSUMER GOODS PAVED THE WAY FOR A NEW APPRECIATION OF COLOUR, TEXTURE AND PATTERN

By the late 1940s – after years of austerity and economy – there was a growing appetite for colour, pattern and a lighter, more expressive approach to home decoration and interiors. The war years marked a seismic shift in the design world, and in the years that followed the spirit was both escapist and experimental, energized by the twin engines of reconstruction and a consumer revolution that saw an unprecedented level of spending on both the home and a whole range of consumer goods, particularly in mid-century America.

This was, above all, a period of reinvention and new beginnings. Sometimes this might mean taking on a whole new life, perhaps in a new country such as the United States, following the American dream. Or it might be a new career, a new company, a new home – or perhaps simply a makeover for the home you already had; something that made it feel fresh again. There was a break with the past and, in the new era of optimism and reinvention, colour and pattern played a big part.

By the 1950s colour seemed to be everywhere. There were colour magazines, full of adverts with bright bold messages reinforced by giant billboards and street advertising. In Alfred Hitchcock's *Spellbound* of 1945 the film-maker experimented with a hand-colouring technique, and by 1947 just over 10% of feature films used colour; just seven years later 50% of films were being made in colour. Colour televisions were first introduced in the States in 1953 and by the mid-1960s they were selling in big numbers.

In the home, colour was also playing a very important role. The modernist pioneers of the 1930s were not afraid of colour and even the multi-talented Le Corbusier* famously liked to brighten things up with a self-painted mural. But there was a sense of purity and restraint to pre-war modernist houses in comparison with the architecture and interiors of the mid-century era. In the 1950s the focus was on more organic colours, materials and textures, combined with large expanses of glass and a strong connection with nature and the world outside. By the 1960s, colour was being used in a far more exuberant and flamboyant manner, mirroring the way pattern was being welcomed in the worlds of fashion and art.

For many architects and designers of the period, colour, texture and pattern were always important considerations. HARRY SEIDLER (see under 'Houses and Interiors') used murals – as well as colourful, diaphanous curtains – to enliven his Rose Seidler house of 1950. CHARLES & RAY EAMES (see under 'Furniture') introduced brightly coloured panels to the exterior of their self-designed home in Pacific Palisades in 1949. LINA BO BARDI (see under 'Houses and Interiors') used bright mosaic tiles on the floors of her Glass House in São Paulo.

Furniture design, too, was an increasingly colourful business, with the likes of ALEXANDER GIRARD pioneering new and vibrantly expressive designs to bring added character to upholstered sofas and chairs, as well as designing wall hangings and other cheerful components for the home. Carpets, rugs, curtains, wallpapers and upholstery fabrics – along with newer materials like linoleum – all played their part in the modern home, although in a very different way from traditional period houses. Their use was more selective and informal, offering accents and highlights within the fresh open-plan spaces of the mid-century home, where the backdrop tended to be more neutral, often in the form of natural materials such as timber, plywood, brick and stone. Greater emphasis was placed upon creating contrasts between different fabrics and the use of 'complementary colours' rather than creating carefully co-ordinated synergies between very similar shades and tones.

Curtains tended to be lighter and more ethereal, so as not to overwhelm those expanses of glass. Wallpapers were used sparingly or to enliven spaces once seen as subservient but now becoming more pivotal – particularly kitchens, playrooms and bedrooms.

OPPOSITE Graphica furnishing fabric pattern by Lucienne Day for Heal's. 1954.

for Alan Veteres's apartment,
New York, with Arabic
wallpaper and Celtic rug, 1971.

Designers like JACK LENOR LARSEN and Alexander Girard were well aware of the
nature of modernist interiors, having trained as architects. In addition, architects such as
ALVAR AALTO (see under 'Houses and Interiors') occasionally designed textiles, as did other
designers such as VERNER PANTON (see under 'Furniture'), who also happened to have
trained as an architect.

In the 1950s, textile design was – by and large – more organic in nature. LUCIENNE
DAY, JOSEF FRANK, Maija Isola and others took inspiration from the natural world, working
seed heads, tree branches and other such forms into their designs. The colours, too,
tended to be more earthy in tone. Other common motifs in contemporary textiles included
whimsical folk art imagery, as well as architectural representations of buildings – seen in
works by Robert Nicholson, Saul Steinberg, Eduardo Paolozzi, Piero Fornasetti* and others.

But all were put through the common filter of abstraction, which saw representational
images simplified and rendered in new ways. Wallpaper and textile design sometimes shared
tendencies with contemporary fine art. Abstract Expressionism – particularly by artists
such as Mark Rothko and Barnett Newman – helped influence the work of many textile
designers in the late 1940s and 1950s, while a number of fine artists and sculptors also
worked in pattern and fabric design. Marc Chagall, Pablo Picasso, Henri Matisse, Henry
Moore, Joan Miró and others saw their work translated into textile designs during the 1950s.

By the 1960s both art and textiles were moving on, while mass-production techniques
were making new patterns more widely available. Colours were more vivid and saturated;
Pop Art influences and cross-overs can be seen in Maija Isola's most famous abstract prints
for MARIMEKKO. Op Art was another major movement that helped bring a sense of rhythmic
movement, geometrical precision and visual dynamism to textile and wallpaper designs,
which were now more linear and controlled in comparison to the more relaxed, free-hand
feel of many designs from a decade before. Common threads can be seen in the kinetic
work of artists such as Bridget Riley or Victor Vasarely when compared with 1960s patterns
by Lucienne Day, FLORENCE BROADHURST and others. The work of DAVID HICKS was partly
defined by his signature geometric carpets and wallpapers, which spliced Op Art elements
and Moorish patterns, and which shook up many period homes as well as modernist interiors.

There was also a growing synergy in the 1960s between the worlds of textile design
and graphic design – as seen in some of Girard's work – as well as closer communion with

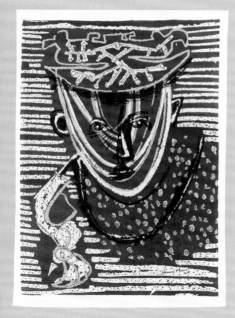

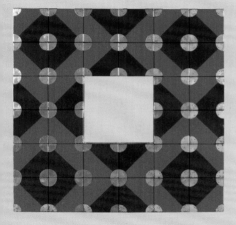

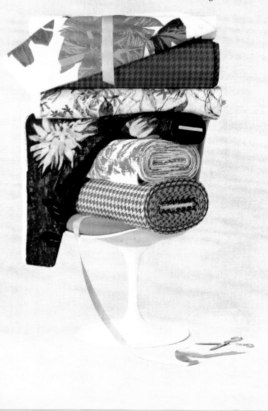

Florals and checks with a modern look.
Screen prints by Sanderson of Berners Street.
Meet five of the newest arrivals in the range...

TOP Head of Man cotton
headscarf by Henry Moore
for Ascher Ltd, London, 1947.

ABOVE Mirror by Alexander
Girard, using fabric over
wood, with brass, produced
by Herman Miller, 1961, for its
Textiles & Objects collection.

ABOVE RIGHT Advertisement
for Sanderson, published in
The Architectural Review,
August 1964.

the world of fashion. Armi Ratia and Vuokko Eskolin-Nurmesniemi of Marimekko combined screen-printed fabric designs for home furnishings with a highly successful clothing range that used the same flamboyant, characterful patterns. The vivid fashion prints of Emilio Pucci – the 'prince of prints' – helped influence upholstery and home furnishing fabrics, particularly the more psychedelic prints of the 1960s; much later Pucci's own prints were used by Cappellini to cover armchairs and other furniture. Within the global village, ethnic influences also became increasingly important in the 1960s and '70s, with Jack Lenor Larsen, Jim Thompson and others looking to India, North Africa and Asia to enrich their collections with patterns and hand-woven weaves and threads.

Textile design in the 1950s and the decade that followed differed in many ways. But there were commonalities, particularly experimentation with colour and a move towards abstraction. These designs graced houses that were very different in nature from the cluttered interiors of the Victorian and even Edwardian ages. Now the purity of spaces and proportions was clearly expressed; nature became a vivid backdrop through banks of glass and easy indoor/outdoor connections; the sculptural lines of furniture and lighting were given room to breathe. But these were still houses that were rich in colour and texture. Many mid-century patterns are still in use, bringing energy and exuberance to the homes of today.

UTILITY TO CONTEMPORARY: TEXTILES IN THE MID-CENTURY HOME

DANIEL HEATH

When reflecting upon the mid-century home one instantly considers the influx of consumer goods and gadgets such as the television that helped to define a generation. The heart of the home was shifting from the kitchen to the living room (or into a combination of the two, as post-war architecture often created contemporary open-plan spaces) and so the consumer-spend in these entertaining spaces often went on trend-following decorative fabrics and wallpapers to adorn them. This essay highlights the many ways in which technology, industry, consumer trends and the national psychology affected the use of domestic pattern and textiles.

In Britain, after years of 'make do and mend' during the war and the restrained age of austerity that followed it, consumers were crying out for interesting new design. The Utility* furniture scheme had been put in place in 1942 to restrict the consumption of furniture in the home, in light of scarce resources. Utility furniture was designed to be functional and sturdy, with a uniform aesthetic that was inspired by the pre-war Arts & Crafts movement, and it was manufactured by approval of the Utility Furniture Advisory Committee. During the war these furnishings, although well designed, were the only pieces available, meaning that the British home was often bereft of any individualism and personal taste became difficult to define. Post-war, a new sense of optimism and hope for the future was perpetuated and fed to a willing public, partly through major design events such as 'Britain Can Make It' in 1946 and the Festival of Britain* in 1951.

Textile design and the production of textiles became revolutionary, with pattern and colour becoming an indicator of new consumer attitudes and options afforded by an end to the age of austerity. The industry had focused on production for the war effort and was in desperate need of a boost, so the re-opening of international trade and export opportunities was a priority and Britain was keen to showcase new talent as well as the established manufacturers that the country had been known for prior to the war. There is no doubt that the nation and the economy were on their knees, swamped by war debt and housing shortages, but the people were ready for change, primed for optimism with the jolly mantra of 'Keep Calm and Carry On' drilled into them by endless pro-Britain war propaganda that invigorated their enthusiasm for the new, for re-birth and growth, and that allowed them to imagine a brighter future.

New technologies and the creation of man-made fibres caused the 'synthetics boom', fuelled by Courtaulds opening a vast processing plant in the UK in 1951 and by the 1960s the launch of a new transfer-printing process that had been developed to put pattern onto synthetic cloth. Another advance in manufacturing was the development of mechanized screen-printing from the 1950s onwards, which provided cheaper fabrics. These processes allowed both the price of production to become lower and the rate of manufacture to become quicker compared to roller printing, which required the costly process of roller engraving. Due to this flexibility, fabrics could be created in line with modern trends and imagery could explore scales that were previously unattainable. New, bolder patterns

BELOW Robert Sevant's 8.25
Insulin for John Line & Sons,
London, 1951.

BELOW RIGHT Surrey,
design for furnishing
fabric by Marianne Straub,
manufactured by Warner
& Sons Ltd, London, 1951.

were explored by British designers, influenced by Scandinavian design from the likes of
MARIMEKKO and colourful fabrics from the continent.

Popular themes explored in designs of the 1950s were often developments of existing
motifs through abstraction, stylized within a contemporary aesthetic. Floral or natural
themes were interpreted using abstract forms and geometric lines, often simplified and
flattened within the design. New and dynamic themes also emerged that were influenced
by the Jet Age and revolutions in science. The public were not only subject to domestic
change, but the merits of scientific developments were also being heartily endorsed at
the Festival of Britain, and in recognition of this the organizers formed the Festival Pattern
Group to help translate the theme of crystallography (crystal-structure diagrams that
recorded the arrangements of atoms in various substances) to commissioned artworks,
designs and installations throughout many of the sites and exhibition halls of the event.
In addition to endorsing the scientific merits of Britain, the theme also made science more
palatable as the imagery was explored across a wide range of products including textiles
for the interior, such as the curtains designed by Marianne Straub*, head designer at Warner
& Sons Ltd, displayed within the setting of the Regatta Restaurant at the Southbank Centre.

The Festival Pattern Group was made up of 28 British manufacturers, 11 of whom were
textiles manufacturers. Each specialized in a different area and so the companies were
asked to work together to create continuity across the exhibition. For the first time, Britain,
or at least the 8.5 million visitors to the Festival of Britain site, could see how pattern could
be coordinated within the home across upholstery, drapes, linens, wallpaper and ceramics
– or hard-surface applications, like printed Formica – to great effect.

Events such as the Festival of Britain pitched the work of a new breed of designers
who were coming out of design schools, such as the Royal College of Art and the Central
schools. Design education had expanded considerably in post-war Britain and the new
consumer demographic that consisted of younger homeowners with modern tastes gave

these young graduates opportunities. David Whitehead* was the market leader in interior textiles, making fabric for the mass market and championing the new 'contemporary' style by taking on board fresh talents, including Jacqueline Groag and Marian Mahler.

Designs such as LUCIENNE DAY's Dandelion Clocks and her Calyx – designed for the Festival of Britain in 1951 and commissioned by Heal's* – were icons of the time, epitomizing the contemporary style. They became big sellers, embodying the 'big is beautiful' rhetoric favoured by designers who were creating for mass production, mass consumption and affordability. Day was a supporter of affordable design and primarily created for the mass market rather than collectors. She believed that everyone should be able to have beautiful textiles within their interiors: 'I wanted the work I was doing to be seen by people and used by people.' She understood that people had been 'starved of interesting things for their homes in the war years'.

By the mid-1950s the UK economy had started to grow, and even the working classes were now in a position to buy products that would previously have only been available to affluent homeowners. Although the furniture being designed, made and desired was influenced by or imported from places such as Italy and Denmark and came in at a high price, homeowners could put their stamp on an interior with flair by making a substantially smaller investment in fabrics to re-upholster their still-going-strong Utility furnishings or to create an on-trend contrasting accent wall adorned with wallpaper depicting bold patterns of 'spasms' and 'boomerangs'.

JOSEF FRANK was one of the key designers who exemplified the new 'Swedish Modern' style, which he had been instrumental in introducing to the world marketplace with Swedish company Svenskt Tenn through the World Exposition in New York in 1939. The designs showcased at the fair were unlike the popular puritanical modernist designs and explored a colourful palette with rich narrative imagery that contrasted with the monochromatic geometric patterns used widely in interiors of the time. Much like Lucienne Day, Frank viewed textiles as an opportunity for consumers to apply individuality to an interior. This ideology was to resonate globally and, once the technology in process and manufacture allowed, these ideas were rolled out for mass dissemination by Frank's contemporaries and successors.

BELOW Sofa designed by Josef Frank in the mid-1930s, upholstered in Textile Hawaii furnishing fabric, designed by Josef Frank for Svenskt Tenn in 1943–45.

The US textiles industry was undergoing a rapid transformation of its own in the 1950s, and revolutionary new man-made fibres and fabrics were being produced with exciting colours and textures, fuelled by the nation's growing post-war consumerism. Many international designers had established themselves in America to escape Europe in the war years, and with them they brought new design perspectives, folk heritage and foreign influences born of traditions unfamiliar to the US consumer. A key designer in American textiles history is the Italian-raised ALEXANDER GIRARD, for example. Hired to head the Herman Miller* textiles division in 1952, he notably worked with CHARLES & RAY EAMES (see under 'Furniture') to create upholstery fabrics for their furniture. Girard was influenced by folk art, employing bright colours and narrative imagery that were inspired by his travels all over the world.

Alongside the influx of new talent and new technology there came a new affordable aesthetic that relied on bold patterning printed onto cheaper ground fabrics. In America this shift in ideals was particularly evident and enabled new companies to form, producing their cloth on low budgets. Many of the manufacturers established before the war were unable or unwilling to take a risk on the new style and were held to larger production runs using their established methods. By the 1960s people were starting to question the ethics of this kind of consumerism and so a new age of textiles was born where small batch production and traditional craft skills were coveted once more, although this model already existed alongside the well-established mass-production model.

In Britain, the Hull Traders formed in 1958 and aligned themselves with the art world, placing a greater value upon the craft element but also on the 'name-dropping' that elevated designers to household celebrity status. Hull Traders worked with artists such as Eduardo Paolozzi to create limited-run, exclusive designs that were screen-printed using pigment dyes. In many ways this development mirrored the approach taken by the Edinburgh Weavers* – an experimental offshoot of Morton Sundour, formed in the 1920s to create artist-designed fabrics for specific architectural projects or interiors. Fabrics created by the Hull Traders explored the new range of textures available, and their approach to artist collaboration began a trend picked up on by mass-market manufacturers, Sanderson. Sanderson commissioned the artist John Piper* to design five patterns for their centenary collection in 1960, fully utilizing the screen-printing process to translate painterly marks and brush strokes to fabric.

The 1960s introduced the duvet to the now stable British economy, giving consumers another area to fill with brightly coloured, large-scale print to dominate the bedroom. In the living room, Sanderson had introduced the concept of coordination with their Triad range (1962) that matched pattern across wallpaper, upholstery fabrics and drapes in 68 different pattern varieties. Influenced by the US, British consumers now had the option to fill a room with pattern, but without the worry that styles might clash. This trend reflected how taste had evolved towards a more sophisticated and harmonious interior than was evident in the post-war excitement of the early 1950s and the beginnings of Pop culture.

Sanderson, Ikea, Marimekko and Svenskt Tenn (among many more) have all re-invented or re-launched many of their previous mid-century successes in recent years in order to bring them to new audiences in alignment with the consumer desire for 'retro' design. These heirloom textiles, celebrated at the time, are still as fresh and contemporary as when they were released, sitting well in modern homes. A reassuring comfort or trust can be instilled in these 'design classics' and their validity has been quantified by decades of appreciation. Designs of the mid-century have become a staple for the homes of today.

BELOW Northern Cathedral furnishing fabric, John Piper for Sanderson, 1961.

ARTIST-DESIGNED TEXTILES: 1945–1970
SUE PRICHARD

The artist-designed textiles of the late 1940s and 1950s emerged from a complex set of economic, political and social issues which created a more relaxed approach to modern living. In Britain, the Industrial Art movement of the 1930s introduced established artists to forward-thinking textile manufacturers keen to reinvigorate the industry with innovative design ideas.[1] After World War II, a new generation of art school-educated[2] and progressive designers joined forces with artists and manufacturers to democratize the avant-garde, creating well-designed, affordable fabrics for the mass market, thereby proving that 'cheap need not be cheap and nasty'.[3]

The emerging trend for pure abstraction in the fine arts acted as a stimulus for many European and American designers and challenged the more conventional approach to interior decoration, traditionally reliant on a rehash of the floral chintzes beloved of the Edwardians. Technological progress, particularly in the field of mechanized screen-printing[4] and the development of pigments and man-made fibres, facilitated the quest for a new aesthetic,[5] which would reject manufacturers' archives and pattern books in favour of the fluid, organic and colourful motifs employed by the Spanish Surrealist Joan Miró and the wiry structures of American sculptor and painter Alexander Calder*. The influence of Calder's brightly coloured mobiles is most evident in the imaginative and inventive patterns showcased by manufacturers of both wallpaper and printed and woven dress and furnishing fabrics at the Festival of Britain* (1951).

Affordable, good design was encouraged by government and national agencies, such as the British Council of Industrial Design, whose members included the sculptor Henry Moore and the war artist Paul Nash. A series of promotional exhibitions were staged to help the public embrace the abstract forms and vivid colourways that epitomized the contemporary style. The 'Britain Can Make It' exhibition (1946) featured headscarves designed by Moore and the war artist Graham Sutherland, commissioned by the Czech émigré and textile converter Zika Ascher.

In addition, Ascher commissioned designs for fashion fabric from Moore and the Polish émigré Feliks Topolski. The latter based his designs for a screen-printed rayon twill on motifs drawn from his wartime sketchbooks, while Moore's eclectic and sometimes light-hearted wax drawings with watercolour washes combined safety pins, barbed wire, clock hands and caterpillars in linear designs, reproduced in various colourways and screen-printed on rayon, cotton and wool. Like many of his peers, Moore felt strongly that art should function as an intrinsic part of daily life: curtains made from both Heads (1945–46) and Horse's Head and Boomerang (1944–45) decorated his family home in Hertfordshire.

Ascher launched a further collection of limited-edition, artist-designed scarves at the Lefevre Gallery, London (1947). The front cover of the catalogue listed collaborations with the ageing French painter Henri Matisse and Moore, as well as designs by Sutherland, the French artist and printmaker Marie Laurencin, and Moore's contemporaries Barbara Hepworth and Ben Nicholson among others. Ascher did not put a design by Pablo Picasso

OPPOSITE ABOVE Landscape
Sculpture silk twill headscarf
by Barbara Hepworth for
Ascher Ltd, 1947.

OPPOSITE CENTRE
Alexander Calder's La Mer
silk twill headscarf for Ascher
Ltd, 1947.

OPPOSITE BELOW Écharpe
silk twill headscarf by Henri
Matisse, 1947, for Ascher Ltd.

BELOW Cocktail dress by
Horrockses Fashion, c. 1953,
textile design based on a
painting by Eduardo Paolozzi.

BELOW RIGHT Red Mobiles
by Marian Mahler, 1952, from
The Brown-Wiltse Collection
of British Textiles.

into production, but Picasso did subsequently design a headsquare featuring bulls, suns and sunflowers to be used as a fundraiser for the Institute of Contemporary Arts (ICA), London. Matisse's Écharpe (1947) proved popular with the press and public alike. Nicholson stated that 'though very different from my original colour, [Moonlight] has obtained the feeling that I wanted and I am very pleased with it'.[6]

Ascher collaborated with Moore and Matisse on a more ambitious project, creating a series of limited-edition large wall panels, designed for the domestic interior. Matisse's Océanie – Le Ciel and Océanie – La Mer (both 1947) were inspired by his experiences at sea in the 1930s. Moore's monumental Standing Figures (1948) and Reclining Figure (1949) focused on the human form and anticipate his later tapestry designs and collaborations with the Edinburgh-based Dovecot Studios and West Dean Tapestry Studio, Chichester.

In the decade following World War II, aspiring homemakers were aided in their quest for a modern style via magazines, journals, books and television programmes – all providing helpful instructions on how to combine modernity with functionality. The influential trade journal The Ambassador helped to consolidate the relationship between fine art and design. Founders and co-editors-in-chief, Hans and Elsbeth Juda, consistently promoted art as inspiration for design, publishing articles juxtaposing furnishing fabrics designed by artists alongside examples of their work and illustrating textile designs on front covers. Hans Juda's seminal 'Painting into Textiles' exhibition (1953), held at the ICA and supported by the Surrealist artist and historian Roland Penrose, was designed to publicize the close and dynamic relationship between art and design.[7]

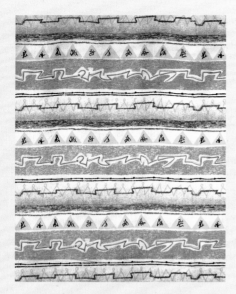

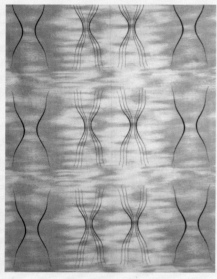

TOP Henry Moore, Triangles and Lines, produced by David Whitehead Ltd, 1954.

ABOVE Paule Vézelay, Elegance, for Heal's, c. 1955.

OPPOSITE ABOVE Henry Moore, Three Seated Figures, for Ascher Ltd, 1947.

OPPOSITE CENTRE John Piper, Foliate Head, produced by David Whitehead Ltd, 1954.

OPPOSITE BELOW Two printed cotton textiles designed by Shirley Craven for Hull Traders Ltd, 1968.

Moore once again featured heavily in the project: his design for fabric, Zigzag (1950), was used for the cover of *The Ambassador*[8] and for the cover of the exhibition catalogue. The exhibition spawned a new confidence in the potential of artist-designed textiles to reinvigorate the British textile market, with some of the 20th century's most influential firms commissioning work directly from artists. David Whitehead put Moore's Zigzag and his Triangles and Lines (1954) into production. They also produced designs from William Scott and from John Piper, who continued to work with the company until 1970.[9]

Horrockses Fashion, one of the most successful ready-to-wear labels of the period, snapped up a mixed-media design by Scottish artist and sculptor Eduardo Paolozzi, his eclectic collage inspired by natural and found objects reminiscent of Moore's seemingly random but more linear juxtapositions of insect wings, piano keys and abstract signs and symbols. Paolozzi, together with the photographer Nigel Henderson, founded Hammer Prints Limited in 1954, supplying textile and wallpaper designs to be retailed through the radical and highly experimental firm, Hull Traders.

Alastair Morton, painter and Design Director at Edinburgh Weavers*, also acquired artwork from the exhibition and subsequently Edinburgh Weavers took up where it had left off in the 1930s, commissioning an exclusive range of woven and printed fabrics designed by artists. Morton re-established his relationships with the mural painter Hans Tisdall and with Ben Nicholson, whose bold large-scale designs featuring circles and squares anticipated the motifs that dominated pattern design in the 1960s. Liberty's relationship with Scottish artist Robert Steward, Head of Printed Textiles at Glasgow School of Art from 1949 to 1978, created a cornucopia of quirky figurative and vivid abstract designs set against a striking colour palette, which were featured in design journals such as *Art and Industry* (1956); Piper's mystical Foliate Head design for Whitehead, based on the popular 'green man' motif, appeared in *The Ambassador* (1955) and Blenheim Gate in *Design* (1957). The energetic Tom Worthington, Managing Director of Heal* Fabrics, worked closely with Paule Vézelay, widely credited as the first female abstract artist. Her series of graphically simple, repeating designs featuring strangely hypnotic floating shapes recall the work of the Surrealist artists Jean Arp and André Breton, while her titles 'Elegance' (c. 1955), 'Harmony' (c. 1956) and 'Modulation' (c. 1956) serve to emphasize a mood of peace and tranquillity.

In the States, Schiffer Prints is singled out as producing one of the most important artist-designed collections of the post-war period – the 'Stimulus Collection', including designs by Salvador Dalí and RAY EAMES (see under 'Furniture'). Fuller Fabrics, Inc. also released a 'Modern Master Print' series (1955): unlike the British collaborations, these patterns comprised a series of recognizable motifs drawn from the artists' paintings, drawings and prints produced under licence. The range included designs inspired by the work of Marc Chagall, Raoul Dufy, Fernand Léger, Picasso and Miró. The small-scale motifs derived from the latter's paintings proved extremely successful when produced as a printed cotton dress fabric, Women and Birds (c. 1955–56).

In New York, Associated American Artists launched its first dress collection in 1952, followed by furnishing fabrics a year later. The 'Signature Fabrics' were marketed at affordable prices without compromising design or quality, and were promoted via a series of exhibitions entitled 'The Painter as Designer'. Artist and sculptor Angelo Testa and painter Ben Rose – both products of Chicago's excellent art and design education system – produced fabrics that embraced abstraction while still aimed at accessibility.

Some of the most influential artists of the 20th century explored the unique characteristics of warp and weft, including Le Corbusier*, Matisse, Chagall and Calder. Unlike historic tapestries, which traditionally relied on paintings as source material and were contained within a woven frame, modern tapestries were much more dependent upon a collaborative relationship between artist and weaver. Back in the 1930s, the French artist

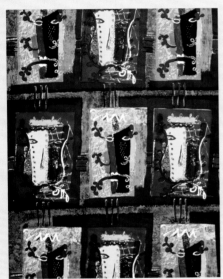

Jean Lurçat had recognized the medium's potential to transform the modern interior and had helped to revitalize the old Aubusson workshops in France.

Inspired by the French model, Dovecot Studios, under the artistic directorship of first Sax Shaw and subsequently Archie Brennan, gained a reputation for combining traditional skills with an imaginative approach to design. Stanley Spencer, Graham Sutherland, John Piper and Henry Moore all produced designs that were small in scale and suited to the domestic interior. The Dovecot weavers, working in close collaboration with the artists, interpreted the designs, forming part of the creative process, which in turn stimulated innovation and experimentation. The spontaneity of the designs, and the themes and images of the period, are apparent in the work of Sutherland and reflect his interest in alterations from small-scale sketches to large-scale tapestry, and the weavers' ability to translate the dense brush strokes and intense colours of the original designs. In the 1960s, Dovecot Studios wove a number of high-profile, site-specific commissions, including a design by painter Harold Cohen, commissioned by British Petroleum for their flagship new headquarters (1966). The Studios also embarked on a unique collaboration with Gloria Rose for a series of limited-edition tapestries based on the paintings of Robert Motherwell.

Throughout the 1950s art, architecture and pattern design continued to be closely aligned. The delicate, doodle-like compositions based on fundamental plant forms such as twigs, stems, leaves and seed heads were replaced by large-scale painterly designs with single repeats. LUCIENNE DAY expanded her pattern repertoire, her motifs becoming bigger and bolder in keeping with an engagement with the architecture of buildings. Her stunning large-scale abstract and geometric designs were influenced by the American Abstract Expressionist movement and the work of Jackson Pollock and Willem de Kooning. Piper continued his exploration of pattern design via architectural motifs: his monumental Stones of Bath (1959) and Northern Cathedral (1961) designs for Sanderson's Centenary were particularly suited to the move towards furnishing large, open-plan areas of corporate and public buildings.

The popularization of post-war International Style* interiors also helped to put Scandinavian textiles firmly on the map. In Sweden, the influential designer Astrid Sampe* championed the symbiotic relationship between architecture and textile design, commissioning the architect ALVAR AALTO (see under 'Houses and Interiors') and abstract artists Olle Bærtling and Karl Axel Pehrson to contribute to the 'Signed Collection' (1954) for Nordiska Kompaniet Textilkammare. Sampe, who studied at the RCA London, anticipated the trend for pure abstraction in pattern design in the 1960s, creating dynamic and geometric designs based on vertical and horizontal stripes and rhythmic diagonals.

Influenced by Op Art and Pop Art, and inspired by the swirling lines epitomized by the work of British painter Bridget Riley and French artist Victor Vasarely, these large-scale furnishing fabrics were the equivalent of modern-day textile hangings and were aimed at an aspiring youth market. Shirley Craven, Chief Designer and Director of Hull Traders, articulated the design ethos of the company: 'Textiles should be an artistic field, not just a commercial transaction.'[10]

By 1970 the changing economic, political and social climate meant that many artists were engaged in pursuing their own ambitions and goals, at the expense of designing for the applied arts. Forward-thinking individuals such as Alastair Morton, Zika Ascher and Hans Juda would be recognized as pioneers of their generation, committed to producing and promoting artist-designed textiles as the most democratic of art forms.

FLORENCE BROADHURST
1899–1977

HIGHLY ORIGINAL AUSTRALIAN
DESIGNER FAMOUS FOR HER
COLOURFUL, BOLD,
FREE-SPIRITED DESIGNS

Florence Broadhurst had an extraordinary talent for reinvention. A singer, fashion designer, painter and art teacher, she was an eccentric character who achieved international fame with her textile and wallpaper designs, which were just as bold as their creator.

Born on a cattle station in Queensland, Australia, Broadhurst could not be contained by the outback for long. As a singer in the 1920s, she travelled widely in South East Asia and China, her experiences ultimately helping to shape her later designs. She established a singing and dancing school in Shanghai before moving to London in the early 1930s, where she ran her own dress shop, Madame Pellier. After the war, she returned to Australia, where she worked and exhibited as a landscape and portrait painter.

In 1959, she moved in another new direction and founded her wallpaper and textile company, Florence Broadhurst Wallpapers. The spirit of Jazz Age Shanghai influenced many of her early papers and fabrics, which featured oversized peacocks and feathers, as well as cranes and egrets. The papers were hand-printed in vibrant colours, carefully selected by Broadhurst, and she also experimented with metallic finishes that reinforced the Deco flavour of a certain strand of her output. She also prided herself on tailoring colour choices to her clients' needs.

Other patterns have a more modernist, mid-century feel, with abstract fans repeated in her Kabuki fabric, while her distinctive Japanese Floral pattern transformed the flowers into oversized ethereal plumes. These prints featured startling images that gradually became more graphic in character.

By the 1960s, Broadhurst's work was more geometric, sharing some of the qualities found in the pattern designs of DAVID HICKS. Her Honeycomb pattern, in particular, had a powerful Op Art flavour, as did Pagoda, which seemed to splice touches of Vasarely and elements of Moorish tile design. Her Curly Swirls and Waterswirls designs showed a decidedly pyschedelic aspect, along with her Solar wallpaper. Patterns would emerge from her mind at 'all hours of the day', she once said.

Broadhurst's innately glamorous designs made her a household name in Australia and were being exported internationally by the 1970s. Her success came to an abrupt halt in 1977, when she was murdered in her studio in Sydney. One of Australia's most original design voices was silenced in mysterious circumstances and the killer was never found.

Signature Prints in Australia has reissued many of Broadhurst's designs, while a range of Broadhurst carpets has also been put into production. American designer Kate Spade is also among those who have adopted Broadhurst patterns in their own work.

LEFT Japanese Bamboo pattern, reissued by Signature Prints, Australia.

OPPOSITE Japanese Floral pattern, reissued by Signature Prints, Australia.

ABOVE Peacock Feathers,
reissued by Signature Prints,
Australia.

RIGHT Aubrey design,
reissued by Signature Prints,
Australia.

OPPOSITE Kabuki, reissued
by Signature Prints, Australia.

LUCIENNE DAY
1917–2010

REVERED BRITISH TEXTILE
DESIGNER NOTED FOR
HER OUTSTANDING USE
OF ORGANIC, NATURAL
FORMS AND STRUCTURES

As a textile designer, Lucienne Day took particular inspiration from the natural world. She had a detailed knowledge of flora and fauna, weaving seed heads and stems, forests and leaves into her work. In this respect she was part of a long and noble tradition, but she passed the motifs through a unique filter, creating patterns that echoed the work of abstract artists such as Alexander Calder*, Paul Klee and Joan Miró. Day also had a painter's knowledge and understanding of colour, restricting her textiles to a limited palette of complementary shades and tones.

In more ways than one, Day wanted to bring character and colour into people's lives. Along with her husband, ROBIN DAY (see under 'Furniture'), she reacted against the drab uniformity and austerity of the war years and was determined to make a difference through design. 'There was a growing feeling of optimism and an anticipation of a bright new world and we thought that progressive design could contribute to the quality of people's lives,' the pair declared. 'We were both supported by our mutual desire to produce designs that would overcome the dreariness of the previous decade, and make it possible for the many – rather than the few – to enjoy pleasant surroundings at a reasonable price.'[11]

Born Lucienne Conradi, she studied at the Croydon School of Art and then the Royal Academy, where she met her future husband. Sometimes compared with another pair of design celebrities, CHARLES & RAY EAMES (see under 'Furniture'), the Days seldom collaborated, although they did often share a studio. One exception was the Festival of Britain* in 1951, which sealed both of their reputations. Robin Day designed interiors for the Homes & Gardens pavilion where Lucienne hung one of her very first fabric designs. Still perhaps the most famous, it was called Calyx – the term for the delicate, cup-like cradle that surrounds a budding flower. Day's design offered a sequence of these abstract cups in

black, white, orange and yellow floating against an olive background. It was a pattern that helped define the Festival itself, with all of its forward-looking, celebratory spirit.

Heal* Fabrics began producing Calyx, but without much confidence that the design would take off. They were soon proved wrong and a few years later were adding Day's signature alongside her designs – a rare honour. A number of early Day designs from the 1950s for Heal's and British Celanese also played with motifs drawn from nature, including Perpetua and Palisade from 1953. Others, such as Flotilla and Foreshore, drew upon marine themes in the most abstract fashion.

But Day was also exploring more graphic and linear elements, sometimes in combination with naturalistic forms, as in Flower Show, where the spindly, feathery plant shapes are contained within irregular rectangles. At times, she was drawn towards more geometric patterns, as with her Graphica screen-printed cotton of 1954 (see p. 224) and Isosceles the following year.

In the 1960s Day's work took a fresh direction. Like many of her contemporaries, she was seduced by the energy, dynamism and implied sense of movement within the work of Op Art painters, such as Bridget Riley and Victor Vasarely. Her Apex fabric of 1967 and Sunrise of 1969 have just this sense of precise, geometric excitement and clarity, and are very different in character from the more fluid and light-hearted designs of a decade earlier.

Day continued working with Heal's for many years, but also designed for other companies, including Edinburgh Weavers*. There were also carpets, wallpapers and ceramics, with her work much in demand throughout the mid-century period. Later, Day became interested in tapestry design, using a complex 'silk mosaic' technique. A number of her textile designs have been reissued in recent years by Classic Textiles.

OVERLEAF LEFT Calyx,
screen-printed linen
furnishing fabric,
manufactured by Heal's, 1951.

OVERLEAF RIGHT Spectators,
screen-printed cotton, linen
and rayon, 1953, reissued by
Classic Textiles.

OPPOSITE ABOVE Dandelion
Clocks, screen-printed linen
and cotton, 1953.

OPPOSITE BELOW Flower
Show, roller-printed cotton,
1954, from The Brown-Wiltse
Collection of British Textiles.

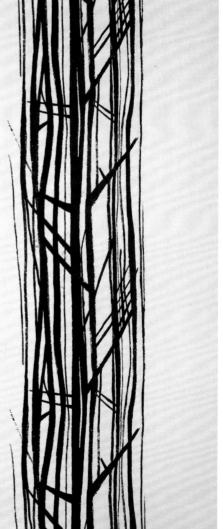

ABOVE Apollo, screen-printed cotton, 1964, from The Brown-Wiltse Collection of British Textiles.

RIGHT Sequoia, screen-printed cotton crepe, 1959, from The Brown-Wiltse Collection of British Textiles.

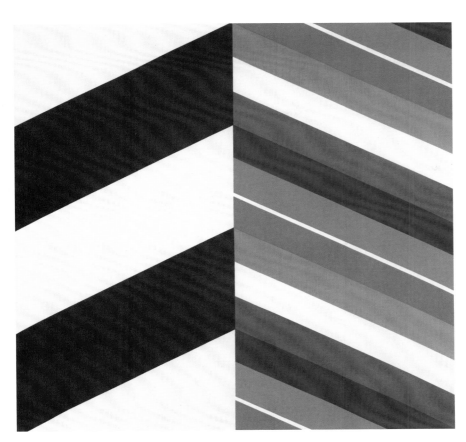

LEFT Chevron, screen-printed cotton, 1968, from The Brown-Wiltse Collection of British Textiles.

BELOW LEFT Sunrise (pink), screen-printed cotton, 1969, originally produced by Heal's and reissued by Classic Textiles.

BELOW Apex (red), screen-printed cotton, 1967, reissued by Classic Textiles.

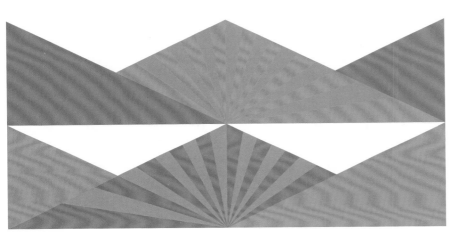

JOSEF FRANK
1885–1967

AUSTRIAN-BORN DESIGNER AND
ARCHITECT, MOST FAMOUS
FOR HIS VIBRANT, COLOURFUL
DESIGNS FOR SVENSKT TENN

BELOW Celotocaulis,
designed by Josef Frank in
the 1920s, used to upholster a
Svenskt Tenn 3031 four-seated
Long Sofa, designed by Frank
in the 1940s.

On the cusp of the mid-century era, an Austrian-born architect and designer with Swedish citizenship living in New York offered his dear friend Estrid Ericson a birthday gift. In September 1944, Ericson was fifty years old and Josef Frank – who had already been working for her company, Svenskt Tenn, for many years – presented her with fifty new textile designs. These vivid patterns were among the most successful of Frank's career and helped to define the look of both Svenskt Tenn and the soft, humanist modernism we associate with Scandinavian mid-century design. At the same time, the complex multicultural layering of Frank's background was indicative of the evolution of a more international, cross-border design world that would establish itself in the post-war years.

Many of Frank's designs drew inspiration from nature, especially flora, fauna, jungle, river and forest scenes. Sometimes his patterns also included exotic birds or butterflies. There was a clear influence from the Arts & Crafts designs of William Morris and others on the one hand, but also a folkloric influence on the other, with an almost child-like sense of naïve abstraction of form as well as an absolute delight in bold and even garish colours. In Frank's hands this was a magical combination and his textiles were filled with the kind of dynamic, vivacious exuberance that had wide appeal for a post-war society desperate for colour, warmth and visual excitement.

Bright blue rivers combined with trees full of blossom and fantastical birds, as in Gröna Fålgar (Green Birds); interwoven flowers, creepers and leaves danced with one another in sinuous formations in La Plata or Loops (all from the 1940s). The images had a bold, abstract quality, and a sense of wonder seemed to flow freely and easily.

Frank trained and worked as an architect in Vienna, as well as teaching and running a home-furnishings business. His architecture was modernist in style and he also designed furniture that fused modernist and neo-classical influences. He took a humanist view, with a strong belief in individuality, comfort and self-expression that put him at odds with the pure, machine-like clarity of certain pioneering modernist exponents.

In 1911 he married a Swede, Anna Sebenius, and in 1934 – as the political situation in Austria and Germany became more extreme – he emigrated to Sweden. Here he met Estrid Ericson, the founder of Svenskt Tenn, an interiors store in Stockholm. It was the beginning of a great creative partnership, combining Frank's design talents and Ericson's talent for curating, presenting and marketing.

Ericson had opened her store in 1924, specializing initially in pewterware (the name means 'Swedish pewter'). But she soon began expanding into other areas of design and with Frank she began collating a collection of furniture and, of course, fabrics.

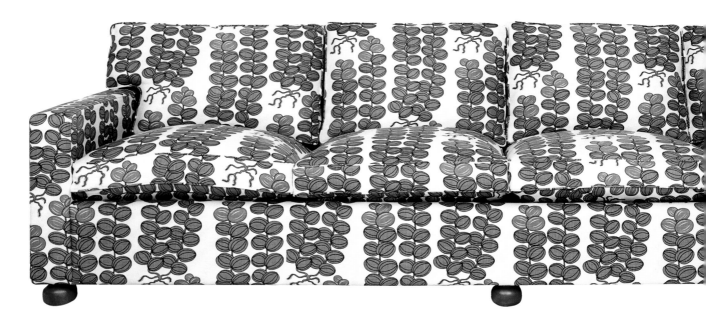

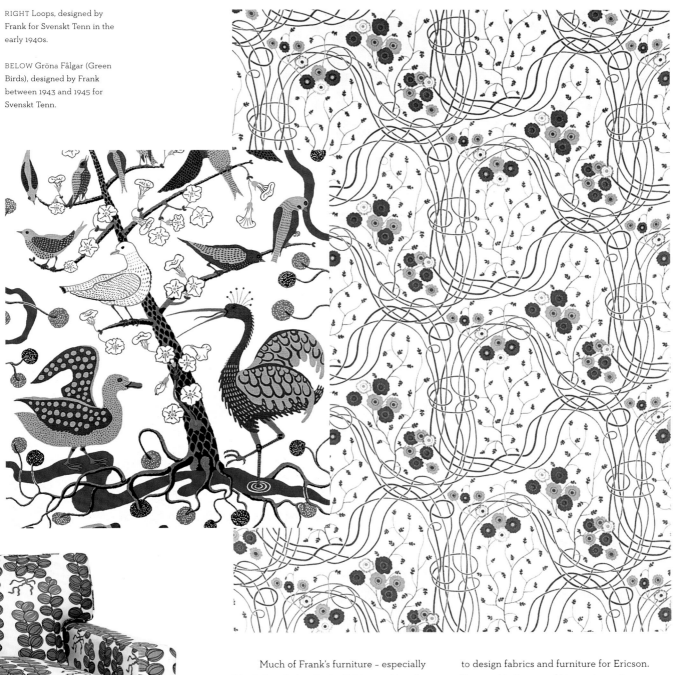

RIGHT Loops, designed by
Frank for Svenskt Tenn in the
early 1940s.

BELOW Gröna Fålgar (Green
Birds), designed by Frank
between 1943 and 1945 for
Svenskt Tenn.

Much of Frank's furniture – especially his dining chairs – had a lightness of touch, as Frank believed that such pieces should not dominate a space. But the sofas he designed for Svenskt Tenn were deep, comfortable and inviting, upholstered in bright Frank fabrics. They were a world away from the precise, linear quality of a design by Florence Knoll* or GEORGE NELSON (see under 'Furniture').

From 1942 to 1945, Frank lived in New York, where he taught at the New School for Social Research, while also continuing to design fabrics and furniture for Ericson. It proved to be one of his most creative periods, despite the worries of the war years, with an escapist, romantic quality pervading his textiles. La Plata was named after a river estuary near Buenos Aires, while other designs were called Brazil and Hawaii (see also p. 230). The designs spoke of faraway places, exoticism and sunny days – yet at the same time they were distinctively Swedish in character.

Some Frank designs of the 1940s, however, do reflect a different approach.

There was a series of more abstract designs, such as the Manhattan fabric inspired by grid maps of New York, or the Terrazzo design of the same period, which offered colourful stones against a grey aggregate backdrop. These images suggest how far Frank had come as a textile designer, now exploring modern forms that had much more in common with the work of LUCIENNE DAY from the 1950s than the work of William Morris from the 1870s.

Most importantly, Frank and Ericson's fabrics had a sense of the unique. Frank's patterns were special to him, and are instantly recognizable as Svenskt Tenn designs. Imitations – and there have been many – seem to pale in comparison. Svenskt Tenn patterns remain much in demand, infused with that highly particular, optimistic, endearing sense of wonder at the beauty of the natural world, rendered in vivid, enticing forms.

BELOW Frank's Liljevalch armchair, designed in 1934, upholstered in a Brazil textile.

BOTTOM A three-seated 3031 Long Sofa, designed by Frank for Svenskt Tenn, in a Hawaii fabric, designed between 1943 and 1945.

ABOVE A Manhattan linen used for a Svenskt Tenn cushion; the fabric was designed by Frank in New York between 1942 and 1946.

TOP RIGHT A cushion in Frank's Terrazzo linen, produced by Svenskt Tenn, designed c. 1944.

RIGHT A 969 mahogany armchair, designed by Frank for Svenskt Tenn, 1939, shown with Hawaii upholstery in a brown colourway.

ALEXANDER GIRARD
1907–1993

US-BASED TEXTILE DESIGNER
WHO PLAYED ON HIS TWIN
LOVES OF FOLK ART AND
MODERNISM TO CREATE
EXUBERANT, ENDEARING
DESIGNS

'The whole world is hometown' was an Italian proverb that designer Alexander Girard liked to repeat every now and then. It pointed not only to his own peripatetic upbringing and education, but also to the multicultural influences and reference points that fed into his work, and particularly his textile designs.

Girard was fascinated by modernism – collaborating closely with friends and colleagues such as CHARLES & RAY EAMES, EERO SAARINEN and GEORGE NELSON (see under 'Furniture') – but he was also captivated by the colours, patterns, craftsmanship and vitality he found in folk art. Over his lifetime, he assembled a vast collection of objects and textiles – many sourced on trips to Mexico – which were eventually donated to the Museum of International Folk Art in Santa Fe, where Girard designed a new wing to house his gift.

His work as a designer fused his dual passions within fabric collections that were full of colour and exuberance. He created over three hundred textile designs that ranged from vivid stripes, dots and circles, through abstract florals, to eyecatching, geometric patterns with a dynamic sense of movement – early examples of the vogue for Op Art-inspired imagery that took hold in the 1960s.

Girard also designed wall hangings and panels infused with endearing, folk-influenced imagery, as in his Daisy Face, Palace and Old Sun designs for Herman Miller*, which were bright and light, with a child-like sense of delight. 'I saw [folk art] as a way to recapture

RIGHT A wall hanging for
Herman Miller, silkscreen
on canvas, 1971.

OPPOSITE Alphabet in
turquoise and crimson, 1952,
for Herman Miller; reissued
by Maharam.

&FSPBJ8NC
ZQ1WAH4EI
GKUY67DX9
R3MOT2V5L
&FSPBJ8NC
ZQ1WAH4EI
GKUY67DX9
R3MOT2V5L
&FSPBJ8NC
ZQ1WAH4EI
GKUY67D
R3MOT2V

all the wonderful enthusiasm and the spirit of discovery that we experience as children but generally lose as we grow older,' he said.[12]

Girard himself came from a rich and mixed background, with an American mother and Italian father. He grew up largely in Italy and studied architecture in Rome, London and New York. He opened his first architectural and design office in Florence, but moved to the States in the early 1930s, where he worked in interior design, creating offices for Ford and the interiors of the iconic Miller House in Columbus, Indiana, designed by Saarinen (1957).

In 1952 Girard began working as director of the fabric division at Herman Miller, after being introduced to the company by Eames and Nelson. He designed a number of pieces of furniture and the interiors of the San Francisco showroom, but he concentrated predominantly on fabrics for upholstery, as well as wallpapers and printed panels used to add a decorative element and colour to Herman Miller's office furniture systems.

As well as the colourful stripes that he designed, including Jacob's Coat (1959) and Millerstripe (1973), there were linear floral patterns, such as Mikado – which recalls some of Maija Isola's prints for MARIMEKKO – and Quatrefoil (both 1954).

A series of black and white geometric designs – such as Double Triangles (1952) and Checker Split (1965) – were more precise and controlled in nature but still carried a sense of rhythmic energy and exercised the eye. Girard also blurred the line between textile and graphic design with a number of designs, including the Alphabet fabric of 1952, which used oversized letters in striking colours, and the Names design of 1957, featuring an interconnected calligraphic swirl, rather like an abstract section of a child's joined-up handwriting. Girard's much-imitated Love Heart design (1967) played with white text within a heart-shaped formation on a vivid red background, with variations also produced along a similar theme.

In 1961, Girard created a Textiles & Objects store in New York under the Herman Miller umbrella, for which he designed many pieces, including a colourful series of mirrors with patterned frames. But the store was not a financial success and was soon closed. A few years later a major commission for Braniff Airlines was much more successful, with Girard designing many pieces, from sofas and armchairs to sugar packets. Herman Miller put a number of the furniture designs into production in 1967, including the Model 66303 sofa.

Girard's work also extended into poster and catalogue design, while for La Fonda del Sol restaurant (1956) he designed not only the interiors but also the menus – again drawing upon folk art imagery, with a range of naïve depictions of a solar face. Girard also collaborated upon a 'Day of the Dead' documentary film (1956) with Charles Eames.

The wit and vibrancy of Girard's designs have been recognized with many recent reissues, as well as books and exhibitions dedicated to his rich and varied work.

OPPOSITE ABOVE LEFT
Double Triangles, 1952,
reissued by Maharam.

OPPOSITE ABOVE RIGHT
Facets, 1952, reissued by
Maharam.

OPPOSITE BELOW LEFT
Checker, 1965, for Herman
Miller; reissued by Maharam.

OPPOSITE BELOW RIGHT
Checker Split, 1965, for
Herman Miller; reissued
by Maharam.

ABOVE A Quatrefoil pattern
for Herman Miller, 1954;
reissued by Maharam.

LEFT Model 66332 ottoman
from Herman Miller, in cast
aluminium and Checker
upholstery, 1967.

DAVID HICKS
1929–1998

FLAMBOYANT BRITISH
DESIGNER WITH AN ECLECTIC
YET TAILORED AND GRAPHIC
APPROACH THAT SET HIM APART
FROM HIS CONTEMPORARIES

OPPOSITE La Fiorentina
printed linen from 'David Hicks
by Ashley Hicks' for Lee Jofa,
2001 (design originally made as
a carpet by David Hicks, 1968).

ABOVE Book cover for *David
Hicks on decoration – with
fabrics*, published by Britwell
Books, London, 1971.

RIGHT London drawing room
of John Panchaud, 1969, with
Londonderry carpet, sofas
with fabric-wrapped feet, leather
and glass coffee table and
chrome side tables, all by Hicks.

At its height the David Hicks empire spread right around the world. During the 1960s and '70s, at the summit of his fame, Hicks designed for household names such as Vidal Sassoon and Helena Rubenstein, as well as royalty. He became a household name himself, one of the first superstar interior designers to achieve an international reputation with a string of shops, products and licensing deals. He spread his highly individual philosophy of design through his many books and was always keen to publish his work in style and interiors magazines. A flamboyant figurehead who was never easy to pigeonhole, he fitted only into a special compartment marked 'Hicks'.

The Hicks look was very daring but at the same time strictly controlled. The designer had an opinion on almost every subject and a highly detailed approach, yet he also delighted in stretching and breaking the rules. He brought new life and energy to neo-classical mansions and London townhouses by throwing out the chintz and embracing bold, modern colours and patterns, while mixing period and contemporary furniture.

The sitting room of Lord and Lady Londonderry's Georgian townhouse in Hampstead, which Hicks decorated in 1965, was a prime example of his mastery of this combination of old and new, with the period cornicing and fireplace mixing with a typically bold, geometric Hicks carpet, modern sofas, an 18th-century armchair covered in a striking damask, a contemporary glass-topped coffee table and a graphic modern painting on the wall. 'An early love of modernism, which was my starting point, was a reaction to the Victorian clutter seen everywhere in the over-furnished homes of my parents' generation,' Hicks wrote. 'My instinct for striking colour combinations arose out of a desire to move away from the restraint of the war years.'[13]

Hicks was masterful in the way that he brought new life to the homes of his wealthy clients, while also turning his attention to hotels, yachts and even the nightclub on the *QE2* ocean liner. He helped to shape the aesthetic approach of countless admirers, but his most enduring legacy lay within his unique approach to colour and pattern.

Hicks became interested in design and architecture at a young age and trained at the London School of Arts and Crafts. He worked briefly as a graphic designer but in his mid-20s switched his focus to interior design. His own 19th-century London home, complete with bespoke wallpaper and specially mixed colours as well as fabrics sourced from theatrical suppliers, was published in *House & Garden* magazine and launched his career.

He began designing the first patterns for his signature range of geometric carpets in 1960, when he found that there was nothing suitable for his needs on the market. His first designs were in a Y-shaped motif, based on a pattern from a Persian mosque. The wool carpets were produced in a factory in Yorkshire in a Brussels weave and it was not long before Hicks was asked to produce a commercial collection.

He found inspiration in everything from manhole covers to Japanese heraldic motifs, arranging his patterns in vibrant, precise and highly graphic formations that echoed the move towards crisp, geometrical modernity seen in many 1960s textile designs. But at the same time these were instantly recognizable as Hicks designs, with hexagonal motifs being a particular favourite.

Other designs took inspiration from Hicks's constant travels, referencing ethnic and Moorish patterns, but always updated, reinterpreted, simplified and produced in an eyecatching selection of colours. Hicks's own distinctive and abstract H-shaped logo was also applied to fabrics, wallpapers and bed linens.

These unique patterns spoke of modernity and sat well in a variety of interiors. While the work may have seemed a world away from the crisp, architectural purity of the Californian Case Study* look, its flamboyant glamour and revolutionary approach to colour helped make Hicks an icon nonetheless.

Today, his textiles are being rediscovered. His son, Ashley, has reworked a number of the designs for fabrics, wallpapers and floor tiles, manufactured by Lee Jofa and others. They remain fresh in feel and full of the dynamic energy that we associate with 1960s design.

OPPOSITE Peter Saunders's study/bath/dressing room at Easton Grey in Wiltshire, 1965, with walls in aubergine tweed bordered with gilt fillet; carpet and chrome trestle desk by Hicks.

ABOVE LEFT Clinch, printed cotton, 1970.

ABOVE A selection of designs and samples from 1963 to 1971, from the David Hicks Archive.

FAR LEFT Hicksonian pattern (featuring Hicks's logo of 4 H's) recoloured by Ashley Hicks for his book *David Hicks: Designer*, 2004.

LEFT Hicks geometric carpet on stairs, 1971.

I am going to be in New York on the 25th Oct
and am giving a Cocktail Party in the Decora
and Design Building at 979   he in t
Rug Gallery of the Harmon   pora
at 5 pm. It would be very   ere a
to come as I should like to   d show
my new carpet designs and   'Davi
Hicks on Decoration' and '   Clan
my portrait drawings, prin   ture.

Perhaps you would drop my   line
say whether you are able to   Har
Carpet Corporation 979 Thi   .Y.

I shall very much hope to s

DAVID HICKS

OPPOSITE ABOVE A selection of designs and samples from 1963 to 1968, with an invitation note printed on brown wrapping paper, from the David Hicks Archive.

OPPOSITE Hicks's first geometric carpet, Y, woven for his own bathroom, 1963.

BELOW RIGHT Interlace carpet, 1969.

BELOW Roquebrune chenille weave from 'David Hicks by Ashley Hicks' for Lee Jofa, 2001 (design originally for printed sheets and towels for American licensee Stevens-Utica, 1970).

BOTTOM Sergeant, printed cotton, 1970.

JACK LENOR LARSEN
BORN 1927

AMERICAN SELF-DESCRIBED 'WEAVER', WHOSE TEXTILES DREW UPON THEMES, REFERENCES AND CRAFT EXPERTISE FROM AROUND THE GLOBE

Having trained as an architect, Jack Lenor Larsen – one of the great innovators of 20th-century textiles – always kept in mind the way that his work would relate to interiors, architectural space and the needs of his clients. His work combined a sense of pragmatism with a mastery of colour and technical prowess. He also famously collaborated with artisans from many different countries, including India, Haiti, Morocco, Thailand and Korea, and was a key figure in the introduction of ethnically influenced textiles and patterns into the American and European design worlds, particularly in the 1960s.

Crucially, Larsen also managed to combine his passion for the quality of hand-produced textiles with an innovative use of new technologies. 'Mass production is never very interesting in textiles because it is so economical in materials and it is done very quickly,' he said. 'Mine, we either made ourselves or we worked with craftsmen in other parts of the world, often with handspun yarn....'[14]

Many of Larsen's textiles of the 1950s and '60s reveal a deep-rooted love for the distinctive character to be found in particular threads and weaves. Aware of the expanses of glass and openness of mid-century architecture, for example, he experimented with sheer and translucent fabrics, as in Bahia Blind (1959), made in Thailand using linen, silk and rayon.

Other Larsen designs were saturated with colour and vibrancy, including Happiness (1967), used for drapery, upholstery and rugs, and inspired by the patterns of a Chinese robe. Samarkand (1968) was similarly colourful and exotic, with a pattern supposedly suggested by spring flowers unfurling on the Asiatic steppes.

A number of Larsen's designs from the period are reminiscent of post-war Abstract Expressionist art, but cross-referenced with multicultural craft techniques and motifs. In the 1960s, there is a more psychedelic flavour to patterns such as Oriental Stripe (1966), Ballet Russe (1966–69) and Rapture (1969), while Larsen also produced an innovative and dynamic stretch upholstery fabric used to cover the Ribbon chair by PIERRE PAULIN (see under 'Furniture'). Most striking of all, looking over Larsen's work, is its sheer breadth and diversity.

RIGHT Samarkand, cotton fabric, Larsen Design Studio, 1968.

OPPOSITE ABOVE Happiness, 1967, rayon, cotton and mohair, Larsen Design Studio.

OPPOSITE BELOW A Dux sofa from Sweden, c. 1970, upholstered in Lenor Larsen fabric.

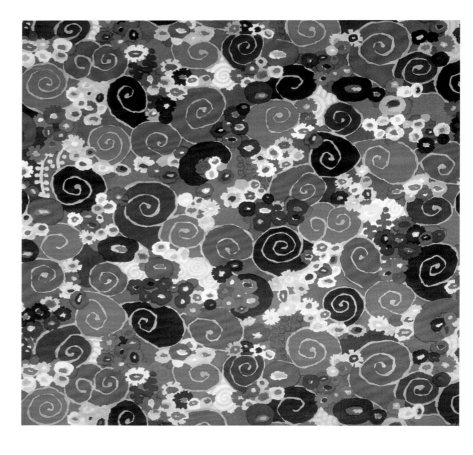

Larsen was born in Seattle and began studying architecture at the University of Washington. But even then, he was tempted into the weaving studio and began a process of experimentation and innovation that would carry him forwards for the rest of his life. He won a scholarship to Cranbrook Academy of Art*, then moved to New York shortly after graduating, opening his own studio in 1951.

Just a year later he was commissioned to produce draperies for Lever House – a pioneering New York skyscraper designed by Gordon Bunshaft* of Skidmore, Owings & Merrill*. Much of Larsen's early work took the form of custom commissions, but he soon realized that he would need to start producing fabrics on a more commercial basis. 'Not knowing how to follow, I led,' he later wrote. 'What I excelled in was doing something new and then finding a following for it.'[15]

Larsen produced textiles abroad extensively, as well as using his own mill in New Jersey, where he worked on achieving a hand-crafted finish while using machine-production techniques. In 1958 he created fabrics for Pan Am used in the first generation of jet airliners and soon afterwards he was experimenting with stretch fabrics and velvet. By 1963, his company had expanded to Europe. In 1997 it merged with Cowtan & Tout (a subsidiary of Colefax & Fowler), with Larsen continuing to work as a consultant. By then he had also established a renowned garden in East Hampton, the natural world being another constant source of inspiration.

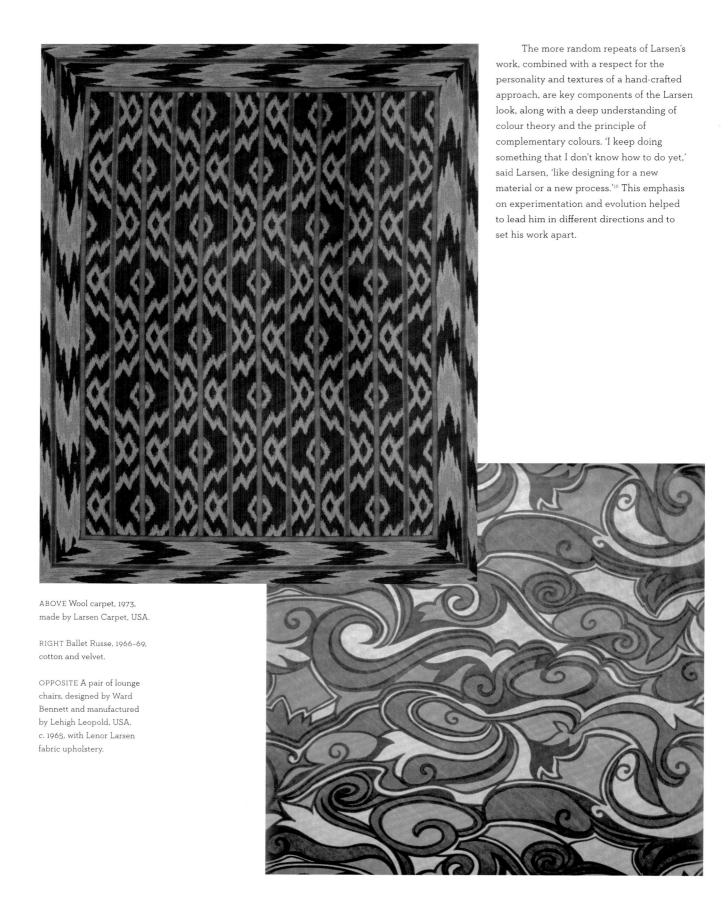

The more random repeats of Larsen's work, combined with a respect for the personality and textures of a hand-crafted approach, are key components of the Larsen look, along with a deep understanding of colour theory and the principle of complementary colours. 'I keep doing something that I don't know how to do yet,' said Larsen, 'like designing for a new material or a new process.'[16] This emphasis on experimentation and evolution helped to lead him in different directions and to set his work apart.

ABOVE Wool carpet, 1973, made by Larsen Carpet, USA.

RIGHT Ballet Russe, 1966-69, cotton and velvet.

OPPOSITE A pair of lounge chairs, designed by Ward Bennett and manufactured by Lehigh Leopold, USA, c. 1965, with Lenor Larsen fabric upholstery.

MARIMEKKO
FOUNDED 1951

PIONEERING FINNISH COMPANY,
WHOSE BRIGHT, DYNAMIC
DESIGNS FOR FABRICS, FASHION
AND INTERIOR DECORATION
ITEMS ENCAPSULATE
THE MID-CENTURY PERIOD

If a single pattern can sum up the vitality, dynamism and colourful experimentalism of the 1960s, then it might well be Maija Isola's Unikko fabric designed for Marimekko in 1964. This sequence of oversized, abstract poppies speaks of the age of 'flower power', with its saturated colours and vivid imagery. Originally a screen-printed cotton fabric – like the majority of Marimekko's textile output – it has since been used for wallpapers, trays and other merchandise. Ironically, floral patterns were discouraged in the early days of the company, but Maija Isola paid no heed. Eight of her designs were put into production, including Unikko, and by the 1960s they had helped to define the company's character and unique version of warm Scandinavian modernity.

Marimekko also forged a close synergy between the worlds of home furnishings and fashion, applying its textile designs to a range of clothing that became an integral part of the brand. In 1960 Jacqueline Kennedy famously bought seven Marimekko dresses and was pictured wearing them on magazine covers, boosting the company's popularity worldwide.

Marimekko was launched by Armi Ratia in 1951. Born in Karelia, she studied textile design at Helsinki's Central School for Applied Arts. Before the war she ran a small textiles workshop, then in 1949 her husband, Viljo Ratia, bought an oil-cloth factory called Printex. Two years later Armi launched Marimekko alongside Printex and guided the expansion of the new company, acting as managing director, art director and publicist. She developed the Marimekko aesthetic alongside a key group of freelance and staff designers, but she was also a brilliant marketing woman. To launch the company's collections she held a fashion show with clothes made using Printex textiles, aiming to inspire customers to use the fabrics in the home and for making their own dresses. But the public wanted the clothes themselves and Ratia had no hesitation in obliging them.

Vuokko Eskolin-Nurmesniemi was appointed as a textile designer in 1953 and designed a number of key patterns, including Tiibet (1953), Indus (1953) and Galleria (1954). Eskolin-Nurmesniemi – who sometimes collaborated on projects with her husband, interior designer Antti Nurmesniemi* – was also responsible for shaping the Marimekko clothing range in the 1950s. She left in 1960 to found her own company, Vuokko Oy.

But it was Maija Isola who worked with the Ratias from the beginning and designed many of Marimekko's most recognizable and popular mid-century fabrics. Having studied textile design in Helsinki, she created over five hundred prints, drawing inspiration from art, nature and her many travels. Some of her

LEFT Unikko, designed
by Maija Isola, 1964.

early patterns show the influence of naïve and folk art, but by the late 1950s she was increasingly looking to natural forms such as seed heads, leaves and twigs to inform her work, as with the Tuulenpesä, Sananjalka and Putkinotko patterns (1957) from the 'Luonto' silhouette series. Designs such as Pidot and Tantsu (both 1960), from the 'Ornamentti' series, were partly inspired by Slovakian folk textiles. Isola was also drawn to patterns found in 17th- and 18th-century Italian brocades.

In the early 1960s she began to move in a fresh direction, developing a series of more rhythmic patterns, with a reduced number of abstract elements produced on a large scale. These fabrics were even more graphic in character, and early examples include Lokki (1961), a series of broad undulating waves, and Melooni (1963), which reduced each fruit to a series of vivid rings, most vividly captured in blue, white and red.

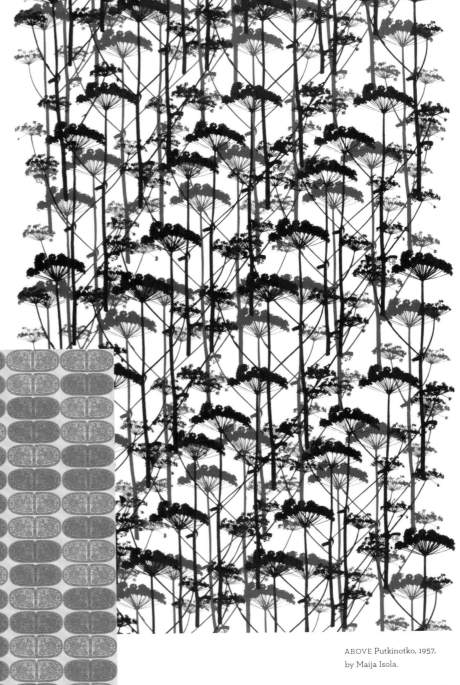

ABOVE Putkinotko, 1957, by Maija Isola.

LEFT Tantsu, 1960, by Maija Isola.

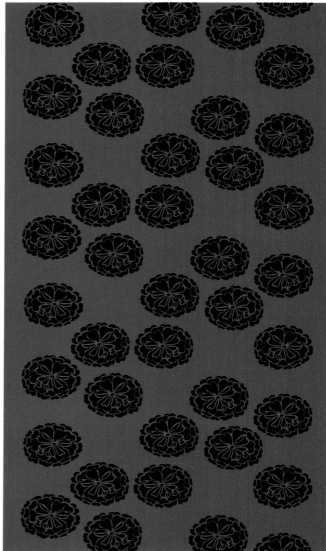
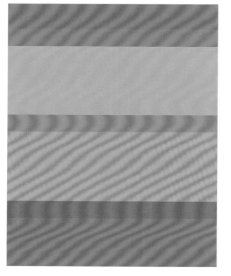

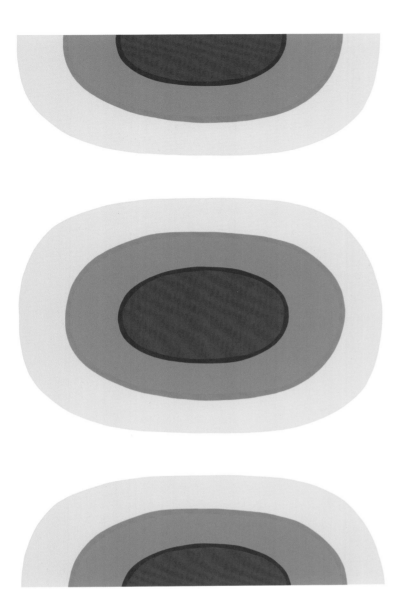

Many of Isola's designs of this period play with intense colours and arresting abstract imagery with a Pop Art sensibility. Florals and fruits were favourite motifs, but other key designs were even more abstract, reducing forms down to warm, sensual rivers and pools of colour. A number of patterns from the late 1960s, such as Husaari and Keisarinkruunu (both 1966), have Op Art connotations.

Marimekko has continued to add to its fabric and fashion ranges, working with a number of other designers. Yet Isola's 1960s patterns in particular still have great appeal and remain a key part of the collection, sitting among the brightest elements of the vintage palette and bringing colourful dynamism right into the heart of the mid-century home.

OPPOSITE ABOVE LEFT
Istuva härka, 1966, designed by Maija Isola.

OPPOSITE ABOVE RIGHT
Poloneesi, 1963, by Maija Isola.

OPPOSITE BELOW LEFT
Hennika, 1964, by Vuokko Eskolin-Nurmesniemi.

OPPOSITE BELOW CENTRE
Silkkikuikka, 1961, by Maija Isola.

OPPOSITE BELOW RIGHT
Lokki, 1961, by Maija Isola.

ABOVE LEFT Melooni, 1963, by Maija Isola.

ABOVE Keisarinkruunu, 1966, by Maija Isola.

PRODUCT
AND
INDUSTRIAL
DESIGN

BEOGRAM 1200

RAPID ADVANCES IN TECHNOLOGY, COMBINED WITH A NEW CONSUMER CONFIDENCE, RESULTED IN A PERIOD OF EXTRAORDINARY INNOVATION IN PRODUCT DESIGN

The pace of change in the mid-century period was startling. Just as nations had competed fiercely against one another for technological and military advantage during the course of World War II, now companies and international corporations battled for commercial supremacy as they looked to bring a new generation of pioneering consumer products to the market. The 1950s and '60s marked the beginning of a technological revolution or – as some prefer to describe it – a second industrial revolution, fed by post-war reconstruction and revival in Europe and a consumer boom in America. The effects and consequences of this revolution are still being felt today.

In the 1950s and '60s, it felt as though life itself was accelerating. This was a period of extraordinary innovation that saw rapid advances in nuclear power, jet travel, satellites and space missions, as well as many other fields of science, technology and design. In the late 1940s the first transistors were invented, along with Polaroid cameras and Tupperware. By the late 1950s, we had the first televisions from Sony*, the launch of Sputnik, lasers, hovercrafts and the first integrated circuit, or microchip.

Transistors and microchips helped generate a whole new wave of electronic products, while also enabling designers and manufacturers – such as DIETER RAMS and Braun*, or JACOB JENSEN and Bang & Olufsen* – to redesign and miniaturize products such as radios and record players. In just a few decades, the radio shifted from being a piece of furniture in the corner of the living room to something you could carry around in your pocket.

At the same time, manufacturers were becoming increasingly aware of the importance of good design as a way of attracting buyers, who were themselves increasingly aware of aesthetics and more demanding than ever. This applied not just to major purchases like cars; it spread to many other kinds of consumer product, from refrigerators to coffee machines and hair dryers. There was a renewed concentration upon the appearance and styling of products, and it was no longer enough to say that form simply follows function.

The relationship between form and function certainly became more complex in the mid-century period, particularly in terms of industrial and product design. RAYMOND LOEWY and his contemporaries pioneered the idea of streamlining – designing the outward shell of a product with aerodynamic, rounded curves within a seductive aesthetic approach. This was a philosophy initially applied to cars, trains and buses, but in the 1950s it gradually crept into many areas of product design. Refrigerators, Coca-Cola bottles and cutlery were all streamlined.

In many instances, streamlining represented a desire to improve and remodel a product by a logical process of reduction and editing. The superfluous was removed and both the essential beauty and function of a product were improved. Mechanics and workings were increasingly disguised and hidden away behind protective shells, whether this applied to a Vespa motor scooter designed by CORRADINO D'ASCANIO or an Olivetti typewriter designed by MARCELLO NIZZOLI or ETTORE SOTTSASS. Form was guided by function but was not a slave to it.

Yet at the same time streamlining became associated with another aspect of design that has become increasingly familiar to consumers and was – on the face of it – at odds with the process of reduction and editing outlined above. Looking to seduce customers into a regular cycle of upgrades, trade-ins and renewals, the big motor manufacturers of Detroit developed the idea of an annual refresh of an existing car model. This was usually little more than a matter of fins and chrome – an adjustment of the outward styling of the vehicle but one that was enough to tempt many consumers looking for the latest thing. Such cosmetic upgrades are indelibly associated with Harley Earl of General Motors, who established a styling department at GM and took the business of 'Borax'* to new extremes.

OPPOSITE Beogram 1200 by Jacob Jensen, launched in 1969 for Bang & Olufsen.

THIS WAS THE AGE OF THE ASSEMBLY LINE AND MASS MANUFACTURE, BUT AESTHETIC QUALITY WAS AS HIGH ON THE AGENDA AS FUNCTIONAL CAPABILITY

This was the birth of the idea of 'planned obsolescence' – the notion that a product would have a deliberately limited life and relevance, and would then need to be replaced.

Many major mid-century designers – including Raymond Loewy and Dieter Rams – hated the idea of Borax and Detroit chrome. Rams, in particular, wanted to step away from fashion in his work and the notion of constant superficial renewal. Many of his pioneering products for Braun still feel fresh and have had a profound influence on the form and aesthetics of the electronic consumer products of today. Rams stressed the importance of function and logic, but, like many of his contemporaries, he also recognized the value of outward appearance. A beautiful product, to put it simply, would always sell better than an ugly one. Rams's hi-fi systems were not only thoughtfully conceived, easy to use and high in functional capability, they were also beautiful to look at and could even be hung on the wall like a work of art.

Rams also helped develop the concept of modularity – the design of a series of components and standardized elements that could be used alone or combined, whether a seating system, shelving or hi-fi equipment. Modularity was a concept also explored by GEORGE NELSON (see under 'Furniture') at Herman Miller*, in his seating designs, but Rams took the principle further than ever.

Modularity carried echoes of the production line itself – the dominant system of mass manufacture that flourished in the mid-century period. Assembly-line techniques, first developed by the car maker and industrial pioneer Henry Ford, saw workers (or machines) concentrate on making or attaching one particular, standardized component that would become an integral part of a whole product at the end of the line. The efficiency of assembly-line techniques was applied to many mass-manufactured products in the post-war period.

Yet there was also a renewed emphasis on the value of design itself among manufacturers and makers in the 1950s and '60s. Many innovative and highly successful companies recognized the essential part that imaginative designers would have to play in the evolution of new consumer products and the growth of the companies themselves,

ABOVE Bang & Olufsen's first main catalogue, designed by Werner Neertoft, 1960.

RIGHT Raymond Loewy (second left) making some adjustments to a painted plaster model of a new Studebaker at the company's manufacturing plant, South Bend, Indiana, 1946.

Veröffentlichung in der Zeitschrift
„Schöner Wohnen", Ausgabe Oktober 69.
Seite 85 und 125

Publication in the magazine
"Schöner Wohnen", October 69 issue,
pages 85 and 125

Publication dans la revue
«Schöner Wohnen». Édition d'octobre 69,
pages 85 et 125

Pubblicazione nella rivista
„Schöner Wohnen" numero d'ottobre 69,
pagine 85 e 125

ABOVE German interiors magazine *Schöner Wohnen*, 1969, featuring the then-titled RZ60 shelving system propped with then-modern artifacts (the beagle was owned by a friend of Niels Vitsœ).

allied to a fresh focus on branding, corporate identity, marketing and advertising. Olivetti, Braun, Bang & Olufsen, Brionvega*, Piaggio and others saw the tremendous value that designers could bring to their business and the pivotal role they must have in realizing the company's ambitions. In many respects, this was a good time to be a designer, with many businesses courting and encouraging design talent.

Alongside this important, collaborative relationship there was a considerable investment in research and development, and a willingness to take risks in the hunt for innovative products. It was an age of invention and new materials, particularly plastics. The use of thermoplastics took off in the 1960s and formed an integral aspect of the new generation of consumer and electronic products.

During the post-war period, industrial and product design shifted and evolved from a utilitarian approach grounded in the austerity of the 1940s to a highly optimistic, progressive approach by the 1960s, full of imagination, innovation and a bold aesthetic. Designers were shaping the future, creating products that spoke of modernity. The organic, sculptural shapes and streamlining of the 1950s gave way to the brave experimentalism of the 1960s. The new generation of electronics, at its best, was clean and precise, futuristic and fresh, seductive and sophisticated.

Consumers, meanwhile, began to wake up to their own power to make or break a product. Some of the greatest success stories of the mid-century period – the Fiat 500, the Mini, the Vespa – sold in their millions and continue to do so today, refined and refreshed. The enduring influence of many other products and their designers is still apparent. The mid-century era was a golden age for industrial and product design.

FROM COMPUTERS TO CORPORATE IDENTITY: COLD WAR-ERA DESIGN

JANA SCHOLZE

In 1953, CHARLES AND RAY EAMES (see under 'Furniture) made the award-winning film *A Communications Primer*, based on a book by Claude E. Shannon and Warren Weaver, *The Mathematical Theory of Communication* (1949). With a playful combination of live action, still photography and animation, the film introduced communication theory, including concepts such as code, transmission and noise. The Eames' intention was to motivate architects and planners to use communication theory as a tool in their work. The film, however, was welcomed by a much wider audience, and not only did Claude Shannon – often called the 'Father of Information Theory' – start using it in his classes at MIT, but the IBM Corporation bought several copies to familiarize their staff with the new theory.

Concerns about computers were still huge in this early post-war period. Most people only had a vague idea of what the machines were doing, where they would be applied and who would operate them. Few imagined their implementation in a private setting. IBM was one of the first to tackle the mass market for personal computers. In an attempt to change public attitude and perception, they transformed first their own image by redesigning the company's 'corporate character'.[1] The chosen design team reads like a 'Who's Who' of American post-war design history: PAUL RAND (see under 'Graphics and Posters') was responsible for corporate identity and advertising; GEORGE NELSON (see under 'Furniture') and critic Edgar Kaufmann, Jr. consulted on the design of computers, sales and exhibitions; Eliot Noyes* worked on the design of all products and architectural commissions.[2] Noyes applied his knowledge of architecture to solve challenges in computer design. Rather than overwhelming the user with details about transistors, tubes and connectors, only minimal information about the inner workings was revealed. This basic principle became known as 'interface' and was first fully realized in the IBM System/360 (1964) – a so-called mainframe computer used by governmental and corporate organizations. However, the machine was not enough to calm the public's discomfort regarding computers, which had first come into public consciousness during World War II, when electronic and communication devices received increasing prominence and played a role in determining the outcome of the war.

Following the success of *A Communications Primer*, Noyes initiated a collaboration between IBM and the Eames office. The film had offered a friendly and human impression of communication processes that could be integrated into all facets of modern life. Several films were commissioned from the Eames office on cybernetics and technological history but also on astronomy and biology, among them *The Information Machine: Creative Man and the Data Processor* (1957) and *Introduction to Feedback* (1960). These films explained the computer and its operations in the context of 'centuries of tools and systems man had developed to process information'.[3]

Eames, along with many of his contemporaries, saw in the formal logic of communication and information theory an objective basis to transform design and design theory. In parallel, many post-war designers and architects had a strong interest in completing the work of the Modern movement. John Harwood describes this early post-war period as the moment

BELOW Emerson radio in walnut plywood, plastic and Bakelite, designed by Charles & Ray Eames and manufactured by Evans Products, 1946.

when 'design became a generalised problem-solving technique'.[4] Despite sharing this understanding, its interpretation and application in design practice and education was fundamentally different when applied along Cold War lines.

The Cold War was dominated by the strained rivalry between the two superpowers, the US and the Soviet Union. But the competition divided not just superpowers but most of the world, as military pacts and economic alliances confirmed. The devastation of World War II was interpreted by architects and designers as an enormous challenge but it also offered a huge opportunity. Destruction and damage provided the chance to build the radical new world that the pre-war generation had imagined. The crucial difference between the two generations was the experience of total war, with the Holocaust and nuclear destruction as its lowest points.

This background served as justification for a rather pessimistic view about technological and social progress. As David Crowley and Jane Pavitt have argued: 'Post-war attitudes to technology were … gauges of contemporary anxieties.'[5] As a consequence, design was called upon to respond to the changing social and political environment. The institution that most strictly complied with this request was the Hochschule für Gestaltung (HfG) in Ulm*, whose aim was to equip young designers with the ability to merge vocational skills with political responsibility and cultural awareness.[6]

Building a democratic society by situating design within a moral and aesthetic discourse was, however, soon challenged. Technological innovations – despite their connection to military research and deployment – needed to be embraced and engaged with: the question was how to use the new materials and technologies. In addition, the Cold War setting played a decisive role in accelerating developments, with special attention given to broadcast and electronic media. Rooted in this environment, one of the most important partners for the HfG became the leading radio manufacturer, Braun*.

RIGHT An operator using an IBM 360 computer, Somerville, New Jersey, 1969.

ABOVE Home economist Anne Anderson posing in a modern kitchen constructed for the American National Exhibition in Moscow, 1959; unpublished photo by Bob Lerner, taken for the *LOOK* magazine article, 'Miracle Kitchen: What the Russians Will See'.

An early focus at HfG on graphic design – with appointments ranging from MAX BILL (see under 'Graphics and Posters') to Anthony Froshaug and Tomás Maldonado – had paved the way for an emphasis on communication and corporate design. Braun's new design department, headed by Fritz Eichler, initiated the collaboration in late 1954, aimed at Braun's design policy of integrating corporate identity as well as products and exhibitions. The head of the product design department, Hans Gugelot*, together with young architect DIETER RAMS and established designer (and former Bauhaus* student) Herbert Hirche, developed the foundation for Braun's new corporate image strongly in the tradition of modernism. The implementation of rational and functionalist principles took centre stage and became a signature for Rams's long career at Braun.

The HfG and Braun, however, did not represent the standard attitude and approach of post-war German design. Germany was not just divided into four Allied Occupation Zones between 1945 and 1949; it became a permanently divided country and a prime battleground of the Cold War. Art and design were drawn into this conflict.

Following the example of the Soviet Union, all socialist countries in the East introduced a new rigid style, 'Socialist Realism', which rejected all pre-war modernist principles. It was efficiently introduced in the fine arts and architecture, but it is questionable how much influence the style had on product design, as its tendency towards realist representation and propaganda was difficult to apply to household appliances and office devices.[7] Undoubtedly, the major focus in design was related to the space and arms races, but domestic appliances, electronic products, cars, fashion and furniture – which reflected actual living conditions – were also a constant battleground between the two superpowers.

Nothing confirmed this better than the infamous 'kitchen debate' between USSR First Secretary Nikita Khrushchev and US Vice President Richard Nixon, which occurred in front of a model kitchen at the American National Exhibition in Moscow in 1959. After a powerful exchange, Nixon challenged Khrushchev: 'Would it not be better to compete in the relative merits of washing machines than in the strength of rockets?'[8] The exhibition had only been possible at this moment of Khrushchev's politics, known as 'Thaw', which initiated dramatic transformations in Soviet (and Eastern) politics and society. Its announcement of peaceful coexistence between nations provided the platform for the American exhibition in Moscow. However, the presentations of affluence generated first and foremost reactions of consumer desire (and envy).

The US-initiated European Recovery Programme (better known as the Marshall Plan) had a similar effect. Between 1948 and 1952 the plan offered support for Europe's reconstruction and a programme of re-education and democratization with a specific focus on former fascist countries. A comprehensive programme of exhibitions, events and films promoted the plan effectively. These presented desirable consumer goods and products that employed a certain formal, functional and aesthetic language.

A similar scheme of US investment and recovery was sketched out for Japan during the US occupation between 1945 and 1952. The US sanctioned a programme of training and technology that led to a widespread consumer boom. By the late 1950s, modern living in Japan had become synonymous with domestic electronic goods, namely televisions, washing machines and refrigerators. The company that best met the desire for home products as well as consumer electronics was Sony*. Having started with repairing and appropriating radios,[9] the company turned its focus exclusively to electronic products, which had substantial effects on Japan's industry, society and culture.

Such products were not only distinguished by the implementation of the latest technology but also by a design characterized by simplicity, high performance and reliability. Early attention to design was confirmed by the creation of Sony's Design Centre in 1961. As the writer Paul Kunkel explains: '[T]he Design Centre does not only create new

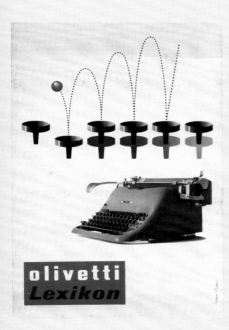

ABOVE A poster by Giovanni Pintori for the Olivetti Lexikon typewriter, designed by Marcello Nizzoli, 1953.

BELOW An 8 301 W portable television, manufactured by the Sony Corporation, Tokyo, 1959.

products, it provides a vision that all of Sony draws upon, turning industrial and consumer products into the purest form of culture while propelling humanity into an era of change the likes of which we have never seen before.'[10] Remarkably, its designers were given freedom to invent and create according to their own interests and judgments, rather than follow market research and analyses. From the outset, and formulated in Masaru Ibuka's handwritten founding document, Sony had a desire to 'always do what has never been done before'.[11] The company understood that a distinctive design quality paired with consistency were key factors for success, which explains why they hired young graduates and taught them the 'Sony style'.

A comparable dedication to innovative product design could be seen at the Italian manufacturer Olivetti, founded by Camillo Olivetti in 1908. After the war his son Adriano continued to manufacture typewriters, adding and calculating machines, and tele-typewriters. He understood industrial design as an ideal conjunction of functionality and aesthetics. All Olivetti products consequently display a formal attitude, a so-called *linea di gusto*, distinguished by attention to the smallest detail. In contrast to Sony's joint venture, most of Olivetti's distinguished products were designed by MARCELLO NIZZOLI.

Formerly fascist Italy received substantial support through the Marshall Plan, and the success of its programme was publicized back in the US. However, Olivetti proved to be a special case. Already before the war, Adriano Olivetti had rationalized production further to his experiences on a long trip to the US. But he also championed exceptionally high ethical standards based on the understanding of the close connection between the wellbeing of his staff and the expansion of both production and the company in general. As a result, he instituted an exemplary programme of corporate welfare, ranging from the introduction of the five-day working week to housing, maternity and child support, and medical, educational and holiday facilities.

Olivetti's theory was validated by the rapid growth of the company, and by a monograph Olivetti show at the Museum of Modern Art in New York as early as 1952. Not surprisingly, Olivetti also became one of the first companies in Europe to engage with the production of computers. A young ETTORE SOTTSASS designed the Olivetti's mainframe Elea 9003 in 1959. Conscious of public anxieties towards the computer, he created a colourful visual interface driven by the aim of humanizing technology.[12] But even more significantly, just five years later, Olivetti finished work on the world's first personal computer – the Programma 101, designed by Mario Bellini*. To the company's surprise this desktop computer received overwhelming attention at the World's Fair in New York in 1965. For the first time a computer had an accessible size, was transportable and seemed suitable for home usage. Olivetti sold around 40,000 units, with ten bought by NASA and used for the Apollo 11 moon landing in 1969.

The developments of computer technology during the post-war period anticipated the most significant transformation of the 20th century: the change from consumption to information. The early post-war years saw the successful peacetime application of wartime inventions, and purposeful and progressive design – combined with a focus on mass production – pushed a new generation of products into consumer society. The long-term technical investments of the Cold War not only supported the arms and space races but also ushered in a new wave of groundbreaking domestic products and electronic devices.

MID-CENTURY PRODUCT DESIGN IN GERMANY
KLAUS KLEMP

Design in mid-20th-century Germany took place in a country characterized by the damage of a self-inflicted world war, utter military defeat, bombed and devastated cities, a broken infrastructure and isolation on the world stage. To be German was already problematic after the first world war, but after 1945 the image abroad was completely ruined. Naturally this was not the best context in which to contend with questions of design.

In the early post-war years there was very little thinking about design, since almost anything could be sold in Germany as long as it promised utility. The urgent question was how one could turn the discarded steel helmets of soldiers into cooking pots. Design theorists, however, were beginning to think differently. Hans Schwippert, chairman of the Werkbund – an association of entrepreneurs, designers and publicists founded in 1907 with the remit of improving the design quality of German products[13] – warned in the newly relaunched *Werkbund* newspaper 'against the abuse of human power and material, against the inhumanity of ill-suited things, against the deception within the material, against the lie within the form, against the nonsense of pomp even in a new guise, against the impurity of bad work, against the glistening or borrowed representation of boastful houses and their façades'.[14] After twelve years of immorality, über-morality had been reinstated in Germany.

Plainness was propagated everywhere, though certainly not always lived out. Then came the currency reform of 1948, which created a remarkable recovery and signalled an end to privation. What the Germans liked to refer to as an 'economic miracle' was actually less a miracle than the result of a craft knowledge coming into contact with the traditional Prussian virtues of hard work and discipline – a work ethic that had already played an important role during the industrialization of 19th-century Germany. This combination helped the country begin to recover from the shock of its monumental ethical failures.

From the mid-1950s Germany saw a glut of new products (even if many were trivial in their design: the icon of the time was a pallet table on three splayed legs, the so-called 'kidney-shaped table'). Initiatives were launched to seek out a more sophisticated design culture. As early as 1946 Mercedes-Benz in Stuttgart organized an export trade show. In 1951, the German Bundestag created a design council, assigned to the Ministry for Economy and established to advise manufacturing companies on design issues and to improve German competitiveness in the export sector. Other moves to promote design included the inauguration at the Hanover Fair, from 1953 onwards, of a special exhibition called 'The Shape of Good Industry', with which the Federal Association of German Industry was involved, as were many other associations. Though design could not always keep pace with technical quality, it was intended that 'Designed in Germany' – alongside 'Made in Germany' – should always appear on home-made products.

In fact, the best-known West German post-war product, the VW Beetle, was not a German design nor a German construction at all; it was based on a concept developed by the Austro-Hungarian engineer Béla Barényi back in the 1920s, although he had not applied for a patent. Born in 1907, Barényi first had Austrian citizenship, then Czechoslovakian and finally German. In 1953 a German court granted him authorship of large parts of the VW Beetle. The legendary Ferdinand Porsche, similarly, came from Bohemia, which was Austrian at the time and Czechoslovakian after World War I (Porsche also changed his nationality twice). German product design was clearly not a parochial matter.

Indeed, Germany as a nation only dates back to 1871, and even then the form was different from today. Then it was made up of many small states, with baroque Catholic Austria dominant in the empire, followed by the rise of Prussia with its frugal Protestant ethic, and not least some close ties to Central and Eastern Europe. At the same time Germany was influenced culturally by a range of its neighbours on all sides.

Before World War I the country was politically reactionary but highly successful economically and culturally, then after the war it became economically unstable though home to the most advanced modern design. This phase – so-called 'Classical Modernism', and unthinkable without the contributions of Germany's neighbours, Russian Constructivism and the Dutch De Stijl – attracted international artists and designers, and American and Japanese students enrolled at the Bauhaus*. Foreigners such as Piet Mondrian, Theo van Doesburg, Mart Stam, MARCEL BREUER (see under 'Houses and Interiors'), El Lissitzky, Le Corbusier*, László Moholy-Nagy*, Wassily Kandinsky and Hannes Meyer had a great influence on the German design scene between the world wars, enabling a familiar exchange; what the German sociologist Wolfgang Welsch defined with the concept of 'transculturation'.[15]

The Bauhaus and the Werkbund were both dissolved in 1933, but many of their design principles were adopted by the new regime, as seen in the lamps of Bauhaus master Christian Dell or the highly functional Arzberg 1382 dinnerware designed by Hermann Gretsch, which was awarded a gold medal at the Paris Exposition of 1937 and became a staple item in National Socialist households. Other pioneers of modernism, such as Heinrich Löffelhardt, Wilhelm Wagenfeld and Walter Zapp, were able to produce their works during the Nazi era. A special department, called 'Beauty of Work', pursued the objectives of simplicity, clarity, standardization and typification. While a new and pathetically grandiose 'dictator classicism' emerged in state architecture, everyday objects were subjected to a more middle-class penchant for usefulness. Nevertheless, one cannot speak of an evolution of modern design during the Nazi era in Germany, but rather of a dull infirmity of modern residual forms, because the basis and the conditions for further

RIGHT A VW Beetle, 1957.

development had been lost. In this regard the United States offered a new and more profitable field, both in relation to the willingness of consumers and in terms of the academic environment. In addition to the New Bauhaus initiated by László Moholy-Nagy*, there was the Cranbrook Academy of Art* and the Black Mountain College, all three enriched by European émigrés.

The generation of designers in Germany during the 1940s and '50s was similarly heterogeneous. After 1945, ex-pats influenced the nation – particularly those from the USA, such as Gropius, who gave his blessing to the Hochschule für Gestaltung (HfG) in Ulm*, one of the first community colleges in Germany. The exiled modernist movement of the 1920s also influenced Germany through companies: Knoll* International opened its first overseas showroom in Stuttgart in 1951, with Hans Knoll, who had emigrated in 1938 from Stuttgart to New York, and his wife Florence, successfully marketing works by exiled German architects and designers such as Gropius, Breuer and LUDWIG MIES VAN DER ROHE (see under 'Houses and Interiors').

A similar return to German reformist modernism came after 1945 from Switzerland, the second most important place of exile. Here, both graphic and furniture design – which had always been in close touch with developments in Germany – had progressed further and were highly respected as 'Swiss design'. MAX BILL (see under 'Graphics and Posters') redefined the pre-war term 'functionalism' in his speech 'Beauty from function and as function' and put everyday objects in a larger cultural context. In 1949, as evidence of this new combination of functionality and beauty, Bill organized the travelling exhibition 'Good Design'.

At the same time Inge Scholl – older sister of the anti-Nazi resistance fighters Hans and Sophie Scholl, who were executed in 1943 – co-founded the HfG in Ulm. Since 1947, Scholl had worked with her husband, OTL AICHER (see under 'Graphics and Posters'), on a concept for a new design academy, which was to promote the re-democratization process. From 1948 the couple were in contact with Max Bill, who became founding director in 1953.

Along with the schools of applied art that began emerging in 1949 and that were in part also based on the Bauhaus* legacy, the HfG under Max Bill saw itself as the direct successor to the Bauhaus. Indeed, Bill obtained approval from Gropius in America to call the new institute 'Bauhaus Ulm', but Scholl and Aicher were against it. They finally agreed on the subtitle from Dessau: 'College of Design'. The first teachers that were appointed – in addition to former Bauhaus members Josef Albers*, Walter Peterhans, Johannes Itten and Helene Nonné-Schmidt – were Otl Aicher, Hans Gugelot* and Tomás Maldonado.

Only three years after the HfG had been founded a quarrel erupted with Max Bill. The younger generation wanted to emancipate itself from the Bauhaus idea, discarding artistic references and treating design not as a matter of form but as order created by use of rational methods. The adoption of a scientific approach and research into design methodology became the central preoccupation and took up more than half of the teaching programme. Study of mathematics, sociology, cybernetics and semiotics, rather than the work of the workshops, became the object. Bill departed in 1957, and there then followed a period of neglect of the aesthetic component. Students no longer focused on actual products, but more on life and functional relationships. Still, the foundations for a contemporary design process were laid in Ulm and have become the standard of the design profession.

The main designers at Ulm were Hans Gugelot in the area of product design and Otl Aicher in the field of visual communications. Both had also increasingly been working on their own designs since the late 1950s. Gugelot had developed his idea of system furniture, M 125, back in Switzerland, then developed it further at HfG. Before his unexpected death at the age of 45, a number of products were developed in his research group, while his Carousel projector designed for Kodak had a special role.

Otl Aicher worked for Brown, Bulthaup, German Airbus, Dresdner Bank, ERCO, Norman Foster, FSB and the second German television station ZDF, and was responsible for the image of Lufthansa from 1960 to 1987. In 1972, he became the undisputed giant of the West German graphic design scene with his work for the Summer Olympics in Munich. He developed a unique position in favour of clear and consistent graphic design, largely based on harmonic grids. The charismatic designer worked – as Peter Behrens had before World War I – on an equal footing with his clients, which often involved an extensive and sometimes radical re-evaluation of the company image. Ulm also extended the definition of design in this respect, as it increased the self-confidence of designers with lasting effect.

Gugelot and Aicher's main project in the 1950s was working for the company Braun* in Frankfurt. In Braun, Ulm found its first major industrial partner. From early 1955, Gugelot designed new radios in light wood, and Aicher created functional presentation and communication systems. By the summer of 1955, Braun had employed a young interior designer called DIETER RAMS, who, together with Gerd A. Müller, gradually transformed the in-house design department. These two graduates of the Wiesbaden Arts and Crafts School, who had become familiar with the functional approach of the Bauhaus through Wiesbaden's founding director Hans Soeder, were at first only junior partners in the process, but within just a few years they had liberated themselves from the influence of Ulm. This happened above all because of their close relationship with Braun's in-house engineers.

Engineers and designers were equals at Braun because the management understood that this was the only way to create truly innovative technical equipment. By the early 1960s, the in-house and by then considerably larger design department had assumed sole responsibility for Braun's product design under Rams's direction. To talk about the 'Braun model' was to define it structurally by an equal emphasis on factors such as management, technology, marketing and design, all working together to create ease of use, durability and long-lasting aesthetics. Contemporary designers such as Naoto Fukasawa and Jonathan Ive of Apple employ this structural model for their work today.

The success and the design language of Braun became synonymous with German design in the 1960s. A crucial aspect was a systematic way of thinking, exemplified by the design of Braun's hi-fi systems in particular. This never became schematic; each element had a self-contained and coherent design, and the individual components were visually strong. Braun managed the transition from a machine aesthetic to a kind of civilian aesthetic with highly visual durability. Ultimately, all its products were self-explanatory. Braun became a model for other German manufacturers, such as Krups and Rowenta, though they were never able to reach comparable peaks of design.

German car design, on the other hand, had some highlights in the 1950s, such as the Mercedes 300 SL Gullwing of 1954 and the BMW 507 launched by Albrecht Graf von Goertz in 1956. Car design then became rather mainstream until Claus Luthe (later head of design at BMW) designed the revolutionary wedge-shaped RO 80 for the West German firm of NSU in 1967 – an icon of automotive design and the blueprint for almost all modern cars.

Some other exceptional designers emerged in Germany in the mid-century period. In 1959, the graphic designer Willy Fleckhaus became art director of the magazine *Twen* and developed a completely new style of magazine layout; in the same year Peter Raacke created his mono-a cutlery, followed in 1966 by his cardboard furniture; Rido Busse, who had graduated from Ulm in 1959, was a highly succesful external product designer; Ferdinand Alexander Porsche*, had, since 1963, been closely involved in his family's company; Ingo Maurer* founded a company, Design M, that represented an early transition to postmodernism due to Maurer's poetic approach; and between 1964 and 1966 Helmut Bätzner designed the Bofinger Chair BA 1171, one of the first mass-produced plastic chairs and a forerunner of today's ubiquitous and anonymous monobloc chair.

If I record my vote for the NSU RO 80 as the
Car of the Year, ...it is because it seems
to have stability, roadholding qualities
and built-in safety margins superior to
any family car produced so far.

(THE OBSERVER)

AUTO
DES
JAHRES

NSU RO 80

NSU Motorenwerke AG, 7107 Neckarsulm, Abteilung VD I
Wir senden Ihnen gern ausführliches Informationsmaterial

NSU RO 80
Das neue Fahren

ABOVE Advertisement for
the NSU RO 80 car from West
Germany, 1967.

BELOW A Heimsuper Berolina
K radio, designed by Horst
Giese and manufactured
by VEB Stern Radio Berlin,
East Germany, 1957.

However, the new design, and the new way of life and culture, no longer came from Germany, but stemmed from American and British Pop Art, and especially from pop music. By comparison, German design of the post-war period was highly ahistorical and committed to isolated modernism. Looking backwards, German history began with National Socialism and, understandably, no one wanted anything to do with it anymore.

Of course it must be remembered that West Germany was only half of Germany, until hundreds of thousands took to the streets in 1989 to proclaim, 'We are the people'. Due to the altered global political situation, a new constellation emerged, which suddenly had a double heritage. Not much was to remain of the German Democratic Republic (GDR) product culture, because all anyone wanted was to have televisions, video recorders and cars from the West; hardly anyone wanted a Trabant or poor-quality products made out of plastics and elastics. The GDR was subsumed and effectively taken over by West Germany, starting with the political system and extending to the product culture.

The design history that arises out of the GDR is very different from that arising in the Federal Republic of Germany (FRG). In the Soviet Occupation Zone the post-war process of dismantling was far more radical than in the West: every second railway track found its way to Russia and entire factories, including the staff, disappeared to the East. Nevertheless, between 1945 and 1967, there were about 80 manufacturers of valve radios in the GDR and the first device with a new contemporary claim was the valve radio Undine II from VEB Elektro-Apparate-Werke, J. V. Stalin in Berlin-Treptow,[16] designed by the student Erich John under his mentor Rudi Högner. The latter – a doyen in shaping the East – was an architect, graphic designer and plastic designer. He taught in Dresden from 1950 and, from 1953, at the art college (Kunsthochschule) Weissensee, where he became a professor in 1959. He had a long relationship with Stern Radio Berlin, where he placed the Berolina K radio (K for Kunsthochschule), designed by his student Horst Giese, and in 1957 the design for TV Alex by Giese and Jürgen Peters, which went into production in 1959.[17]

In the early post-war years, the two design scenes were still open to one another. Mart Stam from the Netherlands was rector at Weissensee from 1950 until 1952, and the West German Herbert Hirche was professor from 1948 to 1950. However, discussions about formalism, which had begun in the Soviet Union, continued and were intended to distinguish the GDR from the 'Western-decadent art industry'. Common ground ceased to exist, marking the end of the freedom of art. The decision of the Central Committee of the Socialist Unity Party on 17 March 1951 was commented on by GDR Prime Minister Otto Grotewohl: 'Literature and the visual arts are subordinated to politics, but it is clear that they have a strong influence on politics. The idea of art must follow the direction of the march of the political struggle.'[18] Walter Ulbricht proclaimed in his speech before the People's Chamber of the GDR on 31 October 1951:'We don't want to see abstract images in our art schools any longer. The grey-on-grey painting, which is an expression of capitalist decline, stands in sharp contradiction to the new life in the German Democratic Republic.'[19]

From 1959, only one semi-private company, HELI in Chemnitz (founded in 1950), and its owner, the engineer Bodo Hempel, remained ambitious. From 1961 the company produced new radio equipment. Two designers, Clauss Dietel and Lutz Rudolph, who had recently graduated from the Kunsthochschule Weissensee, significantly shaped the products of the organization over the following decades.

The GDR was one of Europe's largest furniture exporters, especially to Eastern Europe, and the Soviet Union in particular. The VEB Möbilkombinat Berlin also worked for IKEA. In addition, the GDR was the world's largest lighting manufacturer. Designs, however, came from abroad. GDR design was not very competitive, not because of the designers' capabilities but because the production structures of a controlled economy did not allow innovation and the designers were dependent on political functionaries. This also became

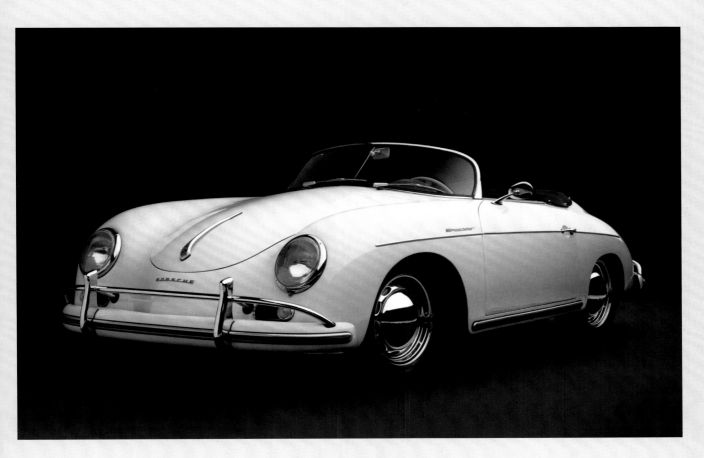

ABOVE Porsche 356
Speedster, Germany, 1958.

apparent when it came to photo equipment, a speciality of the old East German regions, especially Jena. From 1959, the East German camera manufacturer VEB Kombinat Pentacon employed the designer and engineer Manfred Claus, who was responsible for nearly all the company's products.

However, as design expert Günter Höhne – an influential leader of opinion in the GDR – admits, there were no truly outstanding design ideas emerging from East Germany. Ultimately, there was a disconnection between designers and buyers, the latter being the ones to decide what was acceptable and what was not. In the GDR, there were no choices. Consequently, consumers resorted to the successful designs from the West, which eventually led to a simulated product culture.

German design in the mid-20th century meant a reappearance of the great tradition of the 1920s, interpreted by the West and by the East. But it was the 'new' that broke the machine mentality of the Bauhaus and developed it further. This 'civil design' – clear, objective and user-oriented – is now experiencing a significant re-discovery.

CORRADINO D'ASCANIO
1891–1981

AMBITIOUS AERONAUTICAL
ENGINEER WHO CREATED
THE VESPA SCOOTER, AN ICON
OF POST-WAR ITALIAN DESIGN

In many respects, the Vespa motor scooter represented a new beginning. It became a key emblem of the Italian design renaissance in the post-war years and a positive symbol of industrial reconstruction. It offered Italians and Europeans more generally a cheap, accessible but beautifully designed way of getting around their towns and cities – many still badly damaged by the war years – and thus it was a significant engine of personal freedom. For the young especially, the Vespa was a gift, adopted and adapted by aficionados who saw a way to liberate themselves – and often their partners – from the chains of work, home and routine.

For the designer of the Vespa, Corradino D'Ascanio, the scooter may have been the most significant success of his life, but it represented neither his primary ambition nor what he would most have liked to be remembered for. D'Ascanio was primarily an aeronautical engineer and a pioneer of helicopter design and technology. His passion for aeronautics began at an early age and he studied mechanical engineering at Torino Polytechnic before joining an aviation division of the Italian army during World War I.

After the war and a brief period working in the States, D'Ascanio settled in Popoli and began developing helicopter designs, including the D'AT3 commissioned by the Ministry for Aeronautics. In 1932, after the collapse of his own company, he went to work for Enrico Piaggio at Piaggio Aero. The company had been founded by Piaggio's father in 1884 and was initially focused on the production of trains and railway carriages. It moved into aircraft manufacturing during World War I and during World War II produced bomber planes.

In 1945, both D'Ascanio and Piaggio found themselves having to start again. The Piaggio factory had been destroyed in the war and Italian aerospace was stalled by a ten-year embargo on development imposed upon the country. Both men turned their attention to fulfilling the growing need for affordable transport. Although D'Ascanio disliked motorbikes, he applied his experience to creating a scooter that avoided many of the drawbacks of standard motorcycles.

D'Ascanio's original 98cc Vespa of 1945/46 was a new kind of scooter. It was streamlined and elegant, with a sleek mono shell that encompassed the wide front shield, the floor plate and the rear casing that protected the engine and petrol tank, topped with a neat seat on a spring. Enrico Piaggio famously decided that the scooter, with its distinctive silhouette, looked like a wasp – or *vespa*. Its small wheels were inspired by the modest tyres used on airplane landing gear.

The generous scooter shield protected the rider from wind and puddles, while the

cowling around the rear engine hid away any messy or dangerous moving parts. Being easy to ride, practical and endearing in appearance, the Vespa attracted both men and women and soon became an icon of the *dolce vita*. The scooters were manufactured on highly efficient factory assembly lines and a number of improved models were added in the years that followed. By 1956, ten years after its launch, a million Vespas had been sold. By 2011, as many as 17 million had been sold internationally.

In Britain in the 1950s and '60s, Vespas and Lambrettas were adopted by the 'mods', who loved all things Italian, including Italian suits and scooters. They added mirrors and chrome detailing to their beloved Vespas and wore big parka coats to protect their clothes when they were on the road. By the time of the mod revival of the 1970s, the Vespa had become a symbol for this counter-culture movement.

D'Ascanio continued working with Piaggio until the mid-1960s. He then joined the Agusta Group to continue working in aviation design, although relatively few of his designs made it from drawing board to reality. Despite his frustration, he remains known for a design that was destined for the roads rather than the skies – a design that became one of the most recognizable and successful products to emerge from post-war Italy.

ABOVE SmarTee poster showing models with Vespas, 1960s.

OPPOSITE A 1950s Vespa.

LEFT A 1940s Vespa.

KENNETH GRANGE
BORN 1929

BRITISH INDUSTRIAL DESIGNER
RESPONSIBLE FOR A WIDE RANGE
OF PRODUCTS AND GOODS,
FROM TRAINS TO CAMERAS

'Like the cathedral for the architect,' Kenneth Grange once wrote, 'the design of a train comes rarely in the lifetime of an industrial designer.'[20] Grange was the chief designer of one of Britain's most familiar and beloved trains – the Inter-City 125, designed in the late 1960s and still in service in the 21st century. The sleek look of this high-speed train spoke of modernity and the future. It was nothing short of revolutionary in a country used to blunt-nosed diesel engines spilling smoke onto station platforms. It was the kind of train to revive faith in the railway system itself.

Grange's central role came by being in the right place at the right time. British Rail had a rare opportunity to design a highly advanced train from scratch. Initially Grange was asked to design the livery for a train already created by the in-house design team. But he was disappointed by the shape and 'brutal efficiency' of the proposed design and felt he could improve on it. He worked with an aerodynamic consultant, developing a train

that was highly efficient as well as pleasing to the eye. 'Every day we'd make a new model and every night we'd test it in the wind tunnel,' he recalled, 'until we'd got a shape that didn't just look better, it was aerodynamically better than the one they started with.'[21]

The train was introduced into service in the 1970s. It was one of many different products designed by Grange that spliced functionality and pleasure within a modernist-inspired design philosophy. Grange always stressed the importance of practicality and making products 'better', yet there was a welcome degree of warmth to his work, which set him apart from the more 'Germanic' approach of some of his contemporaries.

He started out by studying drawing at Willesden School of Art, followed by work as an architectural assistant in various practices. He contributed to the Festival of Britain* in 1951 before moving into freelance exhibition design. In 1958, he founded Kenneth Grange Design, inspired by modernism, by American

Multiple unit liveries
**HST Diesel electric power car
Class 253**

sheet no		4/19
issued		Aug 1977

HST Diesel electric power car Class 253

Diesel electric power car 1680 kW BR Bo-Bo
Length 17 798mm overall, 10 300mm bogie centres
Width 2 740mm over body, 2 810mm maximum width
Height 3 906mm maximum
Weight 70.10 tonnes (working order)
Engine Ruston-Paxman 12RP200L 12 cylinder 4-stroke
Maximum continuous rated output 1680 kW
Main alternator Brush BL 91-32
Traction motors, four, fully suspended, single
reduction gear drive
Maximum tractive effort 80 000N at 11.6 per cent
adhesion at 1490A traction current

Continuous tractive effort 45 950N at 103.3 km/h
at 1000A traction current
Power at rail (continuous rating) 1320 kW
Full engine output available between 56 and 200 km/h
Automatic air braking for power car and for train,
brake force as percentage of (working order) car weight
0—145 km/h 50 per cent, 145—200 km/h 34 per cent
Minimum radius curves
Horizontal without widening 80m
Horizontal with 20mm gauge widening 65m
Vertical convex 200m
Vertical concave 200m

Maximum permitted service speed 200 km/h
Train heating equipment Brush BL 91-20
electric alternator driven by engine,
280 kW continuous output at 900V
Fuel tank capacity 4682 litres
Painting:
Rail Blue BS 381C No.114
Rail Grey BS 381C No.627
Yellow BS 381C No.356
Roof, undergear and bogies Black
Symbol and outline lettering Silver
Service systems to Code DBS 5946

product design and by the spirit of optimism that had taken root in Britain. 'If you were lucky, and were the right age and in the right place,' he wrote, 'you too could be swept into the thrilling and dynamic enterprise that was Modern Britain.'[22]

One of his first successful collaborations was with the kitchen appliance company founded by Ken Maynard Wood in 1947. Grange was asked to redesign its food mixer using a dynamic approach in plastic and enamelled metal. The sleek appearance and wipe-down functionality of the Kenwood Chef helped establish the product as a key staple of the British kitchen in the early 1960s.

Another important commission developed, like the Inter-City 125, almost by accident. Grange was working on exhibition designs for Kodak, when he passed comment on the rather ugly design and styling of their cameras. The next day Kodak's head of development called and asked Grange to design his first camera. He began with the Brownie 44A of

1960 and later, in 1968, created the Instamatic 33 – a compact, easy-to-use, pared-down design with easily loadable film cartridges. The cameras have often been compared to the Braun* products developed by DIETER RAMS, but they also had an ergonomic warmth and a unique sense of character.

Other products designed by Grange included Parker pens, irons for Morphy Richards and razors for Wilkinson Sword. Another key transport commission was his redesign of the iconic London black cab in 1996. In 1972, along with ALAN FLETCHER and other partners, he founded the interdisciplinary design practice Pentagram. He also served as a visiting professor at the Royal College of Art.

LEFT Kodak 'Brownie' Vecta camera, 1964.

BELOW Courier electric shaver, 1963.

OPPOSITE Kodak Instamatic 233, 133 and 33 cameras, designed in the 1960s.

ALEC ISSIGONIS
1906–1988

GREEK-BORN DESIGNER WHOSE
WORK ON THE ICONIC MINI
AND MORRIS MINOR BECAME
KEY REFERENCE POINTS IN CAR
MANUFACTURING AND DESIGN

OPPOSITE British Leyland
advertising image of the Mini
1000 from the 1970s.

BELOW Side view of a Morris
Mini Minor, 1959.

In late 1950s Britain it was decided that small was beautiful. The country's car manufacturers had grown worried about the increasing popularity of compact foreign cars, particularly the VW Beetle, first produced in 1938, and the Fiat 500, launched in 1957. Both were affordable, modern and stylish, and were beginning to attract a great sense of loyalty and affection. Britain needed its own compact car.

Alec Issigonis, working at the British Motor Corporation (BMC) in the mid-1950s, was developing three experimental cars of different sizes when word came down to get the smallest of these ready for production as rapidly as possible. This was the car that became the Morris Mini Minor, Austin Seven, Austin Mini Seven, or – as it was finally and more simply known – the Mini.

The design that Issigonis developed was revolutionary for the times. Turning the engine within the bonnet to a transverse formation was a key space-saving measure, freeing up 80% of the car body for the driver and three passengers, as well as a small boot. The car was front wheel drive, using an innovative rubber suspension system, and ran on small tyres not much larger than those used on a Vespa. Finally, the car was three metres long – the

same size as a Fiat 500. Yet the design was distinctly Issigonis and distinctly English.

Launched in 1959, the Mini attracted all kinds of buyers and was immortalized in the 1969 film, The Italian Job. It was relaunched, with great success, by BMW at the start of the 21st century. Multiple variations, including the Mini Cooper (developed with racing-car constructor John Cooper), had been added over the intervening decades.

Issigonis was born in the Greek port of Smyrna. The family was evacuated during the Greco-Turkish War of 1919–22 and, after the death of his father, Issigonis and his mother moved to England. Issigonis studied engineering at Battersea Polytechnic, then after a tour of Europe in a car that broke down constantly, he took a job as a draughtsman for Roote Motors in Coventry. He also worked on the development of his own racing car, which he himself raced for many years.

Then in 1936, he was offered a job at Morris Motors. During the war years he was excused service and stayed on at Morris developing military vehicles. But time was also put aside for him to continue developing a low-cost compact car. The result was the Morris Minor, largely designed by Issigonis.

The NEW **MORRIS** MINOR

The World's Supreme Small Car

From 1942 onwards, he worked on a prototype of the car, although the founder of the company famously described it as 'a poached egg' when it was presented to him. The styling of the Morris Minor was influenced by American car design of the period, but was very different in scale, by comparison to the family cars being built in the States. The Morris Minor was modest in every way, but easy to drive and – in an age of rationing, which lasted until 1957 in Britain – also economical. The car was produced until 1971 and, like the Mini, endeared itself to a wide audience.

When Morris Minor merged with Austin in 1952 to become BMC, Issigonis resigned and spent a short period with Alvis before being tempted back and starting work on the development of the Mini. Later he developed the Austin 1100 in collaboration with the Pininfarina design studio in Italy. He retired in 1971. In 1986, the five millionth Mini was driven off the production line at Longbridge.

ABOVE Image from a Morris Minor sales catalogue, August 1948.

JACOB JENSEN
BORN 1926

DANISH DESIGNER WHOSE
PIONEERING WORK FOR
BANG & OLUFSEN
REVOLUTIONIZED SOUND
SYSTEMS IN THE 20TH CENTURY

The mid-century period saw many revolutions. One was in sound and vision, which, during the 1960s in particular, changed radically. Up to that point, sound and vision in the home had revolved around televisions, radios and gramophones that often resembled cumbersome pieces of furniture and felt archaic, despite their 20th-century technology.

In the 1960s, developments in electronics meant that designers such as Jacob Jensen and DIETER RAMS could reinvent equipment on modernist principles – reducing a radio or record player down to a compact and functional product that was also aesthetically pleasing and desirable. In many respects, the sound and vision revolution represented one of the most all-encompassing and pervasive processes of reinvention within any field of 20th-century design.

Although the author of a wide range of products, Jensen is intimately associated with the Danish company Bang & Olufsen*. From the 1950s onwards the firm embraced new electronics, miniaturization and alliances with progressive designers. Jensen developed a series of products for the company from the mid-1960s through to the 1990s and is widely credited with developing the distinctive B&O aesthetic that is still a key part of the brand identity today. Products include the Beovox 2500 speaker of 1967 – an abstract sculpture that also produced high-quality sound – and the Beolit 400 portable radio of 1971, manufactured in a range of coloured speaker fascias and a world away from the antiquated 'Listen with Mother' radios of the 1950s.

The BeoMaster 1200 tuner/amplifier of 1969 began to develop the idea of an electronic countertop – a sleek, futuristic piece of equipment with a Space Age quality. In place of all the traditional radio dials, the BeoMaster introduced a flush desktop design with a sliding scale tuner and a set of 'easy touch' buttons sitting neatly within the metallic surface of the box-like equipment, its labelling in a crisp Helvetica typeface. The Beogram 4000 record player embraced the same approach, with a crisp metallic plane forming a single surface encased by a sleek translucent protective cover. Jensen continued to develop the B&O range in the following years with other landmark designs such as the BeoMaster 1900 radio receiver of 1976.

Jensen was born in Copenhagen and worked at his father's upholstery workshop before studying at the Copenhagen School of Arts & Crafts (one of his contemporaries was POUL KJÆRHOLM; see under 'Furniture'). After graduating in 1952, Jensen joined the Bjørn & Bernadotte design studio, working alongside Sigvard Bernadotte – the son of the Swedish monarch – until the late 1950s. Here he designed the Margrethe mixing bowl, which is still produced today.

In 1959, Jensen moved to America and began working in the office of RAYMOND LOEWY in New York, followed by a period in Chicago as a partner with Latham, Tyler & Jensen. In the early 1960s he returned to Copenhagen and founded his own design studio. His relationship with B&O began in 1964. Other projects included telephones for Alcatel and wristwatches for Georg Jensen*. In 1990 leadership of the studio passed to Jensen's son, Timothy. The studio remains active, continuing to develop new products.

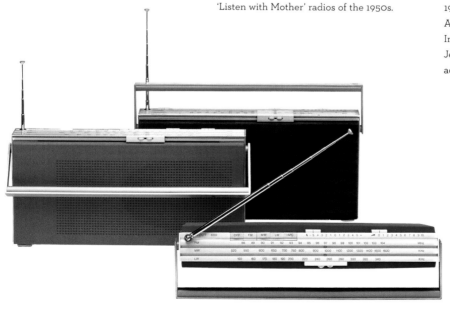

LEFT Beolit 400-600
portable FM radios, first
launched by Bang & Olufsen
in 1971.

OPPOSITE Beovox 2500
'Cube' speakers, produced
by Bang & Olufsen from
1967 to 1972.

RIGHT AND BELOW
Beosystem 1200 (BeoGram
1200 record deck, BeoCord
1200 reel-to-reel tape deck
and BeoMaster 1200 tuner/
amplifier), launched in 1969
by Bang & Olufsen.

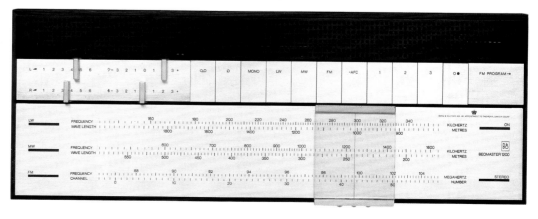

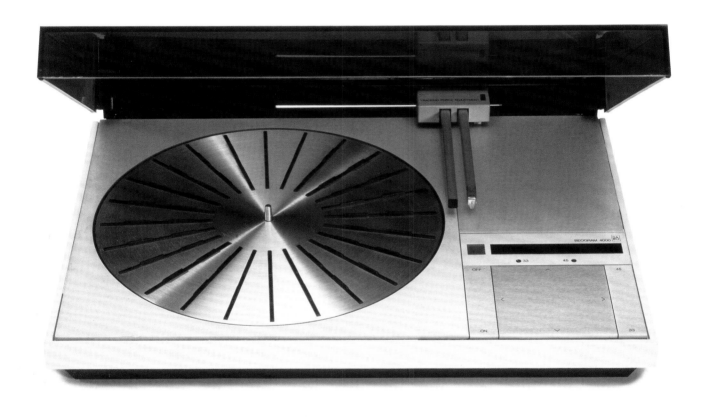

ABOVE Beogram 4000 record
player, launched in 1972 by
Bang & Olufsen.

RAYMOND LOEWY
1893–1986

GROUNDBREAKING INDUSTRIAL
DESIGNER WHO 'STREAMLINED'
AMERICA, MAKING AN
IMPACT WITH A HUGE RANGE
OF CONSUMER GOODS

From Studebakers to space stations, from refrigerators to railway trains, and from cameras to cigarette packets, Raymond Loewy changed the look of America. No other industrial designer of the 20th century exhibited the range, dexterity or imagination of Loewy, who helped pioneer the concept of 'streamlining' and applied it to a wide range of consumer products.

He lived by the maxim of 'most advanced, yet acceptable', recognizing the need to push the boundaries of design while avoiding the danger of alienating consumers. For Loewy the idea that 'form follows function' was not enough, as it failed to encapsulate the truism that if consumers have a choice between similar products in terms of 'price, function and quality, the better looking will outsell the other'.

As a designer, Loewy stressed the importance of outward appearance – whether of a car or a pencil sharpener. But he was never simply a stylist, and he railed at the superfluous 'tinsel and trash' that crept into 20th-century design. With his work in the car industry, in particular, streamlining was not simply an aesthetic exercise but was allied to aerodynamics, fuel economy and efficiency.

Born in Paris, Loewy studied engineering at the city's École de Lanneau and served in the French army during World War I. In 1919 he travelled to America, where he took up work as a store window dresser and fashion illustrator. But he was ambitious to do more and set up his own design practice in New York in 1929.

Early successes included the redesign of a duplicating machine for Sigmund Gestetner and the Coldspot refrigerator for Sears Roebuck. Both combined a strong visual appeal with practicality and ease of production. Within just a few years, Loewy was receiving major commissions and his team was expanding rapidly. There was a series of railroad successes, including the GG-1 electric train of 1936, with streamlined, bullet-nosed locomotives that looked as though they had swept in from the future itself.

Around the same time Loewy began a long relationship with Studebaker that produced some of the most influential car designs of the mid-century period. During World War II, Studebaker diverted production into making military trucks but by 1947 the company was actively producing and promoting Loewy's designs. These included the Starliner of 1953, with a sleek form and a distinctive rounded nose that drew inspiration from airplane design. Often described as the first American sports car, it was glamorous and youthful, fresh and fun, and a world away from the vast

RIGHT A 1953 Studebaker
Commander V-8 Starliner
hard-top convertible in front
of the Eiffel Tower, Paris.

fin-tailed machines being produced by
Studebaker's competitors. In 1962 came the
Avanti – another car that felt ahead of its time,
with a strong European influence.

    During the 1940s and '50s Loewy and his
office applied themselves to a wide range of
commissions, such as the redesign of the iconic
Lucky Strike cigarette packet and work for
Coca-Cola, including bottle design and
dispensing machines. There were boats and
tractors, and a collaboration with ANDREW
GELLER (see under 'Houses and Interiors') on
the design of Leisurama vacation homes on
Long Island. There was also the design of the
Greyhound Scenicruiser bus – one of the great
emblems of dynamic mid-century America.

GREYHOUND SCENICRUISER.

Introducing a great New Era in highway travel!

ABOVE A publicity brochure for the Greyhound Scenicruiser bus, 1954.

By the 1960s, Loewy was also increasingly involved in corporate identity projects. He created logos for Exxon and Shell, as well as the famous eagle logo of 1970 for the United States Postal Service. In addition, he designed the livery for Air Force One in the early 1960s and the racing stripe logo and livery for the United States Coast Guard.

Loewy achieved the aim of designing for the masses with a philosophy of 'beauty through function and simplification'. He appeared on the cover of *Time* magazine in 1949 and his fame continued to grow, with satellite Loewy offices opening in Europe and other parts of the world.

In the 1970s, with the American office increasingly focused on store design, Loewy

began spending more time in Europe. Another key project of the late 1960s and early 1970s was a NASA commission for concept work on the interiors of the new Skylab space station. Loewy died in Monte Carlo in 1986.

His legacy was profound. He had played a highly significant role in establishing industrial design as a profession in its own right, while emphasizing the importance of functionality on the one hand and aesthetic appeal on the other. It was the success of this progressive balancing act that made Loewy a pioneering figure in the field of design.

When you've been in and had a swim,
A cigarette tastes great.
But Luckies taste the best of all,
So, friend — why hesitate?

(Luckies taste better than any other cigarette!)

Be Happy-
Go Lucky!

LUCKIES TASTE BETTER
THAN ANY OTHER CIGARETTE!

Fine tobacco—and only fine tobacco—can give
you the enjoyment of a better-tasting cigarette.
And L.S./M.F.T.—Lucky Strike *means* fine
tobacco. That's why you'll find that Luckies
taste better than any other cigarette. So,
Be Happy—Go Lucky! Get a carton today.

At Anacostia Station, folks,
There is a favorite brand —
It's Lucky Strike that we all like,
The smoke that sure tastes grand!

(Luckies taste better than any other cigarette!)

A LUCKY STRIKE
FOR ALL AMERICA!
BUY
U.S. DEFENSE
BONDS

LUCKY
STRIKE
"IT'S TOASTED"

CIGARETTES

L.S./M.F.T.

COPR., THE AMERICAN TOBACCO COMPANY

LUCKIES TASTE BETTER THAN ANY OTHER CIGARETTE because...
L.S./M.F.T.-Lucky Strike Means Fine Tobacco

ABOVE An advertisement
for Lucky Strike cigarettes,
USA, 1951.

DAVID MELLOR
1930–2009

BRITISH DESIGNER MOST FAMOUS
FOR HIS CUTLERY, BLENDING
THE BEST OF TRADITIONAL
LOCAL SKILLS WITH THE FINEST
CONTEMPORARY DESIGN

One of the great challenges facing the world of industry in the post-war period was how to remain both competitive and relevant. Traditional industries in Britain and other parts of Europe emerged from a world of wartime manufacturing to face increasingly intense global competition and a demand for products that were both innovative and well made. The only way for companies to survive was through a dual process of constant reinvention and the encouragement of new talent in the fields of design and manufacturing.

In Britain, the story of designer David Mellor and his relationship with his home town of Sheffield – world-famous for its cutlery and steel-making workshops and factories – was emblematic of the way in which a combination of progressive design and traditional skills could not only ensure the survival of old industries but also result in products that could compete with the best in the world.

Mellor was born in Sheffield, where his father worked as a tool-maker for the Sheffield Twist Drill Company. He enrolled in the Junior Art Department of the Sheffield College of Art at the age of 12 and immersed himself in the study of art and craft. In 1946, he visited the 'Britain Can Make It' exhibition at the Victoria & Albert Museum, and his interest in design and modernism was further encouraged by later trips to Italy and Scandinavia.

In 1950, after national service, Mellor took up a place at the Royal College of Art, where he excelled. He wrote a thesis on the evolution of the English cutlery-making industry and designed his first set of cutlery, Pride, in 1953, while still a student. The collection combined a contemporary quality with a timeless elegance and a spirit of sophisticated simplicity – hallmarks of Mellor's work to come. A fellow student, Peter Inchbold, recommended Pride to his family firm in Sheffield, Walker & Hall, which not only put Pride into production but also asked Mellor to be a freelance design consultant.

Mellor returned to the Peak District in 1954, where he continued to base himself for the rest of his life. He set up his own silversmithing workshop and an industrial design office, working across a number of areas of design throughout the 1950s and '60s.

Inspired by street lighting that he had seen on a visit to Rome, he designed his own system using tubular steel. These designs were manufactured in the mid-1950s by Abacus. The company went on to manufacture a bus shelter of Mellor's design in 1959. As many as 100,000 of the shelters were eventually produced.

In the mid-1960s, Mellor was asked to produce a square post box for the Post Office – a design met with some alarm by traditionalist supporters of the classic round post box. In 1966, Mellor also developed a traffic light design for the Ministry of Transport, using new plastics and plastic-coating techniques to provide a system that was durable and would minimize damage and injury in the event of an accident.

At the same time, Mellor was working on cutlery design, and by the early 1970s focusing exclusively on cutlery and kitchen ware. His designs encompassed a wide price range, from silver-plated collections, through a Thrift collection commissioned by the Ministry of Public Works for canteen use (1965), to a set of disposable plastic cutlery for mass production (1969). Mellor became the 'cutlery king'. Throughout, he remained focused on manufacturing in Sheffield and the Peak District, and in 1960 commissioned a house, workshop and studio – partly inspired by the Eames House in California – from architects Gollins Melvin Ward.

OPPOSITE ABOVE Pride (Stainless steel) eight-piece set, 1953.

OPPOSITE BELOW Pride (White) eight-piece set, 1953.

BELOW Pride (White) knife, 1953.

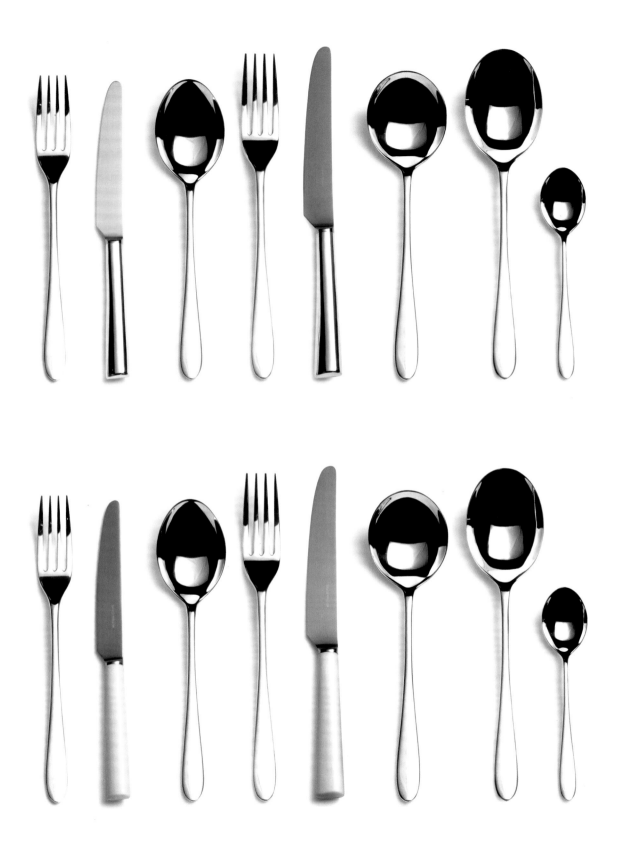

By the late 1960s the famous Sheffield factories, including Walker & Hall, were suffering in the face of international competition and either shutting shop or merging with former rivals. Mellor's work began to encompass design and production, and in 1973 he bought Broom Hall – a large period building – to provide more manufacturing and production space. In 1990, he expanded again and moved to the Round Building in Hathersage – a gasworks building converted by architect Michael Hopkins.

From 1969, Mellor also moved into retail, selling his own work and complementary pieces. He opened his first shop in London, selling kitchen and table ware, followed by two other stores in London and Manchester. Self-produced collections included the Provençal cutlery range of 1973, featuring rosewood or acetal resin handles, and the Chinese Ivory set of 1977. Many other designs followed over the years, with Mellor drawn increasingly to a high-end, design-conscious market.

His work thrived not only on the basis of quality and craftsmanship but also on the inventive modernity of the designs. The company continues on under the creative leadership of Mellor's son, Corin.

OPPOSITE ABOVE
Tubular steel street light,
manufactured by Abacus,
mid-1950s.

OPPOSITE BELOW LEFT
Bus shelter for Abacus, 1959.

OPPOSITE BELOW RIGHT
Post Office box, mid-1960s.

BELOW Chinese Ivory (Green)
set, 1977.

BOTTOM Provençal cutlery,
full set, 1973.

MARCELLO NIZZOLI
1887–1969

A KEY FIGURE IN MID-CENTURY ITALIAN PRODUCT DESIGN, NOTED FOR HIS WORK WITH OLIVETTI

During the 1950s the Italian typewriter and calculator company Olivetti was at the forefront of a progressive revolution by design. The head of the company, Adriano Olivetti, was an enlightened entrepreneur who placed great importance on the value of good design as well as exploring utopian ideals through his management of the company and his interest in community planning. He was a good businessman – organizing his factories with great efficiency and growing the company rapidly in the post-war era – and he also saw the benefits of collaborating with some of the best designers, architects and graphic designers in Italy and beyond as he worked to shape Olivetti's products and its image.

Olivetti, whose father had founded the company near Turin in 1908, declared that 'there is nothing in me but the future' and sought to establish the company as an international brand. He commissioned Carlo Scarpa* to design the showroom in Venice, where Olivetti products were exhibited like sculptures in a gallery. And indeed there was a sculptural and original quality to Olivetti's typewriters of the 1950s, with many of them designed by Marcello Nizzoli, who led the creative direction of the company from the 1940s through to the 1960s.

Born in Boretto, Nizzoli studied art and architecture at the Scuola di Belle Arti in Parma. He exhibited paintings in a Futurist style and created a number of tapestries before establishing his own design office in Milan in 1918. Over the following years there

was a broad range of work, including poster and exhibition design and architectural projects in collaboration with Edoardo Persico and Giuseppe Terragni, as well as a store in Milan for Parker Pens (1934).

The relationship with Olivetti began in the early 1930s, with freelance graphic design commissions, but by the mid-1930s Nizzoli had become Olivetti's chief product designer. One of his most famous designs was the Lettera 22 typewriter of 1950, with its sleek, sculptural case. It made for a robust and portable design with very wide appeal. As with CORRADINO D'ASCANIO's Vespa and RAYMOND LOEWY'S cars, refrigerators and locomotives, the streamlined shell of the product was a carefully styled and seductive envelope that encased the machinery and workings within.

This emphasis on outward appearance and styling helped set Olivetti apart during the mid-century period and provided a model for other design and technology companies that followed, such as Braun* and Apple. Other Nizzoli products for Olivetti included the Lexikon 80 typewriter of 1948 and a number of calculating machines, such as the Divisumma 14 (also 1948).

Nizzoli's role at Olivetti was wide-ranging, including architectural projects, but he did not work exclusively for the company. In 1956, he designed the Mirella sewing machine for Necchi, which remained in production until the 1970s. Here again, the design was streamlined and ergonomic, with most of the working parts tucked away behind a hard-wearing plastic shell, which came in a choice of colours. The machine was electric but had a manual hand-crank option, and was both easy to use and light in weight. As with the Lettera 22 typewriter, portability was a consideration.

Nizzoli also designed petrol pumps for Agip and lighters for Ronson, as well as the 2+7 telephone for Safnat, with a round dial and a neat row of buttons for internal calls that gave it something of a typewriter look.

BELOW 2+7 telephone made using cellulose acetate, rubber, metal and paper, by Safnat, 1958.

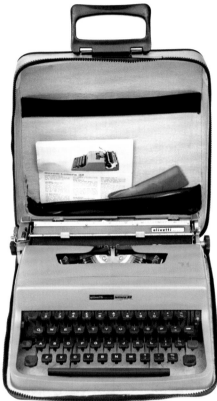

LEFT An advertisement designed by Paul Rand, 1953, for the Olivetti Lettera 22.

BELOW An Olivetti Lettera 32 portable typewriter, 1963.

BOTTOM A Mirella sewing machine, Necchi, 1956.

After Adriano Olivetti's death in 1960, the company remained ambitious and design-focused, later commissioning ETTORE SOTTSASS to design products, including the Valentine typewriter of 1969, and working with architects such as Le Corbusier*, Louis Kahn* and MARCO ZANUSO. The transition to the Computer Age was not smooth, however, despite the fact that the company produced Italy's first electronic computer in 1959. In the late 20th century, in the face of increasing international competition, Olivetti struggled to match the record for innovation established by Adriano Olivetti in the post-war era.

DIETER RAMS
BORN 1932

PRE-EMINENT GERMAN
INDUSTRIAL DESIGNER, WHO,
WORKING WITH BRAUN,
CREATED MANY OF THE MOST
INNOVATIVE PRODUCTS OF
THE 1960S, '70S AND '80S

The powerful and influential career of designer Dieter Rams is intricately interwoven with the success of the German electronics company, Braun*. Rams even met his wife, Ingeborg, at the company, while his self-designed house at Kronberg was built on land originally acquired by Braun for its workers (the lower level held a small design studio, where Rams developed a number of Braun products in secret). Millions of consumers were touched by these products – whether radios, hi-fis, coffee grinders or hair dryers – usually without having any idea who the author might be.

Rams's work for the company was governed by a particular set of tenets, which he carefully articulated and copyrighted. His ten principles of good design were that it should be innovative, aesthetic, unobtrusive, honest, long-lasting, thorough and environmentally friendly, and it should make a product comprehensible and useful, while involving as little 'design' as possible.

Rams is associated not only with the rebirth of German design in the post-war era, but also with the reassertion or reinterpretation of certain Bauhaus* and modernist ideals,

updated and adapted for the mid-century world. While LUDWIG MIES VAN DER ROHE (see under 'Houses and Interiors') declared that 'less is more', Rams argued that 'less is better'. 'My aim,' he said, 'is to omit everything superfluous so that the essential is shown to the best possible advantage.'[23]

Rams was born in Wiesbaden, Germany. He studied architecture at the local art and design school but also served a three-year apprenticeship as a carpenter. He worked in Otto Apel's architecture practice in Frankfurt in the early 1950s, then joined Braun, initially as an architect and interior designer, in 1955.

Braun had always been a pioneering company. It was, for instance, one of the first to produce a combined record player and radio in the early 1930s, and it manufactured the first electric shaver in 1950. After the founder Max Braun's death in 1951, his sons Artur and Erwin were intent on nurturing and enhancing the company's reputation for innovation and placing design excellence at the forefront of their research and development programme.

In 1954, just before Rams arrived, Braun began working with tutors from the

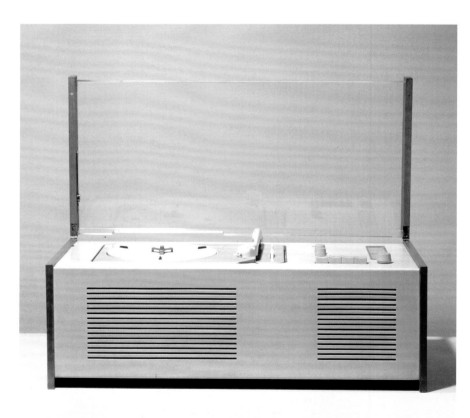

RIGHT A Braun PhonoSuper
SK4 record player and radio,
designed by Dieter Rams and
Hans Gugelot, plastic and
maple, 1956.

Hochschule für Gestaltung in Ulm*. Hans Gugelot* had already begun working on radio designs for Braun, but in 1956 he and Rams developed a combined radio and record player. The SK4 was a crisp, grey box, bookended by timber side panels and protected by a fold-down acrylic lid. Competitors and critics called it 'Snow White's Coffin', but it was wildly successful and marked a great shift away from the cumbersome radio and phonograph 'furniture' of the past and towards appliances that were compact, geometric and functional. The modern grey fascia, minimal but simple controls, and use of clear, concise typography set a pattern for future Braun products, and the transparent lid became a staple of modern hi-fi equipment. It was the first of hundreds of products that Rams developed for Braun.

Over the coming years the company established a clear and unique aesthetic language for its products, much in the same way that JACOB JENSEN did at Bang & Olufsen* some years later. Rams, driven by his design principles, aimed for a timeless approach and was critical of anything that might be led by fashion, or that involved

superfluous styling or built-in obsolescence. He noted: 'We make every effort to impart a simple, clear and balanced beauty to Braun products, so that they will retain fascination and appeal for years to come. For us, the aesthetic quality of a product is ultimately a part of its utility.'[24]

In the mid-century period Rams was also able to take advantage of technical advances in transistors which made miniaturization possible. Key products included a number of pioneering portable devices, including the truly revolutionary TP1 and TP2 compact, hand-held, combined radio/record players of 1959 and c. 1961, capable of playing small records and direct forerunners of the Sony* Walkman and the Apple iPod.

The Rams/Braun approach was applied to a wide range of products, including televisions, calculators and kitchen equipment. Rams was at the forefront of the evolution of modular hi-fi systems and sound and vision equipment – such as the TS45/TG60/L450 speaker/recorder/radio-amplifier combination of the early 1960s, which could be set on a table-top or mounted on a wall.

Modularity was a key concept of the mid-century period, applied not just to audio equipment but also to furniture and shelving. In 1960 Rams developed his 606 Universal Shelving for Vitsœ – a highly flexible and innovative storage and display system. Two years later he designed his 620 seating for Vitsœ, with leather upholstery sitting upon a fibreglass base. Again, the range was designed with modularity in mind and could be used in various combinations.

Over a long and highly productive career Rams established himself as a figurehead of German invention and creativity, and his articulate design philosophy continues to inspire younger generations of designers.

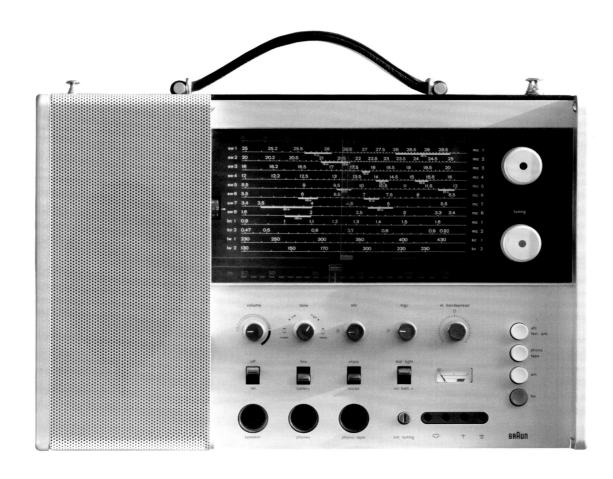

ABOVE Braun Station T1000
CD World Receiver radio, 1965.

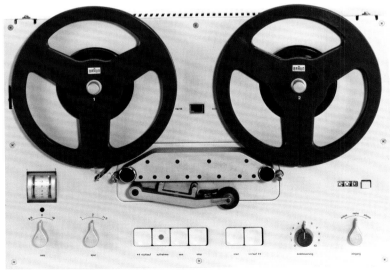

ABOVE 606 Universal
Shelving for Vitsœ, 1960.

LEFT Braun TG60 tape
recorder, 1965.

RICHARD SAPPER
BORN 1932
& MARCO ZANUSO
1916–2001

CREATIVE PARTNERSHIP WHOSE
REVOLUTIONARY DESIGNS
FOR DOMESTIC EQUIPMENT
REINVIGORATED ITALIAN
POST-WAR DESIGN

In the 1960s, from their base in Milan, the German product designer Richard Sapper and the Italian architect and innovator Marco Zanuso forged a highly creative working partnership. Together, they changed the face of both television and the telephone, as well as bringing new energy and excitement to Italian design and helping to progress the fortunes of Italian manufacturers.

Sapper and Zanuso's new-generation televisions for Brionvega* spoke of the future rather than resembling antiquated pieces of domestic furniture. The same could be said of their Grillo telephone for Siemens, which used a plastic clam-shell form to hold a revolutionary design that shifted the direction and aesthetic of the telephone, leaving the traditional cradle and handset far behind.

Richard Sapper was born in Munich and studied engineering and economics at the city's university. He worked with Mercedes-Benz in Stuttgart before deciding to move to Milan. There he worked in the studio of GIO PONTI (see under 'Furniture') before, in 1957, forming a partnership with Marco Zanuso.

Zanuso had trained as an architect at the Politecnico di Milano and established his own studio in Milan in 1945, combining architectural commissions with product and furniture design, as well as editing *Domus* and *Casabella* magazines during the late 1940s. He began exploring the possibilities offered by plastics in the early 1950s and – after joining forces with Sapper – created the steel-cast Lambda chair for Gavina/Knoll*, followed by a stacking plastic chair for children, produced by Kartell* from 1964 through to the late 1970s.

But it was their work in product design for which they became best known. Brionvega had only just expanded into manufacturing televisions when Sapper and Zanuso designed the Doney 14 (1962), which offered a design that was portable and playful within a compact format made possible by new space-saving transistor technology. The Doney was like an open eye, with a sinuous, sleek casing wrapped around a cathode ray tube, sitting on a pair of slim tubular steel supports. This was a stylish equivalent of Sony's* first portable televisions, developed a few years earlier, but much more endearing and available in black, white, orange or a translucent acrylic.

The Doney was followed by the Algol television of 1964, with its angled screen projecting outwards from a modest rectangular body. The Black ST 201 television of 1969 took the product into a new realm of abstraction: a black box with a screen forming one face of the cube and the rest of the body made in a semi-transparent acrylic. This was a television for the Space Age and a precursor of the slick, black devices that now dominate the medium.

Sapper and Zanuso also designed the innovative TS 502 portable radio for Brionvega – a rounded rectangle that split in half and

BELOW Algol television sets of 1964 for Brionvega.

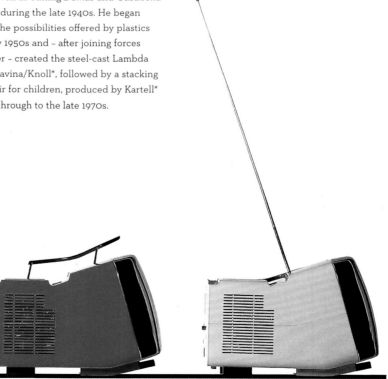

LEFT AND BELOW The TS 522
relaunch (2010) of the original
TS 502 portable radio of 1964
for Brionvega.

BOTTOM Grillo phone, 1966,
for Siemens.

opened out on hinges to reveal a speaker cube
on one side and receiver on the other. The most
popular colour choice was a vivid blood red.

The Grillo telephone embodied another
radical break from established forms and
common perceptions of what a phone should
look like. This compact product was a fraction
of the size of conventional telephones and
was engaging, functional and fresh. In its
resting position it was an abstract form, rather
like a computer mouse. Pick it up and the
mouthpiece flips out while opening the line,
the number dial being neatly contained in
the space between the ear and mouth pieces.
This flip-out innovation shaped the evolution
of a certain type of mobile phone. The ring
tone lent the product its name: Grillo, or 'cricket'.

Zanuso continued working as an
architect, designing production plants for
Olivetti and IBM, as well as creating furniture
for Zanotta* and others. Sapper went on to
design the iconic Tizio desk lamp for Artemide*
(1972), as well as designing for Alessi*, Knoll
and others. A number of Sapper-Zanuso pieces
for Brionvega were updated and reissued at
the start of the 21st century.

ETTORE SOTTSASS
1917–2007

AVANT-GARDE AND MULTI-
DISCIPLINARY DESIGNER,
NOTED FOR HIS COLOURFUL
AND PROVOCATIVE AESTHETIC
APPROACH

The Italian designer Ettore Sottsass was a master of many mediums: architecture, ceramics, glassware and, of course, product design. But more than this, he was one of the great design thinkers; an *agent provocateur*, who encouraged people to question what architecture and design were all about and what kind of form they might take. For him, design was never simply a matter of function. Like many of his contemporaries, he saw that design should also be 'sensual and exciting', generating an emotional response as well as a grateful acceptance of a product's purpose.

Often at the forefront of new innovations and directions in design, Sottsass gave shape to one of the first mainframe computers in the late 1950s, and in the early 1980s became a founding father of postmodern design, co-founding the Memphis collective, which helped shape an original and provocative aesthetic approach that borrowed from all corners of design history yet produced something fresh and iconoclastic. Between the two periods lay a lifetime's work across many fields of design.

Sottsass was born in Innsbruck, Austria, to an Italian father, in 1917. The family moved to Italy, where Sottsass – like so many Italian

designers – studied architecture. He graduated from the Politecnico di Torino just before the start of World War II. He served in the Italian army and spent part of the war in a concentration camp in Sarajevo. Afterwards, he established his own design and architectural office in Milan.

In 1956, he travelled to New York and worked briefly with GEORGE NELSON (see under 'Furniture'). America gave Sottsass a fresh perspective and a more international outlook, which he applied to his work when he returned to Milan. Back in Italy, he took on a number of roles, including artistic director for Poltronova*, for whom he produced furniture and lighting. In 1958, he also began working as a design consultant for Olivetti, building upon the design legacy established by Adriano Olivetti and MARCELLO NIZZOLI.

At Olivetti, Sottsass helped to design Italy's first mainframe computer – the Elea 9003 – in the form of a series of almost architectural modules, like a city in miniature. He also created typewriters, such as the bright red Valentine – released on Valentine's Day, 1970 – accompanied by advertising images showing models happily typing away at the beach or café. The Valentine was a Pop product – glossy, loud and enticing – but at the same time it was practical, compact and portable. The notion of the 'sophisticated toy' – a colourful, vibrant and entertaining work of consumer-oriented design – was soon embraced by other electronics and consumer product companies. Other Olivetti designs included the Logos 27 calculator of 1963 and the Praxis 48 typewriter of 1968.

LEFT A Summa calculator
for Olivetti, c. 1965.

RIGHT Valentine typewriter bas relief, for use in advertising, produced by Olivetti, 1969.

BELOW Valentine typewriter in plastic and enamelled metal, manufactured by Olivetti, 1969.

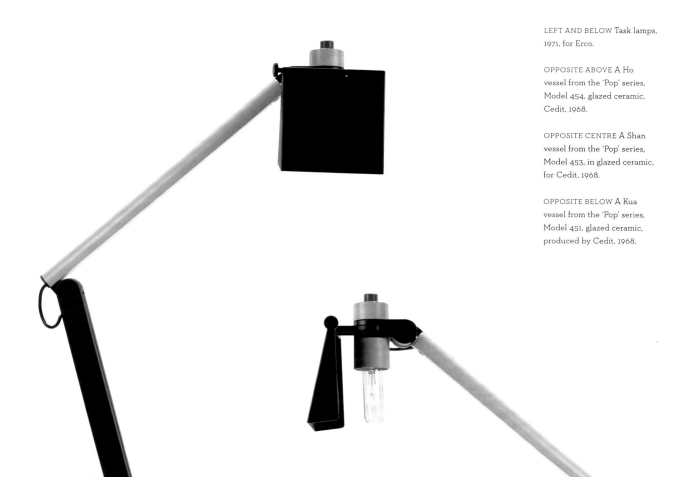

LEFT AND BELOW Task lamps, 1971, for Erco.

OPPOSITE ABOVE A Ho vessel from the 'Pop' series, Model 454, glazed ceramic, Cedit, 1968.

OPPOSITE CENTRE A Shan vessel from the 'Pop' series, Model 453, in glazed ceramic, for Cedit, 1968.

OPPOSITE BELOW A Kua vessel from the 'Pop' series, Model 451, glazed ceramic, produced by Cedit, 1968.

In the late 1960s, Sottsass began experimenting with ceramic and glass 'totems' for Bitossi, Vistosi, Venini and others. These were multi-layered, abstract pieces – in a totem pole configuration – with a highly sculptural quality, as Sottsass began veering away from function and towards more expressive, artistic forms. Other vase collections for Bitossi and Edizioni Arte Design had a more architectural quality, taking the form of abstract towers and geometric motifs. Key Sottsass lighting designs of the mid-century period included the task lamp of 1971 for Erco and the Asteroide lamp of 1968 for Poltronova (see p. 131). Sottsass was also a leading designer for Alessi*.

He was involved with Memphis from 1980 to 1985 – a short but highly influential period. Key pieces from this time include the Carlton bookcase of 1981: a colourful, multi-layered design that was an evolution of the totems he had been exploring in ceramics and glass. As an architect, he also remained active and produced many projects with Sottsass Associati, including private residences around the world and substantial commissions such as Malpensa airport in Milan (2000). Along the way, Sottsass co-founded a literary journal with Allen Ginsberg and established a design school. Always a leader, he set the direction of the times.

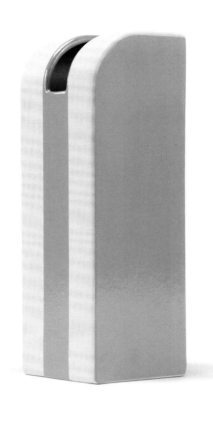

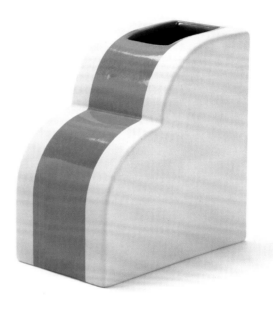

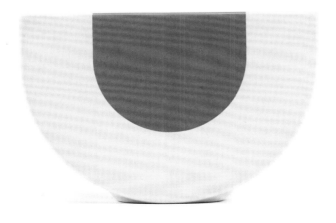

GRAPHICS AND POSTERS

IN THE INCREASINGLY COMPLEX 'GLOBAL VILLAGE', MADE POSSIBLE BY FAST-EVOLVING TRANSPORT AND COMMUNICATIONS SYSTEMS, GRAPHIC DESIGN FLOURISHED

The post-war world was an increasingly complicated place in which to live. The planet was in motion as never before, with super-cities growing at an extraordinary rate, served by multi-layered public transit systems, while the highways filled with commuters sitting in cars made more available through mass production and cheaper sale prices. Businessmen and entrepreneurs took their companies and corporations onto a national and then international level, helped by the growing sophistication of communications systems and the new era of jet travel, which also encouraged an explosion of cross-border tourism. This was the birth of the global village, but living within that village was anything but simple.

Metro systems, roadways, airports, stations, schools, sports stadiums and hospitals grew in scale and ambition, with labyrinthine networks and arteries. Something was needed to bring order and logic to this post-war complexity, and this offered a key challenge to the new and fast-evolving profession of graphic design. In the 1950s and '60s, a relatively disparate group of commercial artists and typographical innovators coalesced into graphic design studios, encouraged by the example of PAUL RAND and others, who established a philosophical clarity around their work as well as a professional framework.

This ordered foundation was echoed by a thoughtful logicality developing within both typography and graphic layouts. The model was the Swiss Style*, championed by MAX BILL, ADRIAN FRUTIGER, Jan Tschichold, Josef Müller-Brockmann* and others. The Swiss typefaces – such as Frutiger's Univers and MAX MIEDINGER's Helvetica – were crisp sans serif fonts, infused with a progressive character. Max Bill and OTL AICHER's highly influential school – the Hochschule für Gestaltung, Ulm* – promoted a design philosophy grounded in the Swiss Style, using precise working grids to give greater structure to both type and images, while advocating geometric forms and a minimalist, less-is-more approach.

The Swiss Style was adopted and adapted across the Atlantic in America, where it was more commonly known as the International Typographic Style. Designers such as HERBERT MATTER and Massimo Vignelli* themselves crossed the Atlantic and began to work in New York, reinforcing the growing prevalence of the style in their own individual ways.

The Swiss and International Styles – founded upon much the same principles – spoke of modernism and modernity, feeding into the growing desire to 'make it new'. But they were also perfectly suited to the crucial challenge of bringing order, clarity and logic to the ports, stations and temples of the global village. The new sans serif fonts were accessible and easily legible, even at speed, leading to their adoption for highway, metro and airport signage from the early 1960s onwards. In Britain, JOCK KINNEIR & MARGARET CALVERT developed their own Transport sans serif typeface – based on Swiss Style fonts – and used it for signage across the growing road and motorway network. They also developed a new set of graphic pictograms that helped warn drivers of possible hazards. Otl Aicher, some years later, developed his own set of pictograms to help athletes and visitors from countless countries navigate their way around the 1972 Munich Olympics.

Increasingly, graphic design was used as a marketing and communication tool that could cross borders, cultures and language barriers. Travel posters were a key medium of the period explored by ABRAM GAMES, Herbert Matter and others, and airlines and countless other corporations that began to spread their wings both nationally and internationally had to think of marketing and promoting themselves on a scale that was almost unprecedented in the private sector.

Corporate branding programmes had to consider how a particular graphic look and logo might be perceived in New York, Paris and Tokyo. Trademarks became more important than ever, establishing clear graphic symbols that would be instantly recognizable, while

OPPOSITE Football pictogram devised by Otl Aicher for the 1972 Munich Olympics.

crossing language barriers and conveying the essential characteristics of a company. 'If in the business of communications, image is king, the essence of this image, the logo, is the jewel in the crown,' wrote Paul Rand,[1] a key practitioner in the art of modern logo design.

Rand's work for companies such as IBM progressed the concept of brand identity with the creation of a cohesive and comprehensive rule and style book for the company in question that could be applied to marketing, promotions and packaging around the world and across every aspect of the business. Such an approach became an essential part of corporate culture, particularly for multinationals, in the mid-century period, and became increasingly important in subsequent decades.

This was part of a larger process of 'making it new' that involved a sweeping away of any branding and packaging that seemed outdated or out of step with the post-war world. Archaic typefaces were phased out, overly ornamental flourishes were abandoned and cohesion ruled. But that is not to say that the nascent profession of graphic design did not allow for colour, fun or wit. The work of Rand, Matter, CHARLEY HARPER, Raymond Savignac* and others is rich in all three, but sits within a carefully ordered and directed design methodology. Matter's work for Knoll*, for instance, uses humour, surrealism, juxtapositions of scale and other devices to promote the company's furniture, but his images sit within a corporate line and a neatly functional graphic and typographic approach.

A playful quality and an adventurous usage of colour and illustration are defining characteristics of so much mid-century graphic design, drawing inspiration from artistic movements ranging from Surrealism and Russian Constructivism to Op Art and Pop Art. The relationship between commercial art and fine art was notoriously blurred during the period, with artists such as Charley Harper and Peter Blake crossing between the two worlds. Even designers such as WIM CROUWEL, who is regarded as one of the most functional and formal of mid-century pioneers, experimented with vibrant colour choices and contrasts within his many exhibition poster designs which had both a great sense of artistry and touches of Abstract Expressionist inspiration.

Many design studios and designers – from Paul Rand to ALAN FLETCHER – managed to serve multiple markets at the same time, whether creating logos for global corporations, or consumer packaging, or book jackets for novels and monographs. During the 1950s and

> CLARITY, LOGIC AND COHESION BECAME ALL-IMPORTANT, ALTHOUGH GRAPHIC DESIGN IN THE MID-CENTURY PERIOD ALSO ACHIEVED A PEAK OF EXUBERANCE AND VIBRANCY

RIGHT 1950s billboard over a parking lot, equating Chevron Skypower gasoline to jet power.

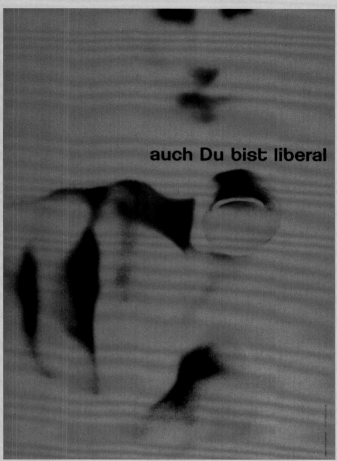

auch Du bist liberal

'60s book cover design established itself as one of the most exciting mediums to be working in, offering a degree of creative latitude that could seldom be found in corporate work. Album cover design also became a new frontier by the 1960s, with record sleeves becoming a powerful mode of expression.

During the 1960s, of course, a counter-culture also established itself and sought its own identity while setting itself apart from mainstream culture. This meant finding a new aesthetic that offered a vibrant alternative to the International Style and could be applied to mediums such as concert ads. Victor Moscoso in California was one of the best-known exponents of a psychedelic style that spliced organic Art Nouveau imagery, Op Art visual kinetics and drug culture surrealism. Protest posters and kitchen-table magazines of the period often had a hand-made/basement-printed feel, which stood in opposition to the increasingly sophisticated marketing and promotional approach being fed to consumers.

Yet even within mid-century mainstream advertising there is a great sense of energy and experimentalism. Designers were playing with many different tools and techniques, from photomontage to collage, as well as theatrical shifts of scale and perspective. There was something of a gold rush feel to the period, particularly in the 1950s, that gave the graphic design industry and advertising a sense of momentum and dynamism. Importantly, there were also receptive consumers with money in their pockets who were waiting to be seduced. Today we are more jaded, more cynical and over-exposed to ever-present sales tactics, yet even so – looking back – so much of the imagery and techniques of the 1950s and '60s still has the power somehow to mesmerize and entice.

MID-CENTURY CONFLUENCES:
TYPE, DESIGN AND TECHNOLOGY
STEVEN HELLER

The 1950s and '60s were incredible periods for technology, art and design, the confluence of which was the nexus of graphic design in industrial countries throughout the world. The focus of this essay is on the US as the wellspring and recipient of many developments.

The profound influence of Europeans and European émigrés (Herbert Bayer, László Moholy-Nagy, Ladislav Sutnar, György Kepes, HERBERT MATTER, Leo Lionni and Will Burtin) and the American moderns who established themselves in the very late 1930s and early 1940s (PAUL RAND, Lester Beall, Bradbury Thompson*, William Golden, Alvin Lustig* and Cipe Pineles), some of whom were still active during the 1950s and '60s, contributed directly and indirectly to three paramount American design methods of the period: rational (or modern), eclectic (or historical), and anarchic (or underground).

Under each of the above rubric, however, are disparate subsets, as well as individual designers who cannot be conveniently pigeonholed. For example, under Rational/Modern are the 'strict formalists', representing the International School and including John Massey, Rudolph de Harak and Massimo Vignelli*, who practised objectified, systematic design. There are also the 'exuberant moderns', such as SAUL BASS, Lou Dorfsman, George Lois, Gene Federico and Herb Lubalin, who were known for making visual ideas come alive through type. The 'eclectic moderns', on the other hand, such as Robert Brownjohn, Ivan Chermayeff & Thomas Geismar, Tony Palladino, James Miho and Bob Gill, routinely broke the rules and veered away from the dominant styles. The 'crypto moderns', such as the corporate identity firms of Walter Landor and Lippincott & Margulies, made generalized identity systems using ambient forms. Then, straddling the fence between Modern and Eclectic, were the 'magazine moderns', such as Alexey Brodovitch, Henry Wolf, Alan Hurlburt, Peter Palazzo, Marvin Israel, Bea Feitler and Ruth Ansel, who used rationally designed formats as a means to present a wide variety of subjects with exuberance.

Under the Eclectic banner the subcategories run the gamut from historically revivalist to idiosyncratically playful. Push Pin Studios was the most devoutly eclectic (and most profoundly influential), having revived the denigrated styles of Victorian, Art Nouveau and Art Deco, and reintroduced narrative illustration to the design equation. Tom Daly and Peter Max (Daly & Max) and Phil Gips (Gips & Danne) did likewise through their use of stylized illustration and rare woodtypes. Quite a few art directors and designers also fit into this general category, among them Bob Cato and John Berg, whose CBS album cover designs were archetypes of the genre; Neil Fujita and Robert Scudellari, who did book jackets that knew no stylistic constraints; Otto Storch, whose format for *McCalls* magazine was alternately the paradigm of the new ornamentation and a paean to functionalism; Art Paul, whose approach to *Playboy* magazine was to invest in conceptual art; Arnold Varga, whose advertisements for Joseph Horne Co. updated the passé art of decoupage; and Ed Benguiat, who injected a 19th-century spirit into 20th-century typography.

To further confuse matters of categorization some of the Modern pioneers became Eclectic when it suited them. Despite Herbert Bayer's excoriation of Victorian ornamental

typefaces in advertising as 'bad taste under the disguise of functionalism *par excellence*', he designed posters for Aspen, Colorado, using ornamental typography combined with modernistic collage; Bradbury Thompson routinely used 18th-century engravings from Diderot as a foil for his modern typography; and Herb Lubalin, the master of talking-type, also did his share of Victorian layouts ... when, of course, the subject called for it.

Patterns resulting in these aesthetics developed along generational lines. Many of the graphic designers who began working before World War II were Depression-era children from immigrant or poor families, introduced to commercial art in high school and engaged as an alternative to mundane labour. One influential teacher, Leon Friend, head of the graphics department at Brooklyn's Abraham Lincoln High School, exposed his students (Gene Federico, Alex Steinweiss and Seymour Chwast) to the great European graphic designers and taught them to emulate the masters' creative approaches. Modern design symbolized a break from the previous generation's Old World ties. Teachers such as Howard Trafton at the Art Students League, and Herschel Levitt and Tom Benrimo at Pratt Institute in New York, further opened doors to the expressive realms of graphic design.

After World War II, new design schools attracted European émigré faculty members. Programmes such as those at Yale University in New Haven, MIT in Cambridge and the Art Institute of Chicago offered a neo-Bauhaus approach. The Chouinard Art Institute in Los Angeles and the School of Visual Arts, Parsons School of Design and Cooper Union in New York graduated some of the decade's leading Moderns and Eclectics.

Graphic design was at first a dialectic: the proponents of Modern versus advocates of Eclectic form. As the root of post-war American design, European modernism attracted those interested in more than just mechanical commercial art. As a teenager in the 1930s Paul Rand was introduced to the Bauhaus* and speaks for many of his contemporaries about its influence: 'I was intrigued with that kind of work which focused on ideas and not banalities; which stressed painting, architecture, typography and showed how they interrelated.'[2] He and others took design out of the print shop and forged a real profession.

Belief in 'the rightness of form' was key to the mid-century modern design revolution, but not at the expense of wit or humour. The Moderns practised economy, promoted the virtues of white space and imbued their work with measured expression. Yet some rejected expressionist approaches, favouring a systematic Swiss method of visual organization being applied to corporate communications, product design and exhibition design, where order was imperative. But an increase in making posters, record covers and book jackets demanded a wide range of design and typographic methods.

Typefaces and typography are never created in a vacuum. Practical and commercial motivations prevail, but theoretical and artistic rationales are never entirely in the shadows. Type design and typographical applications are routinely informed by the designers' conscious concerns and unconscious impulses, which inevitably change with time. When examining the principal typefaces and dominant styles of the 1950s and '60s the entire continuum of type comes into play, yet the periods that are bundled together have certain distinct characteristics, too.

The Moderns, those who more or less followed the lead of the Bauhaus and the so-called New Typography, preferred sans serif faces, especially Akzidenz Grotesk, to express messages with clarity, simplicity and ideological – typographically, that is – purity. Reduction of visual noise in everything from advertisements to book design was the stated goal, and the Modern mission was as aggressively practised as the Swiss/International Style. But it didn't reach its critical mass until the introduction of one particular typeface named after the famously neutral nation.

Arguably the most indelible typographic mark of the period was Helvetica (aka Swiss), designed in 1957 by MAX MIEDINGER. Some adored the new typeface, others hated it, often for the same reason – its cool neutrality. A response to the unsatisfactory optical imperfections found in earlier grotesks, it represented both a clear Platonic ideal and a turgid, generic sterility. 'Conceived in the Swiss typographic idiom, the new Helvetica offers an excitingly different tool to the American graphic designer and typographer,' read the promotional text in a D. Stempel AG Typefoundry specimen sheet (c. 1958). 'Here is not simply another sans serif type but a carefully and judiciously considered refinement of the grotesk letter form.'

Readable, versatile and modest, Helvetica embodied the democratization of visual communication, and was more successful at this than Futura (the fabled 'type of tomorrow'). Following its introduction first in Europe and then the United States, Helvetica emerged as the typeface of choice for business throughout the multinational world. When the Soviet Union Ministry of Commerce needed to put a Western gloss on its 'for export only' publications and advertisements, Helvetica was used. When the New York City Department of Sanitation wanted to clean up its typographic image, it specified Helvetica for its trucks. When the Urban League, America's foremost inner-city civil rights advocacy group, wanted to appeal to white middle-class donors, Helvetica came to the fore. Conversely, even though Helvetica broke down national borders and exuded a democratic air, it was also of course used to obfuscate corrupt corporate messages. Such is neutrality's double-edged sword.

The new typeface was perfectly consistent with the new needs of corporate identity. Rather than local business, global influence was now the key to economic stability. One

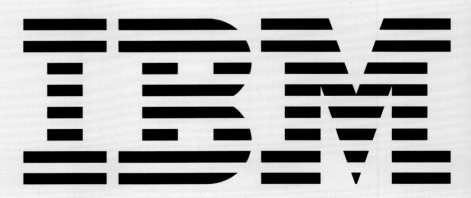

End Bad Breath.

ABOVE A poster design
by Seymour Chwast, 1967.

of the prime movers in realizing the value of design – graphic and industrial – to the new business environment was IBM. Its chief during the 1950s, Thomas Watson, famously announced, 'Good design is good business.' IBM was not the only design-savvy corporation, but when it hired Eliot Noyes* as its design consultant and he, in turn, recruited Paul Rand to revamp the company's graphics, American corporate identity was truly born.

IBM's first logo (with contoured lettering in the shape of a globe) was designed in 1924, when 'high-tech' business machines came with Queen Anne legs and mahogany cabinetry. So it is not so ironic that a typeface derived from 19th-century slab serifs came to symbolize the Computer Age. After all, the future was scary. In fact, in the 1930s, when the logo was redesigned using Beton, visions of the future were actually amalgams of the old and slightly newer. IBM did not embrace modernism until the early 1950s, when Noyes replaced Queen Anne with progressive product and industrial design. In 1956, Rand redesigned the logo using a Constructivist-inspired slab serif called City, designed in 1930 by Georg Trump, because he felt it was important to retain something of IBM's earlier Beton identity. In 1962, when Rand added emblematic stripes, the old font was transformed into a typeface that symbolized a company with its eye on the future, slab serifs and all. The stripes were not simply a mnemonic: they implied that a logo was more than a mash-up of stylized letters or word and image – a logo was a symbolic entity that embodied a corporate legacy and reputation. And the 1950s and '60s was the era of these new communicative entities.

Needless to say, for every action there is a reaction. Modernism – or corporate modernism – came under fire from a growing number of Eclectic designers for its cool sterility on the one hand (although Rand's work was never sterile) and for its social and political conservatism on the other. In the mainstream, this reaction (or rebellion) was represented notably by Push Pin Studios, founded in 1955 by Milton Glaser* and Seymour Chwast. Their inventive methods awoke a somnambulant post-war field and altered advertising and book design. Although Push Pin was not fanatically avant-garde, through its reinvention of discarded mannerisms it did spark profound shifts in commercial art, away from the cold rationalism of the corporate modern movement and the staid conventions of common commercial practice, towards new realms of pictorial expression. Push Pin did not merely copy Victorian, Art Nouveau and Art Deco (two decades before post-modernism encouraged similar reappraisals of the past and passé); the work was decidedly contemporary in formal conceptual outlook. It was not nostalgic or faddish but created a foundation on which graphic design could be practised beyond Push Pin's own sphere of influence, which was international.

Push Pin's mission was not solely an attack on modernism. Like the Moderns, Push Pin believed design could make a difference to the well-being of society, not only by making messages more accessible through clear systems but also by brightening daily life through expressive form. The means of achieving this goal was through visibility in the marketplace. Building their commercial identity, and obtaining prestigious clients in the process, was therefore paramount to Push Pin's aims. Besides taking on the role of experimental hot-house for illustration and design, the studio was in business to do business.

While Push Pin ushered in reprises of Victorian and Art Nouveau as the basis for contemporary visual language, a unique new offshoot known as psychedelia (because it was influenced by hallucinogenic drugs) became the sweet code of youth during the late 1960s. Art Nouveau had exerted an influence on typography throughout Europe from the early 1890s to before World War I. Type designers George Auriol, Eugène Grasset, Peter Behrens and Otto Eckmann, among others, filled foundry specimen books with curvilinear and eccentric calligraphic conceits. The style did not represent a political revolution, but Art Nouveau (in France), Jugendstil (in Germany), Stile Liberty (in Italy) and Vienna Secession

(in Austria) were youth-inspired social upheavals that altered visual language and spawned new moral and aesthetic values. Visual taboos – including a prodigious amount of nudity – nudged out conventional images. Sinuous Art Nouveau typefaces and ornaments were also overtly erotic. Yet not long after Art Nouveau was introduced it found mainstream acceptance, particularly in architecture, furniture, fashion and graphics. In France and Belgium, Art Nouveau was the *de facto* national style. Even today, kitsch French signs and posters include Art Nouveau alphabets. In the early 1960s Push Pin Studios reprised Art Nouveau lettering, which later influenced psychedelic poster artists in San Francisco, who adopted it as the code for the sex, drugs and rock 'n' roll generation. Art Nouveau's youth culture underpinnings were nonetheless not the sole motivation.

BELOW Film title sequence
designed by Pablo Ferro for
The Thomas Crown Affair,
directed by Norman Jewison,
United Artists, 1968.

Victor Moscoso, Mouse & Kelley, Rick Griffin and others were the pioneers of psychedelic posters. They enjoyed the formal intricacies of the letterforms and became obsessed drawing the ornate negative spaces between letters. The lettering for their original posters was hand-drawn, designed to vibrate and shimmy. As with original Art Nouveau, what started out underground was instantly adopted by the mainstream when Photo-Lettering, Inc., America's largest type house, introduced 'Psychedelitypes', a collection of faux zany Art Nouveau faces. Today, few people recall Jugendstil and Secession, but the emblematic alphabets will be forever linked to the 1960s.

Psychedelic design was integrated into the mainstream at breakneck speed, if only to capture the audience who responded to the youth culture clamour. But there was another more significant typographic shift endemic to the late 1950s and 1960s – phototype technology – and its maestro was Herb Lubalin.

Back in the early 1960s BC (before computer), Lubalin became known for expressive or illustrative typography that was made possible through photo manipulations. He was also an 'eclectic modernist', as evidenced by his typeface Avant Garde, which more than any other was the emblem of the '60s. But even more than the physical face, he predicted that, since type was rapidly moving off the page and onto the television screen, typographers needed to rethink the aesthetics of type. He argued that typographers should abandon delicate Bodonis, the subtleties of which were lost on the cathode ray tube, and rely instead on bold, more readable sans serifs. He further argued that large print advertisements on the sides of moving vehicles explained why passers-by had become conditioned to reading fleeting messages. With the public's eyes pulled in different directions on message-laden streets, it was incumbent on graphic designers to devise new kinetic reading methods that were at once legible, eye-catching and stylish. Passive typography – the kind that quietly and sometimes elegantly sat on a page – was not viable in a telekinetic world. Like the screaming headlines on tabloid newspapers, television demanded increasingly dramatic type displays. Technology had been influencing typographic aesthetics since the days of Gutenberg, but the act of moving typefaces around in telekinetic space demanded that typographers reappraise the essential cultural role of type. Was it still a neutral vessel for words and ideas, or a component of – indeed a player in – a larger communications drama? One thing was certain: type in motion could never be entirely neutral.

It was not until a decade after Lubalin's death in 1981 that the Macintosh computer, announced in 1984, enabled graphic designers to make type move without the benefit of complex optical effects and high-end computer programmes such as Paintbox. Another few years passed before programmes like Flash and After Effects gave designers the power to create animation on their own computers. Prior to the Macintosh, motion typography was so costly and time-consuming that only designers with patience and ambition even attempted to make type perform on the screen. In the 1960s, film title sequence designers, including Saul Bass and Pablo Ferro, laboriously experimented with type on screen. Ferro also introduced dancing type for eccentric TV commercials that combined cartoon lettering with Victorian circus type into improvisational compositions. By utilizing quick-cut editing, stop-frame animation and simultaneously projected images, he helped condition viewers to receive multiple graphics and produced typographic *tours de force*.

The 1950s and '60s were decades of ecological shifts in the broad landscape of graphic design and typography. The players and their roles are numerous and intersecting. It could be considered a formative period or a transitional one, the bridge from the pre-computer to the computer eras (which is arguably as significant as any epoch change). This time and its outputs led to the next, which influenced the following. The continuum of design history proceeds apace.

THE TRAVEL POSTER IN THE MID-CENTURY
SOPHIE CHURCHER

Collectors are drawn to posters for a rich variety of reasons. Posters offer a reflection of society, capture a specific moment in time and impart a critical understanding of the development of design. Above all, they have an immediate impact, their original function being to stimulate, distract and communicate in an instant.

The travel poster, in particular, provides us with some of the most powerfully evocative imagery from the late 19th and early 20th centuries. Travelling for leisure grew in popularity in the early 1900s with the advent of large-scale rail travel and long-distance ocean liner voyages. Transportation changed rapidly during this period, mirroring the industrial advances of the 20th century. At the same time, advances in lithographic printing enabled colourful posters to be produced on a scale never before witnessed. Railway, shipping and aviation companies embarked upon thrilling poster campaigns to compete for the attention of the traveller in search of an adventure. Highly regarded artists and illustrators were commissioned to create designs that conveyed the luxury and prestige of travelling, and their creations filled bustling cities and transport hubs. Today imagery that conveys what is referred to as the 'golden age' of travel has become highly collectable for buyers who are drawn to Art Deco and modernist graphics, high-quality lithography and limited print runs.

Following World War II, and into the 1950s and '60s, both the advertising and travel industries saw dramatic changes, not just in terms of advancing technology but also in consumer appetites. These two factors contributed to a gradual shift in the function and style of the travel poster. Post-war, communication was required to be more direct than ever before. Only the most essential words and images were used in order to produce an instantaneous and memorable effect. Shock, surprise and importantly humour were key tools for the propaganda campaigns of many nations, and continued as vital devices for the poster into the late 1940s and 1950s. Post-war humour differed from that of the 1920s and '30s, particularly in Britain. It became darker, acknowledging the horrors of war and a more menacing side to society. British designers embraced bizarre visuals, utilizing an object with multiple meanings or juxtaposing objects that were at once familiar and alien. ABRAM GAMES, in particular, embraced the surreal, while notably ensuring that his work was able to communicate and resonate with the public.

This was a time in which aviation, particularly, witnessed huge changes. Faster routes, including a rapid transatlantic service, were required during conflict, which ushered in a new era in air travel. Into the 1950s air travel was no longer the preserve of the super-rich. While the cost of 'surface' transport continued to increase, air travel was the only method of transport that was decreasing. Consequently in the United States, airline passenger numbers more than doubled during the decade as the increasingly affluent population could afford to fly. Competition to provide the fastest and most comfortable service intensified. Strict rules, however, governed passenger rates and facilities, which meant that airlines were not able to advertise cheaper seats on routes covered by rival companies. Designers reacted by conceiving advertisements that distinguished one airline from another

RIGHT Offset colour lithograph
travel poster, designed by
Stan Galli (aka Stanley Walter),
c. 1955.

in order to build brand loyalty. It was more important than ever for ads to be conceptual.
No longer could a dream be sold via beautiful artwork: the travel poster was now forced
to capture the imagination via a 'big idea'.

The primary method for airlines to compete directly against one another was to imply
a faster or more reliable service. Airlines employed artists who could convey the huge
advances in speed in the most imaginative way possible. Artists embraced the opportunity
to play with the altered relationship between time and space brought about by the rapidity
of the airplane. Lewitt-Him for American Overseas Airlines (AOA) and Abram Games for

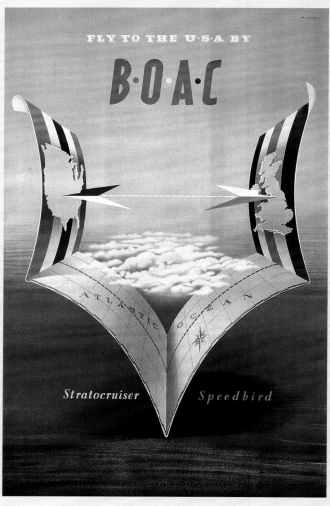

the British Overseas Airways Corporation (BOAC) drew upon Surrealist art to convey a
phenomenon described by G. O. Austen as the 'shrinkage of time'.[3] Clocks were morphed,
maps were distorted and typography was warped in posters that expressed the technological
advancements of individual airlines. Games frequently used large expanses of sky to exploit
the strangeness and novelty of travelling through the air. Skies that had been the focus of
much conflict were re-appropriated as windows into adventure, freedom and peace. In his
poster to encourage intercontinental travel, he implies that the USA and Britain have been
brought closer together via the *Stratocruiser Speedbird*.

It was also important for airlines to convey the identity of their 'home' nation, which
was why Games, whose graphic style was at the heart of visual culture in post-war Britain,
was chosen to be BOAC's primary designer. In the late 1940s, AOA selected the UK-based
Lewitt-Him (a partnership between Polish-born Jan le Witt and George Him, who came
to London in 1937) over American artists to appeal to British audiences, who were viewed
as having significantly different humour and taste from the 'flashy' Americans.[4] 'AOA USA'
conveys the expanding links from America to Europe, cleverly flattening the globe to
illustrate the speed of the AOA flagships. Typography is also dynamically integrated, giving
an impression of speed – a technique that draws upon the principles of modernism.

By the early 1950s, many airlines focused on portraying the exoticism of their journey's
end, rather than the glamour of the experience of travelling itself. Although this approach

could not differentiate between airline companies, it nevertheless acted as 'collective propaganda'.[5] Each company hoped individually to benefit from the portrayal of unfamiliar, sunny and spectacular destinations that were becoming accessible to the masses. Advertisements exploited the thirst for travel brought on by a desire to escape austerity and the towns and cities ravaged by war in exchange for a colourful adventure. Flat, bright sweeps of colour and heavily stylized images formed optimistic posters that expressed the emotional appeal of sun, sand and sky. Although the use of photography within poster design was quickly becoming more fashionable, many artists viewed expressionist lithography as the best way to convey the exoticism of travel. In this sense, the travel poster offered relative freedom for the artist because the imagery was selling a fantasy.

The freedom of travel poster design also appealed to younger artists as a democratic and inexpensive way to make images. Inspired by the influential models of poster pioneers, both established and new designers set forth to contribute to the discipline. The standard size/format and appeal of having work seen by a large public held a unique allure for artists who wished to channel their creativity through a commercial project. In 1956, Air France employed the designer Jean Carlu to commission a series of ten posters destined for display all over the world. The posters had two functions: to advertise the services of Air France, and to convey the standard and variety of contemporary French graphic design. The aim was to connect Air France to contemporary art and thereby convey it as a truly contemporary brand.[6] The project reveals the value that was placed upon poster design in Europe at the time, not only as a commercial object but also as a work of art with a moral responsibility to educate society.

By the mid-1960s, however, it was widely recognized that the graphic poster was struggling to compete with photographic advertisements. In 1964, the British designer Ashley Havinden commented that 'Graphic Design – and indeed the art of the poster, as we used to know it – seems to have disappeared completely from the hoardings in favour of the "blown up" photograph'.[7] The concept of poster designer disintegrated: posters were no longer signed in the plate by their creators, and large agencies dominated the industry. A large number of the posters that were commissioned were there to support a television campaign, so often a still from the TV ad would suffice. The poster struggled to compete with the mass of visual and audio advertising that the eyes and ears of the consumer were now exposed to on a daily basis.

In spite of the gradual marginalization of graphic and illustrative travel posters during the 1950s and '60s, they still offer a unique insight into the significant technological, cultural and economic changes during this transformative period. Their primary function – to provide clear and immediate communication – ensures that the changing desires and popular tastes of the masses are reflected in a very poignant manner. This combination of cultural significance and visual appeal gives the poster a unique place in the eye of a collector, distinctly setting it apart from other forms of art.

The market for mid-century travel posters is, relatively speaking, in its infancy, and as a collecting field it continually draws in new buyers. A large part of the posters' appeal is that the reductive graphics compliment contemporary uncluttered interior spaces, making them ideal for home decoration. Collectors are also still able to purchase a poster from this period that has high visual impact for a relatively small sum. There are, however, challenges to collecting. Both availability and condition affect value because typically the majority of a print run would have been destroyed after use. As such, examples can be rare and difficult to track down, or the paper is found to be in poor condition. Because posters are not numbered, we often do not know how many were originally printed, let alone have survived, but in many ways it is this unknown quantity that makes collecting so fulfilling.

AOA

USA

The Route of the Flagships

SAUL BASS
1920–1996

AMERICAN MASTER OF GRAPHIC
SYMBOLISM, FETED FOR HIS
GROUNDBREAKING FILM TITLE
SEQUENCES AND MOVIE POSTERS

Saul Bass was a master of graphic symbolism. He knew how to distil the essence of a story, concept or corporation down to a vivid, engaging, visual image. Most famously, he applied his unique version of symbolism to the world of film posters and movie titles. In doing so he not only reinvigorated poster design in the 1950s and '60s – taking it in a very fresh direction, with an emphasis on abstraction, geometrics and bold colour choices – but he also revolutionized the whole nature of film title sequences.

In the world before Bass, film titles were essentially wasted space – a reel of bland type for which projectionists often left the movie theatre curtains closed. But Bass took the images he had created for poster campaigns and brought them to life with kinetic or animated sequences that were visually enticing and also introduced the film itself, setting the tone and establishing key themes. The titles became something not to be missed – a vital ingredient of the movie experience. Bass had created a new art form.

'What is most important is that the introduction to the film – which is what a title is – be true to its content and to its intent,' said Bass. 'Therefore, something has to be created that is expressive of that. A more profound relationship must exist beyond a superficiality of style.'[8]

Bass began working for the film industry after meeting director Otto Preminger in Hollywood in the early 1950s. Preminger asked Bass to create the poster design and title sequence for his 1954 film *Carmen Jones*. This was followed by one of the most important commissions of Bass's career a year later – the poster and title sequence for Preminger's *The Man With the Golden Arm*, the story of a jazz musician with an addiction to heroin, starring Frank Sinatra and Kim Novak. Bass designed a distorted and disjointed arm within a geometric framework – an arresting symbol of the addiction that plagues the central

character's life. The imagery was used for the film poster, the soundtrack album by Elmer Bernstein and the movie's title sequence. It was a radical departure, and one that Preminger fought for in battles with studio executives.

Other Preminger/Bass film collaborations followed: *Saint Joan* (1957), *Bonjour Tristesse* (1958), *Anatomy of a Murder* (1959) and *Exodus* (1960). Bass went on to work with – among others – Billy Wilder and Alfred Hitchcock, creating the infamous spiral patterns on the posters and titles for *Vertigo* (1958), and also working on *North by Northwest* (1959) and *Psycho* (1960), for which broken type and pulsing graphics suggested the deranged nature of Norman Bates's character; Bass also assisted Hitchcock with the staccato shower scene within the film itself.

Bass was born in New York, the son of an émigré furrier from Eastern Europe. He attended the Art Students League and also took night classes with the Hungarian graphic designer György Kepes – a key mentor – at Brooklyn College. Bass worked as an apprentice with a number of New York firms before freelancing as a graphic designer. In 1946, he moved to Los Angeles and he set up his own studio in 1950. Much of the work that followed in the 1950s and '60s was film-related, and Bass moved into film-making himself with a series of short movies and a feature film called *Phase IV* (1974), which was not a commercial success.

But Bass also made an important contribution to the evolution of corporate graphics, working in the sphere of commercial design and creating a very different set of pioneering symbols and logos for a wide spectrum of household-name companies. There were corporate identity programmes and logos for Continental Airlines (1967), Quaker cereals (1969), the communications giant Bell (1969) and United Airlines (1974). Many of the corporate graphic identities that Bass created are still in use today.

RIGHT Logo designed
for United Airlines, 1974

FAR RIGHT Logo for Bell, 1969.

He also designed record covers, illustrated a children's book (*Henri's Walk to Paris*, 1962), worked on covers for John Entenza's* *Arts & Architecture* magazine, and collaborated with architects Buff, Straub & Hensman* on the design of his house (Case Study #20, 1958).

But it was his movie graphics that he will be best remembered for, and Bass title sequences and poster designs have been widely imitated and referenced in recent years. Martin Scorsese approached Bass to work on titles for a sequence of films in the 1990s, including *Goodfellas* (1990) and *Cape Fear* (1991). These movies helped remind everyone of Bass's gifts and the way in which graphic design could be moulded to encompass symbolic and narrative weight.

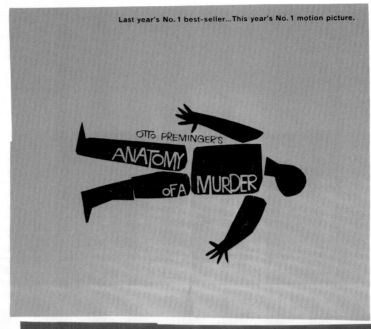

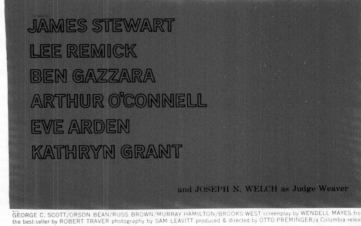

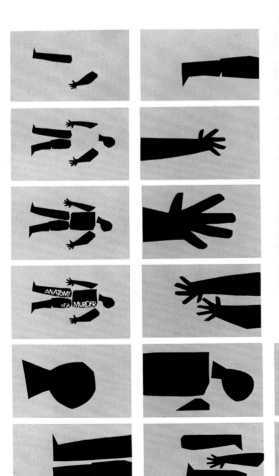

ABOVE Film poster, 1959.

LEFT Black and white film sequence from *Anatomy of a Murder*, 1959.

FRANK SINATRA · ELEANOR PARKER · KIM NOVAK

THE MAN WITH THE GOLDEN ARM

A FILM BY OTTO PREMINGER

With Arnold Stang, Darren McGavin, Robert Strauss, John Conte, Doro Merande, George E. Stone, George Mathews, Leonid Kinskey, Emile Meyer, Shorty Rogers, Shelly Manne, Screenplay by Walter Newman & Lewis Meltzer, From the novel by Nelson Algren, Music by Elmer Bernstein, Produced & Directed by Otto Preminger, Released by United Artists

OPPOSITE Film poster, 1955.

ABOVE Film poster, 1958.

MAX BILL
1908–1994
& OTL AICHER
1922–1991

SWISS-GERMAN DUO NOTED
FOR THEIR RIGOROUS, HIGHLY
CONTROLLED APPROACH
TO GRAPHIC DESIGN

An architect, artist and graphic designer, as well as a furniture and product designer, Max Bill was one of those multi-talented, polymath figures who seem to dominate the mid-century period. Born in Switzerland, he served an apprenticeship as a silversmith before going on to study at the Bauhaus*, where his tutors included Wassily Kandinsky and Paul Klee. His education shaped his design, and he is known for the mathematical purity of his approach to all media, from buildings to watches and clocks.

As an artist, Bill was a key figure in the Concrete Art movement – an affiliation of artists who put an emphasis on order, precision and geometry within work that was abstract to the point of having no obvious connection to the world beyond. Within Bill's colourful but always highly controlled compositions there were also many similarities to Op Art.

When it came to graphic design and typography, Bill remained a purist. He sought to clarify and systematize graphic design within the framework of the Swiss Style* or International Typographic Style, both owing much to the rigorous modernist approach of the Bauhaus in the pre-war years. Bill argued

in favour of a grid framework system that would give order to creative graphics, and he advocated sans serif typography and the use of photography as a key component. It was a Northern European, Swiss-German approach that was to prove highly influential, offering a very different way of working compared to the more liberated, playful approach of designers such as SAUL BASS and HERBERT MATTER working in the United States in the 1950s.

In 1951, Bill co-founded the Hochschule für Gestaltung* in Germany with designer Otl Aicher, who had been born in Ulm and had opened his own graphic studio in the city four years earlier. Bill designed the buildings for the school, as well as his famous Ulmer Hocker stool – typically formal and functional. He also served as the school director, while Aicher headed the visual communication department. In many ways, Ulm was inspired by the model of the Bauhaus while its tutors placed graphic design within a clear theoretical and philosophical context, including semiotics – the study of signs and symbols. Bill served as director until 1957, while Aicher stayed on until the mid-1960s when the school closed and he moved to Munich to relaunch his own studio.

ABOVE Wristwatch designed by Max Bill for Junghans, 1961.

RIGHT Wall clock designed by Max Bill for Junghans, 1950s.

Aicher's work of the late 1960s and
1970s showed the Ulm model at its best,
combining clarity and purity with a high level
of innovation and creativity. He became
involved in corporate identity and branding,
particularly in the field of transport, using
MAX MIEDINGER's Helvetica typeface to design
the logo for Lufthansa in 1969. Then in 1972
he was commissioned to work on the Munich
Olympics. His system of pictograms for
different athletic events offered clear graphic
signage without the need for words, allowing
visitors from around the world to make easy
and instant sense of them. His symbols
established a model that has been widely
replicated and adapted ever since, as well
as mirrored by signage for roads and airports.

Aicher also designed a series of posters
for the Olympics. There was a trademark sense
of clarity, but also a refreshing and vibrant
use of colour within semi-abstract images of
athletes, infused with a sense of kinetic energy.
The posters were fresh, dynamic and engaging.
In addition, Aicher designed a range of
associated material for the Olympics, from
maps to cultural event posters, all tied together
by a similar use of typography and a disciplined
use of colour and graphic devices. Visually,
it created one of the most striking portfolios
of Olympic images ever produced, born of
the ideas and philosophy set out within the
relatively short-lived but still highly influential
Ulm school.

BELOW Pictograms for archery,
riding and ballet, designed by
Otl Aicher for the 1972 Munich
Olympic Games.

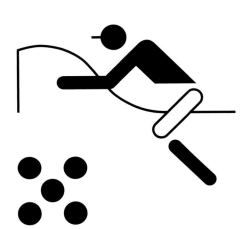

München ◯◯◯◯◯ 1972

ABOVE AND OPPOSITE
Olympic Games posters
designed by Otl Aicher, 1971.

München ⭕⭕⭕⭕⭕ 1972

WIM CROUWEL
BORN 1928

DUTCH INNOVATOR RENOWNED
FOR HIS BESPOKE TYPEFACES,
GRID-BASED SYSTEMS AND VIVID
USE OF COLOUR

There is an intriguing contradiction at the heart of Wim Crouwel's work. On the one hand, his method of working was highly formal and functional, operating within clear parameters (he had long employed the structural framework of a grid system, as advocated by, among others, Josef Müller-Brockmann*, a key influence on Crouwel), and his posters, catalogues and stamp designs largely avoid the use of photography or illustration, allowing bespoke typefaces to present his message, or that of his clients. On the other hand, there is a humanist quality to Crouwel's work, a deep-rooted respect for artistry, craft and expression that feeds into his fonts, many of which were drawn by hand and are full of character and individuality. His vivid use of colour, too, has an often intense and painterly quality, stemming perhaps from Crouwel's first career as an Expressionist artist.

This contradiction can best be seen in the series of exhibition posters and catalogues that Crouwel created for the Stedelijk van Abbemuseum in Eindhoven in the 1950s, and then for the Stedelijk Museum in Amsterdam from the early 1960s onwards. His poster for a collection of artworks depicting Hiroshima (1957), for example, offered a distinctive sans serif typeface, bold and black, on a blood-red background.

'I always used the main word – or name – as the focus of the poster, and then tried to use that word to translate the idea of the exhibition,' said Crouwel. 'The work was always done by hand, always by doing a lot of drawing.... The Hiroshima exhibition consisted of paintings and drawings about the horror of Hiroshima by a Japanese artist. So I thought I should make it bright orange, or red, with very heavy black type to give an impression of the horror of the bombing of Hiroshima. I always used one word to make an image – a kind of image-based typography....'[9]

Crouwel himself was brought up in a world of type. His father was a block-maker in the printing industry in the Dutch city of Groningen. Crouwel studied fine art at the city's Minerva Academy, within one of the first modernist buildings in Holland – an environment that made a deep impression on him. In the early 1950s he moved to Amsterdam and continued painting for a number of years before starting work with an exhibition design company. He also began attending evening classes in graphic design and typography at the Rietveld Academy.

LEFT 'Hiroshima' exhibition
poster, 1957.

In 1956, Crouwel founded an office with interior designer Kho Liang Le, again focusing on exhibition design, with Crouwel concentrating on graphics. Around the same time Edy de Wilde, director of the Stedelijk van Abbemuseum Eindhoven, began commissioning exhibition posters and catalogues. When de Wilde moved on to the Stedelijk in Amsterdam, Crouwel moved with him and began work on a groundbreaking series of typographic posters that helped establish a new identity for the museum and Dutch graphic design as a whole, featuring Crouwel's unique blend of expressive typography, bold colour choices and a systematic grid-based approach. Occasionally, as in the 'Vormgevers' exhibition poster of 1968, the grid became a visible part of the design itself.

Most of the bespoke fonts that Crouwel created for his exhibition posters were never drawn up into full font runs. But Crouwel did famously experiment with a number of new full alphabetic fonts, including his New Alphabet. This was an experimental font developed in 1967 as a response to the pixellated, computerized types appearing in digital formats. The pared-down font eradicated rounded lines, creating a futuristic set of lettering wherein certain curved letters – such as 'a' – were reduced to abstract symbols. The New Alphabet was highly influential and remains so today, also proving the power of

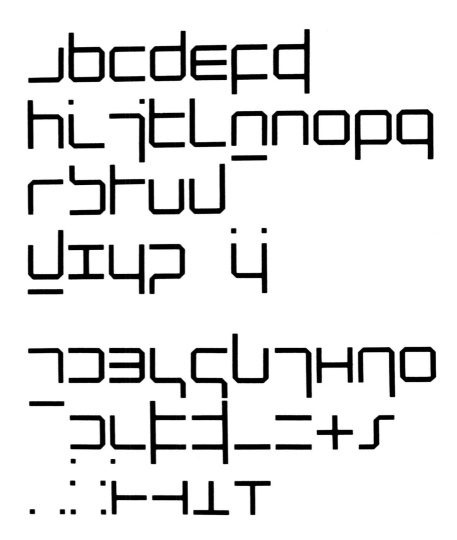

the human brain to fill in missing typographical information within an ordered system as long as the rules are cohesive and consistent. The typeface was later used on Joy Division's famous *Substance* album cover (1988), designed by Peter Saville and Brett Wickens.

In 1963, Crouwel co-founded the multi-disciplinary design studio Total Design in Amsterdam, continuing to serve as a consultant after stepping back from his partnership in the 1980s. Key projects included a series of stamps for the Dutch post office in the 1970s, which used Crouwel's Gridnik font, first designed for Olivetti electric typewriters in the early 1970s but never used for its original purpose.

ABOVE New Alphabet, developed in 1967.

LEFT 'Vormgevers' exhibition poster, 1968.

ALAN FLETCHER
1931–2006

DYNAMIC GRAPHIC DESIGNER
WHO, INSPIRED BY AMERICAN
MODELS, BROUGHT MULTI-
DISCIPLINARY VERVE TO
POST-WAR BRITAIN

In so many fields of creativity, from architecture to the novel, America seemed to possess a golden energy in the 1950s. To a Europe still suffering from the war years, it represented an alluring alternative to austerity. Many creative thinkers visited the States on exchange programmes or self-funded trips and came back enthused, inspired and perhaps a little jealous of the vibrant state of America's economy and its ongoing consumer boom.

One such visitor was graphic designer Alan Fletcher. Born in Kenya, to British parents, he moved to England as a five-year-old and went to boarding school in Sussex. He attended Hammersmith School of Art, then the Central School of Art and Design, where he met Colin Forbes and Theo Crosby – friends who would later become his business partners. He went

on to the Royal College of Art, where he edited *ARK*, the college magazine, and met artists such as Peter Blake and Joe Tilson.

But America was calling. In 1956, Fletcher was awarded a travel scholarship and was invited to attend classes at Yale University, where his tutors included PAUL RAND and Josef Albers*. He also worked in the office of SAUL BASS in Los Angeles and won a number of early commissions, including a cover design for *Fortune* magazine and some work for IBM.

Returning to England was not a joyful prospect. 'Everybody was still doing the same thing: little black and white jobs with 8pt type. If it had a second colour it was red, or possibly blue. When I arrived back in London in the early 1960s, it was with a portfolio of full-colour jobs and ambitious hopes.'[10]

RIGHT 'The Launch of
Sputnik' cover design for
Fortune magazine, 1958.

Fletcher also brought with him imagination and a fresh approach. He formed a partnership with Colin Forbes and Bob Gill, an American living in London (in 1965 Gill was replaced by Theo Crosby). They began developing their practice on the American model, creating a multi-disciplinary design agency and consultancy.

Early projects included covers for Penguin books, but then larger and more involved commissions began to arrive from BP, Shell and other companies. By the early 1970s the practice had evolved into Pentagram: a truly multi-faceted creative enterprise that included not only graphic designers but also architects and the celebrated KENNETH GRANGE (see under 'Product and Industrial Design'). Pentagram's founders also considered structures found in legal practices and management consultancies, with each partner supported by a group of affiliated designers. This structure allowed for a degree of independence within the collective but also creative collaboration between partners and teams with various skills and talents.

One of Fletcher's strengths was designing or adapting typefaces tailored to individual clients, such as Pirelli, Kodak and Rank Xerox. He worked on corporate identity programmes, information design and posters. One of his most famous commissions was for the news agency Reuters, for whom he created a logotype

LEFT Book cover for Penguin Books, 1961.

BELOW LEFT Book cover for Penguin Books, 1962.

composed of dots, echoing the punched tickertape feeds that supplied the news rooms. His poster designs also experimented with typographic games, including a series for Lyons tea rooms that explored different typefaces within brightly coloured designs.

A playful approach to design also expressed itself in adverts for Pirelli slippers, where Fletcher created a banner poster for doubledecker Routemaster buses that made it look as though the passengers on the upper deck were wearing the slippers in the ad; Bob Gill designed similarly humorous display cards that made it look as though cartoon dogs were holding the slippers in their mouths.

But Fletcher – and Pentagram – were able to turn their talents in many different directions. This sophisticated flexibility, as well as multi-layered creativity, made it stand out. The model still holds good today.

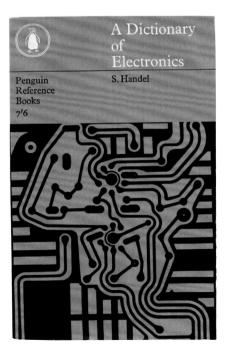

TOP Logotype for Reuters, 1965.

ABOVE Articulated imagery for Pirelli Cintura, 1972 (collaborator: Jessica Strang).

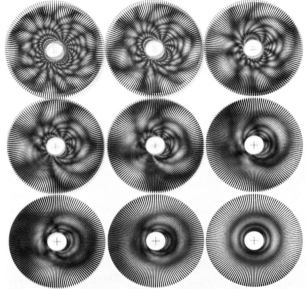

ABOVE Poster advertising
Pirelli slippers, 1962.

ADRIAN FRUTIGER
BORN 1928

SWISS INVENTOR OF
PIONEERING, MODERNIST
TYPEFACES, INCLUDING
UNIVERS AND FRUTIGER

The working career of leading Swiss Style* designer Adrian Frutiger encompassed three very different worlds of type. He started out in the days of individual metal letters and compositors' trays, was fêted in the era of photosetting and then carefully refined his typefaces for the digital age. His fonts offer instant clarity, but also have an innate modernist character with a sense of elegance and sophistication. They have become key elements in the ongoing struggle to make sense of an increasingly complex and information-loaded world. 'The most important thing I have learned,' Frutiger said, 'is that legibility and beauty stand close together and that type design, in its restraint, should be only felt but not perceived by the reader.'[11]

Born in the Swiss town of Unterseen, he was interested in calligraphy and sculpture from a young age. He served an apprenticeship with a printer in nearby Interlaken and then studied at the School of Applied Arts in Zurich. After finishing his studies in 1951, he secured a position with the prestigious Deberny & Peignot type foundry in Paris. Early Frutiger typefaces included a serif font with a rather gothic feel, called President, and another called Ondine, meaning 'wave', which had a calligraphic, arabesque, free-hand quality.

But Deberny & Peignot were also experimenting with photosetting technology and seeking a new generation of clearly defined typefaces that would sit well with the new printing methods. Frutiger's new typeface, Univers, appeared in 1957 and is still used widely today. It was based – like MAX MIEDINGER's Helvetica, with which it

is sometimes confused – on the Akzidenz Grotesk typeface, first introduced by a German foundry in 1898 and influential in the evolution of a number of landmark mid-century fonts, including Transport developed by JOCK KINNEIR & MARGARET CALVERT in Britain.

Univers was a sans serif typeface with letters of a uniform height and proportion within their lower-case and upper-case families. It also came with a revolutionary new colour-coded and numerical system – emblematic of the precise and logical Swiss Style – that carefully mapped the different weights and widths of the full range of type within the Univers family.

The font was widely adopted in the 1960s and '70s, sometimes with slight variations. It was used by the Paris Metro system and Deutsche Bank, and for Rand McNally and Ordnance Survey maps. OTL AICHER also used it on many of his much-lauded posters for the 1972 Munich Olympics. Apple adopted it for their computer keyboards up until 2007.

In 1968, Frutiger was handed another complex information design commission. This was the new signage system for the Charles de Gaulle airport in Roissy, just outside Paris. His new sans serif typeface was originally called Roissy, but was later renamed simply Frutiger. Once again, it is distinct and legible, but with a warmer, more casual nature than Univers. It can be read easily and quickly, making it highly suitable for airport signage, road signs (the Swiss, naturally, adopted it for theirs, along with the French) as well as football shirts. It has since become almost as prevalent across the everyday contemporary world as Helvetica.

BELOW Sample of the Univers typeface, released in 1957.

Univers Bold

abcdefghijklmnopqrstuvwxyz
ABCDEFGHIJKLMNOPQRSTUVWXYZ
1234567890
abcdefghijklmnopqrstuvwxyz

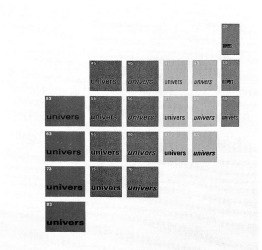

LEFT AND BELOW RIGHT
Specimen pages for the
Univers typeface.

BELOW LEFT The Univers
type family.

stuvwxyz

OPQRSTUVWXYZ

&.,:;!?[]*

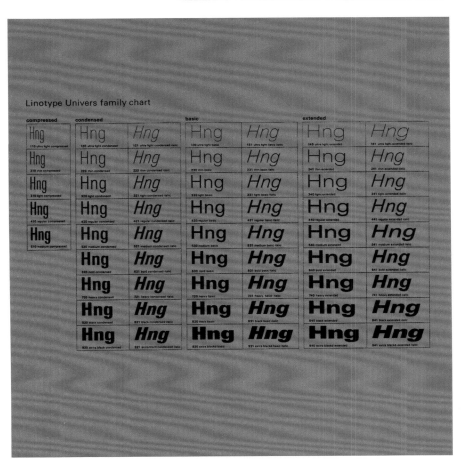

Frutiger

ABOVE Sample of the Frutiger typeface, designed in 1968.

RIGHT AND BELOW Frutiger, as designed for the signage system of Charles de Gaulle airport, and also used for the Swiss Post Office and the French motorway system.

La signalisation de l'Aéroport Charles-de-Gaulle

Le choix d'un caractère

Panneaux jaune foncé, le Français en noir, l'Anglaise en blanc

Départs
Departures

La couleur jaune est la seule non chargée de significations (rouge « interdiction, vert « secours, bleu » indications auxiliaires)

1 Dans une signalisation basée sur la rapidité des empattements «brouillent» la lecture.

2 Des lettres du type Univers sont trop fermées (voir a, e).

3 Une lettre purement construite (rondes au compas) manque de noblesse.

4 Le grandissement des lettres diminue la lisibilité, les signes ont une plus grande ressemblance.

5 Pour toutes ces raisons la création d'un nouveau style s'imposait.

Les premières applications du caractère « Frutiger » par les PTT Suisse et les autoroutes françaises

Les bureaux de poste des PTT Suisse (conception Kurt Wälti)

Sur les autobus des PTT

L'animation touristique des autoroutes (conception Jean Widmer)

Le «Frutiger» adapté pour les textes imprimés

L'aspect de chaque caractère d'imprimerie est une chose complexe, où forme, mouvement rhytme, et donc aussi les proportions, le réglage des approches, etc., ne se laissent plus dissocier. Dans tous les rapports formels et autres relations il s'agit de phénomènes optiques irréductibles aux règles mathématiques et que seule pourra percevoir et fixer la sensibilité visuelle, qu'il s'agisse des détails de chaque même caractère, ou de la graduation distinguant réciproquement les diverses séries

L'aspect de chaque caractère d'imprimerie est une chose complexe, où forme, mouvement rhytme, et donc aussi les proportions, le réglage des approches, etc., ne se laissent plus dissocier. Dans tous les rapports formels et autres relations il s'agit de phénomènes optiques irréductibles aux règles mathématiques et que seule pourra percevoir et fixer la sensibilité visuelle, qu'il s'agisse des détails de chaque même caractère, ou de la graduation distinguant réciproquement les div

L'aspect de chaque caractère d'imprimerie est une chose complexe, où forme, mouvement rhytme, et donc aussi les proportions, le réglage des approches, etc., ne se laissent plus dissocier. Dans tous les rapports formels et autres relations il s'agit de phénomènes optiques irréductibles aux règles mathématiques et que seule pourra percevoir et fixer la sensibilité visuelle, qu'il s'agisse des détails de chaque série du même caractère, ou de la graduation distinguant réciproquement les div

Frutiger Roman

abcdefghijklmnopqrstuvwxyz
ABCDEFGHIJKLMNOPQRSTUVWXYZ
1234567890
abcdefghijklmnopqrstuvwxyz

Frutiger Bold

abcdefghijklmnopqrstuvwxyz
ABCDEFGHIJKLMNOPQRSTUVWXYZ
1234567890
abcdefghijklmnopqrstuvwxyz

Frutiger Black

abcdefghijklmnopqrstuvwxyz
ABCDEFGHIJKLMNOPQRSTUVWXYZ
1234567890
abcdefghijklmnopqrstuvwxyz

ABOVE Samples of different weights of Frutiger.

ABRAM GAMES
1914–1996

DESIGNER RESPONSIBLE FOR
SOME OF THE MOST MEMORABLE
GRAPHIC IMAGES AND POSTERS
OF MID-CENTURY BRITAIN

The Festival of Britain* in 1951 was a national celebration of the country's collective talents in the fields of the arts, design and architecture as well as science and technology. Centred upon the South Bank of the Thames in London, it was intended as both a reminder of what made Britain 'Great' and an optimistic overview of future positives, looking forward to the many achievements that were just around the corner as the country slowly began to emerge from an age of austerity and reconstruction.

The symbol of the Festival, designed by Abram Games, had to somehow summon up all these elements, encompassing past, present and future. His emblem, used on posters and catalogues, was dubbed the 'Festival Star', with four dynamic swirling arrows radiating from a circle that contained the focal symbol – a four-pointed compass draped with bunting, the northern point morphing into the profile of Britannia. The design had a sense of kinetic energy and was celebratory and colourful, while redrawing Britain - through Games's new Britannia - in modern form.

Like so much of the designer's work, the Festival symbol and posters stood out all the more within the context of the grey realities of life in Britain in the 1940s and early 1950s. Games's work had energy, wit and colour. His posters, in particular, had much in common with the playful images being explored on the Continent by Raymond Savignac*, Jacques Auriac and others. Like HERBERT MATTER,

Games had been inspired by Russian Constructivists, Surrealists and the posters of pioneering French graphic artists such as A. M. Cassandre. Yet he also kept in mind his mantra of 'maximum meaning, minimum means', approaching his work with a 'less is more' sense of restraint and looking for clarity within images that might be spoilt by excess.

Games was the son of a Latvian photographer and a Russo-Polish seamstress, who had settled in the East End of London. After school in Hackney, he spent two terms studying at St Martin's School of Art, but decided that he could not afford to continue. He went to work as an assistant with a commercial art studio called Askew Younge in 1932, but lost his job a few years later and began working freelance. Commissions came in from London Transport, the Post Office and Shell, whose design director became a great supporter.

During the war, Games became a dedicated war artist and began working on a series of posters that would seal his reputation. Among his many dramatic and highly imaginative wartime images was a 'Grow Your Own Food' poster from 1942, encouraging people to be self-sufficient rather than rely on merchant shipping which was under constant attack by the German navy.

Another famous poster warning of loose talk showed a spiralling swirl of speech emerging from a soldier's mouth and then

RIGHT Land Travelling
Exhibition at City Hall,
Manchester, 1951 (one
of the nationwide events
organized as part of
the Festival of Britain),
showing Abram Games's
symbol for the Festival.

becoming a red sword that impales three of his comrades. Games's sense of movement, combined with graphic surrealism, seems way ahead of its time. Other images had a transatlantic quality, particularly the rather glamorous posters advertising the merits of the Auxiliary Territorial Service (ATS).

In the post-war years, Games was able to turn his talents in a different direction. As well as the Festival commission, there were posters for the Metropolitan Police, Guinness and the *Financial Times*. But some of his most powerful designs from the 1950s were put to the service of the growing tourism and airline industries. A lighthearted image for Blackpool tourism showed the city's famous tower rebuilt in sand on the beach. Posters for British European Airways and the British Overseas Airways Corporation were often more sophisticated in nature. One poster showed a set of airline steps transforming into a map of the world, continuing with the surrealist techniques of Games's war-time work, tied to an accomplished level of original artistry and illustration.

Other projects included one of the first animated identity graphics for the BBC. Games also experimented with industrial design, creating a successful coffee maker for Cona. There was also a tile mural for London Underground, adding to earlier poster commissions for the capital's transport system.

BELOW A Festival of Britain catalogue, 1951.

ABOVE Poster advertising
Orient Line passenger cruises,
UK, 1951.

ABOVE RIGHT 'Grow Your
Own Food' war poster,
UK, 1942.

OPPOSITE Recruitment poster
for the Auxiliary Territorial
Service, c. 1941.

JOIN THE

ATS

ASK FOR INFORMATION AT THE NEAREST EMPLOYMENT EXCHANGE OR AT ANY ARMY OR A.T.S. RECRUITING CENTRE

PRINTED FOR H.M. STATIONERY OFFICE BY FOSH & CROSS LTD., LONDON   (51/1065)

CHARLEY HARPER
1922–2007

AMERICAN ILLUSTRATOR WHOSE
INSTANTLY RECOGNIZABLE,
NATURE-INSPIRED WORK SHOWS
A MASTERFUL UNDERSTANDING
OF COLOUR AND A GRAPHIC
SENSE OF CLARITY

A sense of delight with nature and art itself is threaded through the illustrations, posters and paintings of Charley Harper. His work offers an endearing, pared-down view of the natural world through vividly coloured images in which the composition is reduced to a limited number of shapes and patterns. But these are not cartoon images: Harper disliked the genre, along with the idea of imposing human characteristics upon animals.

Harper called his style 'minimal realism' – a way of creating a vivid representational image halfway between reality and abstraction. In some respects there was a crossover with Pop Art, spliced with a folk art quality, but Harper's style was unique and highly original.

His aviaries of prints and paintings have, above all, come to define his career. These emerged during a thirty-year relationship with *Ford Times* magazine – a travel journal published by the Ford Motor Company, to which Harper began contributing illustrations in the late 1940s. Arthur Lougee, the art director, was a great supporter, mentor and friend, and came up with the idea of offering readers affordable screen-prints ordered direct from the artist. Harper began producing the prints on a hand-press in his basement, while continuing to expand his range of bird images.

His birds were always beautifully observed and informative, the essential characteristics of each picked out within purposefully two-dimensional images.

Sometimes, they became geometric forms in a highly graphic arrangement – as with his *Bank Swallows* (1959) or *Family of Chicadees* (1968). In some of his paintings, too, the backdrop environment became an abstract geometric pattern, like a textile repeat, suggesting leaves or falling rain. 'Always I try to express the personality of the bird by exaggerating yet simplifying its colour and form,' Harper wrote. 'And I maintain a designer's concern for the total area of the picture, trying to make it a satisfying arrangement of colours and shapes.'[12]

Harper was born in West Virginia and raised on his father's farm in the foothills of the Appalachian mountains. He began to draw at an early age, then studied at the Cincinnati Art Academy before joining an intelligence and reconnaissance platoon during the war years. Even during military service in France and Germany, he managed to continue sketching.

After the war, he moved to New York but soon found that city living was not to his taste. He returned to the Cincinnati Art Academy and, upon graduation, won a travel scholarship – a painting trip across the American West, which also became his honeymoon.

Around this time, Harper began to define his own style and to move away from realism. 'I concentrated on trying to simplify the great natural forms and symbolize the design underlying the surface clutter. It was a giant step forward for me.... I began to search for something particularly me – a style,

RIGHT *Bank Swallows*,
serigraph, 1959.

OPPOSITE *Creatures of
the Far North*, gouache,
1961, for the *World Book
Encyclopedia*, published
by Field Enterprises.

LEFT *Life Story of a Plant*, gouache and watercolour, 1961, for *The Golden Book of Biology*, published by Western Publishing.

BELOW LEFT *The Pond*, gouache and watercolour, 1961, for *The Golden Book of Biology*.

BOTTOM *Fleeing from a Prairie Fire*, gouache and watercolour, 1961, for *The Golden Book of Biology*.

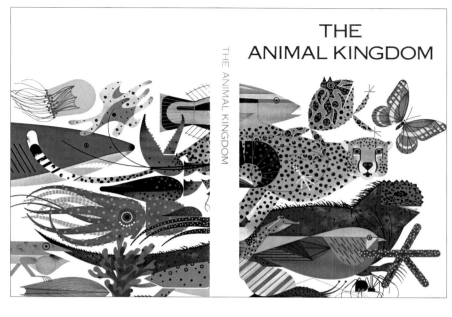

THE
ANIMAL KINGDOM

THE ANIMAL KINGDOM

a technique, a point of view – and gradually
it emerged: the impulse to caricature and
simplify at the same time.'[13]

Harper's illustration work for *Ford
Times* – including travel scenes, landscapes,
cityscapes, animals, insects and birds – formed
a foundation for his life as an independent
artist. There were over four hundred images
in all, often accompanied by Harper's texts
as he was also a gifted writer. He illustrated
a number of books, including Betty Crocker's
Dinner for Two Cookbook (1958) and two
children's textbooks, *The Golden Book of
Biology* (1961) and *The Animal Kingdom* (1968).

At the same time, he became increasingly
involved with advertising, creating as many
as 100,000 images for a whole range of
commercial clients. He worked hard and fast,
encompassing a wide variety of subjects,
playing to greater or lesser degrees with
caricatures, abstraction and a more graphic

approach. Commissions ranged from food
illustration to multivitamin tablets to posters
for a Brazilian airline. Such work funded
Harper's independence, allowing him time
to pursue his own paintings.

In the late 1970s, he began working on
a series of ambitious posters for county and
national parks, along with other conservancies
and natural attractions, which took his affinity
for the natural world to a new level. He
applied his artistry to a more formal, grid-like
framework into which he fed a menagerie of
natural treasures. From 1964 onwards he also
developed a series of full-scale mosaic murals,
beginning with an installation at the Federal
Building in Cincinnati.

In recent years Harper's work has
been championed by designer and author
Todd Oldham. It now helps to inspire a new
generation of artists and illustrators – adults
and children alike.

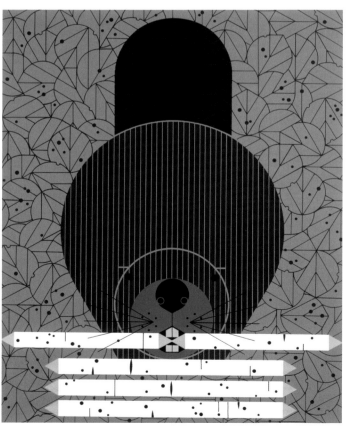

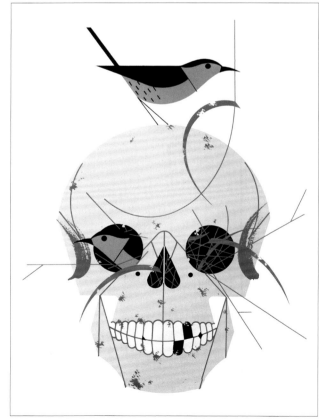

OPPOSITE ABOVE *Two Salamanders*, gouache, 1961, for *The Golden Book of Biology*.

OPPOSITE BELOW LEFT *Dam Diligent*, serigraph, 1975, for the Frame House Gallery in Louisville, Kentucky.

OPPOSITE BELOW RIGHT *Wrented*, serigraph, 1968, for the Frame House Gallery.

ABOVE *Water Ouzel (Dipper)*, gouache, 1955, for the Ford Motor Company's *Ford Times* magazine.

RIGHT *My Name is Puffin*, serigraph, 1971, for the Frame House Gallery.

JOCK KINNEIR
1917–1994
& MARGARET
CALVERT
BORN 1936

WORKING PARTNERSHIP WHO,
WITH THEIR ROAD SIGNAGE
FOR A NEWLY MOBILE BRITAIN,
PLAYED A MAJOR ROLE IN
THE EVOLUTION OF
INFORMATION DESIGN

In the 1950s and '60s, the whole idea of mobility became a key social and cultural theme. There was the notion of upward mobility – the ambition to raise yourself and your family to a better place, in an era of growing production and prosperity. But there was also the idea of personal mobility in the more literal sense, with national and international travel seeing an extraordinary period of expansion. A new breed of airliners and airlines fed the increasing appetite for global adventure and the growth of international business. Car ownership also boomed as mass-production techniques made cars more affordable, and cheaper models – such as the Mini, designed by ALEC ISSIGONIS (see under 'Product and Industrial Design'), or the Fiat 500 – made the prospect of owning a car a more realistic prospect, offering a greater sense of personal freedom and providing an alternative to public transport.

More cars meant, of course, a rapid expansion of road systems and also the evolution of 'information design' as a way of making sense of these increasingly complex networks. This was particularly true of Britain, where drivers of the 1950s were struggling to make sense of a system that had developed in a piecemeal fashion with a whole range of different kinds of signage, depending on which part of the country and what kind of road you might find yourself. The situation was further complicated by the creation of a new class of

super-highroads, or motorways, the first section of the M1 motorway opening in 1959.

It was this that prompted a review of road signage, and graphic designer and typographer Jock Kinneir was entrusted with the task of bringing sense to the system. Kinneir had worked for the Central Office for Information and the Design Research Unit before founding his own design practice in 1956, while also teaching at the Chelsea School of Art. He had asked one of his brightest students, Margaret Calvert, to assist him with one of his first major commissions – designing signage for the new Gatwick airport, south of London. An ambitious design information project, Gatwick proved a positive learning experience for both Calvert and Kinneir.

One job that came out of Gatwick was a commission to redesign the baggage labelling for the P&O shipping company. The chairman of P&O, Colin Anderson, was appointed head of the government committee investigating signage for the new motorways and instantly thought of Kinneir – and Calvert, who was becoming an increasingly important part of Kinneir's office and was appointed an equal partner of Kinneir Calvert Associates in 1964.

Kinneir and Calvert developed a brand new system of signage for the motorways, with clear signs that could easily be read and understood at speed. They developed a new sans serif typeface – an adaptation of Akzidenz Grotesk, known, appropriately enough, as

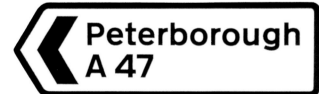

ABOVE 'Children crossing' sign, 1964.

LEFT Directional road signs, 1957–67.

RIGHT A British Rail poster (artist unknown), showing 26 locomotives, one for each service of the day between Birmingham and London, 1972.

BELOW Samples of the new road signage typeface, 1964.

An Inter-City Express leaves Birmingham for London every half-hour

The 112 mile journey takes just over 90 minutes

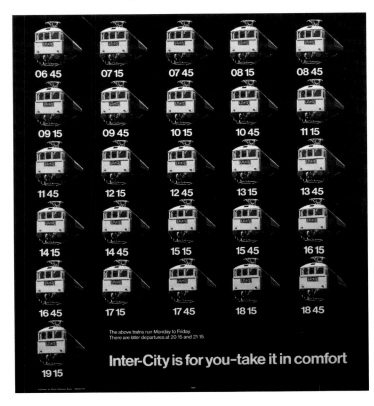

ABCDEFGHI
JKLMNOPQ
RSTUVWXYZ
abcdefghijk
lmnopqrstuv
wxyz'.-,()

Transport. The type was clear and legible, printed in white on a blue background. There was a certain elegance to the signage, but it was also functional and distinct, clearly imparting the necessary information without distracting the driver. The legibility of the signs was proved through tests in an underground car park and in Hyde Park in London. The signage was approved in 1958.

Kinneir and Calvert were then asked to create a system for the entire British road network. This included white letters on a green background for A roads (principal routes) and black lettering on a white backdrop for all other routes. The pair worked within the accepted European convention of using triangular signs for warnings, circles for

commands and rectangular signs for conveying all other information, along with the principle of using pictograms as warning symbols. Like the Transport typeface, the pictograms developed by Kinneir and Calvert adopted the same principles of graphic clarity and high visual impact, while never seeking to distract or confuse an audience in motion.

Among Calvert's pictograms was the 'children crossing' sign, with the taller of the two children based on an old photograph of Calvert herself as a child. 'The ones with human forms and animals were mine,' she explained. 'The cow was based on Patience, who was on the relatives' farm in Warwickshire where my mother and sister and I went when we arrived off the boat from South Africa in

1950. The deer and horse I based on Eadweard Muybridge photographs of animals at speed.'[14]

The new signage system has become part of British identity – a familiar presence that is now taken for granted. But it played a major role in the evolution of information design and also became a model for signage systems in many other parts of the world.

Other key commissions included typography for British Rail and signage for the British Airports Authority and the Tyne & Wear Metro. Both Kinneir and Calvert also taught graphic design at the Royal College of Art.

HERBERT MATTER
1907–1984

SWISS-BORN AMERICAN GRAPHIC
DESIGNER AND PHOTOGRAPHER,
RENOWNED FOR HIS INNOVATIVE
USE OF PHOTOMONTAGE

Like so many of the creative pioneers of the mid-century period, Herbert Matter refused to recognize the boundaries between different disciplines of art and design. In his world, photography and graphic design were two sides of the same coin and his talents in the two fields fused with great originality and technical expertise. He was also a documentary film maker and a Yale professor. Other projects included co-designing the Swiss Pavilion for the 1939 World's Fair, creating a mural in 1958 for the Seagram Building, designed by LUDWIG MIES VAN DER ROHE (see under 'Houses and Interiors'), and creating logos for the New Haven and Boston & Maine railroads.

Matter also had the gift of being in the right place at the right time. He was in Paris during the 1920s and then in New York during the 1950s – two of the great focal points of 20th-century art and design, when new movements and forms of expression were being forged. Matter's creative journey intersected with many of the great names of art and design as he learnt his craft and developed an individual and innovative approach.

Matter was born in the Swiss town of Engelberg, which evolved into a highly fashionable ski resort during his childhood years. He studied at the École des Beaux-Arts in Geneva before starting work as a poster artist. But he was soon tempted to Paris and enrolled at the Académie Moderne, where one of his tutors was the artist Fernand Léger. Afterwards he joined the famous Deberny & Peignot type foundry, but he also worked as a freelance designer and photographer, assisting the legendary Art Deco poster artist A. M. Cassandre and also working briefly with Le Corbusier*.

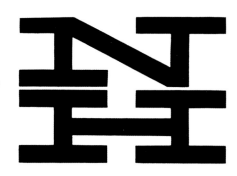

In 1932, Matter returned to Switzerland, where he began working on a series of groundbreaking posters for the Swiss Tourist Office, including promotional images for his own home town. A gifted photographer, Matter skilfully juxtaposed his images in advertising campaigns that pioneered photomontage techniques, experimented with scale and perspective, and used colour sparingly but to powerful effect. Matter's work also had an endearing playfulness, with a strong sense of implied narrative underpinning the strength of the visual surface. Some of his posters offered a dynamic sense of movement, one portraying a passenger plane sweeping over a landscape of snowcapped peaks.

The airplane poster was echoed by a wartime commission, created after Matter moved to the States in 1936. This Civilian Defense poster depicts a soaring eagle, with graphic strokes of red and blue suggesting speed and kinetic energy. Matter continued his career in America with great success, one of his first ports of call being the office of art director Alexey Brodovitch, who happened to have some of Matter's Swiss posters on his wall and began commissioning photography from him for *Harper's Bazaar*.

ABOVE New Haven Railroad logo, 1954.

RIGHT Cover and inside spreads from a booklet released by the Swiss national tourist office, 1935; Herbert Matter also contributed some photographs.

Matter also worked in California for a time, creating covers for John Entenza's* *Arts & Architecture* magazine and working with CHARLES & RAY EAMES (see under 'Furniture').

In 1946, Matter began a long and fruitful working relationship with Knoll*, collaborating closely with Florence Knoll as a design and advertising consultant. As with ALEXANDER GIRARD (see under 'Textiles') at Herman Miller*, Matter's approach was multidisciplinary, but his key tools were photography and typography, as he continued to explore photomontage and narrative techniques. Some of his images were surreal – two tiny workmen on a gantry putting the finishing touches to a pair of oversized HARRY BERTOIA (see under 'Furniture') Diamond chairs; others evinced a form of storytelling that was a key part of many of Matter's advertisements – there was a story being explored beyond the product itself that made you stop and think. In other Matter advertising images, the product itself is used as a graphic element: additional Matter adverts for Bertoia chairs transformed their colourful seat pads into vivid, abstract patterns that become an integral part of the overall image.

RIGHT Tourism poster, designed in 1935.

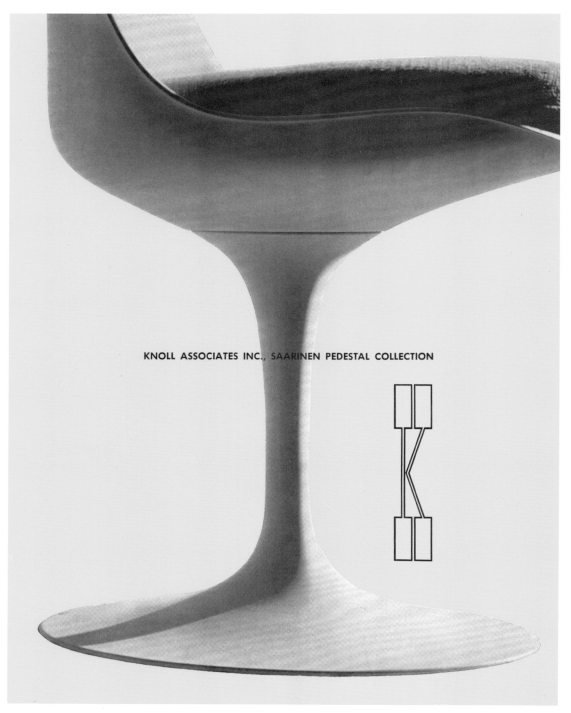

KNOLL ASSOCIATES INC., SAARINEN PEDESTAL COLLECTION

Matter worked with Knoll for twenty years before passing the baton to Massimo Vignelli* in the late 1960s. As well as his many advertisements – infused with a playful, teasing spirit and a powerful visual identity – Matter worked on the graphic design of Knoll catalogues, such as the 1954 Index of Contemporary Design.

Later projects included a documentary film on Alexander Calder* and a photographic essay on another friend, Alberto Giacometti*. Summing up Matter's work, PAUL RAND said, 'It has that timeless, unerring quality one recognizes instinctively. It speaks to all tongues, with one tongue. It is uncomplicated, to the point, familiar, and yet unexpected.'[15]

BELOW Knoll advertisements, promoting the Bertoia Collection, c. 1953.

RIGHT A Knoll advertisement for Eero Saarinen's Womb chair, c. 1951.

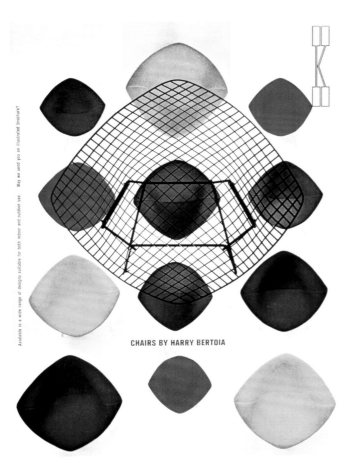

CHAIRS BY HARRY BERTOIA

MAX MIEDINGER
1910–1980

SWISS TYPOGRAPHER
RESPONSIBLE FOR HELVETICA,
THE ARCHETYPAL MID-CENTURY
MODERNIST TYPEFACE

Today, we think of Max Miedinger's Helvetica as a modernist type, and one that felt highly original and innovative in the 1950s and '60s. It became a symbol in itself of a progressive, forward-thinking approach and a font for the future. But it was actually one of a group of typefaces, including ADRIAN FRUTIGER's Univers, that evolved from Akzidenz Grotesk, or Standard Medium as it is sometimes known. This sans serif type was originally introduced back in 1898 by the German type foundry Berthold AG and became a great favourite among German and Swiss typographers and designers, including MAX BILL.

Today its offspring, Helvetica, is a global default font. It is the most recognizable and widely used of the mid-century modernist typefaces, with a character that suggests reliability, practicality, uniformity and – despite its history – modernity. While continuing to feel fresh and contemporary, it has also become so widespread that it has a familiar, reassuring presence. Its clarity and legibility make it a perfect choice for signage and corporate graphics on the one hand and for computer screens on the other.

In the late 1950s Eduard Hoffmann, manager of the Haas type foundry in Münchenstein, began to plan a new variant of an existing font. For the development of the typeface he commissioned Max Miedinger. A native of Zurich, Miedinger had completed an apprenticeship in typesetting and worked in typesetting and typography for a number

RIGHT Promotional material
for Helvetica, early 1960s.

of companies before joining Haas. In the mid-1950s he became a freelance graphic designer and typographer, but continued to produce a number of typefaces for Hoffmann and Haas.

The new font Miedinger developed was initially called Neue Haas Grotesk, but in 1960 it began to be licensed in other countries as Helvetica and was also adopted as a Linotype font. By the mid-1960s it had invaded America and was used increasingly by designers and companies on both sides of the Atlantic. Graphic designer Massimo Vignelli* was a key supporter in the States, using Helvetica in his work for Knoll*, the New York subway system and other organizations.

Perhaps more than any other font, Helvetica has made the transition into the

ABOVE Road safety poster designed by Hans Hartmann, Switzerland, 1963, using Helvetica.

ABOVE RIGHT The cover of a Helvetica specimen book, published by the Haas type foundry, Switzerland.

digital age with ease and grace. No wonder, then, that it surrounds us in our day-to-day life. It is an obvious and safe workhorse used by transit systems and airports, as well as corporations ranging from American Airlines to Gap. It is a truly international typeface, seen the world over, with versions available for many different languages from Hebrew to Hindi. Yet at the same time it is the leading light of the Swiss Style* – the name itself is the Latin for 'Swiss' – and its sans serif nature speaks of a no-nonsense, efficient and functional design philosophy infused with a degree of warmth, humanity and tradition.

From the 1980s onwards the Helvetica family began to grow. A number of variants were introduced, many geared to digital use. The font has been the subject of a landmark film by Gary Hustwit, and entire books have been dedicated to the typeface. Having become more than ubiquitous, Helvetica is now treated with passion, indifference and contempt. Today, it is easy to forget just how enticing the font must have seemed in the early 1960s, when it became a key tool for mid-century designers looking to 'make it new' and to sweep away decades' worth of fussy ornament and indulgent excess.

PAUL RAND
1914–1996

PROLIFIC AMERICAN GRAPHIC
DESIGNER WHO EXPLORED A
NUMBER OF DISCIPLINES WITH
GREAT SUCCESS

The very first task of rebranding performed by Paul Rand was upon himself. Born Peretz Rosenbaum, the graphic designer was just starting out when he decided something simpler and more accessible was called for. He abbreviated his first name to Paul and borrowed the surname from an uncle, creating a neat combination of two succinct and harmonious four-letter words. It was a brand that was to last the course of four or five careers and that continues to endure today, with Rand's philosophy of design still much studied and respected, while many of his corporate logos and identity programmes are still in use.

These include the UPS logo (1961), its shield topped by a wrapped parcel tied with string (Rand famously tested the concept on his young daughter, who immediately recognized the graphic representation). Perhaps his most celebrated collaboration was with a company called International Business Machines Corporation, or IBM. Rand's comprehensive brand identity programme brought the many different aspects of the company's printed and graphic output within one cohesive rule book; in addition, the new logo he developed became a symbol not only of a company that had to be seen to be looking to the future but also of the hi-tech revolution.

The first IBM logo that Rand developed in the late 1950s was little more than a subtle evolution of the existing branding. But in 1962 he created a more ambitious alternative – a striped version, whose black and white banding helped unify the three letters and offered a sense of movement and energy, like pulsing

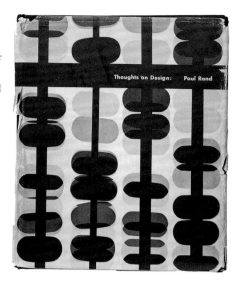

bands of electricity or the lanes of a super highway (see p. 324). 'It not only satisfied the conceptual problem, but also satisfied the visual problem of tying the three letters together, which tended to fall apart,' said Rand. 'Since each letter was different, the fact that all the lines were the same was the element of harmony that brought them together. It's since been used to symbolize the computer industry, and that's only because it's been used by IBM. There's nothing inherent in horizontal or vertical lines that says "computer"....'[16]

Rand was born in Brooklyn, the son of a grocery store owner. He showed an interest in design from an early age, painting signs for his father and for his school. As a teenager he began looking at European design magazines and started drawing inspiration from Swiss Style* designers such as Jan Tschichold, as well as pioneering figures such as A. M. Cassandre. He was also influenced by architects and artists from the Bauhaus*, as well as a wide range of creative innovators who included Le Corbusier*, Pablo Picasso and Fernand Léger.

ABOVE Book cover, self-designed by Paul Rand, published by Wittenborn, Schultz, Inc., USA, 1946.

FAR LEFT A series of logos designed for IBM.

LEFT Logo created for the American Broadcasting Corporation (ABC), 1962.

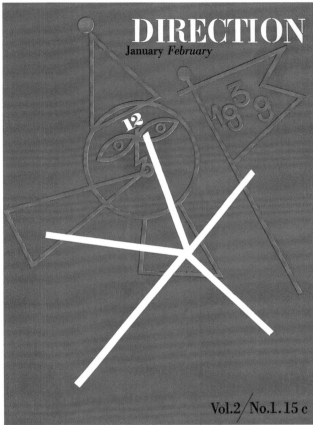

Rand studied at the Pratt Institute, the Parsons School of Design and the Art Students League before assembling a portfolio with freelance assignments and a part-time job with a stock graphics agency. His first career in magazine art direction began in 1937, when he was still only in his early 20s, producing covers and other layouts for *Apparel Arts* magazine and *Direction*.

Rand then moved into advertising, developing posters, billboards and magazine ads for a broad spectrum of clients from Dubonnet and Coronet through to Olivetti and Stafford Fabrics. His advertising work was arresting and colourful, but also infused with wit and humour, playing with startling imagery and intriguing juxtapositions.

Rand explored other ambitions with a large portfolio of book jacket design – working with authors from Thomas Mann to Philip Roth – as well as illustrating a number of children's books written by his second wife, Ann Rand.

By the mid-1950s he was ready for a new challenge, moving into corporate identity as a freelance designer and consultant. His many clients included IBM, ABC television and publishers such as Yale University Press and Alfred A. Knopf. 'A trademark is the signature of a company as opposed to the signature of an individual,' Rand wrote. 'It should as closely as possible embody in the simplest form the essential characteristics of the product or institution being advertised. It should be easy to identify, and it should serve to glorify the merchandise in question, which is often dull and utilitarian in nature.'[17] One of Rand's later commissions was creating a logo and branding for Steve Jobs's NeXT educational computer company in the 1980s.

From computers to light bulbs to engine parts, Rand's work spanned them all. He played a key part in pioneering the development of graphic design as a clearly defined profession, leaving the notion of the jobbing commercial artist far behind. He wrote about his profession and approach to design eloquently in a series of his own books and also found time to teach at Yale University, where HERBERT MATTER was also a professor. Through his many careers, Rand helped to shape the world of design itself.

ABOVE LEFT An interior page from *Apparel Arts* magazine, 1939.

ABOVE Cover of *Direction* magazine, 1939.

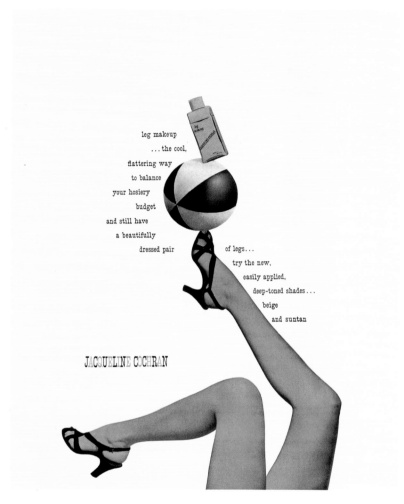

leg makeup
...the cool,
flattering way
to balance
your hosiery
budget
and still have
a beautifully
dressed pair   of legs...
try the new,
easily applied,
deep-toned shades...
beige
and suntan

JACQUELINE COCHRAN

I always feel like traveling

with an **EL PRODUCTO**

ABOVE Advertisement for
Jacqueline Cochran, 1943-46.

ABOVE RIGHT Advertisement
for El Producto, 1953-57.

RIGHT Advertisement for
The Architectural Forum, 1945.

The building market in 1 package

architects & engineers

realty owners & managers

builders & contractors

lending institutions

public officials

distributors & dealers

The Architectural

FORUM

The Anatomy of Revolution

Crane Brinton

A Vintage Book
K 44 $1 25
in Canada $1 35

Paul Rand

OPPOSITE Book cover for
Vintage Books/Random
House, 1956.

RIGHT Book jacket design
for Alfred A. Knopf, 1956.

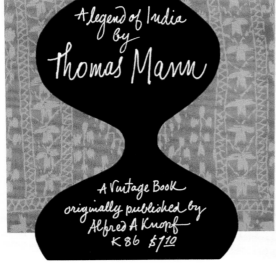

ABOVE Book cover for
Vintage Books/Random
House, 1959.

RIGHT Book cover for
Meridian, 1959.

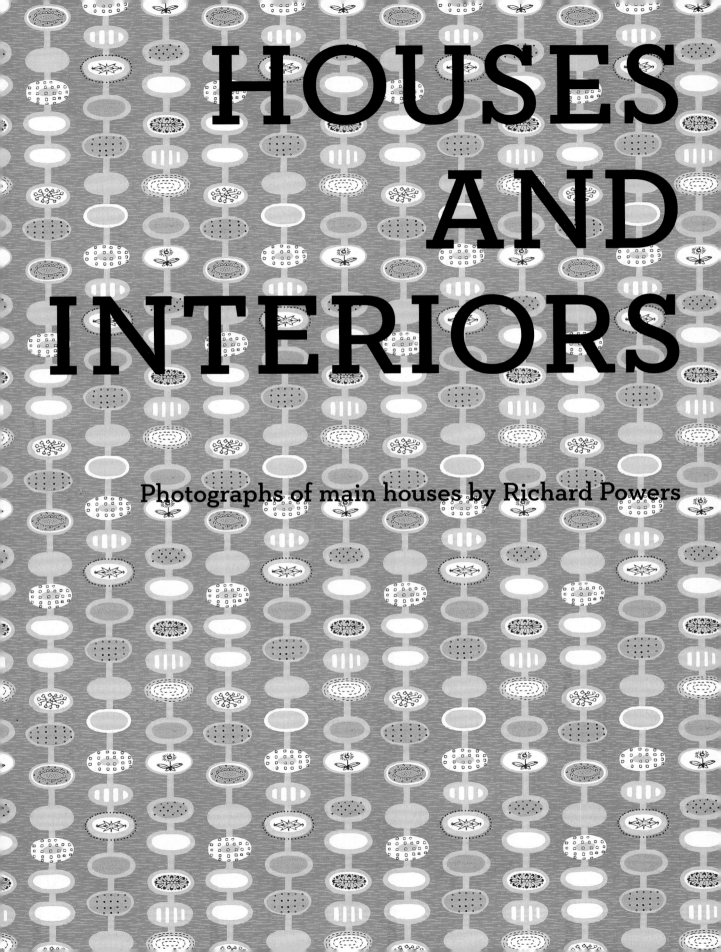

HOUSES
AND
INTERIORS

Photographs of main houses by Richard Powers

INNOVATIONS IN THE MID-CENTURY ERA BROUGHT RADICAL CHANGES TO THE WAYS IN WHICH PEOPLE LIVED, AND THIS WAS REFLECTED IN THE VERY FABRIC OF THEIR HOMES

The 1950s and '60s constituted a period of extraordinary experimentation across all aspects of design. This was particularly true of the home, which was radically reshaped and reinvented. Many of the key characteristics of the way we live today – open-plan living spaces, integrated kitchens, indoor/outdoor living, and so on – were either formulated or refined during the period. The modern home truly came of age in these key design decades.

The modern movement offered a new approach to residential design as early as the 1920s and '30s, when highly influential houses such as Rudolph Schindler's Schindler House in Los Angeles (1922), LUDWIG MIES VAN DER ROHE's Tugendhat House in the Czech Republic (1930) and Le Corbusier's* Villa Savoye in Poissy, France (1931), began to suggest a fresh way of thinking about the organization and construction of our homes. These were buildings that were fluid, open, linear and light, and full of innovative ideas.

By the late 1940s and early 1950s, however, the world had moved on again and in so many different ways. A combination of advanced engineering and technical innovations in the usage of glass, steel and concrete had opened up new possibilities for architects and designers, while prefabrication was also being used as a way of speeding up and streamlining the building process. Home technology in terms of appliances and labour-saving devices – from refrigerators to washing machines – was advancing rapidly, and more and more 'white goods' were making their way into the home.

But just as importantly, by the mid-century period a whole new mentality had established itself when it came to ordering and planning houses. Home life was increasingly informal compared to the early years of the 20th century and few could afford the servants who had serviced so many family homes in the Edwardian and Victorian periods or the

BELOW Inside/outside living at Craig Ellwood's Steinman House, Malibu, California, USA, 1956.

space required to accommodate them. Rather than creating a series of compartments and distinct rooms set aside for one specific purpose or another, architects, designers and their clients began to think about universal spaces and free-flowing floor plans that combined and condensed areas for dining, entertaining and relaxing. Kitchens were no longer simply service spaces hidden away at the back of the home; they became more integral than ever – stocked up with all those new appliances and finished with innovative new materials such as Formica, Vitrolite and Masonite.

Two closely related houses – PHILIP JOHNSON's Glass House (1949) and Mies van der Rohe's Farnsworth House (1951) – pushed the idea of open-plan living further than ever. Using steel frames and banks of floor-to-ceiling glass, these pioneering and highly influential buildings were largely transparent, allowing an intense sense of connection with the surrounding landscape. The steel frame took all the structural load of the building, doing away with the need for a load-bearing façade or any internal supporting walls, and so the floor plan was completely liberated. In the Farnsworth House, Mies famously used a service core – like a monolithic piece of furniture – to contain a kitchenette, bathroom and storage, while the rest of the space was lightly zoned through the arrangement of furniture and rugs, and the eye passed through the pavilion unhindered. Johnson took a similar approach at the Glass House, where a modest cylinder holds a fireplace and compact bathroom, and other services are contained in a twin building nearby – the Brick House. In Brazil, LINA BO BARDI experimented with her own Glass House in São Paulo – an elevated pavilion among the treetops, dominated by a vast open-plan living area opening up to nature and the landscape.

These were striking and – for the times at least - extreme examples of universal space and transparency at work within a 'curtain wall' building, where the façade is liberated from its structural role. Discreet steel frames were used to great effect in California by RICHARD

ABOVE A detail of the colourful windows of the Garcia House, by John Lautner, in Los Angeles, 1962.

NEUTRA, CHARLES & RAY EAMES (see under 'Furniture') and others to create houses with a particular lightness of touch and internal spaces that were flexible and fluid. Neutra's Kaufmann Desert House in Palm Springs (1947) was a particular icon of the age and for many represents the modernist dream house at its best. The largely single-storey house pivots around a light and open central living space, graced with a retractable glass wall leading to terraces and the swimming pool alongside. Guest quarters and service areas are contained within separate wings, while up on the roof Neutra designed a 'gloriette' – a semi-sheltered outdoor room for making the most of the epic views.

Many houses in the famous Californian Case Study Program* – a collection of exemplary houses supported and promoted by John Entenza's *Arts & Architecture* magazine from 1945 to 1966 – used steel or timber frames to create the archetypal 'contemporary' mid-century home. These were linear pavilions, often only a single storey and a flat roof, with fluid, informal layouts, a degree of transparency, and strong connections between indoor and outdoor living. Buildings by Neutra, CRAIG ELLWOOD, Pierre Koenig* and others opened themselves up to the landscape and offered outdoor living rooms in the form of decks, verandas and roof terraces. These were thoughtful residences with clean lines and an unfussy approach, yet they were also ergonomic and practical as well as often playful and colourful. These were not crisp, white, modernist boxes nor machines for living in. They were living homes and full of character and warmth.

Perhaps it is the essential character and warmth of the mid-century home that makes it so inspirational and appealing, especially in comparison to the crisp modernity of many pioneering houses of the pre-war years. On the East Coast, ANDREW GELLER created a series of timber-framed weekend and holiday houses out on Long Island that were infused with a playful spirit and woven into vibrant, sculptural forms. MARCEL BREUER – a Bauhaus* émigré, like Mies and Walter Gropius* – was inspired by the context and materials of New England, and his houses of the 1950s and '60s use timber and field stone combined with linear outlines and innovative thinking to create buildings of great integrity, elegance and organic friendliness.

It was the combination of innovation, contextuality and organic materials that gave rise to some of the most appealing houses of the mid-century period – houses that continue to fascinate and inspire. JAKOB HALLDOR GUNNLØGSSON's own home in Denmark (1958) is a beautifully crafted example in a spectacular setting, overlooking the Øresund Strait. ALVAR AALTO's work was always beautifully executed, using a wealth of natural materials within a contextual response to the landscape and site; his Maison Louis Carré in France (1959), in particular, was a *Gesamtkunstwerk*, for which Aalto designed almost every detail, including the lighting and furniture. HARRY SEIDLER and BRUCE RICKARD in Australia, too, developed a warm, crafted approach within their homes and interiors.

In the 1960s a more dynamic, sculptural approach emerged that lent a new energy and impetus to residential design. The master of energetic '60s design was JOHN LAUTNER, whose gravity-defying concrete, steel and glass houses were balanced on Californian hillsides and mountain tops. Lautner's Elrod House in Palm Springs (1968) was the futuristic setting for a James Bond film, while CHARLES DEATON's Sculptured House in Colorado (1965) represented the future in Woody Allen's sci-fi comedy, *Sleeper*.

The 1960s in particular was also a time of great experimentation in apartment buildings and social housing tower blocks. Many concrete towers in Europe and beyond – partly inspired by the ideas of Le Corbusier and his Unité d'Habitation in Marseilles – may have been well intentioned but were spectacular failures. Yet their architects, such as BASIL SPENCE and ALISON & PETER SMITHSON, salvaged their reputations elsewhere and also produced some very thoughtful homes for themselves along the way, blessed with a softer modernist approach.

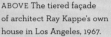

ABOVE The tiered façade of architect Ray Kappe's own house in Los Angeles, 1967.

ABOVE RIGHT Polymath designer Russel Wright's home, Dragon Rock, near Garrison, New York State (1961), the dinner table laid with his American Modern ceramics.

In many ways, the mid-century style that we look to for inspiration today is characterized by soft modernism. It is a way of living that is warm and playful but also informal and contemporary. Mid-century homes challenged convention and tradition, yet so often embraced craftsmanship and contextual, vernacular themes.

Interiors were clean and uncluttered, yet also full of texture and colour. They embraced new materials and fresh ideas, integrating the new wave of home technology – including hi-fis and televisions, which turned the house into a place of entertainment more than ever before. Many elements – from fitted kitchens to storage and furniture – were integrated into the fabric of the house itself, rather than floating freely. Increasingly, within more open-plan layouts, cabinets, storage units and other pieces of furniture were used to help gently delineate separate parts of the home from one another.

As well as being informal, there was a general modesty and accessibility to the scale of mid-century homes, and even highly significant buildings such as the Kaufmann Desert House feel manageable and comfortable. Many of the new breed of mid-century homes were weekend houses and holiday cabins, reflecting not just a new era of affluence post-war but the rise and rise of leisure time itself in the 1950s and '60s.

The evolution of a new generation of architectural and home-making magazines catered for a growing appetite for information and inspiration on every aspect of the home and spread the word about ideas, trends, products and styles more quickly than ever, reinforced by marketing and advertising drives. Disposable income combined with a greater awareness of contemporary architecture, design and interiors among consumers ready to 'make it new' and to forge a different kind of home life, a new way of living, from those embraced by their parents and grandparents. Mid-century style, then, involved a process of not only embracing the future but also – to varying degrees – rebelling against the past. In an era so focused upon revolution and change, it is no wonder that the nature and identity of home shifted so radically in a way that still shapes the way we live today.

COLLECTING THE MID-CENTURY HOUSE
MATT GIBBERD

ABOVE The façade of Louis Kahn's Esherick House, Chestnut Hill, Philadelphia, Pennsylvania, completed in 1961.

While the art market has boomed in the early years of the 21st century, the world of real estate has often proved turbulent. But what about that niche area of investment that straddles the two – the buying and selling of the world's greatest modernist houses, those masterpieces of architecture for which collectors clamber over casual homebuyers?

The auction by Christie's of RICHARD NEUTRA's exquisite Kaufmann Desert House (1947) in Palm Springs, with the lofty estimate of $15–$25m in 2008, was intended to signal the arrival of 'architecture as art' as a serious field for investment. Although the house went under the hammer at just over $16m, the money failed to materialize and the sale never went through. Louis Kahn's* Esherick House (1961) also failed to find a buyer when it was put up for auction by Wright in Chicago in the same year. All this despite an intense level of marketing by both auction houses for the respective sales: Wright commissioned photographer and artist Todd Eberle to produce an elaborate photographic essay on the Esherick house, while Christie's put together the glossiest of brochures which included the offer of 'complimentary air transportation from the Los Angeles International Airport' to all potential buyers.

Despite these high-profile setbacks, there is evidence that superior mid-century modern architecture does have an inherent value above and beyond the local price per square foot (indeed, with such a staggering estimate on the Kaufmann house, it could be argued that Christie's tried to make the market run when it had only just learned to walk). In 2003, Sotheby's sold LUDWIG MIES VAN DER ROHE's seminal but not sizeable Farnsworth House (1951) for the princely sum of $7.5m. At the time, the best houses in that area (Plano, Illinois) were going for around $150,000. The seller was the British property developer and philanthropist Lord Palumbo, who is perhaps the most high-profile collector of modern houses in the world. He owns Kentuck Knob (1956), a Frank Lloyd Wright* masterpiece, and previously acquired two Le Corbusiers* and a Mies van der Rohe apartment overlooking Lake Michigan.

Sotheby's were also responsible for what is thought to be the first offering of modern architecture by a major auction house – the 1989 sale of a Manhattan townhouse designed by PHILIP JOHNSON for $3.5m. It was bought by Anthony d'Offay, the celebrated London art dealer, who clearly knows a good investment when he sees one: he sold the property a decade later for almost four times what he paid for it. The purchaser? Ronald Lauder, chairman of the Museum of Modern Art in New York. The case for architecture being sold as art could not ask for a more convincing case study.

Other notable transactions include Wright's sale of Pierre Koenig's* Case Study House #21 (1958, also known as the Bailey House) in Los Angeles for more than $3.5m (the property cost around $20,000 to build in the late 1950s), and the private purchase of Pierre Chareau's celebrated Maison de Verre (1932) in Paris by the Wall Street banker turned architecture scholar Robert Rubin in 2006. There is also the Christie's sale of one of JEAN PROUVÉ's (see under 'Furniture') Maison Tropicale prototype houses to the hotelier

André Balazs for $5m in 2008; Rubin had also bought another of Prouvé's Maison Tropicale houses some years earlier.

Balazs's famous Chateau Marmont hotel is a short drive from one of Los Angeles's most exalted modern houses, Case Study House #22 by Pierre Koenig (1960, also known as the Stahl House). This single-storey property measures little more than 2,000 square feet and has just two bedrooms, yet the Stahl family – who commissioned the house and still own it – have turned down an offer of $15m. Why is it so covetable? Because it has a perceived value significantly beyond its component parts. The Stahl House is LA's original dream home; the building that came to define the modern city. It was immortalized with a single black-and-white image taken by the photographer Julius Shulman*. The shot shows two glamorously attired women engaged in conversation in a living room that appears to float above the Los Angeles basin. The vertiginous viewpoint contrasts with the relaxed atmosphere of the house's interior, testifying to the ability of the modernist architect to transcend the limits of the natural world. Handily for the Stahl family, thanks to its iconic status the house also does rather well as a location for film and photo shoots. The chances are you will have seen it in an advertisement without even realizing it. It could be argued that it's not really a house at all any more; it's a set of sorts, a glamorous backdrop for conveying the ultimate modern lifestyle.

The same might be said of the 1949 JOHN LAUTNER house that appears in Tom Ford's stylized film, *A Single Man* (2009). The movie's main protagonist, played by a brooding Colin Firth, has a vintage Mercedes, impeccable suits and dashing spectacles, but it is his modernist residence that steals the show. There can't be many people who came away from the cinema and didn't long to own it. So why, when the house came up for sale soon afterwards, did it sit on the market, unsold, for several years? The truth is that it could never live up to its motion-picture billing. And no matter how enticing the property itself might be, buyers will always be swayed by location. The celluloid version of the house is in a suburban-chic section of Santa Monica, whereas the real thing is hidden in a wooded valley at the foot of the Verdugo mountains in Glendale.

It might be the major auction-house sales that grab the headlines, but numerous deals involving less high-profile properties have been brokered in recent years by specialist estate agents such as Mossler Doe in California and The Modern House in the UK, which my business partner Albert Hill and I have run since 2004. The fact that buyers aren't charged a premium is a significant advantage (this being the way the real-estate market works, as opposed to the auction market where the buyer pays a significant commission). Indeed, those running the auction houses readily admit that this is what will always hold them back when selling property: 'the high transaction costs for the buyers' was one of the reasons cited by Wright for the failure of the Esherick House sale.

What is the attraction of such purchases? Compared to, say, a sculpture or a piece of antique furniture, a house eats up a lot more in maintenance charges. Its site specificity also makes it vulnerable to the vagaries of environmental change – a multi-storey car park being built opposite, for instance, or a rise in river levels. But there is also the fact that you can take a holiday in a house, you can occupy it, you can improve it. A building has a romance beyond anything that a Regency armoire or a tribal headdress can offer.

What of the market for modernist property in Britain? The Modern House agency is something of an anomaly within the property industry, focusing not on a particular location but on the design quality of the properties themselves. Having realized the scope of the modern architectural heritage this side of the Atlantic, the agency now provides a forum for it, hosting a database of houses and flats that currently numbers several thousand. It is also noticeable that appreciation for mid-century homes among the British public has increased immeasurably over recent years.

BELOW An iconic period image of Pierre Koenig's Case Study House #22 (the Stahl House), 1960, taken by legendary mid-century photographer Julius Shulman.

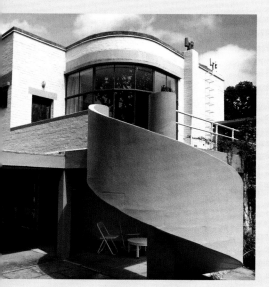

ABOVE An exterior view of artist Augustus John's studio, designed by architect Christopher Nicholson, 1933, in Fordingbridge, Hampshire, UK.

Memorable sales include the studio of the painter Augustus John (1933), designed for him by Christopher Nicholson, which was sold to a well-known sculptor. There was the only house in the UK designed by MARCEL BREUER (Sea Lane House, West Sussex, 1936), which was acquired by a prominent figure in the fashion industry who recognized the value of its singularity. There was the aptly named Space House (1963) by Peter Foggo and David Thomas, one of the few buildings in Britain that stands comparison with the Case Study houses in California. And there are any number of Eric Lyons*-designed 'Span' houses from the 1950s and '60s – modest, carefully detailed homes in little clusters on beautifully landscaped estates throughout southern England.

A few years ago a senior architect at Foster + Partners bought one of the most distinguished modern houses in Britain – the Williams Residence in Suffolk (1963), designed by Sir Philip Dowson. Pointing out that 'it is so difficult to get planning permission for good contemporary buildings in the British countryside now', the buyer realized that the house was one of a rare breed that is only likely to get rarer. Despite the fact that he paid substantially more per square foot than the going rate in the area, he rightly identified that it transcended the local market.

Valuing such architectural one-offs is a challenging task. One must not only consider local prices (in fact, in some cases these are almost irrelevant) but also assess where the property sits in the pantheon of modern houses throughout the country. Regardless of any agency's experience in valuing properties, it is often a matter of setting a guide price and seeing where the market takes it.

Although many of the best examples in the UK have been razed to the ground to make way for short-sighted development projects, advances are being made and English Heritage is listing increasing numbers of buildings from the era. Interestingly, the National Trust took on the custody of one of Britain's finest modernist houses, the Homewood, designed by Patrick Gwynne (1939). Restored to its rectilinear glory, this now resides in the Trust's portfolio alongside medieval castles and Tudor mansions.

The restoration of the Homewood was overseen by John Allan of Avanti Architects, who has made a name for himself as a mid-century specialist. Among many others, he has revived two of the most important houses in Hampstead, North London: Ernö Goldfinger's* house on Willow Road (1939, also owned by the National Trust), and 66 Frognal (1938) designed by Colin Lucas, where the original colour scheme was reinstated.

For projects like this to be successful, significant financial and emotional commitment is required on the part of the owner. Thoughtless extensions and refits to key mid-century buildings, often carried out in the 1960s and '70s, have undermined the authenticity of many of the best examples, as well as their value. Restoring such houses is a specialist task, which can be time-consuming and expensive, especially where there may be structural problems or where the house is listed or closely monitored by the planning authorities. Inevitably, these are buildings that require care and a tailored treatment.

Arguably the finest early modern movement house in the UK is High & Over in Buckinghamshire (1929), a resplendent ocean liner of a building. Bizarrely, it was divided into two parts in 1962, a crude act that destroyed the proportions of the interior. On my first visit I climbed the elegant spiral staircase and banged my head on a plasterboard ceiling on the way up. The roof terrace had been assigned to the other half of the property, so the stairs served no purpose. When the two parts of the building were finally united a number of years later, we sold the house to a couple who set about restoring it to its former glory.

I believe that houses such as these will only increase in value as we become increasingly nostalgic about them. As modernist properties get older and we gain greater historical perspective, the finest examples should be placed on an equal footing with the great Georgian or Victorian houses. They are our heritage of the future.

ABOVE The swimming pool
at 66 Frognal, Hampstead,
London, designed by
architect Colin Lucas of
Connell, Ward & Lucas, 1938.

RIGHT High & Over in
Amersham, Buckinghamshire,
UK, 1929, by Amyas Connell
and Basil Ward (who joined
forces with Colin Lucas in 1934).

ON RESTORING MODERNISM:
THE PURIST AND THE PRAGMATIST

MICHAEL BOYD

In architectural restoration, the purist seeks total authenticity. The idea is to turn back the hands of time; to erase the wear and tear and harsh reality that the elements and owners' use (and sometimes abuse) have brought over many years. Materials fail; lustre fades. Unfortunately, the only material that seems truly to last is the granite used in nearly every remodel during the 1980s. Through either neglect or the simple passage of time, structures can be compromised. To the purist, however, there is no expense too great to stabilize, reclaim or revive a modernist architectural masterpiece.

Not every design worth saving is necessarily groundbreaking: there are numerous examples of highly competent historical modernist buildings. The practitioners who created these perhaps did not come up with some unique principle or idea first, yet their work still informs the present and also the future of building livable and logical structures. So if Victorian and Federal architectural works are protected by preservation laws, then modern architecture should also be guarded by local and national codes and by a responsible caretaker. This informed custodian must also know the limits of what can be added or extended, and – most importantly – what cannot.

The pragmatist knows that the 'price is no object' approach cannot always be followed in reality. Some embedded, antiquated technologies are better off abandoned or at least not brought forward. Some engineering feats are too much to imagine for current conditions. When foundations are failing or compromised, it can be impossible to get access for repairs with the weight and solidity of all that burdens a structure from above. Time, the elements, and unsympathetic owners and custodians can all spell trouble for buildings. Most of this is reversible ... but not all.

Mother Nature can undermine houses in a cruel way, and site-specific issues can arise. California – and Los Angeles, in particular – is *terra firma* challenged. In an area with a high concentration of modernist domestic architecture, one must examine sloped sites carefully and make prudent assessments, taking the unforeseen into account, especially moving ground. There are expensive procedures that are perhaps not necessary, just as there are inexpensive and easy fixes that can make an enormous difference. In short, there are many stumbling blocks on the way to restoring a Californian Frank Lloyd Wright* Mayan concrete block building in an earthquake zone.

At a certain point a narrative must develop that reconciles the possible with the actual, the historical with the contemporary, the real with the imagined. It might seem surprising that in the face of design realities, current and historical, a kind of fiction ever enters into architectural restoration, but in truth it can. These 'stories' are sometimes more interesting and offer more meaningful insights into the process and practice of restoration than a dry list of tasks. The purist approach must be merged with the pragmatic. One must be mindful that people are to inhabit these structures, and the responsible caretaker must come to terms with the challenges of day-to-day living, home ownership and real-estate factors. Practical considerations push heavily into the zone of purist philosophy.

OPPOSITE ABOVE The terrace at Craig Ellwood's Steinman House in Malibu, California, originally commissioned in 1956.

OPPOSITE BELOW Cork flooring in the renovated Steinman House.

When I was composing scores for television and film in the 1990s, I often worked at Skywalker Ranch, George Lucas's facility in Marin County for post-production. It was impressive and beautiful, and had many buildings and structures that spread throughout the property. I worked in the audio building, where Skywalker Sound was housed. One day we ate in a building that seemed older, and on that day an original Hector Guimard fireplace was being installed in the main entry hall. Eventually I learnt that, in fact, many of the buildings were not old, although they looked like well preserved or restored relics. Not only were many of the structures brand new, they each had attached to them a fabricated story that mythologized their existence. As a design purist, I was slightly shocked at first. It seemed unnecessary, even wrong. For example, one tale would be that the audio building was originally built in 1850 by early settlers with a Western bent, remodelled in 1920 with a Deco-inspired interior and then modified again in the 1950s, or something to that effect. I thought to myself, 'How strange.' But at the same time something about it worked quite well. It was undeniably pleasing as a building project and finished space.

Many years later, when I was restoring the Steinman House by CRAIG ELLWOOD on the Malibu coast, it occurred to me that in fact we were also creating fictitious stories in the narrative of our work. The house was commissioned in 1956 by a school principal with a love of the ideal modernist box structures designed by Ellwood and his main associate at the time, Jerry Lomax. When Steinman approached the Ellwood office, he was told that the steel box plans he admired were out of his price range. Steinman persisted and ultimately a 1,600 square foot box was made with wood beams in place of steel. Steinman's budget was modest, but his architecture was superb. Given that money was tight, he planted jade succulents and other inexpensive plants right next to the house. This offered privacy, to be sure, and was easy to maintain, but almost an acre of Malibu sat overgrown and unused. Surely there was a more practical and productive way to utilize the lot.

The new owner and I began to weave a story that went something like: 'What if the Steinman House project had had a larger budget? Ellwood and Lomax would have put in a pool and cabana, and they would have hardscaped and planted the entire property.' I immediately contacted Lomax and he agreed with our projected plans. In other words, we made up a story. When replacing the floor material, we had conversations along the lines of: 'Terrazzo would be beautiful but inappropriate with the modest wood beams and scale of the house. White linoleum would be classic but possibly overpowering. Cork is perfect and in concert with the original commission, yet an upgrade from the plywood sub-floor and wall-to-wall carpet.' This is the kind of lore a pragmatist can conjure up. But the purist can be satisfied as well. No liberties were taken with the original structure or plan, and the consent of the creator was in place. In fact, Lomax and Ellwood themselves returned to the project in 1960 to add a covered carport and to enclose the former garage for additional sleeping quarters. So there was an evolution already underway that we merely continued.

The purist would certainly be shocked by the findings at Paul Rudolph's* townhouse on Beekman Place in New York City. In restoring that project, my wife Gabrielle and I retained architects who had worked on the project in Rudolph's office, in an attempt to keep the restoration on a pure path. But when we found the original drawings and began surgical demolition, it became clear that the plans that Rudolph had submitted to the city bore little resemblance to what had actually been built. Rudolph evidently had a better idea/solution for a given design issue when at the site, and he was going to be the one to inhabit the space. But the house had been left in a state that was impossible to leave 'as is'. There had been endless additions and re-workings, and the building was uninhabitable when we arrived. This was not a Sir John Soane type of situation, with a house left intact by the architect, and something we could memorialize. It was a laboratory for perennial experimentation, and this left us in the position of having to invent or edit a 'story'.

ABOVE Details of the
renovated New York City
townhouse originally designed
by Paul Rudolph.

There was the 1975 chapter that was a very Halston-like, white-on-white example of high tone taste (Rudolph had, in fact, just completed a project around the corner for the American fashion designer so popular in the 1970s). There was also the c. 1980 Studio 54-type chapter, when disco balls and mirrored Mylar covered the place. Then there was the 1990 chapter of plastic replacing white Thassos marble when budgets were limited. And let's not forget the original story: this was a townhouse from 1915. What to do? We navigated carefully through the levels of urban archaeology, and – honouring Rudolph throughout, but making pragmatic decisions – we came up with a legible, livable solution. Since all the Mylar had to be removed for restoration, we decided to play down the Studio 54 version of the building's history, while amplifying the elegance of the Halston white marble and steel rendition, alluding to Rudolph's original vision and legacy of purist modernism in Florida.

We are always careful, and there are plenty of standard procedures on our job sites. Hardware is stored and numbered. Original doors, case goods, windows and vintage fixtures are saved, catalogued and restored non-invasively whenever possible. Hairline cracks in stone and concrete are accepted, and only structural issues suggest complete re-dos. The purity of the architect's original intent is paramount when engaging in such projects, but the pragmatism required to prepare a habitation for a new owner also plays a part. Today new technologies are available, so are they to be installed and hard-wired in the walls, as they are in new construction? Perhaps not, but wireless could be an option. These are the kinds of questions that arise and lead to an interior dialogue; the internal two-sided conversation between the purist and the pragmatist.

When we first began work on OSCAR NIEMEYER's Strick House of 1964, we were faced with the fact that the landscape had already been stripped in preparation for demolition of the house. The City of Santa Monica Landmarks Commission intervened to save the house, preventing a developer from proceeding with the building of a McMansion or Tuscan behemoth. The silver lining was that we could begin the landscaping with a clean slate. We wanted to infuse the project with the sense of a Brazilian environment, in general, and the exuberant gardens of Roberto Burle-Marx, a frequent Niemeyer collaborator, in particular. Luckily, the house itself did not require major architectural changes, as it was unaltered. But the wall-to-wall carpet and linoleum floors needed replacing: in accordance with our story's tropical narrative we introduced palm-wood floors. In preserving the architectural past, we needed to leave space for the building to evolve, enabling new stories to be told. The inside is now outside and the outside inside, as was Niemeyer's original plan.

He himself never physically came to the site: all the work was carried out by sub-contractors suggested by John Entenza, editor of *Arts & Architecture* magazine and patron of the Case Study Program*. Many of the architectural details are reminiscent of RICHARD NEUTRA's projects, which made it simpler to attain appropriate salvage hardware and vintage materials. This design DNA connection has been noted by the architectural historian Thomas S. Hines, who has referred to the Strick House as an unofficial Case Study House project.

Although some lingering lore can be eliminated or tamped down, it is not of course the case that any story will do. There is more freedom to invent in new construction, as in the case of Skywalker Ranch, but in building renovation and restoration one has to fit into and follow the existing narrative created by the architect's original vision and scheme, as well as the one that revolves around the question, 'What can be done from this point on?' For example, I arrived one morning to begin work at a Neutra house near UCLA to find that the owner, in the short time since our last meeting, had taken it upon himself to re-plaster and paint the house mac-'n'-cheese orange, inspired by a trip to Tuscany. The plaster was smooth-trowled and sloped at the base, like the vernacular rustic buildings he had seen. I had the Neutra specifications in hand that called for a specific sand finish. Fortunately, I was able to persuade the owner that Neutra knew best, especially when it came to his own buildings, and that superimposing an Italian story onto a Californian mid-century masterpiece just didn't work. The house now stands proudly in its intended crisp International Style white sand-finish stucco. Sometimes there is only one possible 'story'.

Restoration involves peeling back the insensitive and disparate layers of additions and re-workings, getting into the mindset and vocabulary of the original designer or architect, and extrapolating with care, thought and delicacy. The new 'story' is written by the lives that take over the space after the restorer has stabilized the gem-like building. Living in the space is the creative exercise, not the resurrection of the building.

Of course this attitude would be cavalier when approaching Josef Hoffman's Sanatorium Purkersdorf in Vienna (1906), or Charles Rennie Mackintosh's Glasgow School of Art (1897–1909), or any number of magnificent manifestations of modernism. These are masterworks on public display with museum-piece status. They have never descended into a state of ruin and there is copious literature, archival drawings and plans, as well as photographic evidence, to set the course for maintenance and rehabilitation.

The good fortune of working on residences by JOHN LAUTNER, Craig Ellwood, Oscar Niemeyer, Paul Rudolph, Richard Neutra, Rudolph Schindler and others is that – unlike the public masterworks – these will all ultimately be owner-occupied. We must not make any irreversible changes, yet we must make room in the present incarnation of the house for the modern conveniences needed for growing families and inspired connoisseurs.

A balance is needed between a purist approach and a pragmatic approach; between art and life. The role of a homeowner must be reconciled with that of a guardian. There is both the responsibility that comes with ownership of an irreplaceable treasure and the freedom that comes with living life in a unique space. One can tread lightly, almost invisibly, on architecture and still live fully. Of course new custodians of important buildings must be cautious and diligent, and must bring forward the original architect's design, but they must also remember the creator's ultimate intention: a living space offering health, happiness and relative ease. Exaltation and inspiration, even awe, are part of the recipe in embracing vintage modern design, but the other key ingredients are compromise and practicality. It comes down to a measured system of balancing the opposing purist and pragmatic philosophies. When Le Corbusier* was challenged about the apartment buildings at Chandigarh, his visionary city in India, and the fact that all of the luminous polychrome exterior decks so carefully calibrated and planned by his office were now, some years later, filled with a cacophony of bicycles and personal clutter, he responded: 'Life is always right.'

BELOW The renovated Strick House in Santa Monica, originally designed by Oscar Niemeyer in 1964.

ALVAR AALTO
MAISON LOUIS CARRÉ, FRANCE, 1959

A HIGHLY CRAFTED AND
REMARKABLY INTEGRATED
SYNTHESIS OF ARCHITECTURE,
FURNISHINGS, FITTINGS
AND LIGHTING

For Finnish architect and designer Alvar Aalto no detail seemed too small to merit attention. A polymath with a cohesive, all-encompassing vision, he preferred to create buildings that were true *Gesamtkunstwerks* – total works of art. This included architecture, interiors, furniture, lighting and detailing, right down to hand rails and wash basins.

It was Aalto's design for a tuberculosis sanitorium in Paimio, Finland (1933), that first secured his international reputation. Here, on a substantial scale, he concerned himself with every facet of the project, seeking to create a building where design was placed at the service of health, and a warm, welcoming, colourful environment was intended to encourage the rehabilitation and well-being of patients. Aalto made the most of the spectacular location, designing balconies that looked out over pine forests. He also designed a range of furniture for the project, including his famous Paimio (Model 41) chair (1932).

A few years later Aalto co-founded his own furniture company, Artek*, with his wife Aino Aalto* – a successful designer in her own right – and Nils-Gustav Hahl and Maire Gullichsen. Artek continues to produce and market Aalto's designs, particularly from the 1930s and '40s.

Maire Gullichsen was the daughter of Finnish industrialist Walter Ahlström and shared – with her husband Harry – a love of modern art and architecture. They were among Aalto's key patrons, as well as business partners, and commissioned the Villa Mairea, one of

Aalto's most famous houses. Completed in 1939, this summer villa in Noormarkku on a rural Ahlström estate was an extraordinary collaboration between architect and client. Every aspect was considered and discussed, and a powerful relationship was established between the house and its country setting.

There are clear echoes of Villa Mairea and its highly creative genesis in the story of Aalto's best respected house of the 1950s: the Maison Louis Carré. Again, Aalto found an energetic and sophisticated client willing to grant him creative freedom while encouraging ever greater achievement; and, again, the level of bespoke detailing was profound and the connections to the natural context of the house were key.

Louis Carré, a dealer in modern art, first met Aalto in Venice in 1956, where the latter had designed the Finnish Pavilion at the Biennale. The pair got on well from the start, and, even though Carré knew Le Corbusier* well, he favoured Aalto's approach and his love of natural materials. Carré asked for a pitched roof, but this was one of the few stipulations.

The house sits on a hillside, southwest of Paris, not far from Versailles. The monopitch roof is in French slate from Trélazé and echoes the gradient of the site, while the house itself is constructed of a base layer of Chartres limestone topped with white-painted brick and timber detailing.

The entrance area is one of the most dramatic moments, with a sinuous free-form vaulted ceiling in the shape of a wave, made

PREVIOUS PAGES The open living room is arranged around a fireplace, with nearly all the furniture, as well as the lighting, designed by Alvar Aalto himself.

BELOW The slope of the roof forms a clear line that echoes the natural slope of the hill, although the land to one side has been terraced to form dramatic steps with the feel of an amphitheatre.

of strips of Finnish red pine. The warmth of the timber is brought out by high clerestory windows positioned over the front door. Carré declared the hallway a masterpiece in itself.

The hallway is the true junction of the house, marking the point of separation between the building's different sectors. There is a natural progression down a small rank of steps to a generous living room, with a series of windows opening up to the view down the hill to the countryside beyond – now partially obscured by mature trees bordering the grounds. A wall of timber coat cupboards in the hallway disguises the entrance to the more private side of the house, with his-and-her master suites for Carré and his wife, while the kitchen and service spaces are positioned to the rear. Additional bedrooms are positioned on a modest upper level. As well as this contrast between the more 'public' and private areas of the house, there is a distinction between the openness of the hallway and sitting room and the more intimate evening retreats, such as the library and dining room.

As with Villa Mairea, Aalto's all-pervasive approach to furnishings and detailing – as well as landscaping and additional elements, such as the pool and pool pavilion – gives the house a cohesive charm, while his signature emphasis on refined natural materials lends the house a great sense of warmth and character. Carré travelled to Finland a number of times to select Aalto designs from the Artek line, but many pieces – from furniture down to door handles – are bespoke creations.

While the house served as Carré's residence, it featured artworks by Pablo Picasso, Paul Klee, Fernand Léger, Alberto Giacometti* and Alexander Calder*. Aalto paid great attention to creating surfaces where these artworks could be displayed, as well as bespoke lighting to illuminate them, such as the multi-directional pendant lights over the dining table.

It is a house that suggests, like so much of Aalto's work, a true sensitivity and sympathy for natural materials, a deep-rooted appreciation of contextuality and landscape, and a great understanding of functionality and ergonomics. Maison Louis Carré, now a historic monument, represents one of Aalto's most significant accomplishments.

ABOVE The wooden gate in the entrance hallway, at the top of the steps from the living room, marks the boundary between the more 'public' and private realms of the house.

LEFT High clerestory windows throw sunlight on the undulating ceiling of the entrance hall, coated in Finnish red pine.

ABOVE The kitchen sits to the rear of the house, within a self-contained section that also includes a staff room.

ABOVE RIGHT The living room looks out over the sloping grounds and to the landscape beyond.

RIGHT The nest of tables and the ceiling light in this corner of the living room are Alvar Aalto designs.

ABOVE The dining room is a comparatively intimate evening space to one side of the main entrance. The dining table is a bespoke Aalto design and the chairs are Artek pieces designed by Aalto.

RIGHT The ceiling lights in the dining room are bespoke Aalto designs, designed to direct light both downwards onto the table and across to the artworks on the wall.

FAR RIGHT One of the door handles specially designed for the house, in brass with a leather sheath attached.

LINA BO BARDI
GLASS HOUSE, BRAZIL, 1951

AN INNOVATIVE BELVEDERE
IN THE TREETOPS THAT INSPIRED
A NEW WAVE OF VIBRANT
BRAZILIAN ARCHITECTURE
AND INTERIORS

Lina Bo Bardi was fascinated by the idea of floating buildings. Her most famous design – on Avenida Paulista in the heart of downtown São Paulo – is the Museum of Art of São Paulo (MASP), completed in 1968. This extraordinary gravity-defying structure has four vast crimson columns that continue along the roof line until they meet and join, supporting a crisp, floating rectangle of glass and concrete. Beneath the museum sits a piazza, partially shaded by the great mass hovering above the ground.

It is, in a sense, an extreme reinterpretation of Le Corbusier's* own obsession with elevated architecture, explored most famously with Villa Savoye – his pioneering house in Poissy from 1931, raised up above a pristine lawn by a series of steel piloti, or columns. LUDWIG MIES VAN DER ROHE's Farnsworth House of 1951 also appears to float but in a more gentle way, raised a modest five feet above the floodplain of the Fox River in Illinois. Bo Bardi took these ideas further, not only with MASP but with her own São Paulo home, the Glass House, also completed in 1951.

Raised up on slender steel columns on a hillside site, surrounded by greenery and towering trees, the Glass House is an observatory for viewing both nature and the city in the distance. In the 1950s the district of Morumbi was still relatively untamed and Bo Bardi delighted in the wildlife to be found around the house: armadillos, deer, sloths and birds of all kinds. 'Many frogs and toads would croak at night,' she wrote. 'There were also some very beautiful snakes and many cicadas.'[1]

Today Morumbi has long been swallowed by the vast metropolis of São Paulo, but the sense of theatre surrounding the Glass House – and its immediate setting within a natural enclave – remains. It was a very individual retreat for Bo Bardi and her husband, full of drama, character and ritual. Steps ascend from under the belly of the house, with a landing halfway, and lead directly into a vast open studio with a blue mosaic floor: an open-plan living space among the treetops with space for a dining area, library and lounge. The sense of elevation was accentuated further by a suspended courtyard to one side of the studio, with a mature tree piercing the opening. It was a dramatic backdrop for an eclectic and very personal collection of art, period furniture, statuary and pieces designed by Bo Bardi herself, including her famous Bowl chair (1951).

Although she took Brazilian citizenship and is widely regarded as one of the greatest figureheads of Brazilian modernism, Bo Bardi's formative years were spent in Italy, where she was born. She studied architecture at Rome University and then moved to Milan, where she went to work for the great Italian

PREVIOUS PAGES AND ABOVE The main living room is a light-filled space with a mosaic floor and a mixture of period pieces, mid-century furniture and many of Lina Bo Bardi's own designs.

polymath GIO PONTI (see under 'Furniture'), serving an apprenticeship that covered all aspects of design. She went on to establish her own practice, while also working as a journalist and illustrator. During the war years she briefly edited *Domus* magazine and then joined the Resistance.

In 1946, after all the destruction of the war years – which Bo Bardi documented on a tour around Italy – she married the journalist, art curator and collector Pietro Bo Bardi and they decided to set sail for Brazil, taking with them a library, artworks and furniture in the hold of the liner *Almirante Jaceguay* – pieces that were to inhabit the Glass House.

In Brazil, Bo Bardi felt liberated: 'I felt myself in an unimaginable country, where everything was possible.'[2] The Glass House was the most personal expression of this new sense of freedom, and soared upwards – quite literally – over a landscape that she embraced.

Yet, perhaps in contrast to the transparent simplicity and purity of Mies's Farnsworth House, Bo Bardi's home was not a space that revealed itself in one open gesture. She contrasted the sense of transparency in her own Glass House with other elements that revealed themselves by degrees. The studio room, overlooking São Paulo, was open and light, sheltered only by diaphanous curtains, when needed, but beyond this was a sequence of bedrooms and bathrooms, meeting the rising slope of the hillside. Beyond these was a courtyard with a sequence of service spaces to the rear, while the kitchen lay away to one side. Within the grounds themselves there was a separate studio, a porter's lodge and garaging.

The interiors, too, were full of unexpected delights and discoveries, with the greenery outside offset by the shining surface of the marine-coloured mosaics of the floors. The choice of furnishings introduced organic textures through leather, timber and stone. There was a place for art, curios and treasures of all kinds, and each had space to breathe.

Bo Bardi's house, then, was full of life and personality. Architecturally, it was one of the key houses that lent power and originality to a vibrant modernist scene at the heart of mid-century Brazilian design.

ABOVE The elevated house sits high among the trees, which grow around and through the very centre of the building.

ABOVE A bespoke fireplace
forms a focal point in
the main living space,
with a dining area beyond.
Diaphanous curtains can
be used to diffuse the light.

LEFT Sculptural lighting
and warm colours help bring
additional character to the
house.

ABOVE LEFT Bo Bardi's own
furniture designs in the house
include her Bowl chair of 1951.

ABOVE The kitchen sits
towards the rear of the house,
warmed by a playful use
of colour and mosaic floors.

LEFT The recliner and
ottoman by Charles & Ray
Eames contrast with the
many self-authored pieces
and period touches.

ANTONIO BONET
LA RICARDA, SPAIN, 1963

A CLASSIC OF MODULAR,
COMPOUND LIVING, THIS HIGHLY
TAILORED HOME CONSISTS OF
THREE INTERLINKED PAVILIONS

It seems that in the 1950s and '60s the world of design was far less compartmentalized than it is today. The word 'designer' embraced a whole plethora of products and environments, while artists designed lights, sculptors designed furniture, and architects turned their hand to almost anything that interested them. One thinks of ALVAR AALTO and of ARNE JACOBSEN and EERO SAARINEN (see under 'Furniture'). Another name that comes to mind is Antonio Bonet Castellana, a gifted and imaginative designer of furniture and interiors as well as an architect.

One of Bonet's most famous designs was actually one of his simplest. The Butterfly chair of 1938 (also known as Model 198, or the BKF chair), a modern reinterpretation of a 19th-century campaign chair, was designed with associates Jorge Ferrari-Hardoy and Juan Kurchan. It used two loops of tubular steel to create a strong frame, with a sling seat in leather or canvas. This lightweight easy chair for indoor or outdoor use was produced by Knoll* in the late 1940s, but was dropped after the company lost a copyright infringement case. The chair is now ubiquitous, manufactured with a whole range of seats.

At the other end of the spectrum stands one of Bonet's most accomplished, cohesive and sophisticated buildings, La Ricarda, in Barcelona. Here Bonet not only designed a modular country retreat, consisting of a triptych of interlinked pavilions, but also created interiors of great warmth and character, and designed much of the furniture.

The building was commissioned by engineer Ricardo Gomes and his wife – a couple with a strong interest in architecture, art and music. They wanted a spacious, welcoming and liberating home for themselves and their six children, and chose a spot on a family estate on the outskirts of the city, close to the sea and a small lagoon, with a small airfield close by. The Gomes family first commissioned Bonet in the early 1950s, when he was living in South America. Bonet's peripatetic lifestyle and the difficulties of long-range communication meant that the house was not completed until 1963, although Bonet did open an office in Spain in 1958 and moved back to Barcelona permanently in the early 1960s.

Bonet was born in the city and studied at its School of Architecture. He formed the practice MIDVA in 1935 with two fellow students and collaborated with Josep Lluís Sert on the Spanish Republican Pavilion for the 1937 Paris International Exhibition. During the Spanish Civil War, he went to work in Le Corbusier's* office, where he met Ferrari-Hardoy and Kurchan. The three went on to establish a practice in Buenos Aires. Key Spanish projects of the 1960s include La Ricarda and the Meridiana Greyhound Track (1963).

The design of La Ricarda evolved partly as a response to its setting. 'The central concept of the design came from the landscape, which is why I decided to build it as a single storey, in spite of the large scale of the project,' said Bonet. 'The needs of a large family had to be considered along with the ability

PREVIOUS PAGES Latticed windows using glass, stained glass and ceramic tiles are a repeated motif in the house, providing a diffused light and splashes of colour. The furniture around the fireplace was designed by Antonio Bonet.

BELOW The series of low-slung pavilions that form the house are protected by the wave-like roof, with mature trees forming a green backdrop.

of the parents, great music lovers, to separate themselves and have the option of using the living room for holding concerts.'[3]

Two single-storey pavilions were designed for the parents and the children, while the family as a whole congregated in a third that was dominated by generous living spaces. Within the main pavilion there is a large sitting room with a double-vaulted ceiling and large windows introducing a rich quality of controlled light. Rugs over the stone flag floors help to lightly delineate separate seating zones.

Bonet used many varied elements to give character and originality to the architecture and interiors, including internal courtyards and indoor gardens, latticed brick walls and latticed windows studded with stained glass. Much of

ABOVE LEFT Glazed walkways help connect different parts of the house. The two seats are examples of Bonet's famous Butterfly chair from 1938.

ABOVE The window lattice creates a patterned backdrop to this study niche, complete with bespoke fitted desk.

FAR LEFT The roof shelters verandas as well as the main house, creating easily accessible outdoor rooms.

LEFT A view down one of the spine hallways, with two Harry Bertoia for Knoll chairs at the end of the passage.

the furniture is by Bonet himself, including the double-sided suede sofas in the main seating area and the elmwood dining table. There are also many integrated and bespoke elements. Even the most functional areas, such as the kitchen, are enlivened with blue mosaic walls and sky-grey floors.

La Ricarda is a house of great originality and sophistication. The peaceful nature of the retreat has, however, been marred by the transformation of the small airfield next door into an international hub airport. But the Gomes family continue to care for the house and it remains a beautiful example of carefully crafted compound living, where the occupants can choose to set themselves apart or can come together within a communal hub.

OPPOSITE ABOVE An indoor garden set into the floor helps lend an organic note to this side of the main, open-plan living space.

OPPOSITE BELOW Integrated furniture – including desks, storage cupboards and sink units – lends the house cohesion as well as a degree of simplicity and purity.

LEFT Screens and rugs help define this games table to one side of the main living room. The chairs are by Hans Wegner.

BELOW LEFT The elm dining table was designed by Bonet, while the cabinet is a piece by artist Magda Boulmar.

BELOW A tiled courtyard serves as both a bolt of colour and a lightwell, helping to introduce sunlight to more sheltered parts of the house.

MARCEL BREUER
STILLMAN HOUSE II, USA, 1966

HIGHLY CONTEXTUAL HOUSE,
INTEGRATING ORGANIC STONE,
BRICK AND TIMBER WITH
THE ROBUST, RECTANGULAR
OUTLINES ASSOCIATED WITH
THE BAUHAUS

Architects and designers dream of clients like Rufus Stillman. The industrialist was one of Marcel Breuer's most ardent and faithful supporters, commissioning not just one but three houses, all focused on the town of Litchfield in Connecticut. He and his wife Leslie had seen Breuer's exemplar of an affordable modern American home in an exhibition at the Museum of Modern Art in 1948 and their interest was sparked. It was the beginning of a long and close friendship.

Stillman was the vice-president and later chairman of the Torin Corporation, for which Breuer eventually became the architect of choice, designing nine buildings around the world. Stillman also played a pivotal role in Breuer winning the commission for a series of school buildings in the Litchfield area in the 1950s. In addition, Stillman introduced Breuer to a number of friends and associates who placed work at the architect's door.

Breuer built around sixty houses in the post-war period, mostly in Connecticut and New England. They tended to be either linear long houses, often elevated upon hillside locations, or 'bi-nuclear' homes, with a clear sense of separation between public daytime spaces and intimate sleeping and guest zones. His interiors were generally characterized by fluid layouts, with open-plan living areas and a combination of clean lines with organic materials.

Born in Hungary, Breuer studied in Vienna before moving to the Bauhaus*, where he established an enduring friendship with the

director, Walter Gropius*. By the mid-1920s Breuer was head of the Bauhaus furniture workshop and developing his own range of tubular steel furniture, including the famous Wassily armchair, or B3 club chair. In 1935, he moved to England, where he worked briefly with F. R. S. Yorke and also Jack Pritchard's Isokon* furniture company.

Two years later he followed Gropius to America, taking up his mentor's invitation to teach at Harvard and founding an architectural practice with his fellow émigré. By 1946 Breuer had his own practice and had settled with his family in the Connecticut town of New Canaan, becoming known as the senior member of the 'Harvard Five', along with a group of his ex-students. By the time Breuer first began working with Rufus Stillman in the early 1950s, he had developed an interest in the local, vernacular materials of Connecticut and its gentle landscape.

Stillman House II is pushed into a slope in a quiet, rural location just outside Litchfield. The single-storey building sits on a base of field stone, topped by stucco walls pierced with large, sliding glass windows and a flat roof. The main, open-plan living area is at the centre, with space for the kitchen, dining area and a seating zone around a fireplace, while a semi-sheltered terrace sits out in front. The master bedroom is positioned to one side of this central space, with three bedrooms to the other, in a U-shaped plan. A small guest lodge is set apart from the main house, cantilevered over a stone wall that helps form a boundary to the gardens and pool area further up the slope.

The house was highly sophisticated for its time, using radiant underfloor heating, air conditioning vents set into brick floors and windows on a sliding track and ball bearing system developed by Breuer. Many elements, such as benches and the dining table on the terrace, were built-in. Breuer also landscaped the grounds, planting a number of silver birches. His friend Alexander Calder*, who lived nearby, added a mural on a wall further down the site; a signature touch that also graced Stillman's other two Litchfield houses.

Completed in 1966, Stillman House II still feels fresh and innovative. It has recently been restored by creative consultants Barbara Dente and Donna Cristina, who have respected and restored the many original features and elements that make the house so unique.

CHARLES DEATON
SCULPTURED HOUSE, USA, 1965

AN EXUBERANT, CURVILINEAR,
MOUNTAINTOP MASTERPIECE
THAT PAVED THE WAY FOR NEW
FORMS OF RESIDENTIAL SPACE

Across the state of Colorado and beyond, the
Sculptured House has become a landmark.
The sinuous form of this futuristic mountaintop home is clearly visible from the freeway
down in the valley below and has long been a
source of fascination. Designed in the 1960s by
architect Charles Deaton, and based on ideas
first developed in a plaster sculpture made in
his studio, the house was way ahead of its time.

'I knew … when I started the sculpture
that it would develop into a house,' Deaton
said. 'There was, however, no attempt to simply
wrap a shell around a floor plan. In fact, no
scale was set until the sculpture was done.'[4]

The dynamic shape of the construction,
set in a 15-acre site on Genesee Mountain, was
so pioneering that it helped define the future

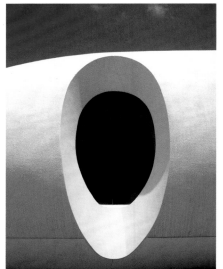

itself when it featured in Woody Allen's sci-fi
comedy film, *Sleeper* (some still call it the
Sleeper House). Deaton finished the exteriors
in 1965, but he was unable to complete the
interiors, which remained empty at his death.

Born in New Mexico, Deaton was a
largely self-taught architectural and product
designer who funded his early studies with
work as a commercial artist. He based himself
in Denver, Colorado, from 1955 onwards and
focused on designing bank buildings and then
stadiums. The Sculptured House was a much
more personal project and the only residential
design of his career.

'The house was never finished,' says his
daughter, interior designer Charlee Deaton,
who with her sister would go along and help

their father paint the house. 'We lived on the same mountain as the house and so I grew up near it and was witness to it being developed and built. It slowly evolved through my childhood but it was stop-start. He was very busy with other projects....'[5]

The house is anchored to the bedrock with a steel and concrete cylindrical pedestal. Its clam-shell upper level is made of a steel frame coated in pumped concrete, with a smooth final layer of synthetic rubber mixed with walnut shells and white pigment. Deaton could not afford to finish the house or hold on to it, so sold it just before his death in 1996.

During his last months he drew up some initial ideas for an addition to the house for its new owners, collaborating with Charlee's husband, architect Nick Antonopoulos. But work on the Sculptured House only restarted in the late 1990s, with the building still little more than a shell. Antonopoulos and Charlee Deaton worked closely together on bringing in services, finishing the interiors and reworking the plans for a large addition, discreetly pushed into the hillside.

The few original interiors elements, such as a striking staircase, were preserved, while Charlee Deaton designed many bespoke pieces of furniture, complemented by mid-century classics. The upper level of the clam shell is dominated by the open-plan living area, leading out onto a large terrace that takes full advantage of the panoramic views. The master bedroom and bathroom are also positioned on this upper level, with further bedrooms on the two lower levels of the main house. Extra living space, service areas and caretaker's quarters are all positioned within the new extension.

'As a family, we weren't in a position to keep the house ourselves and it was painful to see my father have to let it go. But I think he would have been really pleased with the finished house. It truly reflects, as my father would say, the "unencumbered song" that it should sing.'[6]

Restored and refreshed, the Sculptured House has great vitality, with a dynamism that can be compared to some of JOHN LAUTNER's work, or even the 'bubble' houses of Antti Lovag*. It remains a symbol of an optimistic age, when anything seemed possible.

ABOVE An Arne Jacobsen chair and Eero Saarinen pieces sit next to a Corona chair by Poul Volther.

ABOVE RIGHT Splashes of vibrant colour stand out against the white walls in this guest bedroom.

RIGHT A Ribbon chair and ottoman, by Pierre Paulin.

OPPOSITE The master bedroom is in the main part of the house, with views out across the forested hillside. The yellow Marshmallow sofa is by George Nelson.

CRAIG ELLWOOD
PALEVSKY HOUSE, USA, 1970

MODERNIST CALIFORNIAN
DREAM HOUSE, EXEMPLIFYING
ASPECTS OF INDOOR/OUTDOOR
LIVING, COMPOUND LIVING
AND COURTYARD LIVING

A constant thread of glamour wrapped itself around the life and work of Craig Ellwood. In many ways, he lived the Californian dream, driving fast cars and making the most of his natural charm. No wonder some called him the Cary Grant of modernist architecture.

More than this, he was a gifted and instinctive architect and designer, with an understanding of the need for self-promotion. One of his greatest supporters was John Entenza, editor of *Arts & Architecture* magazine, who published a large number of Ellwood's projects. Ellwood also designed three Case Study* houses. These were typically crisp, linear and single-storey, beautifully made and crafted, with an emphasis on free-flowing layouts and indoor/outdoor living, while stocked with every modern amenity.

Ellwood was a self-made man and a largely self-taught architect; even his name was a fabrication. He was born Jon Nelson Burke, the son of a barber. During the war years he enlisted in the US Army Air Corps and afterwards worked as a cost estimator for a construction company while taking night classes in architecture, engineering and design. By the time he set up Craig Ellwood Associates in 1948, he was an expert in steel construction techniques and applied his knowledge and creativity to his designs, which were influenced both by the work of Californian contemporaries such as RICHARD NEUTRA and the lessons of LUDWIG MIES VAN DER ROHE.

One of Ellwood's most loyal clients, Max Palevsky, often thought he should have become an architect, too. Instead, he became a pioneer of the Californian computer industry. In 1961 he founded a company called Scientific Data Systems (SDS), which he later sold to Xerox, helping to fund his interests as a philanthropist, art collector and patron of architecture.

Palevsky commissioned Ellwood to design a production plant for SDS that was completed in 1966, and by then architect and client were good friends. Palevsky already had a weekend and winter apartment in Palm Springs, but it lacked the privacy that he and his wife wanted. So he bought a prime piece of land on the edge of the city, not far from Neutra's Kaufmann Desert House, and asked Ellwood to design him a retreat. Fascinated by the idea of a walled compound, the architect and client – along with their wives – took a trip to Morocco and Tunisia, seeking inspiration from the walled farmsteads and hamlets of North Africa.

Working with associated Alvaro Vallejo, Ellwood designed a rectangular compound around 655 feet by 295. Within this he created a glass-fronted, steel-framed pavilion spanning the width of the site. In front was a pool and pool terrace, leading to a low, transparent barrier open to the desert view. To the rear, Ellwood added a guest house and garaging, separated from the main house by a courtyard garden. The arrangement allowed for privacy – even from guests, if needed – while orienting the main section of the house to views of the extraordinary landscape. The master pavilion was designed with a largely open, fluid layout, with limited partitioning to maximize the flow of light from the windows to both the pool and the courtyard.

It was a key moment in the development of the idea of the courtyard house, providing a way of introducing both light and outdoor living right into the heart of a building. But it was also a pioneering step in the evolution of the compound home, whereby the residence becomes a small, elegant collection of structures rather than one all-purpose building.

Palevsky was delighted with the house, and he added many notable works of 20th-century art. It was one of the last houses that Ellwood designed before retiring and moving to Italy to concentrate on his painting, helped by Palevsky's gift of some stock in a company now known as Intel, which Ellwood eventually cashed in for a healthy profit.

ABOVE The dining and seating area, arranged around a custom fireplace, are within an open-plan space that forms the chief part of the compound's central pavilion.

LEFT The dining area, housing two Wassily chairs by Marcel Breuer and works from Max Palevsky's collection of 20th-century art.

ABOVE The master bathroom and bedroom stand within the main pavilion. Guest bedrooms are contained within a separate structure to the rear of the compound.

ABOVE RIGHT AND RIGHT Details of the master bedroom and bathroom. The owner's art collection was an integrated part of the interiors.

OPPOSITE The bedroom faces outwards to the pool terrace and the landscape beyond, but also draws in light and air from the courtyard between the master and guest pavilions.

ANDREW GELLER

FRANK HOUSE, USA,
1958

MID-CENTURY ARCHITECTURE
ON A MODEST AND AFFORDABLE
SCALE, YET FULL OF INGENIOUS
IDEAS AND POSSIBILITIES

Andrew Geller liked to give nicknames to the
many distinctive, affordable beach houses he
built along the shores of Long Island. There
was the Gull, the Milk Carton and the Cat,
along with the Reclining Picasso. These were
sculptural, quirky, timber-framed houses that
made a big impression along the coast in the
1950s and '60s.

The house that Geller built for Rudolph
and Trudy Frank in 1958 on Fire Island Pines
was known simply as 'the Cube'. Geller wanted
to make good design as available to his clients
as possible, often accepting small budgets.
From the mid-1940s to the mid-1970s his day
job was with the RAYMOND LOEWY (see under
'Product and Industrial Design')/William
Snaith studio, where he worked as an architect
and product designer on everything from
department stores to compact cameras.

But in 1955, Elizabeth Reese, director
of public relations for the legendary Loewy,
asked Geller to design a beach house out at
Sagaponack, Long Isand. It was a modest,
A-frame cabin built for just $7,000, but it was
full of imagination, originality and personal
touches. Reese loved the house so much that
she fed it into her own publicity machine
and soon Geller found commissions rolling in,
which were managed outside working hours
within a busy second career.

A few years later he designed the Milk
Carton House on Fire Island and then received
the commission from the Franks, who had
read about his work. Rudolph Frank managed
an ice cream company in Queens and his
wife was an artist and fashion illustrator. They
had recently been on a trip to the Yucatan
Peninsula in Mexico and were taken by the
Mayan ruins that they saw, showing their
holiday snaps to Geller.

The Frank House, peeking over the trees
from its hilltop location, borrowed something
of the imposing shape and form of Mayan
architecture. But rather than being made of
stone, it was a lightweight house of timber and
glass sitting on wooden piles, with views out to
the sea and across Fire Island Pines. Dominated
by a glorious double-height living space, it had
an elevated catwalk that connected the master
bedroom on the upper level with a fireman's
ladder that projected out from the front of the
building and ran down to the deck below.

The house has recently been restored by painter Philip Monaghan, working with architects Larson & Paul, and it was furnished with a sympathetic selection of vintage designs by Paul McCobb*, CHARLES EAMES and EERO SAARINEN (see under 'Furniture'). Today, it looks just as fresh as it did in pictures from the early 1960s, when it appeared in *Life* magazine.

External changes included replacing the shingles that had at some point been used to coat the house with horizontal cedar boards of a kind that Geller had originally specified; the fireman's ladder at the front of the house was also reinstated. Inside, the positions of the kitchen and guest bedroom on the ground floor were swapped, while a wooden sliding door that can be used to separate the living room and the new kitchen was modelled on Geller's design. Upstairs, a full-height timber wall was added to enclose the master bedroom, once part of an open mezzanine overlooking the living room below; a second guest suite was also added at lower ground level. Geller and the Franks visited the house after the work was done and expressed their delight at the sensitivity of the restoration.

The Frank House is emblematic of the rich imagination of Geller, who liked to respond to his clients' personalities and never wanted to repeat himself. In this post-war period, when New Yorkers increasingly began to yearn for vacation homes and points of escape, Geller provided them with an affordable and enticing solution within bespoke and ingenious designs.

ABOVE The apex of the house forms a dramatic viewing deck, looking out across the landscape of Fire Island Pines and to the sea.

ABOVE The kitchen was designed by Larson & Paul. The stools are by Alvar Aalto for Artek.

RIGHT A George Nelson clock sits above a Minotti sofa in this corner of the sitting room.

FAR RIGHT The Tulip dining table is by Eero Saarinen for Knoll, while the ceiling light is a George Nelson design.

OPPOSITE A leather Butterfly chair designed by Antonio Bonet and associates sits in the main living space, its tall windows open to the leafy backdrop.

JAKOB HALLDOR GUNNLØGSSON

GUNNLØGSSON HOUSE, DENMARK, 1958

EXEMPLAR OF MID-CENTURY
SCANDINAVIAN ARCHITECTURE
- WARM, ERGONOMIC, IN TUNE
WITH NATURE, AND HONOURING
THE INTEGRITY OF MATERIALS
AND CRAFTSMANSHIP

PREVIOUS PAGES The open-
plan living space has a
fireplace wall that creates
a light sense of separation.

BELOW AND BOTTOM
The one-storey house sits low
in the landscape, but opens
up to the private garden at the
rear and the sea at the front.

OPPOSITE ABOVE Natural
materials, including the
Kolmarden marble floors,
bring warmth and texture.

OPPOSITE BELOW Integrated
bookshelves and cupboards
double as partition walls, here
separating off the kitchen.

It was, above all, the organic warmth and considered craftsmanship of Scandinavian design that made it so very influential in the 1950s and '60s. This was soft modernism at its best, displayed in furniture, interiors and architecture by ALVAR AALTO and others. It offered an enticing alternative to modernist design in the International Style*, which was generally associated with purity and minimalism, as well as steel, concrete and glass.

The new aesthetic can be seen in the house that architect Jakob Halldor Gunnløgsson created for himself and his wife, Lillemor, looking out over the Øresund Strait. Their single-storey, timber-framed home responds to its dramatic setting and surrounding gardens with banks of glass at front and back. Inside, marble floors, timber ceilings, and designs by LE KLINT (see under 'Lighting') and Gunnløgsson's friend POUL KJÆRHOLM (see under 'Furniture') offer a palette of textures within simple yet beautifully crafted and conceived interiors.

Gunnløgsson studied architecture at the Royal Danish Academy of Fine Arts in Copenhagen, graduating in 1942 and then spending the rest of the war in Sweden. Upon his return to Denmark he founded a practice with Jørn Nielsen, as well as teaching at the Academy. His most famous projects were Tarnby City Hall (1959) and the Ministry of Foreign Affairs in Copenhagen (1980), while he was also much respected for his houses.

Gunnløgsson began to look for a spot to build a home for himself and his wife

after a lengthy trip to Japan – an extended honeymoon that influenced both the house and Gunnløgsson's approach to design more generally. They found a parcel of land just off the coast road that runs between Copenhagen and Helsingør – an area of country estates and large villas. The Gunnløgssons' home was designed on a more modest scale, forming a discreet presence by the waterside.

The site was excavated gently, both to create a level setting for the building and to create a degree of privacy, which was enhanced by planting around the house and its approach. The main body of the house is essentially just two rooms – a large, open-plan living/dining area and a bedroom, with a sliding door separating the two. A compact galley kitchen, a bathroom and other amenities are contained within a service core.

The open-plan nature of the main living space, with its floor-to-ceiling glazing at either side, creates the impression of a generous belvedere open to the seascape, while also leading to adjoining timber decks. The marble floors are underheated and the mechanics of the house are hidden away from view throughout. Different timber treatments establish a modest series of contrasts: dark beams are offset by fir ceiling slats, while the internal timber coating the brick of the two end walls has been painted black and polished to create the feeling of shining Asian lacquer.

There are many bespoke and fitted elements, such as the leather couch in the living area, the bed and the folding breakfast

table on the deck. The processional quality of the entrance area holds echoes of a Japanese-style *genkan*, and the internal sliding doors to the bedroom are reminiscent of *shoji* screens. These Asian influences combine with the use of local materials – timber and marble – as well as a particular sensitivity to context and landscape.

Splashes of colour – added through paintings, textiles by Vibeke Klint, and hidden accents such as the deep red used for the insides of the storage cupboards in the hall – stand out all the more against a restrained palette of colours and materials. Yet perhaps it is the view of the water and sky that stands out most when one is within the house, which is just as it should be in such a spellbinding setting.

RIGHT The kitchen is a flexible
space at the centre of the
house, either partly open to
the main living spaces or
hidden behind a sliding door.

BELOW Poul Kjærholm's PK25
lounge chairs grace the main
seating area.

BOTTOM LEFT A Poul
Kjærholm PK91 folding stool
doubles as a low table in the
bathroom.

BOTTOM RIGHT The master
bedroom can also be easily
separated from the rest of the
house with a sliding door. The
bespoke bed is Gunnløgsson's
own design.

OPPOSITE The bright red
interiors of the storage
cupboards in the entrance
hall shine out in contrast with
the greys and blacks of stone
and timber.

CHARLES GWATHMEY

GWATHMEY HOUSE & STUDIO, USA, 1965/66

A SCULPTURAL TIMBER HOME
COMPRISING A MEMORABLE
MIX OF ABSTRACTION, PURITY
AND FUNCTIONALITY

PREVIOUS PAGES AND
OPPOSITE ABOVE In the main
living area, with two black
armchairs by Le Corbusier,
high clerestory windows help
introduce light from a number
of directions.

THIS PAGE The house has a
sculptural quality, enhanced
by the way it sits alone on
the flat green lawn, like a
work of art.

OPPOSITE BELOW This
later studio building forms
a complementary structure,
sharing the same design
language as the main house.

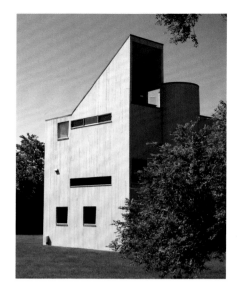

By the early 1960s the southern fork of Long
Island was becoming established as a place
of artistic and architectural experimentation.
Artists such as Robert Motherwell and
Jackson Pollock had homes and studios in
the Hamptons, and there was a constant
buzz of creativity out among the dunes and
potato fields. Architects such as ANDREW
GELLER, PHILIP JOHNSON and the pioneering
modernist master Pierre Chareau explored
fresh forms and bold ideas against a backdrop
that seemed open, accessible and liberating.

Here, in 1964, a young architect called
Charles Gwathmey was asked by his parents
to design a modest home on a duneland site
in Amagansett, set back from the ocean. It was
a commission that was to change Gwathmey's
life, kickstarting an extraordinary career and
establishing a precedent for a particular kind
of pure and sculptural timber home that has
established itself right across the Hamptons of
today. Arguably, Gwathmey's very first building
was his most accomplished and original.

Gwathmey studied at the University of
Pennsylvania and took a master's degree at
Yale before embarking on a tour of Europe,
where he took particular note of Le Corbusier's*
work, and especially the powerful, sculpted
form of his Chapel of Notre Dame du Haut
at Ronchamp (1954). Upon his return to the
States, Gwathmey took a job in the office of
Edward Larrabee Barnes*, but at the age of
only 25 he resigned his post to work on the
xommission offered by his parents, while also
teaching at the Pratt Institute in New York.

His father, Robert Gwathmey, was a painter and his mother Rosalie a photographer turmed textile designer. They secured a one-acre site cheaply and had $35,000 left over to build a house. Beyond asking for a living space, a master bedroom and room enough to squeeze in four grandchildren when required, they offered their son *carte blanche*.

Gwathmey designed a highly sculpted building that was a combination of intersecting cubes and spheres. He had wanted to build the house in concrete, but soon realized this would be far too expensive, so he decided on a timber frame with thin strips of vertical cedar siding. Even then, the estimated costs came in at twice the budget, so Gwathmey himself became lead contractor and project manager, working with a local builder.

A bunk room for the grandchildren was positioned on the ground floor, with a small studio for Gwathmey's mother. The main living room was on the floor above, taking advantage of the views, with a small kitchen alongside. A mezzanine level contained the master suite, offering the best viewpoint in the house. Indoor and outdoor staircases were contained in the cylindrical elements that soften the more linear aspects of the building.

'I was more influenced by Le Corbusier than the American shingle style vernacular,' said Gwathmey. 'Corbu's plans were always very simple but the spaces became very dynamic and spatial and complex, so that was my motivation – I wanted to make a volumetric building.... My parents placed a great deal of trust in me.'[7]

A year later Gwathmey added a secondary, complementary building a short walk from the original house, containing a guest bedroom on the ground floor and a painting studio above for his father. The two structures played off one another delightfully, like two cubist dancers on a crisp green lawn. Soon afterwards, Gwathmey's parents moved out to Long Island full time, as the Hamptons changed around them, becoming the summer playground of well-heeled New Yorkers. After his parents' death, Gwathmey inherited the house and made a few small changes and updates, as well as adding a hedge around the border and a row of linden trees.

The house proved controversial at first and was sometimes likened to a silo or agricultural barn. But the praise was far more vocal and the house was widely published, establishing Gwathmey's reputation. He became one of the 'New York Five', a loose affiliation of like-minded contemporaries: fellow Fives Richard Meier and John Hejduk also built houses in the Hamptons.

In 1968, Gwathmey formed Gwathmey Siegel & Associates. There were many one-off houses, including a number of homes for director Steven Spielberg, as well as museum projects and apartment buildings. But the Gwathmey House & Studio – a piece of sculpture; two objects floating on a flat plane – developed an iconic status. 'It doesn't feel dated,' said Gwathmey in 2008. 'The house is as compelling today as it was in 1965.'[8]

OPPOSITE The mezzanine level containing the master bedroom floats above the main living spaces, helping to define the dining area below and lend it a more intimate scale.

ABOVE LEFT 'It's maple for the cabinets, with white marble floors and cedar siding,' said Gwathmey. 'That's the whole deal.'

ABOVE The spiral staircase is a repeated motif in the main house and the studio, echoed in the rounded elements of the exterior forms of both buildings and softening their otherwise linear nature.

LEFT The bedrooms also explore shifting volumes, while manipulating light with window openings that frame carefully edited views of the landscape outside.

PHILIP JOHNSON

GLASS HOUSE, USA, 1949

THE ULTIMATE GLASS BOX –
ONE OF THE MOST EMBLEMATIC
AND IMITATED HOMES OF THE
MID-CENTURY PERIOD

PREVIOUS PAGES The transparency of the building allows the eye to pass through the house and out into the wooded landscape beyond. The Barcelona chairs and the day bed are by Mies van der Rohe.

BELOW The Glass House sits within an estate populated by a number of Johnson-designed buildings and structures that collectively form a grander residence of many parts.

OPPOSITE Apart from the cylindrical drum containing the bathroom, the house is completely open-plan. The kitchenette is in one corner, close to the dining table.

Philip Johnson was the great architectural chameleon of the 20th century. His work embraced many themes and ideas, ranging from the restrained purity of the International Style* to the self-referential playfulness of postmodernism. He called his own estate at New Canaan, Connecticut, a 'diary' of these changing tastes and predilections, populated by a whole series of buildings added one by one over the decades, as the estate was gradually extended to 47 acres.

These fourteen buildings – developed with Johnson's partner, art curator David Whitney – included a subterranean Painting Gallery (1965), with three rotating Rolodex-style painting stands, a Sculpture Gallery from 1970 and a Library/Study from 1980. There are also architectural follies, such as the scaled-down version of a classical pavilion down by the lakeside (1962) and the Lincoln Kirstein Tower (1985). But the most renowned building by far is one of the first: the Glass House.

Johnson first purchased a parcel of land here – around five acres – in 1946. He picked the exact spot where he would site the Glass House after just five minutes walking across the site. The house that he designed sits on a promontory, overlooking the lake and woodland down in the valley below. It was this landscape that became the 'wallpaper' of the house – 'very expensive wallpaper', as Johnson put it.

The Glass House is an open pavilion for both viewing and drawing in the views. Each of the four glass walls has its own glass door and the interior is almost completely open, with one brick cylinder containing the bathroom and, at the other side of it, a fireplace. Johnson's bed and desk are separated by a half-height line of walnut cabinets, while another unit at the opposite end of the house forms a slim galley kitchen.

The unfitted furniture is by Johnson's friend and associate LUDWIG MIES VAN DER ROHE and includes his Barcelona chairs, a dining table, desk, coffee table and couch – pieces that were largely manufactured by Knoll* from the early 1950s onwards. The Glass House itself clearly owes much to Mies van der Rohe, who Johnson had known for many years and who was commissioned to design Johnson's own New York apartment.

BELOW Brno MR50 chairs sit around the dining table. Diaphanous window blinds can be used to provide a degree of shade.

BELOW RIGHT The main seating area sits at the centre of the pavilion, defined only by the arrangement of the furniture and a rug over the herringbone brick floor.

OPPOSITE ABOVE The cylindrical brick drum holds the fireplace and a bathroom. The master bedroom sits behind a screen of wardrobes that provide a partial partition.

OPPOSITE BELOW The trees are reflected in the glass at certain times of day, softening the outline of the house in the landscape.

Johnson had got to know Mies's work as the founding director of the Department of Architecture at the Museum of Modern Art, where he was responsible for a highly influential 1932 exhibition on International Style. He went on to study architecture at Harvard under Walter Gropius* and MARCEL BREUER, becoming known as one of the Harvard Five.

In the mid-1940s, Mies was already at work on his Farnsworth House, and clearly the two projects have much in common – a high level of transparency, an open plan, a simple but sophisticated modern aesthetic. Debate continues around the extent to which Johnson owed his ideas to Mies; later they would collaborate on the design of the Seagram Building in New York (1959). But there is no doubting the revolutionary qualities of the Glass House, and arguably its dramatic location gives it something of a visual advantage over the Farnsworth House. Its openness and visual power are still scintillating.

The Glass House should also be seen in conjunction with its lesser-known twin, the Brick House, which was completed at the same time and is positioned just a stone's throw away. While the Glass House allowed the landscape to pass right through the building, the Brick House was like an abstract monolith and was almost completely enclosed, apart from a doorway and three circular windows to the rear. It contained guest bedrooms and services – a support capsule, in effect, for the star of the show.

The Glass House – and Johnson's New Canaan estate – is now in the hands of the National Trust for Historic Preservation. It still feels fresh and brave today, and is one of the most widely imitated buildings ever produced.

JOHN LAUTNER
ELROD HOUSE, USA, 1968

SITE-SPECIFIC MASTERPIECE
THAT EXPLORES THE
RELATIONSHIP OF INSIDE
TO OUTSIDE, USING SPATIAL
INNOVATION AND EXTREME
ENGINEERING

PREVIOUS PAGES The curved
glass wall at the front of the
house retracts to allow a
direct relationship with the
pool – which edges into the
interior – as well as the terrace
and the landscape itself.

BELOW LEFT The newer
addition to the house sits
further down the hill, with
a rounded, ship-like prow.

BELOW RIGHT A sculptural
concrete staircase helps
connect the older and newer
sections of the house, with
a skylight above that helps
bring natural light down
to the lower levels.

OPPOSITE ABOVE The
extraordinary concrete and
glass ceiling over the main
living spaces has the look
of a vast propeller or fan,
with radiating solid blades
punctuated by skylights.

OPPOSITE BELOW LEFT
The views out across Palm
Springs and the open desert
landscape are mesmerizing
from the elevated vantage
point that lends additional
drama to the house.

OPPOSITE BELOW RIGHT
A bespoke, drum-like fireplace
in the open-plan living room
provides a key focal point.

Palm Springs was the place to be in the 1950s
and '60s. The desert city, to the east of Los
Angeles, had become an escapist resort for
the fashionable elite, with a fresh wave of hotels
and houses. Bob Hope, Frank Sinatra and
others built homes here, while a number of
progressive architects – including Albert Frey*,
William E. Cody and E. Stewart Williams*
– gave shape and substance to this rapidly
growing enclave of mid-century modernism.

Towards the end of the 1960s, Arthur
Elrod – an interior designer with a prestigious
client list, whose work featured regularly
in *Architectural Digest* – asked John Lautner
to design a house for him on the slopes of
Smoke Tree Mountain. The rugged site was
extraordinary, with views across the city and
Coachella Valley, and a steep, rocky incline
to one side. Here, Lautner designed a house
that is arguably the best known of his career.

Lautner had grown up in Michigan, his
mother a painter and his father a teacher. One
of his first building projects was a timber cabin
that he built with his father on the shores of
Lake Superior. He spent six years working with
Frank Lloyd Wright*, training initially at Taliesin
East and then supervising the construction of
a number of Wright houses, including homes
in Los Angeles, where he settled with his family
and founded his own practice in 1940.

Lautner was always careful, even when
labouring under Wright's shadow, to think out
his own ideas. His early work shows a relative
modesty, using timber and steel to create
pavilions that explored connections between

outside and in. But by 1960 his designs had
become more experimental, daring and
structurally exuberant.

The Malin Residence – or 'Chemosphere'
– in Los Angeles, completed in 1960, was a
milestone. The house is perched upon a single
column, like a mushroom-shaped water tower,
forming a dramatic sculpture placed on a
hillside. Intriguingly, Lautner also designed
a small funicular railway linking the carport
to the house's entrance further up the slope.

The Garcia House of 1962 – also situated
on a Los Angeles hillside – offered another
visual treat, with a sweeping parabolic roof
neatly embracing both internal living spaces
and an integrated terrace. These and houses
that followed – such as the Reiner Residence
(1963) – showed Lautner using advanced
engineering and big ideas to create houses
with drama, ambition and glamour.

Such qualities are all apparent in the
Elrod House. The main living room is one
of the most recognizable spaces in America:
60 feet across, with a panoramic view over
Palm Springs via a retractable curving wall
of glass. The room is sheltered by a vast roof
in the shape of a fan, or propeller, its concrete
blades interspersed by glass skylights.
Huge boulders push into the space, creating
a purposeful contrast between futuristic,
man-made aspects and organic, elemental
notes. The kitchen is positioned to the rear,
and a bespoke concrete fireplace sits to one
side. The room played a starring role in the
1971 James Bond film, *Diamonds are Forever*.

The master bedroom and bathroom sit alongside the main living space: again, rocks push through the glass and walls, as though seeking to reclaim their territory. Later, Lautner was commissioned to add a guest 'wing' a little further down the slope of the hill, accessed by two sets of spiral stairs and topped with a roof deck. The addition takes the form of a curving ship's bow, emerging from the cliff.

This was mid-century style at its most flamboyant and theatrical, but also its most dynamic and original. Later buildings, such as the Arango Residence in Mexico (1973) and the Sheats Goldstein Residence in LA (1963/1989), explored similar themes but with very different solutions. Lautner wanted each of his projects to be unique, and he always fulfilled this promise.

ABOVE The water in the kidney-shaped swimming pool reflects the sky and forms a welcome contrast with the monumental, man-made quality of the house.

ABOVE RIGHT Decorative glasswork by Dale Chihuly adds another dimension and burst of colour to the living room and kitchen.

RIGHT The herringbone brick floors in this bedroom sit well with the texture and patina of the concrete walls.

OPPOSITE The boulders and slabs of rock that surround the building edge into the outline of the house at times, including here in the master bathroom as well as in the living room.

PAULO MENDES DA ROCHA
MILLÁN HOUSE, BRAZIL, 1970

GROUNDBREAKING EXPLORATION OF THE BEAUTY OF BRUTALISM, WITHIN AN UNCOMPROMISING AND OFTEN EXPERIMENTAL AESTHETIC

PREVIOUS PAGES AND
OPPOSITE The spiral staircase
sits at the heart of the
house, forming a sculptural
centrepiece within this
dramatic, gallery-like space.

BELOW The house has an
enigmatic quality when seen
from the street outside, with
a façade that is largely closed
and industrial in character.

BELOW RIGHT The swimming
pool sits close to the entrance
and alongside a dramatic
external staircase leading up
to the roof terrace.

The Brazilian metropolis of São Paulo seems to go on forever. It is a city of delights and dysfunction, endless junctions and urban jungle. It is no surprise, then, that a culture of enclosure and introspection has developed, with high walls, security checkpoints, private courtyards and hidden retreats. The work of Paulo Mendes da Rocha – one of the city's most famous architects – is notably famous for looking inwards rather than outwards, and for its focus on space and volume rather than connections between inside and outside living.

Mendes da Rocha was a leading light in what is known as Paulist brutalism – a movement that can be compared with the work of European brutalist architects of the 1960s and '70s, such as ALISON & PETER SMITHSON and BASIL SPENCE. Mendes da Rocha studied at the Mackenzie University School of Architecture in São Paulo and founded his own practice in 1955. His work – from the Paulistano Athletics Club building of 1955 through to the Brazilian Museum of Sculpture (1988) – has a monumental, heroic sense of scale, largely using unadorned concrete. In 2006, the architect, lecturer and furniture designer was awarded the Pritzker Prize.

One of Mendes da Rocha's most striking private homes was originally designed for art dealer Fernando Millán and completed in 1970. More recently the house was acquired by another art dealer, Eduardo Leme, who worked with the architect on a modest update and renovation. Perhaps it is no surprise, given these clients, that the house has the feel of a

gallery carved out of concrete, with a great sense of volume and a minimalist approach to finishes and colour. The use of large skylights rather than conventional windows reinforces the notion of the home as an introspective zone.

This uncompromising space maximized the use of prefabricated and industrially produced concrete component parts. The house is a rectangular bunker, pushed into a sloping site, with a courtyard garden to the front, along with a sheltered swimming pool, while external steps lead upwards to a roof terrace. The exterior façade to the street beyond is highly enigmatic, with few clues as to whether this might be a private residence or something more industrial in nature.

Inside, the building is a powerful composition of contrasting spaces. More enclosed, single-height volumes on two storeys contrast with a soaring double-height space at the heart of the house, drawing in light from the skylights above. The centrepiece of this open void is a sculptural spiral staircase – also in concrete – that connects the two levels of the house, with the main living room on the ground floor benefiting from the double-height ceilings and the sense of openness in this section of the building.

The power and drama of the house come not from fine materials, elaborate decoration or the landscape and context in which the building is placed; instead, the focus is on the pure grandeur of the spaces and volumes within the house and the manipulation of light, playing upon the raw concrete textures

LEFT The two leather and steel chairs are by Brazilian designer Flávio de Carvalho, 1950.

BELOW The layers of concrete that form the building create an uncompromising façade with the quality of a fortress.

BOTTOM LEFT The internal spaces are brought to life by the careful manipulation of light and shade, as here in the bathroom.

BOTTOM RIGHT A Charles & Ray Eames chair and ottoman grace the bedroom.

and polished cement floors. The main living room includes rounded 1950s chairs in leather and ironwork by Brazilian architect, artist and designer Flávio de Carvalho and crimson armchairs by Swiss-born designer John Graz, who based himself in Brazil from the 1920s onwards.

Mendes da Rocha's buildings continue to inspire a new generation of architects, and not just in Brazil. In many ways his design approach represents a polar opposite to that of the mid-century soft modernists such as ALVAR AALTO, or CHARLES EAMES and ARNE JACOBSEN (see under 'Furniture'). Mendes da Rocha's work appeals to those with a passion for pure materiality, spatial power and raw sculpture.

TOP AND ABOVE
The staircase and main living area sit within an atrium at the heart of the building, toplit by a large skylight.

LEFT The dining area, close to the kitchen, is a sheltered, intimate space to one side of the more open seating area.

LUDWIG MIES VAN DER ROHE
FARNSWORTH HOUSE, USA, 1951

MODEST BUT REVOLUTIONARY
GLASS AND STEEL PAVILION
THAT PIONEERED THE
FREE-FORM INTERIOR AND
A NEW TRANSPARENCY IN
MODERN LIVING

PREVIOUS PAGES AND
BELOW The characteristic
sense of lightness is enhanced
by the way the building 'floats'
above the ground on slim
supporting piloti, intended
to help protect the house
from flooding.

It is hard to overestimate the importance and influence of Ludwig Mies van der Rohe's modest glass and steel pavilion in Plano, Illinois. It was this small building, perhaps more than any other, that established the idea of transparency in the context of the home. This belvedere, open to nature and light, provided an almost spiritual experience, in which the natural world assumed – as Mies intended – 'a more profound significance' when viewed through the picture frame of the building.

More than this, the house proposed a whole new way of living. Within it, Mies perfected the idea of the 'free plan' and the 'floating room'. Essentially, the Farnsworth House was one open, fluid space rather than a series of conventional rooms and compartments.

The kitchen, bathroom, shower room and services – as well as a fireplace – were contained within a compact 'core' that floated within the overall outline of the universal space. Any other sense of separation, or zoning, was provided only by the positioning of furniture and rugs, as well as by a freestanding bespoke wardrobe that helped add some privacy to the one sleeping area at the rear of the building. The Farnsworth House was, in so many respects, revolutionary.

Mies van der Rohe was, like Walter Gropius* and MARCEL BREUER, an émigré architect and designer from Germany, who had been intimately involved with the Bauhaus* (he succeeded Gropius as director in the final years of the school). His greatest early successes in Europe included the Tugendhat House in Brno in the Czech Republic (1930) and the Barcelona Pavilion of 1929. The Pavilion – destroyed in 1930 but later rebuilt – explored many ideas, including transparency and the free plan, that were revisited on a smaller, domestic scale in the Farnsworth House, and combined glass, travertine, marble and other simple slabs of stonework within a crisp, clean and startlingly original, free-flowing composition; Mies's famous Barcelona chair (MR90) was also designed for the Pavilion and was put into production by Knoll* from 1948.

In 1945, seven years after arriving in America, Mies was introduced to Dr Edith Farnsworth, a kidney specialist based in Chicago. Farnsworth had bought a seven-acre site alongside the Fox River, 55 miles southwest of Chicago, and wanted to build a weekend escape there for herself. Client and architect established a close rapport, which may well have become a romance. Farnsworth appeared to embrace Mies's radical ideas for a sophisticated pavilion of purity and simplicity.

To avoid the danger of flood risk from the river, the house was raised up on steel columns so that the floor plate sat five feet above ground level, creating the impression of a floating structure. A significant portion of the outline of the house was devoted to a large veranda at the front, with an additional terrace alongside, four steps down. This erodes the division between inside and outside even further and establishes another, enigmatic element to the overall transparency of the house.

The Farnsworth House has fertilized a thousand imitations and more. One of the first could – arguably – be said to be PHILIP JOHNSON's own Glass House, which owes a clear debt to Mies's thinking. Mies himself was soon much in demand, pioneering the modernist high-rise with his Lake Shore Drive apartments in Chicago (1951) and the Seagram Building in New York (1958). The New National Gallery of Berlin (1968) marked a return to the form of the open pavilion on a much larger and more ambitious scale.

Dr Farnsworth, however, was less than pleased with the product of Mies's extraordinary imagination. Admittedly, certain problems blighted the building, especially repeated flooding. But Farnsworth's attacks upon a once beloved friend may well have been the fallout from a broken love affair. She had once said: 'Such work one can only recognize and cherish – with love and respect.'[9] Later she complained that the house was totally impractical: 'I can't even put a clothes hanger in my house without considering how it affects everything from the outside.'[10]

The battle between architect and client spilled into the open with a court case, as Mies sued for unpaid fees and Farnsworth counter-claimed for budget overruns and a leaking roof. Mies won the case but the two never spoke again. Yet rather than sell up, Farnsworth continued to live in her house until 1972. One can only hope that she eventually found some pleasure in a building that has given so many others such inspiration.

ABOVE AND RIGHT A slim galley kitchen sits within a service core to one side of the pavilion. The core also holds services and storage, freeing up the rest of the space in the house.

ABOVE The arrangement of furniture within the universal space helps define the different functions of the house with the lightest of touches. The Barcelona MR90 chair and the day bed are designs by Mies van der Rohe.

RIGHT The fireplace, which sits within the central service core, helps to define the sitting area.

FAR RIGHT A Brno MR50 chair (1930) sits at the desk by one of the windows.

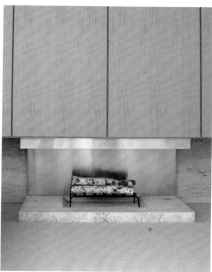

ABOVE The greenery of the landscape serves as a constant backdrop to everyday living in the house.

LEFT Cabinets help separate the bedroom from the rest of the pavilion but without the need for solid, full-height partitions.

RICHARD NEUTRA
KAUFMANN DESERT HOUSE, USA, 1947

THE MOST FAMOUS EXAMPLE
OF CALIFORNIAN MID-CENTURY
DESERT MODERNISM,
INTRODUCING A FRESH
RELATIONSHIP BETWEEN INDOOR
AND OUTDOOR LIVING

PREVIOUS PAGES A powerful
connection between inside
and outside living space is
established via the retracting
glass walls that border the
living room and master
bedroom in the central part
of the house.

BELOW The San Jacinto
Mountains form a dramatic
natural backdrop to the house.
The 'gloriette' on the top floor
is an open-sided, elevated
living room that doubles as
an observation deck.

Few buildings summon up the ideal of the
modernist Californian dream home as
effectively as the Kaufmann Desert House.
In a country just stepping out of the shadow
of the war, Richard Neutra's masterpiece
offered an escapist haven that was alluring,
evocative and original. It opened itself up to an
extraordinary landscape, where the desert met
the San Jacinto Mountains, and broke down
conventional barriers between living indoors
and being outside. Yet Neutra still managed to
establish dramatic contrasts between the light
transparency of certain sections of the house
and the monumental stone walls that cradle
other parts. The building has become one of
the most admired and influential in the world
of mid-century design.

Neutra himself was an émigré, born
in Vienna, where his mentors included Otto
Wagner and Adolf Loos and where he first
befriended his contemporary, Rudolph
Schindler. Neutra settled in Los Angeles in
the early 1920s, working with Frank Lloyd
Wright* and then collaborating with Schindler
before setting up a solo practice. One of his
most famous early commissions was the Lovell
Health House in Los Angeles (1929). The first
steel-framed house in America, it was built
for clients with something of an obsession
for healthy living. It allowed Neutra to develop
his own philosophy about the importance of
the built environment in relation to our physical,
mental and emotional well-being, and the way
in which it can enhance the experience of
everyday living.

Edgar J. Kaufmann, like the Lovells, saw
himself as an architectural patron. A department
store owner, based in Pittsburgh, Kaufmann
had asked Frank Lloyd Wright to design a
house for him at Bear Run, Pennsylvania, a
decade earlier. Fallingwater became arguably
the most famous house of the 20th century.
But for his new house Kaufmann decided to
step in a different direction.

In the mid-1940s Palm Springs was just
beginning to establish itself as a desert resort,
a place where the sun always shone and the
scenery could never fail to impress. Kaufmann's
site was next door to Albert Frey's* Loewy
House, but he only wanted to use the house as
a winter retreat for the month of January, when
the days are still warm but the nights are cold.

Neutra designed a building of sandstone,
steel and glass around a central fireplace, from
which the broad spokes of a pinwheel design
then radiated, with the main section of the
house holding the main living room and master
suite, while other spokes contained service
spaces, utility zones and guest suites, all set
slightly apart from the heart of the building.

Within the main living room the glass
wall leading to the terrace and pool retracts
completely, allowing a seamless transition
between inside and outside. Radiant underfloor
heating was installed to cope with the chill
nights and even extended out to the pool
terrace. Keen to engage all the senses, Neutra
used the semi-sheltered 'breezeway' connecting
the living room and guest quarters to add
integrated planting and a water garden.

Up on the roof, Neutra skirted around planning restrictions on second-storey living space by designing a partially enclosed terrace with a louvred aluminium screen to shelter this outdoor sitting room from the sun. With its own fireplace and dumb waiter, and flanked by the sandstone chimney stack, the 'gloriette' offered enticing views of the desert and mountains.

The Kaufmann House combined modernist thinking with inspiration from Japanese design and landscaping, along with Neutra's love of the shapes and textures of Indian adobe pueblos and the rugged landscape of the desert. As well as eroding traditional boundaries between interior/exterior and house/garden, Neutra created a home that was highly adaptable – a compound that could open itself up to guests or concentrate down to become an intimate space. Natural cross-ventilation cooled the house in the heat of the day but at night the building could be closed up to preserve the warmth inside.

A sensitive restoration and update in the late 1990s by architects Marmol Radziner stripped away unwelcome additions that had crept in over the years, while subtly introducing up-to-date services. Today few houses seem so inviting and glamorous. But the glamour is born from the building's design, setting and ingenuity rather than from outward trappings of luxury. This is a house that picked up on themes that are still resonant today. It is a house that has helped shape the way we think about architectural space and its relationship to the wider world beyond.

ABOVE A Pernilla chaise longue, c. 1950, by Bruno Mathsson sits in one corner of the master bedroom, with the swimming pool beyond.

LEFT Plywood chairs by Charles & Ray Eames populate the seating and dining areas. The stone wall lends texture and character to the space.

OPPOSITE The semi-sheltered
walkways that connect the
different parts of the house
also help frame terraces
that serve as outdoor rooms.

RIGHT The best views are
from the 'gloriette'. This
semi-enclosed pavilion also
has its own fireplace.

BELOW RIGHT The barriers
between inside and outside
space are effectively blurred
throughout, as seen here
with the dining area and
courtyard beyond.

OSCAR NIEMEYER
STRICK HOUSE, USA, 1964

THE LEADING BRAZILIAN
ARCHITECT'S ONLY HOUSE
IN THE US: WARM, ELEGANT,
CHARACTERFUL MID-CENTURY
MODERNISM AT ITS PUREST

PREVIOUS PAGES The main
living area is an open and light
space, with windows to either
side. The two armchairs are
by Jean Prouvé (1942).

BELOW AND BELOW RIGHT
The gardens around the house
were completely redesigned
by Michael Boyd, drawing
inspiration from the work
of Roberto Burle Marx.

OPPOSITE ABOVE The dining
area sits upon a raised platform
overlooking the main seating
area. The dining chairs are
by Jean Prouvé.

OPPOSITE BELOW LEFT
The black chairs in the living
room are by Oscar Niemeyer,
c. 1970.

OPPOSITE BELOW RIGHT
Many of the distinctive lighting
pieces are by Serge Mouille.

The leading Brazilian architect of his generation, and a designer who often seemed well ahead of his time, Oscar Niemeyer has long been an inspirational figurehead. His work is full of originality and imagination, and noted for its warmth and sensuality. Niemeyer helped shape the identity of Brazil itself, particularly with his many landmark buildings for Brasília, including the National Congress (1958) and the Metropolitan Cathedral (1959). But he also worked outside Brazil, and one of his most endearing projects was a house that was largely forgotten for many years but has now been restored and reclaimed for the Niemeyer canon: the Strick House in Los Angeles.

Niemeyer was born in Rio de Janeiro, where he studied at the city's National Art Academy. In the mid-1930s he worked with Lúcio Costa* and Le Corbusier* on the Ministry of Education and Health building in Rio; later, in 1952, he collaborated with Le Corbusier again on the United Nations headquarters* in New York. In the late 1950s Niemeyer was appointed chief architect of Brasília but was forced into exile in France a decade later by the changing political situation in Brazil. He returned in 1982, continuing his work, and was awarded the Pritzker Prize in 1988.

In the early 1960s an American film director named Joseph Strick visited both Brasília and Niemeyer's own Canoas House (1954) after attending a film festival in Argentina. He asked Niemeyer to design a house for himself and his family in Los Angeles but the architect was denied admission to the States because of his Communist sympathies. Strick pushed on with the project, communicating with Niemeyer by mail, but his wife Anne vetoed the first design, while the second – with a layer of subterranean bedrooms – was rejected by the local planning authorities. The house that Strick built, then, was Niemeyer's third scheme, with a linear T-shaped design that maximized the connections between indoor and outdoor living.

The house of brick and glass was constructed by builders who had worked on John Entenza's Case Study Program*. A generous portion is dominated by an open-plan living, kitchen and dining area, with gardens to either side. A slight shift in floor level helps to separate the kitchen and dining zone from the seating area. The adjoining crossbar of the house holds service spaces and bedrooms.

Joseph Strick, however, never got a chance to live in the house. He split from his wife while the house was being built, and it was Anne Strick and their two children who moved in once it was completed. In 2003, the house was saved from demolition by designer and restoration expert Michael Boyd (see p. 384) and his wife Gabrielle, who spent two and half years restoring and updating the property.

The Boyds added a palm-wood floor in the living room and re-landscaped the gardens, taking inspiration from the work of Brazilian landscape architect Roberto Burle Marx, who collaborated with Niemeyer in Brazil. The Boyds also adapted a study and basement garage to create a two-storey library with a

mezzanine gallery. The sensitive renovation won the admiration of Niemeyer himself.

The Boyds also introduced their own collection of highly significant mid-century furniture into the house. Among the many designers represented are GEORGE NELSON, ARNE JACOBSEN, JEAN PROUVÉ and CARLO MOLLINO (see under 'Furniture'), as well as a number of Niemeyer pieces. The 'Maison du Méxique' wall unit (1953) in the living area by Charlotte Perriand, Jean Prouvé and Sonia Delaunay is particularly striking and rare.

The Strick House – Niemeyer's only completed house in America – remains full of grace, elegance and character, despite the fact that the architect himself was never able to visit in person.

ABOVE The cabinet is by
George Nelson for Herman
Miller (c. 1950); the ceramics
are by Stig Lindberg.

ABOVE RIGHT A Jean Prouvé
armchair sits close to the
integrated fireplace.

RIGHT The yellow banquette
in the reading room is a piece
by Jean Prouvé (1954), as is
the green armchair.

OPPOSITE The Marshmallow
sofa is by George Nelson,
while the standing lamp next
to it is by Serge Mouille.

BRUCE RICKARD

MARSHALL HOUSE, AUSTRALIA, 1967

SEMINAL MID-CENTURY
AUSTRALIAN ARCHITECTURE:
NATURAL MATERIALS,
OPEN-PLAN LIVING AND
A STRONG CONNECTION
TO THE OUTDOORS

Where traditional houses tended to present a series of compartmentalized rooms, with a limited sense of connection between inside and outside, buildings in the 1950s and '60s began to offer re-thought living spaces – open-plan areas for seating, dining and entertaining – with fluid connections to decks, terraces and verandas through banks of glazing and sliding glass windows. In California, RICHARD NEUTRA and others famously dissolved the divisions between indoor and outdoor space, but it was also happening in other parts of the world. In Australia one of the greatest pioneers of this fresh way of living was Bruce Rickard.

Rickard studied architecture at the Sydney Technical College and worked in the practice of Sydney Ancher before studying landscape architecture in London. He was then offered a study fellowship at the University of Pennsylvania. During his travels, he was particularly taken by the work of Frank Lloyd Wright* and Wright's 'organic' approach, with an emphasis on contextuality and natural materials.

Returning to Australia in the late 1950s, Rickard founded his own practice and began to develop a personal aesthetic and design philosophy, principally within a series of houses built in and around Sydney. One of the best preserved and most significant is the house that Rickard built for Penny and Greg Marshall, completed in 1967.

The house is positioned on a steeply sloping site in the Clontarf district of Sydney, overlooking the Middle Harbour and the Spit

bridge, which rises periodically to allow yachts to pass through. Despite the difficult topography, Rickard was able to create a design that made the most of the engaging vista and provided a series of outdoor rooms that complemented the living spaces within.

Three compact bedrooms were positioned at lower ground level, pushed into the slope of the hill, all leading out directly onto a long deck: utility and service spaces were also positioned on this lower storey, as well as a workroom which now serves as a study. The main level of the house, accessed via a steep drive and an entrance courtyard, makes the most of the views and the light, with a generous, open-plan living and dining area that has an easy flow through to the courtyard at

one end and an elevated deck at the other. This upper level is almost entirely open, with only a compact, galley-style kitchen hidden behind the brick wall that holds the fireplace. But even the kitchen is open at either end to the rest of the universal space, allowing both light and occupants to circulate freely.

Rickard encouraged the Marshalls to plant native trees and shrubs around the house, including angophora gum trees. Materials throughout have a warm, organic quality, from the recycled sandstock brick walls to the tallow floors and the red cedar used in a shiplap treatment for ceilings and panelling. Also included were many bespoke and built-in elements, from the custom kitchen to fitted desks in the bedrooms; light fittings using linen

and Perspex shades integrated within maple shelving units were another signature touch.

The Marshalls brought up three children in the house before selling it on to author and editor Karen McCartney and her partner, writer and stylist David Harrison. They found that the house had stood the test of time extraordinarily well, including areas of intense day-to-day use such as the kitchen. Their own collection of Scandinavian mid-century furniture – including pieces by HANS WEGNER (see under 'Furniture') and Norman Cherner* – slotted into the house perfectly. They made only minor changes to the carport, organized by Rickard himself, who McCartney and Harrison got to know in the years before his death in 2010. No other changes were necessary and the couple have found the experience of living in the house rewarding.

'As you come upstairs in the morning you can immediately connect with the view and clock what kind of day it is outside,' says McCartney. 'You do have this constant appreciation of nature and what is going on in the world around you.'[11]

ABOVE A day bed by Poul Volther sits in one corner of the main seating area.

LEFT The dining table is a Hans Wegner design, with Wegner CH24 and CH32 chairs produced by Carl Hansen.

OPPOSITE The chair in the study is a Charles & Ray Eames design for Herman Miller. The shelves are a new addition.

RIGHT A CH22 chair by Hans Wegner sits by the window in the sitting room.

FAR RIGHT Chairs and a rectangular table by Harry Bertoia sit on the deck, which benefits from views out across Sydney and its Middle Harbour.

ABOVE The kitchen is a bespoke Bruce Rickard design, with steel-topped counters and coachwood timber units.

LEFT The breakfast table is a contemporary piece designed by David Harrison. The galley kitchen is tucked away just around the corner.

HARRY SEIDLER
ROSE SEIDLER HOUSE, AUSTRALIA, 1950

A PIONEERING MID-CENTURY
MODERNIST AUSTRALIAN HOUSE,
INTEGRATED IN ALL ASPECTS
AND HIGHLY SOPHISTICATED
FOR ITS TIME

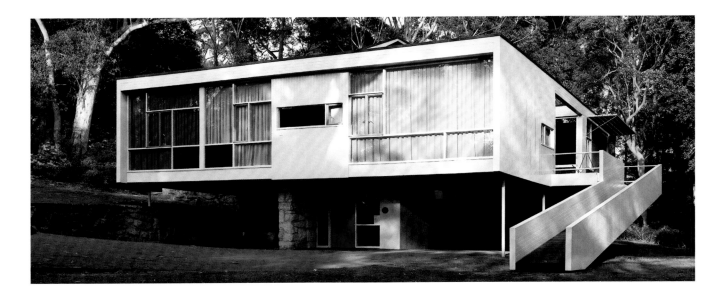

PREVIOUS PAGES The
elevated deck is dominated
by a colourful, Corbusian-
style mural by Harry Seidler.
The Grasshopper chair in
the sitting room is by Eero
Saarinen.

ABOVE The house is raised
up to take advantage of the
views and is accessed via an
elongated ramp that creates
a dramatic, processional
entrance.

On the long and winding road from Austria
to Australia, Harry Seidler took points of
inspiration from some of the great names
of modernist architecture. Seidler was one
of a prestigious group of European émigré
architects and designers who fled Germany
and Austria in the run-up to World War II.
He landed first in the UK but was then shipped
to Canada, where he studied architecture at
the University of Manitoba. At Harvard he was
taught by two other exiles, Walter Gropius*
and MARCEL BREUER, who he later worked for
in New York, after a brief posting with ALVAR
AALTO's American office and a short spell
studying design with Josef Albers*. En route
to Australia, Seidler stopped in Brazil, where
he worked in the studio of OSCAR NIEMEYER.

By the time the young Seidler arrived
in Sydney, then, his CV was already peppered
with the names of masters of design. He
was able to take his lessons, knowledge and
imagination and apply them to this new
country, Australia, introducing his own version
of modernism. Ultimately he became the
country's first architect who could really be
called a household name.

One of the things that Seidler brought
with him to Australia was a house. He carried
it in his mind, almost fully formed – a building
that had first been conceived in New York in
1947 while he was working in Marcel Breuer's
office as his chief assistant. The plans had
even been published in *Arts & Architecture*
magazine. His parents, Rose and Max Seidler,
had encouraged their son to follow them to

Australia with the offer of a commission to
design a home for them. With some adaptations
for site and situation, he offered them the
building he had brought with him.

For an architect still at the beginning
of his career, the Rose Seidler House was a
remarkably mature, assured and sophisticated
composition. It was set in a generous site at
Wahroonga, on the edge of Sydney, with views
across the Ku-ring-gai Chase National Park.
The house is tucked gently into the undulating
landscape, with a backdrop of mature trees.
The living spaces are lifted up into the air by
steel columns and sandstone walls, making
the most of the views, while garaging and
an entrance area are positioned underneath.
A 45-foot ramp sits to one side of the house,
offering an alternative means of access to
the terrace integrated into the outline of the
elevated home. The ramp was to become a
repeated motif in Seidler's later projects and
carries echoes of Le Corbusier's* Villa Savoye
of 1931 in Poissy, France.

The upper level was divided into three
main sections, with areas for living, sleeping
and sitting outdoors on the terrace. This terrace,
complete with a colourful mural painted by
Seidler himself, reinforced connections
between inside and out, and helped introduce
natural light into the heart of the building.
The main living space was open, bright and
fluid, with the main seating area connecting
seamlessly with the dining zone, which sat
alongside a semi-partitioned kitchen, divided
by internal windows and shelving units.

The kitchen itself was highly sophisticated and advanced for the period, accounting for a significant proportion of the cost of the entire project.

Recognizing in his parents the perfect 'captive clients', Seidler encouraged them to part with all their period Viennese furniture and – as well as designing a number of bespoke pieces for the house – he specified almost every choice. There were DCM and LCM dining and lounge chairs by CHARLES & RAY EAMES (see under 'Furniture'), upholstered Grasshopper armchairs by EERO SAARINEN (see under 'Furniture'), and dinnerware and cutlery by RUSSEL WRIGHT (see under 'Glass and Ceramics'), purchased while Seidler was living in New York. His mother refused to part

with her silver cutlery, brought with her from Europe, but would always use the Wright knives and forks when her son came to visit.

The house offered a completely cohesive design statement, combining architecture, art, interiors, siting, landscaping, colour, texture and materials. Seidler went on to build another two houses nearby for other members of the family. The Rose Seidler House – and its furniture – was ultimately bequeathed to the Historic Houses Trust.

Seidler went on to become the godfather of modernist Australian architecture, designing a series of landmark buildings. But the Rose Seidler House continues to have a special place in the mid-century canon: a groundbreaking home tied to an extraordinary landscape.

BELOW Deck, living area and dining area flow naturally into one another, while a fireplace forms a monolithic element that partly separates seating and dining zones.

OPPOSITE The custom kitchen was a sophisticated design with modern appliances and represented a significant part of the budget of the house.

ABOVE LEFT A sense of connection between the kitchen and dining area is established through a long horizontal slot window just above the level of the counter top, with sliding glass panels.

ABOVE AND LEFT Built-in desks and other pieces of integrated furniture sit alongside a choice collection of mid-century pieces by Charles & Ray Eames, Eero Saarinen and others.

ALISON & PETER SMITHSON

UPPER LAWN PAVILION, UK, 1962

A SIMPLE PAVILION THAT
REDEFINED THE AESTHETIC
OF THE RURAL RETREAT,
COMBINING RUSTIC SIMPLICITY
AND LINEAR MODERNISM,
AND INTEGRATING PREVIOUSLY
BUILT STRUCTURES

PREVIOUS PAGES The living area on the upper storey makes the most of the views across open farmland to the woods beyond. The wood-burning stove is a new addition.

ABOVE AND ABOVE RIGHT The Smithsons recycled elements of the original farm labourer's cottage and integrated them into the new house, including the stone boundary wall and the chimney buttress, as well as a tiled floor that became an outdoor terrace.

OPPOSITE ABOVE A simple staircase, little more than a wooden ladder, joins the two storeys together.

OPPOSITE BELOW LEFT The upper level is dominated by the view that runs the length of the house and the long sequence of windows that provides a constant sense of connection with the countryside.

OPPOSITE BELOW RIGHT The interiors are characterized by unpretentious simplicity. Glass doors fold back at the corner of the house to allow a direct relationship with the garden.

The pioneering modernist Le Corbusier* was at his happiest in a small timber cabin that he built for himself by the sea at Cap Martin on the Côte d'Azur. The master claimed to have designed his cabin in just 45 minutes on the corner of a table in 1951 – later adding a small box-like studio alongside – and it became a favoured place for contemplation and escape. Looking at this simple pine cabin, it is hard to believe it came from the same vibrant imagination as the Villa Savoye in Poissy (1931), Unité d'Habitation in Marseilles (1952) or the Chapel of Notre Dame du Haut at Ronchamp (1955). One gets a similar feeling looking at the plain but engaging pavilion that the British modernist power couple Alison & Peter Smithson built for themselves in the Wiltshire countryside.

Described as a 'solar pavilion', this was an escapist belvedere open to an extraordinary landscape, where the architects and their family could track the movement of the sun and the seasons. Simply built and delightfully conceived, it was a place of tranquillity, where the Smithsons did little more than camp. Yet it proved to be one of their most accessible and influential buildings.

Upper Lawn Pavilion certainly stands in marked contrast to the designs that made the Smithsons famous, or – some might say – notorious. There was, above all, Robin Hood Gardens, completed in London in 1972. Like so many social housing projects of the period, the estate of 213 homes in a single multi-storey block was designed in a spirit of optimism,

with the ever-vocal Smithsons describing its balconies and walkways as 'streets in the sky'. But, built by a main road and structurally flawed, the building never looked as impressive as Le Corbusier's Unité d'Habitation, which was a key point of inspiration for the Smithsons and many of their contemporaries.

Born in Sheffield and Stockton-on-Tees respectively, the two architects first met as students at the school of architecture in Newcastle. They founded a practice together in London shortly after their marriage, winning a competition to design Hunstanton Secondary Modern School in North Norfolk (1954) – a building that both launched their careers and set a precedent for the spirit of controversy that always surrounded this outspoken and often eccentric couple. Perhaps their greatest successes were their House of the Future for the 'Ideal Home' exhibition of 1956 – a futuristic plastic building suited to mass production – and the Economist building in London from 1964.

With their own homes in London – specifically their 19th-century terraced home in Priory Walk, South Kensington, and then Cato Lodge, a detached villa dating from 1851, just across the street – they developed the idea of 'found space'. They settled into these homes as if they were shells ready to be inhabited, slotting in new services and bathrooms without disturbing the fundamental character of the spaces. It was an interesting philosophy that was to prove highly influential to a generation who settled into lofts and period houses with a similar approach, keeping interventions and alterations to a minimum.

At Upper Lawn Pavilion the Smithsons took this idea in a different direction. They bought part of a farmstead on the Fonthill estate in 1959, with a derelict labourer's cottage partially built into the boundary of a walled courtyard. Instead of trying to preserve the cottage as a found space, they integrated parts of it into a new house, using elements such as the courtyard wall and an old stone chimney to help support the new pavilion. The old cottage, then, has a ghostly presence within the new pavilion, with the central chimney, a left-over window in the boundary wall and a terrace formed from part of the old internal floor of the farm labourer's cottage.

The upper level was an open-plan living space, arranged around the stone chimney, where the vista could be savoured front and back. The lower storey was meant for cooking, dining and services, although of a rudimentary kind. A simple wooden ladder originally connected the two floors.

In recent years, architects Sergison Bates have undertaken a sensitive restoration and upgrade, introducing some modern comforts such as underfloor heating and woodburning stoves to make the house more practical and functional for year-round use. But the essential character of the pavilion remains, with its banks of sliding teak and glass doors that can retract to open the house up to the gardens and the land.

Like BASIL SPENCE, the Smithsons suffered from bitter recriminations over the failure of their attempts at social housing; the word 'brutalist' was coined in the 1950s by critic Reyner Banham to describe their work. But there is no doubt that the pair were deeply influential figures in the world of post-war British architecture. Upper Lawn Pavilion suggests their softer, more sensitive side, in which the past is respected and endures even within the outline of the new. It is an approach that has its merits, preserving an essential sense of character rather than erasing it to begin afresh.

BASIL SPENCE
SPENCE HOUSE, UK, 1961

QUINTESSENTIALLY 1960S
TAILOR-MADE WEEKEND BOATING
PAVILION, FULL OF WARMTH,
SENSITIVITY AND A COHERENT
SENSE OF PURPOSE

PREVIOUS PAGES An Arne
Jacobsen Egg chair sits near
the spiral staircase that Basil
Spence added to the house
a few years after it was built.

ABOVE The upper level of
the house cantilevers outwards,
providing a shaded zone for
the pool terrace below.

OPPOSITE ABOVE The bespoke
fireplace, and use of stone,
brick and timber, offers texture
in the living space.

OPPOSITE BELOW The spiral
staircase and its drum-like coat
offset the strong, straight lines
of the building.

The reputation of Sir Basil Spence has been
on the ascendant in recent years, as the many
achievements of one of Britain's most
successful and flamboyant post-war architects
are revisited and reassessed. While Spence's
work was inevitably overshadowed by the
failure of his Hutchesontown C tower blocks
in the Gorbals district of Glasgow (1962), partly
inspired by Le Corbusier's* Unité d'Habitation
in Marseilles, there were also many high points.
His ecclesiastical and university buildings
earned him praise, as did the 'Beehive' wing
of the New Zealand parliament in Wellington
(1964) and the British embassy in Rome (1971).
His greatest achievement was his Coventry
Cathedral project, completed in 1962 (see p. 6),
but – on a far more modest scale – the weekend

house that he built for himself in Beaulieu,
Hampshire, was also a real delight.

Born in India and educated in Scotland,
Spence assisted in Edwin Lutyens's London
office for a time. He went on to co-found his
first architectural practice in Edinburgh in 1931,
but re-established himself in London after the
war, when he served in the Camouflage Training
and Development Unit and participated in
the D-Day landings. He designed the Sea and
Ships Pavilion for the Festival of Britain* in 1951
and around the same time won the competition
to rebuild Coventry Cathedral, which had
been heavily damaged during the wartime
bombing campaign.

Spence was the only competing architect
to suggest that the new cathedral sit alongside

the ruins of the old, which were preserved as a monument. The new building, including stained glass by John Piper*, became a favourite with the public, as well as a powerful symbol of both destruction and regeneration. This was post-war modernism at its most endearing, and a polar opposite to the brutalist nature of Spence's work in Glasgow.

His Beaulieu house was a very personal project and infused with an aesthetic that is warm and considered, while also establishing a particular sensitivity to the landscape that surrounds it. Spence was a keen sailor and the house was built on a gently sloping site on the northern bank of the Beaulieu River. A timber pavilion, punctured by a long balcony, was built projecting outwards over a crisp plinth of whitewashed brick.

In the original design, the modest lower level was devoted only to boat storage and a workshop. But just a few years after completing the house, Spence made some significant adjustments to create more living space. On the upper level the balcony was filled in and glazed, while a kitchenette was removed to allow room for an extra bedroom. The lower level was reconfigured to create a new kitchen and dining area. The two floors were connected with a new spiral stairway at the side of the building. A swimming pool to Spence's design was positioned on a terrace at the front of the house, partially sheltered by the overhang of the cantilevered upper level. Inside the house, timber was used throughout, lending a sense of warmth, while a dramatic concrete and brick fireplace, also to Spence's design, dominates the generously proportioned living room.

In many ways, the house is reminiscent of the work of Scandinavian mid-century masters such as ALVAR AALTO, as well as the more contextual New England houses of MARCEL BREUER. It was recently refurbished and restored by architect John Pardey for a private client, who also commissioned a new wing.

Spence only lived in the house for around five years, building a holiday villa in Majorca just a few years later. Towards the end of his life he retired to Yaxley Hall in Suffolk – a period country house. This was not a decision one might expect from a pioneering modernist, but, as the Beaulieu house suggests, Spence was always full of surprises. The architect dubbed his house a simple 'little shack', but it was – in many ways – one of his finest buildings.

ARTHUR WITTHOEFFT
WITTHOEFFT HOUSE, USA, 1957

CLASSIC EXAMPLE OF 1950S
HOME STYLE: A RECTANGULAR,
SINGLE-STOREY STRUCTURE,
WITH FEATURES THAT SHOW
A REMARKABLE ATTENTION
TO DETAIL

PREVIOUS PAGES A Paul
McCobb sectional sofa takes
pride of place in the main
seating area. The cocktail
table is by Milo Baughman.

BELOW The woodland
behind the house forms a
green backdrop. Garaging is
below the main body of the
house, accessed by a sloping
driveway.

OPPOSITE ABOVE
The travertine and steel
fireplace was designed
by Arthur Witthoefft and
his wife. The dining chairs
are by Charles & Ray Eames.

OPPOSITE BELOW LEFT
The Bird chair and ottoman
by the fireplace were
designed by Harry Bertoia
and produced by Knoll.

OPPOSITE BELOW RIGHT
The dining table is a 1970s
piece by an unknown
designer, while the ceiling
light above is by Valerio
Bottin for Foscarini.

Legendary American super-practice Skidmore, Owings & Merrill* (SOM) has designed some of the world's greatest skyscrapers, including Manhattan's Lever House (1952) and Sears Tower in Chicago (1973). One of its architects, Arthur Witthoefft, was also responsible for a more modest gem in the town of Armonk, a few hours north of New York City. Built for himself and his wife Eleanor, the Witthoefft House is a single-storey pavilion of steel, glass and brick, resting on a stone plinth, with a backdrop of forest greenery. Recently restored, it is a classic example of 1950s home style.

Witthoefft studied architecture at the University of Illinois, then took a masters in urban design at the Cranbrook Academy of Art* under Eliel Saarinen*. Briefly, he worked with Minoru Yamasaki* – the architect of the Twin Towers – and then joined SOM's Manhattan office. During his tenure there, he also found time to design the Armonk house, as well as its neighbour and two others in the area.

Sitting on a sloping site in a quiet spot, the house makes the most of the views across the woodland at the back. Banks of glass and sliding glass doors frame the views and establish an easy flow to the terrace at the rear. Garaging and storage is slotted under the main body of the building. Witthoefft collaborated on the interiors with his wife, who was an interior designer in her own right, creating features such as the centrepiece fireplace in the living room.

Witthoefft and his wife lived in the house for thirty years before deciding to sell up and move to Florida. Unfortunately, the house later began to deteriorate and lay empty for seven years, during which time the neglected building suffered from roof leaks and damp. It seemed that the house might be in danger of demolition and replacement when it was bought by two aficionados of mid-century design, creative director Andrew Mandolene and real-estate specialist Todd Goddard.

Mandolene and Goddard have a longstanding passion for 1950s and '60s design and previously lived in a landmark Palm Springs home designed by E. Stewart Williams*. When they decided to move, they began searching for another mid-century home and came across the Witthoefft House.

'It was in such bad shape that we called Arthur Witthoefft in Florida and asked him if the house was worth restoring,' recalls Mandolene. 'He told us that the house is steel-framed and built on solid rock, so it's structurally very strong. It wasn't going anywhere.'[12]

Mandolene and Goddard persuaded Witthoefft himself to help them with a painstaking renovation process. Every detail was carefully researched and as many fixtures and fittings as possible were restored, down to the door handles and light switches. Glass panels and leaking skylights were replaced, the kitchen was updated and two small bedrooms were combined to form one generous study. Services were updated throughout and a shiny bright white polyurethane coating was laid over the concrete floor slab in the living room.

Into the mix went Mandolene and Goddard's collection of mid-century furniture, including a Paul McCobb* sectional sofa in the living room, chairs by CHARLES & RAY EAMES (see under 'Furniture') in the dining area, and in the study a 1953 sofa by Florence Knoll*, a coffee table by HARRY BERTOIA (see under 'Furniture') and a Paul McCobb cabinet.

Witthoefft was delighted by the restoration and sensitive preservation of his work. The layering of vintage pieces reinforces the vintage character of the house, but it has also been carefully updated for 21st-century living. Far from being a showroom or period piece, it is a living home that reflects its new owners' personalities, as well as being a photogenic reminder of the 1950s at its best.

OPPOSITE The armchair and ottoman in the study are Danish, and the orange cabinet is by Paul McCobb. The lamp on the cabinet was manufactured by Prisma.

ABOVE The couch in the study is by Florence Knoll and the coffee table is a Harry Bertoia design for Knoll.

ABOVE RIGHT The round table in the kitchen has an Eero Saarinen table base with a Maurice Burke table top. The photograph on the wall is by Rob Mandolene.

RIGHT The bedside lamps in the master bedroom are by Pierre Cardin and date from the 1960s.

A–Z OF DESIGNERS AND MAKERS

AALTO, AINO 1894-1949

Finnish architect, interior designer and glass designer Aino Aalto (née Marsio) was born in Helsinki, where she studied architecture at the city's Institute of Technology. She married architect and polymath designer ALVAR AALTO in 1924 and began working in his office the same year.

The Aaltos collaborated on many architectural, interiors and design projects up until Aino's death in 1949. Her focus tended to be on interiors and furnishings, although the breadth and depth of her contribution to Alvar Aalto's commissions may have been understated at times.

In 1935, Aino Aalto co-founded the furniture company Artek* along with her husband and business partners Maire Gullichsen and Nils-Gustav Hahl, and was a principal force in the leadership of the business.

She is best known today for her glassware designs. In 1932 she designed the Bölgeblick (Wave View) range, with its distinctive ribbed appearance, for Karhula-Iittala. The collection of glasses, pitchers and bowls is still produced by Iittala*.

AALTO, ALVAR 1898-1976
See p. 388.

AARNIO, EERO b. 1932
See p. 26.

AICHER, OTL 1922-1991
See p. 336.

AIN, GREGORY 1908-1988

Californian architect Gregory Ain worked with RICHARD NEUTRA in the early 1930s and was also strongly influenced by the work of Rudolph Schindler. During World War II he worked with CHARLES & RAY EAMES on the development of plywood products and chairs.

Ain built his first architectural projects in the late 1930s, but was best known for his work on affordable houses and large housing tracts in the post-war period. His work sought to apply modernist design principles to large-scale developments.

ALBERS, ANNI 1899-1994 & JOSEF 1888-1976

Anni Albers (née Annelise Fleischmann) and Josef Albers were both tutors, or 'masters', at the Bauhaus* in the 1920s and early 1930s, at both Weimar and Dessau, with Anni teaching textiles and Josef heading the carpentry workshop. They emigrated to America in 1933, where they pursued their work and teaching.

Both taught at the Black Mountain College in North Carolina, and from 1950 to 1960 Josef Albers headed the design department at Yale University.

Anni Albers was also a textile designer, much respected for her geometric and abstract patterns. From 1959 onwards she designed a number of textiles for Knoll*. Her work had some elements in common with Josef Albers's abstract paintings. As well as being a painter, Josef Albers was a designer, writer and theorist. His work on colour theory was pioneering.

ALBINI, FRANCO 1905-1977

Italian architect and designer Franco Albini studied at the Politecnico di Milano before working in the office of GIO PONTI. He established his own architectural and design studio in Milan in 1930.

His best-known furniture designs date from the 1950s, including his Gala and Margherita wicker chairs of 1950 for Bonacina and his Fiorenza chair of 1952 for Arflex*.

Albini also designed a number of pieces for Cassina*, including the Cicognino side table of 1953 and the Tre Pezzi lounge chair of 1959. He designed the futuristic, tension-mounted Veliero (Sailboat) bookshelf in 1940 – using two angled wooden masts, thin steel hanging rods and glass shelves – but the design was too complex for manufacture at the time and was only put into production by Cassina in 2011.

In the 1960s, Albini concentrated on larger architectural commissions, including stations for the Milan subway system. He also designed a television for Brionvega* and lighting for Arteluce*.

ALESSI

A design-led Italian homeware manufacturer, Alessi was initially founded in 1921 by Giovanni Alessi as a metal foundry. Industrial designer Carlo Alessi and his son Alberto Alessi established the company's reputation for sculptural forms and innovative pieces. Alessi designers have included RICHARD SAPPER, ETTORE SOTTSASS and Alessandro Mendini.

ARABIA

A Finnish ceramics producer founded in 1873 as part of the Rörstrand company, Arabia was the leading European manufacturer in the field in the 1930s. In 1946, KAJ FRANCK was appointed designer-in-chief and held the post until the 1970s. The company is now a division of Iittala*.

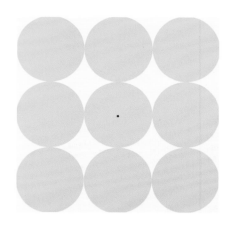

ALBERS, JOSEF
Screenprint from *The Interaction of Colour*, published by Yale University Press, 1963.

ALBINI, FRANCO
A pair of Ca 832 armchairs in walnut and upholstery, produced by Cassina, Italy, 1946.

ARABIA Ceramic clock designed by Birger Kaipiainen for Arabia, c. 1965.

ARFLEX

Established in 1950 as a satellite of the Pirelli rubber and tyre company, Arflex began to explore opportunities to manufacture furniture using foam rubber. Arflex commissioned MARCO ZANUSO to design a number of its early pieces in the 1950s and '60s, including the Lady chair of 1951 and the Martingala chair of 1954. Other Arflex designers of the mid-century period include Franco Albini* and Alberto Rosselli.

ARTEK

Artek is a Finnish furniture company established by ALVAR AALTO, his wife Aino Aalto*, Maire Gullichsen (a significant patron and supporter of the Aaltos) and Nils-Gustav Hahl. The company, which opened its first store in Helsinki in 1936, was founded principally to produce and market Alvar Aalto's furniture designs, although a number of designs by his contemporary, Ilmari Tapiovaara*, also appear in the collection. In recent years Artek has increased its range through adding products by a new generation of designers.

ARTELUCE

This Italian lighting manufacturer was founded in 1939 by GINO SARFATTI, who designed many of the company's iconic lights and lamps of the mid-century period. In 1973 the company was sold to Flos*.

ARTEMIDE

A leading lighting manufacturer, Artemide was established in Milan in 1960 by designer, academic and entrepreneur Ernesto Gismondi. The company, known for its avant-garde approach, was at the forefront of the Italian golden age in lighting design. Artemide worked with many leading Italian lighting and product designers of the post-war era, including VICO MAGISTRETTI, RICHARD SAPPER, Livio Castiglioni* and Gianfranco Frattini.

ARTIFORT

A Dutch furniture-manufacturing company based in Maastricht, Artifort worked closely with PIERRE PAULIN to develop a pioneering range of furniture in the 1950s and '60s using plastics, latex foam and elasticized fabric coverings. The company has also worked with Kho Liang Ie and Geoffrey Harcourt.

AULENTI, GAE 1927-2012

As an architect, furniture and lighting designer, Gae Aulenti created many product pieces that emerged or evolved from architectural commissions. Born in Udine, Italy, Aulenti studied architecture at the Politecnico di Milano, while also contributing to design magazines such as *Casabella*.

As an architect and interior architect, her commissions included showrooms for Olivetti and the conversion of the Gare d'Orsay into one of Paris's major art museums. Her lighting designs include the Pipistrello lamp (1965) and La Ruspa lamp (1968), both for Martinelli Luce, as well as pieces for Artemide*. Her furniture includes the Sgarsul chair for Poltronova* (1962) and the April Model 210 folding chair (1964), with a steel frame and leather seat and back, for Zanotta*.

BANG & OLUFSEN

A Danish producer of radios, hi-fi equipment and televisions, Bang & Olufsen was founded by Peter Bang and Svend Olufsen in 1925. In the 1960s the company began collaborating with leading designers such as JACOB JENSEN and Swedish design studio Bjørn & Bernadotte, while developing a distinctive modern aesthetic for its product range.

BARNES, EDWARD LARRABEE
1915–2004

American architect Edward Larrabee Barnes studied at Harvard University under Walter Gropius* and MARCEL BREUER. He founded his own practice in Manhattan in 1949. He is best known for his many museum and educational buildings from the 1960s through to the 1980s, including the Indianapolis Museum of Art (1969) and the Carnegie Museum of Art in Pittsburgh (1974).

BARRAGÁN, LUIS 1902-1988

Mexican architect Luis Barragán was one of the leading proponents of mid-century regional modernism, perfecting a warm and vibrant approach to his buildings, interiors and landscape design. He combined a love of clarity and spatial precision with a passion for colour, texture and natural materials. Gardens and landscaping were always an integral part of his projects, using high walls, patios and native planting.

Barragán was brought up on his father's ranch in Jalisco, where he developed a passion for horses and horse riding as well as a profound affection for traditional Mexican architecture and haciendas. He studied engineering in Guadalajara, but soon became fascinated with

ARFLEX Weekend lounge chair in beech, leather and brass, designed by Marco Zanuso, 1951.

ARTEMIDE A pair of sconces in chrome-plated brass and glass, 1964, designed by Studio BBPR.

AULENTI, GAE Sgarsul rocking chair, produced by Poltronova/Stendig, Italy, 1962, in lacquered wood and vinyl.

BAUGHMAN, MILO
Sectional sofa and table in rosewood, chrome-plated steel and upholstery, manufactured by Thayer Coggin, USA, c. 1960.

BAUHAUS Study for a Bauhaus poster by Herbert Bayer, 1967, for the exhibition '50 Jahre Bauhaus'.

BELLINI, MARIO
Teneride chair made with moulded polyurethane, lacquered wood and lacquered fibreglass, Cassina, Italy, 1970.

BELLMANN, HANS
Popsicle dining table in laminate and lacquered wood, produced by Knoll, USA, c. 1955.

architecture and garden design. He travelled to Europe in the late 1920s and 1930s, meeting Le Corbusier* and landscape architect Ferdinand Bac, both of whom were to have a lasting influence on his work.

Settling in Mexico City, Barragán soon developed a highly individual version of warm modernism. Key projects include his own house in Mexico City (1948), the sculptural Torri Satélite towers along the Querétaro highway (1957, with Mathias Goeritz) and the iconic Capilla de Tlálpan (1960), where Barragán's mastery of light, colour and materials were perfectly displayed, as well as his ability to create escapist spaces infused with a sense of serenity.

One of his most endearing and widely appreciated projects was the Cuadra San Cristobál ranch (1968) – a seven-acre compound outside Mexico City, where Barragán combined many of his favourite elements and motifs, as well as his love of all things equine.

BASS, SAUL 1920-1996
See p. 332.

BAUGHMAN, MILO 1923-2003
American furniture designer Milo Baughman was born in Kansas and grew up in Long Beach, California. He served in the US Air Force during World War II and then studied architectural and product design in Los Angeles. He was later employed as a designer by the Franks Brothers furniture store.

Baughman opened his own design studio in 1947 in Los Angeles. Early commissions included the Californian Modern furniture collection for Glenn, created in collaboration with Greta Magnusson-Grossman*. In the 1950s he opened his own store with his wife, Olga Lee, a lighting and textile designer.

In 1953, he began a long and highly productive working relationship with furniture manufacturer Thayer Coggin. Many of Baughman's key designs of the mid-century period were produced by the company, including his semi-circular sectional sofa and his crisp but comfortable Model 2165 settee with a rosewood panelled shell.

BAUHAUS
Although the doors of Bauhaus shut in 1933, its design philosophy and legacy were to have a powerful influence on design during the mid-century period. The inter-disciplinary school was founded in Weimar, Germany, in 1919, with Walter Gropius* as its first director. A foundation year was followed by

more detailed study in at least one craft and design discipline under a series of 'masters' who ran their own workshops. The masters included artists, designers and architects.

In 1925, the Bauhaus relocated to Dessau, with new headquarters designed by Gropius himself. Gropius passed the directorship on to Hannes Meyer, who was followed, in 1930, by LUDWIG MIES VAN DER ROHE. Facing political pressure from the National Socialist authorities, the Bauhaus was dissolved in July 1933.

Many of the Bauhaus masters, including Gropius, Mies van der Rohe, Anni & Josef Albers*, MARCEL BREUER and László Moholy-Nagy*, moved to America and began teaching and working there. The functionalist design philosophy taught at the Bauhaus – together with the work and example of its masters and students – helped shape modernist design and architecture, while also influencing the teaching approach of many design schools in the post-war period.

BAWA, GEOFFREY 1919-2003
Born in Ceylon (now Sri Lanka) to Anglo-Asian parents, Bawa studied law at Cambridge University. He practised law briefly before studying at the Architectural Association in London. After qualifying in 1957, he returned to Sri Lanka and established his own architectural practice. He became known for a unique, original and contextual version of 'tropical modernism', or 'soft modernism'. His work has been compared with that of other distinctive regional modernists of the mid-century era, such as Luis Barragán*. Among Bawa's many houses, hotels and public buildings, perhaps the most famous is Lunuganga (1948), his own home and garden in Bentota, Sri Lanka.

BELLINI, MARIO b. 1935
Italian furniture and product designer Mario Bellini was born in Milan, where he studied architecture at the Politecnico di Milano, graduating in 1959. He was design director for the La Rinascente group of department stores in the early 1960s, before co-founding an architectural practice with Marco Romano and then establishing Studio Bellini in Milan in 1973.

In 1963, Bellini became a design consultant for Olivetti and also designed for the Italian electronics company Brionvega*. In parallel with his industrial and product work, he designed furniture. His best-known designs include La Bambole leather armchairs and sofas for B&B Italia

BIANCONI, FULVIO
Forato vases, produced
by Venini, Italy, 1951–52.

BOJESEN, KAY Wooden
animals in oak, teak and
birch, produced by Kay
Bojesen, Denmark, c. 1951.

BORSANI, OSVALDO
P40 lounge chair in
enamelled steel, brass and
upholstery, manufactured
by Tecno, Italy, c. 1955.

BRIONVEGA RR126
stereo designed by Achille
& Pier Giacomo Castiglioni,
in laminated wood,
metal and plastic, 1965.

(1972) and the Cab chair for Cassina*
(1977). Lighting designs include his
Chiara floor lamp for Flos* (1967).

BELLMANN, HANS 1911–1990
Swiss designer Hans Bellmann worked
with LUDWIG MIES VAN DER ROHE
in the 1930s before founding his
own design studio in Zurich in 1946.
His designs include the Model 1000
dining table made by Wohnbedarf
(c. 1947), the Einpunkt plywood dining/
side chair produced by Horgenglarus
(c. 1952) and the Popsicle table for
Knoll* (c. 1955).

BERTOIA, HARRY 1915–1978
See p. 30.

BIANCONI, FULVIO 1915–1996
Italian glassware designer Fulvio
Bianconi was born in Padua,
but moved as a child with his family
to Venice, where he studied at the
Accademia di Belle Arti. In the 1920s
and '30s he worked as a glass painter
and a designer of perfume bottles.
In 1948, he began collaborating
with PAOLO VENINI of the Venini
glassworks in Murano. The pair
collaborated on the design of the
Fazzoletto (Handkerchief) vase of
1949 and Bianconi produced a number
of other innovative pieces for the
company, such as his Pezzato series
of the 1950s with a mosaic effect.
He also designed for Vistosi and had
a second career as a graphic designer.

BILL, MAX 1908–1994
See p. 336.

BO BARDI, LINA 1914–1992
See p. 394.

BOJESEN, KAY 1886–1958
A product designer and silversmith,
Danish designer Kay Bojesen served
an apprenticeship at Georg Jensen*
before establishing his own studio
in 1913. He was a much respected
designer of cutlery and homeware,
but became best known in the post-war
period for his wooden spider monkey
(1951) and other wooden toys designed
with a simple, contemporary and
endearing aesthetic as well as a sense
of warmth and humour.

BONET, ANTONIO 1913–1989
See p. 400.

BORAX
Shorthand for excessive and often
superfluous product styling, and
named after the hard-sell promotional
offers of an American soap company,
Borax was used to describe the

chrome and fins applied to Cadillacs
and other cars by Harley Earl and
his contemporaries in the Detroit
motor industry. Borax was at its
height in the late 1940s and 1950s
and was associated with the American
automobile industry's attempts to
entice customers into annual or
regular upgrades.

BORSANI, OSVALDO 1911–1985
In 1953, Italian furniture designer
Osvaldo Borsani and his twin brother
Fulgenzio founded the Tecno furniture
company in Milan. The company
was established to market Osvaldo
Borsani's own collection of furniture,
which included pieces such as the
adjustable P40 lounge chair of c. 1955
and the D70 sofa from 1954 – another
flexible design that could convert
into a bed. The S80 folding plywood
chair was also launched in 1954. Tecno
opened its first shop in Milan in 1956.
Borsani also co-founded the design
journal *Ottagono* in 1966.

BOYD, ROBIN 1919–1971
One of the most influential mid-
century Australian architects, Robin
Boyd was also a writer and cultural
commentator. He was the son of the
painter Penleigh Boyd and served
an architectural apprenticeship in
Melbourne. He co-founded his own
practice in 1953 – with Frederick
Romberg and Roy Grounds – and was
best known for a series of innovative
houses in and around Melbourne.
These included his own home on
Walsh Street, completed in 1958.

BRAUN
One of the most innovative home
electronics and appliance makers
of the mid-century period, Braun
was founded in Frankfurt in 1921 by
engineer Max Braun. The company
began producing radios in the 1930s
and developed the first electric shaver
in 1950. Under the guidance of Max
Braun's sons, Artur and Erwin, the
company established an in-house
design department, which was headed
by DIETER RAMS from 1961 until his
retirement in 1995.

BREUER, MARCEL 1902–1981
See p. 406.

BRIONVEGA
An innovative Italian electronics
manufacturer, Brionvega was founded
in 1945. The company always placed
great emphasis on design quality
and innovation, working with leading
designers such as RICHARD SAPPER,
MARCO ZANUSO, ACHILLE & PIER

GIACOMO CASTIGLIONI and Mario Bellini*. The company failed to keep pace with the rapid technological advances of the late 20th century and went out of business in 1992, although some Brionvega designs have since been reissued after the brand name was sold on to new owners.

BROADHURST, FLORENCE
1899–1977
See p. 236.

BUFF, STRAUB & HENSMAN
A noted Californian architectural practice in the late 1950s and 1960s, Buff, Straub & Hensman was founded in 1952 by Conrad Buff, Calvin Straub and Donald Hensman. One of their key projects was a house in Altadena for SAUL BASS, which was also Case Study House #20 (1958) within the exemplary house-building programme pioneered and publicized by John Entenza* of *Arts & Architecture* magazine. The practice also designed a residence for actor Steve McQueen in 1962 and a second Case Study house (#28) in 1965.

BUHRICH, HUGH 1911–2004
Born in Hamburg and educated in Munich, Berlin and Danzig, Hugh Buhrich emigrated to Australia in 1939 with his wife, writer Eva Buhrich. He specialized in residential projects in Sydney, as well as designing furniture and interiors. Key projects, such as his own house – Buhrich House II – in Sydney's Castlecrag district – combined these skills in one cohesive and original vision.

BUNSHAFT, GORDON 1909–1990
An architect and partner with the New York office of the architectural firm Skidmore, Owings & Merrill*, Gordon Bunshaft designed Lever House in New York, completed in 1952. This was among the first glass-fronted, curtain-walled skyscrapers in America and marked a turning point in mid-century high-rise design. Bunshaft was awarded the Pritzker Prize in 1988.

CALDAS, JOSÉ ZANINE 1919–2001
A self-taught designer, Brazilian furniture-maker José Zanine Caldas began by building architectural models in Rio de Janeiro for OSCAR NIEMEYER and Lúcio Costa*. He started producing furniture in 1948 and later moved to São Paulo. Early pieces explored fluid forms and experimented with timber and plywood; later pieces of the 1970s onwards assumed a more robust sense of weight, using slabs of timber or cut and carved blocks of wood.

CALDER, ALEXANDER 1898–1976
A sculptor, painter and illustrator, American artist Alexander Calder spanned the border between the worlds of art and design. Most famously, his colourful and kinetic mobiles fused sculpture, engineering and design. As well as his paintings and monumental sculptures, Calder designed jewelry and tapestries, and produced murals; he also painted the exteriors of two airplanes for Braniff International Airways.

CALVERT, MARGARET b. 1936
See p. 360.

CANDELA, FELIX 1910–1997
Born in Spain, where he trained as an architect, Felix Candela emigrated to Mexico at the end of the Spanish Civil War in 1939. He established his own architectural and engineering practice in 1950, pioneering the use of sculptural and fluid concrete shell buildings in Mexico in the 1950s and '60s. Some of his most famous vaulted structures served as churches, but they were also adopted for many other uses. His first hyperbolic project using an ultra-thin reinforced concrete shell was the Cosmic Rays laboratory in Mexico City (1951). Other key projects included his Bacardi Rum factory in Cuautitlán (1960).

CARDIN, PIERRE b. 1922
One of the most influential French fashion designers of the post-war period, the Italian-born Cardin founded his company in Paris in 1950. His mid-century work used strong colours, geometric patterns and futuristic forms, and reflected his interest in designing for 'the world of tomorrow'. His avant-garde collections of the late 1960s reflected his interest in Space Age futurism. Cardin also expanded into other realms of design, including furniture and car design. His home near Cannes, the Palais Bulles, or 'Bubble House' – designed by Antti Lovag* – was begun in the early 1970s but not completed until 1989; much of the furniture was designed by Cardin.

CARL HANSEN
A Danish furniture manufacturer, Carl Hansen is best known as the manufacturer of designs by HANS WEGNER. The company was founded in 1908 by Carl Hansen in Odense, Denmark, and has retained an emphasis on high-quality craftsmanship.

CASE STUDY PROGRAM
Launched in 1945 by John Entenza, editor of *Arts & Architecture*

BUNSHAFT, GORDON
Cabinet in aluminium, marble and glass, c. 1965.

CALDAS, JOSÉ ZANINE
Dining table in reclaimed peroba and brauna timber, c. 1970.

CALDER, ALEXANDER
Tapestry in woven jute, produced by CAC Publications/Bon Art, USA, 1975.

CARL HANSEN Hans Wegner Sawbuck chairs, manufactured by Carl Hansen, Denmark, 1951.

magazine, the Case Study Program championed the design of a series of innovative, prototypical, modernist Californian homes designed by a range of groundbreaking mid-century architects. Curated by Entenza, who teamed up selected architects with clients, the Program consisted of 36 houses – although not all were built – and ended in 1966.

Participating architects included CRAIG ELLWOOD, RICHARD NEUTRA, Raphael Soriano*, Julius Ralph Davidson and practices such as Buff, Straub & Hensman*. Two of the best-known Case Study houses are CHARLES & RAY EAMES's house (#8; 1949, designed in conjunction with EERO SAARINEN) and Pierre Koenig*'s Stahl House (#22; 1960).

CASSINA
The Italian furniture manufacturer Cassina was founded in Meda by Cesare and Umberto Cassina in 1927. In the mid-century period, the company worked with GIO PONTI, VICO MAGISTRETTI, Gaetano Pesce*, Franco Albini*, Angelo Mangiarotti* and others. In 1957, it launched Gio Ponti's iconic Superleggera chair.

CASSON, HUGH 1910-1999
British architect, designer and artist Hugh Casson was director of architecture for the Festival of Britain* in 1951 and played a key role in commissioning London South Bank buildings such as Ralph Tubbs's* Dome of Discovery and Leslie Martin's Royal Festival Hall. His own architectural projects, with his practice Casson Conder, included the Elephant House at London Zoo (1965).

CASTAING, MADELEINE 1894-1992
One of the most eminent and original voices of 20th-century French interior design, Madeleine Castaing was well known for her bold colour choices, eclectic approach and distinctive patterns, such as her signature leopard-print wallpapers and fabrics. One of her most famous projects was the 1947 interior of the 17th-century townhouse in Milly-la-Forêt owned by poet, writer and artist Jean Cocteau, with whom Castaing collaborated closely on the design.

CASTIGLIONI, ACHILLE 1918-2002 & PIER GIACOMO 1913-1968
See p. 132.

CASTIGLIONI, LIVIO 1911-1979
The elder brother of ACHILLE & PIER GIACOMO CASTIGLIONI, Livio Castiglioni was also a successful and prominent designer of the post-war period. He studied architecture at the Politecnico di Milano and co-founded a design studio with Pier Giacomo in 1938, which Achille joined in the mid-1940s. In 1952, however, Livio Castiglioni parted company with his brothers to practise as an independent designer. He worked with companies such as Phonola and Brionvega*, and developed a number of lighting designs. His most famous light was the Boalum (1969), designed in conjunction with Gianfranco Frattini and produced by Artemide*.

CASTLE, WENDELL b. 1932
American designer Wendell Castle began studying sculpture before moving into furniture design. His work has a particularly abstract and sculptural quality, whether in wood or fibreglass. His Molar lounge chairs and coffee tables of 1969 were produced in gel-coated fibreglass in vivid reds and yellows. His segmented Puzzle table (1970) used the same material, but Castle increasingly turned to wood for later designs.

CHAMBERLIN, POWELL & BON
This leading British architectural practice was formed in 1952 by Peter ('Joe') Chamberlin, Geoffry Powell and Christoph Bon. The firm is best known for the design of the Barbican in London, built between 1965 and 1976. The style of the concrete complex is brutalist and uncompromising, yet it remains a successful community. Other projects include the Golden Lane Estate alongside the Barbican, built between 1957 and 1962.

CHERMAYEFF, SERGE 1900-1996
Chermayeff's own house in East Sussex, Bentley Wood, was completed in 1938 but felt ahead of its time and was an important precursor of mid-century style. From 1933 to 1936 Chermayeff worked in partnership with Erich Mendelsohn, and other key projects of this time include the De La Warr Pavilion (1935) and 66 Old Church Street in London (also 1935). In 1940, Chermayeff emigrated to America to begin a new career as a teacher, writer and painter, becoming president of the Institute of Design in Chicago. His son, Ivan Chermayeff, co-founded the influential Chermayeff & Geismar graphic design studio in 1960.

CHERNER, NORMAN 1920-1987
American architect, furniture designer and writer Norman Cherner is best known for his plywood chairs,

CASSINA Model 877 lounge chair and ottoman, designed by Gianfranco Frattini, in walnut and vinyl, 1959.

CASTIGLIONI, LIVIO Boalum lamp made with plastic tubing, Artemide, Italy, 1969, designed by Livio Castiglioni and Gianfranco Frattini.

CASTLE, WENDELL Molar settee in gel-coated fibreglass, c. 1969.

CHERNER, NORMAN

Cherner armchair in
walnut plywood, produced
by Plycraft, USA, 1958.

COLANI, LUIGI Lounge
chair in chrome-plated steel,
aluminium and upholstery,
manufactured by Kusch+Co,
Germany, c. 1968.

CURTIS JERÉ Mirror in
brass and copper, c. 1970.

first designed for Plycraft in 1958.
Now known simply as Cherner chairs,
the pieces included a side chair
and an armchair, with sculptural
plywood wings emerging like taut
bows from the main body; these
chairs were reissued in 1999.
As an architect, Cherner developed
a prefabricated housing system
known as 'Pre-built' in 1957. He also
designed glassware, lighting and
storage systems.

CHRISTIANSEN, POUL
See LE KLINT, p. 140.

COLANI, LUIGI b. 1928
Swiss-born designer Luigi Colani
took the idea of streamlining to new
extremes, within a playful design
approach that placed great emphasis
on aerodynamic, rounded forms.
He studied painting and sculpture
in Berlin and aerodynamics in Paris
before moving into car design in the
1950s, working for Fiat, Alfa Romeo
and BMW, as well as producing his
own kit car.

In the early 1960s he expanded
his portfolio and began to design
furniture. His designs included
lounge chairs for Kusch+Co,
experimental fibreglass chairs for
Fritz Hansen* and others, and a
modular seating system (c. 1970)
for Rosenthal Studio-Line that could
be arranged in conversation-pit
formation. In the decades that
followed, Colani continued to explore
other areas of design and established
an office in Japan.

COLOMBINI, GINO b. 1915
Italian furniture and product designer
Gino Colombini worked with architect
and designer Franco Albini* during
the late 1930s and 1940s. From 1949
to 1961 he served as technical director
for the Italian manufacturer Kartell*.
He designed a number of early Kartell
products during the 1950s, exploring
the versatility of plastics in furniture
and household products.

COLOMBO, JOE 1930–1971
See p. 36.

COPER, HANS 1920–1981
See p. 178.

COSTA, LÚCIO 1902–1998
A leading Brazilian urban planner,
architect and furniture designer
of the post-war period, Lúcio Costa
was born in France to Brazilian
parents and studied in England,
Switzerland and Rio de Janeiro.
He collaborated with Le Corbusier*

and OSCAR NIEMEYER on the design
of the Ministry of Education and
Health building in Rio (1943) and also
designed furniture for the project.
He developed the masterplan for
the new capital of Brasília in the late
1950s, which saw another period of
close collaboration with Niemeyer.
His furniture designs include the
Poltroninha armchair of 1960.

COURRÈGES, ANDRÉ b. 1923
Influenced by Futurism, technology
and modern design, French fashion
designer André Courrèges explored
new materials in his work – including
plastics, PVC and metallics – as well
as bold, primary colours. His Space
Age collection of 1964 helped define
the look of the period and – along
with Mary Quant – Courrèges is
credited with inventing the mini-skirt.
Certain parallels can be drawn with
the work of his contemporary, Pierre
Cardin*, who was also at the height
of his powers in the 1960s.

CRANBROOK ACADEMY OF ART
Founded in 1932 by newspaper baron
and philanthropist George Booth,
the Cranbrook Academy of Art – in
the town of Bloomfield Hills, Michigan
– quickly established itself as one
of the most progressive design schools
in America. Under the presidency
of architect and designer Eliel
Saarinen*, the academy attracted
a talented and learned faculty, while
drawing on some of the principles
established by the Bauhaus*, such
as the interaction between different
disciplines of design. Many leading
American designers of the mid-
century period either attended
Cranbrook or taught there, including
CHARLES & RAY EAMES, HARRY
BERTOIA, EERO SAARINEN, JACK
LENOR LARSEN and Florence Knoll*.

CROUWEL, WIM b. 1928
See p. 340.

CURTIS JERÉ
Curtis Jeré – or C. Jeré – was
the invented signature of designers
Curtis ('Kurt') Freiler and Jerry
Fels. They applied the name to
an ornate, sculptural yet distinctly
modern range of mirrors, lights
and decorative sculptures in the
1960s and '70s. The pair first met
in the 1940s and produced costume
jewelry before launching their own
design company, Artisan House,
in 1964. The metallic finishes and
hand-crafted quality of Curtis Jeré
pieces give them a powerful sense
of sophisticated glamour.

DE HAVILLAND COMET
British Overseas Airways
Corporation (BOAC) Comet,
c. 1952.

**DE PAS, D'URBINO &
LOMAZZI** Joe chair, 1970,
made with polyurethane
foam on a steel frame
and leather upholstery,
Poltronova, Italy.

DITZEL, NANNA
Lounge chair and ottoman,
produced by Kolds
Savværk, Denmark, 1953,
in teak and upholstery.

D'ASCANIO, CORRADINO
1891–1981
See p. 284.

DAVID WHITEHEAD
British textiles company David
Whitehead was established in 1927 as
part of a firm whose history stretched
back to 1815, when it was founded
by the Whitehead family. Under the
guidance of John Murray and Tom
Mellor, David Whitehead became
one of the most progressive and
forward-thinking texiles companies in
Britain during the mid-century period,
working with artists and designers
such as Jacqueline Groag, Marian
Mahler, Eduardo Paolozzi, John Piper*
and a young Terence Conran.

DAY, LUCIENNE 1917–2010
See p. 240.

DAY, ROBIN 1915–2010
See p. 40.

DE HAVILLAND COMET
The world's first commercial passenger
jet airliner, the De Havilland Comet
was introduced into service in 1952
by the British Overseas Airways
Corporation (BOAC). The first
prototype of Comet 1 had flown just
three years earlier. A number of
accidents in the early 1950s led the
plane to be modified, but it heralded
a revolution in commercial jet travel
and the growth of international
tourism and business commuting.

DE PAS, D'URBINO & LOMAZZI
The DDL design studio was founded
in Milan by Jonathan de Pas, Joe
D'Urbino and Paolo Lomazzi. Their
furniture designs of the 1960s are
associated with the playful Pop
culture of the period, particularly
the inflatable plastic Blow chair for
Zanotta* (1967) – one of the first pieces
of its kind. Another key design was
the Joe leather chair of 1970 in the
shape of a giant leather baseball glove
and named after Joe DiMaggio.

DEATON, CHARLES 1921–1996
See p. 410.

DIOR, CHRISTIAN 1905–1957
The inventor of the New Look,
Christian Dior was arguably the
most famous and influential fashion
designer of the post-war period.
He launched his couture house in
1947, and his first collection offered
an escape from years of wartime
austerity with its emphasis on luxury
and glamour and a fresh silhouette
of nipped-in waists, flowing skirts

and enticing, feminine fabrics. The
New Look established the house of
Dior and reasserted Paris's dominant
position on the map of global fashion.

DITZEL, NANNA 1923–2005
Danish furniture and textile designer
Nanna Ditzel (née Hauberg) married
fellow designer Jørgen Ditzel in 1946.
Many of her designs of the 1950s
were collaborations with her husband
(who died in 1961), including lounge
chairs and sofas manufactured by
Knud Willadsen and Kolds Savværk,
as well as the Model 113 chair in
teak and cane (1956). Her wicker
and mahogany bucket-seated
Ditzel chair for Ludvig Pontoppidan
(1950) had an organic, endearing
warmth shared with one of her
most famous designs – the Egg chair
of 1957 for Pierantonio Bonacina,
a cocoon-like wicker hanging chair.
Solo designs from the 1960s include
her Toadstool seats and table (1961),
originally designed for her children.
Ditzel also designed textiles for
Kvadrat and silverware for Georg
Jensen*.

DREYFUSS, HENRY 1904–1972
An industrial and product designer,
best known for his work in the 1930s,
Henry Dreyfuss was an early pioneer
of streamlining, applied to everything
from locomotives to telephones and
vacuum cleaners. His work, which
continued into the 1940s and '50s,
helped establish the importance
of outward aesthetics for functional
consumer products and paved the
way for mid-century product designers
such as RAYMOND LOEWY.

DUQUETTE, TONY 1914–1999
A celebrated interior designer,
as well as a set designer for theatre
and film, Tony Duquette injected
multiple layers of Hollywood glamour
into his work. His 'maximalist' designs
were flamboyant and theatrical
but not elitist, and reflected his
love of fantasy. One of his most
engaging projects was his own home,
Dawnridge, in Beverly Hills (1949).
He was also a furniture and jewelry
designer.

EAMES, CHARLES 1907–1978
& RAY 1912–1988
See p. 44.

EARL, HARLEY 1893–1969
See Borax.

EDINBURGH WEAVERS
Alastair Morton, who came from
a family of entrepreneurial textile

manufacturers, launched Edinburgh Weavers in 1931. The company soon established a reputation for modern patterns with an emphasis on organic designs or geometric abstraction. Morton, who was a painter himself, worked closely with a number of artists who designed textile patterns for the company, including Ben Nicholson, Barbara Hepworth and Victor Vasarely. Other contributing designers included LUCIENNE DAY and Marion Dorn.

EICHLER, JOSEPH 1900-1974
A real-estate developer with a passion for 'Californian Modern' style, Joseph Eichler developed a series of communities in California in the late 1950s and early 1960s. Known simply as 'Eichlers', the houses – which numbered around 11,000 in total – were designed by respected architects such as Robert Anshen, Raphael Soriano* and A. Quincy Jones*, and promoted inside/outside living, open floor-plans and outside rooms. The houses were solidly built but affordable. Eichler's development company ultimately over-extended itself and went out of business in 1967.

EIERMANN, EGON 1904-1970
A German architect, interior and furniture designer, Egon Eiermann established an architectural practice with Robert Hilgers in 1946 and combined his building commissions with the development of many innovative chairs manufactured by Wilde & Spieth. Many of these pieces used plywood, including the distinctive, three-legged SE42 chair (1949) and SE18 chair (1952). Eiermann's buildings included the German Pavilion at the Brussels World Fair of 1958.

EKSTRÖM, YNGVE 1913-1988
Swedish designer Yngve Ekström co-founded the furniture manufacturer Swedese in 1945 with his brother and a third partner. The company still produces many of Ekström's own designs from the mid-century period, including his most famous piece – the Lamino chair (1956). Other designs include the Desirée collection of dining chairs and matching table (1954).

ELLWOOD, CRAIG 1922-1992
See p. 416.

ENTENZA, JOHN 1905-1984
See Case Study Program.

ERCOL
The furniture-making business Ercol was founded in 1920 by designer Lucian Ercolani. Born in Tuscany, Ercolani moved to England with his family as a child. In 1910, he joined the furniture company Parker Knoll and later moved to E. Gomme (the makers of G-Plan* furniture). Government contracts helped see Ercol through the war years and the business thrived in the 1950s, with Ercolani himself designing many of the company's best-known timber designs. These included his organically pleasing Nest of Tables (1956), rounded Windsor dining table (1956) and Butterfly chair (1958). Many Ercolani designs are still produced under the Ercol Originals label.

ESHERICK, WHARTON 1887-1970
A sculptor, illustrator and furniture designer and maker, Wharton Esherick fused sculpture and craft within his work. His long career also encompassed painting and interiors, including the crafted timber kitchen of the Esherick House (1961), designed by Louis Kahn* for Esherick's niece. His own house and studio at Paoli, Pennsylvania, evolved over many years – from the 1920s to the 1960s – to become an extraordinary and highly personal *Gesamtkunstwerk* in the woods, featuring a workshop by Kahn.

EVANS, PAUL 1931-1987
American furniture designer Paul Evans studied at the Cranbrook Academy of Art*. His work fused art, craft, design and sculpture within contemporary pieces hand-made either by his own studio or by the furniture company, Directional. Evans signed and closely supervised the manufacture of his pieces, many of which were custom or limited-edition designs. These included a series of cabinets from the 1960s, either fronted in timber or sculpted metal, sometimes with ornate and abstract patterns. Other designs included sofas, tables and chairs, all with a distinctive and sculptural quality.

FANTONI, MARCELLO b. 1915
An Italian ceramicist and sculptor, Marcello Fantoni founded his own design studio in 1936. His work of the 1950s and '60s included vases and pitchers with sculptural forms and distinctive glazes, sometimes decorated with abstract or naïve patterns with a folk art influence. He also produced a series of earthenware figurines, which spliced Cubist influences, folk art patterns and a contemporary sensibility.

EIERMANN, EGON
Model SE42 chairs in walnut plywood, produced by Wilde & Spieth, Germany, 1949.

EKSTRÖM, YNGVE
A pair of Lamino lounge chairs in teak, beech and leather, manufactured by ESE-Möbler, Sweden, 1956.

ERCOL Nest of Tables designed by Lucian Ercolani, 1956.

EVANS, PAUL Coffee table in steel, slate and gilt wood, produced by Paul Evans Studio, c. 1965.

FARINA, BATTISTA ('PININ')
1893-1966
Battista Farina established his own bodyshop in Turin in 1930 and helped develop a number of key car designs during the 1930s, '40s and '50s. His company, Pininfarina, produced the classic Cisitalia 202 sports car of 1947 and began working with Ferrari in the 1950s. Farina worked on the styling of the Ferrari 250 SWB of 1961 and went on to collaborate with Jaguar in the 1970s. His company also established a research centre and helped develop concept cars, as well as exploring auto aerodynamics.

FASANELLO, RICARDO 1930-1993
A Brazilian furniture designer of the mid-century period, Ricardo Fasanello was based in Rio de Janeiro, where he established his own design studio. His pieces include the Anel chair of 1970 and a series of heavily upholstered, sculptural leather chairs from the late 1960s, including the Esfera armchair and the Fardos chair (both 1968).

FESTIVAL OF BRITAIN
A key event in British culture of the 1950s, the Festival of Britain was held in 1951 on the centenary of the Great Exhibition, which had been hosted by Joseph Paxton's Crystal Palace. Like its exemplary forerunner, the Festival was a national celebration of Britain's past, present and future, with a focus on innovative design and architecture. It was also intended as a moment of escapism from post-war austerity and as an optimistic symbol of recovery and future progress.

The centre point of the Festival was London's South Bank, where a series of landmark modernist buildings were created under the supervision of the Festival's director of architecture, Hugh Casson*. These included Ralph Tubbs*'s innovative Dome of Discovery, the emblematic Skylon tower (designed by Hidalgo Moya, Philip Powell and Felix Samuély) and the Royal Festival Hall, designed by Leslie Martin (with Peter Moro and Robert Matthew). The legacy of the Festival is still felt, and not only within the continuing presence of the Royal Festival Hall.

FLETCHER, ALAN 1931-2006
See p. 342.

FLOS
A pioneering Italian lighting manufacturer, Flos was founded by Dino Gavina and Cesare Cassina in 1962. Flos worked closely with ACHILLE & PIER GIACOMO CASTIGLIONI, producing a number of their iconic lamps and lights, including the Taccia, Arco and Toio lamps of the early 1960s. The Castiglioni brothers also designed the company's Milan showroom in 1968. Flos started working with Tobia Scarpa* in the 1960s, and in 1974 bought Arteluce*, the lighting company founded by GINO SARFATTI.

FONTANA ARTE
An Italian lighting and furniture producer, founded by GIO PONTI in 1932, Fontana Arte manufactured a number of Ponti designs as well as lighting and furniture by Pietro Chiesa and Gae Aulenti*. Max Ingrand was artistic director during the 1950s and also a key designer. The company expanded its design collections from the early 1980s onwards with a new generation of Italian designers.

FORNASETTI, PIERO 1913-1988
One of the most original and distinctive masters of Italian furniture and interior design, Piero Fornasetti was also an artist, illustrator and ceramic designer. He studied at the Accademia di Belle Arti in Milan before becoming a protégé of GIO PONTI, with whom he collaborated on a range of furniture and interiors commissions.

Fornasetti designs were particularly popular in the 1950s and '60s, when his personal portfolio of motifs and themes – including birds and butterflies, classical porticos and façades, suns and clouds, as well as, most famously, the seductive eyes of opera singer Lina Cavalieri – were applied to his furniture, ceramics, wallpapers and textiles.

Fornasetti also designed the interiors of the San Remo Casino (1952), the ocean liner *Andrea Doria* (1952) and his own home, Villa Fornasetti, in Milan (c. 1955). His work has undergone a marked renaissance in recent years and the Fornasetti style is again much in demand.

FRANCK, KAJ 1911-1989
See p. 182.

FRANK, JOSEF 1885-1967
See p. 246.

FREY, ALBERT 1903-1998
Born in Switzerland, Albert Frey worked with Le Corbusier* and contributed to the design of the iconic Villa Savoye (1931) in Poissy, France, before emigrating to America just before its completion. After time in New York a commission took him to

FANTONI, MARCELLO Three vessels in glazed stoneware, c. 1955.

FASANELLO, RICARDO A pair of Anel chairs, in enamelled steel, fibreglass and suede, 1970.

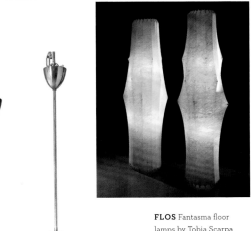

FLOS Fantasma floor lamps by Tobia Scarpa for Flos, made with sprayed fibreglass over a metal frame, 1962.

FONTANA ARTE Model 1933 pendant lamps, in brass and crystal, designed by Max Ingrand, 1961.

FRITZ HANSEN Arne Jacobsen Grand Prix chairs, in chrome-plated steel and leather, 1957.

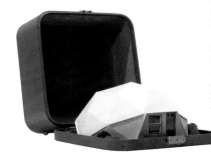

FULLER, RICHARD BUCKMINSTER Model of a geodesic home, used as a salesman's sample, produced by the Pease Woodworking Company, c. 1960.

GARDELLA, IGNAZIO Digamma lounge chairs in enamelled steel, brass and upholstery, produced by Gavina, Italy, 1957.

GEORG JENSEN A pair of Model 1087 silver candlesticks designed by Søren Georg Jensen, 1960.

Palm Springs – the Californian desert city that became his home and where many of his most famous buildings are located.

Frey's distinctive version of 'Desert Modernism' was expressed in a series of houses, including a home for designer RAYMOND LOEWY completed in 1947 and his own modest home (Frey House II) tucked into the side of a mountain and overlooking the city below. Frey also helped shape the more public face of Palm Springs during its mid-century heyday, with projects including Palm Springs City Hall (1957) and the Valley station of the Aerial Tramway (1963).

FRIBERG, BERNDT 1899–1981
See GUSTAVSBERG POTTERY, p. 186.

FRITZ HANSEN
This Danish furniture manufacturer started life in 1872 when Fritz Hansen opened a cabinet-making workshop in Copenhagen. During the 1930s the founder's son, Christian E. Hansen, began to develop new production techniques using steam-bent timber and wood laminates, and also launched the company's first steel furniture. During the 1950s the company worked with ARNE JACOBSEN on an iconic range of furniture, including the plywood Ant chair (1952) and its sister chair, the Model 3107 Series 7 (1955). Jacobsen's Swan and Egg chairs followed in 1958. The company also produces furniture by VERNER PANTON, Bruno Mathsson* and Piet Hein*, as well as pieces designed by POUL KJÆRHOLM across the mid-century period, many of which were originally manufactured by Kold Christensen.

FRUTIGER, ADRIAN b. 1928
See p. 346.

FULLER, RICHARD BUCKMINSTER 1895–1983
One of the most original thinkers in the world of 20th-century architecture and design, Richard Buckminster Fuller was an inventor, designer, writer and theorist. Born in Massachusetts, he was educated at Harvard University but twice expelled. His best-known and most successful architectural innovation was the geodesic dome, which he began working on in the late 1940s and patented in 1954. The first commercial dome was completed in 1953 for the Ford motor company in Dearborn, Michigan. In the years that followed, a whole series of domes were built internationally, including the US Pavilion at the Montreal Expo

of 1967. Some estimates suggest that as many as 300,000 geodesic domes have now been built globally.

Another key interest was prefabricated housing and Buckminster Fuller first began developing ideas for a modular, factory-produced housing system back in the late 1920s. This became the Dymaxion Dwelling Machine, or Wichita House, which was produced as a prototype in 1945. A company was established to produce the Dymaxion but collapsed in 1946 just before production could begin. Buckminster Fuller also developed a three-wheeled Dymaxion car. As a theorist, he pioneered the philosophy of sustainable design and coined the phrase 'spaceship earth'.

G-PLAN
A low-cost range of modern British furniture, G-Plan was produced by E. Gomme and designed by Donald Gomme in 1953. The range could be bought piece by piece over months or years, allowing customers to save up and buy the matching collection one item at a time. The name was coined by the J. Walter Thompson advertising agency, and the success of G-Plan was helped by advertising campaigns and a network of showrooms.

GAMES, ABRAM 1914–1996
See p. 350.

GARDELLA, IGNAZIO 1905–1999
Italian architect, writer, academic, and interior and furniture designer Ignazio Gardella began designing furniture in the 1940s. In 1947, he co-founded the Azucena furniture and lighting store in Milan. He designed for Kartell* and Gavina, who produced his Digamma armchair in 1957. His building projects included offices and a showroom for Olivetti and an office building for Alfa Romeo.

GELLER, ANDREW 1924–2011
See p. 422.

GEORG JENSEN
Georg Jensen founded his eponymous silverware company in Copenhagen, Denmark, in 1904. In the 1950s the company worked closely with designer Henning Koppel* as well as other designers such as Nanna Ditzel*. Jensen's son, Søren Georg Jensen, also contributed designs and was artistic director of the company in the 1960s and early 1970s.

GHYCZY, PETER b. 1940
Hungarian-born designer Peter Ghyczy studied architecture in Germany

GIACOMETTI, ALBERTO Osselet floor lamp in cast bronze with a parchment shade, 1960.

GRAFFI, CARLO Acero timber base for a glass-topped dining table by Franco Campo and Carlo Graffi, c. 1955.

GUARICHE, PIERRE Equilibrium Double-Branch floor lamp, in enamelled steel, brass and aluminium, produced by Disderot, France, 1951.

and lived and worked in the country before settling in the Netherlands. He helped pioneer the evolution of plastic products and furniture in the 1960s. His most famous design is his hinged Garden Egg lounge chair of 1968 for Reuter Products - a clam-shell design in fibreglass that unfolds to reveal an upholstered seat and back-rest.

GIACOMETTI, ALBERTO 1901-1966 **& DIEGO** 1902-1985
The Swiss-born artists and designers Alberto and Diego Giacometti created lighting, candlesticks and other sculptural cast-metal pieces for Jean-Michel Frank in the 1920s in Paris. In the 1950s and '60s Diego Giacometti produced bronze furniture and lighting, while his brother concentrated on sculpture and fine art.

GIRARD, ALEXANDER 1907-1993
See p. 250.

GLASER, MILTON b. 1929
American graphic designer and print and poster artist Milton Glaser co-founded Push Pin Studios in New York in 1954 and *New York* magazine in 1968. In 1974, he launched his own eponymous design studio. His playful posters of the 1960s drew upon a wide range of visual and typographic references and incorporated vivid, psychedelic colours; one of his most famous advertisements was for the Olivetti Valentine typewriter designed by ETTORE SOTTSASS. Glaser also designed or re-designed a number of magazines and worked as a book illustrator.

GOLDFINGER, ERNÖ 1902-1987
Hungarian-born architect Ernö Goldfinger studied in Paris and moved to London in 1934 after his marriage to English heiress Ursula Blackwell. He became one of the key proponents of modernism in the UK and lived in Berthold Lubetkin*'s Highpoint apartment tower block while building his own home in Willow Road, Hampstead, completed in 1938. His post-war work included primary schools, office buildings, a major mixed-use development at Elephant & Castle, and - most memorably - the Trellick Tower high-rise building in West London, which was begun in 1968 and completed in 1972.

GRAFFI, CARLO 1925-1985
Italian designer and architect Carlo Graffi was part of the 'organic school of Turin' and worked with CARLO MOLLINO before setting up a design

studio with Franco Campo. Graffi and Campo's best-known design was their 1951 armchair for Apelli & Varesio, using a sinuous birch plywood and laminate frame with velvet seat cushions. Another key design was their skeletal Millepiedi table (c. 1952), which looked like an upturned boat frame with a crisp glass top: the table was mistakenly attributed to Mollino by some sources.

GRANGE, KENNETH b. 1929
See p. 286.

GROPIUS, WALTER 1883-1969
Founder of the Bauhaus* and a lauded pioneer of modernist architecture and design, Walter Gropius emigrated to Britain in 1934 and then the United States in 1937. He became director of the architecture department at Harvard University and went into practice with colleague and fellow émigré MARCEL BREUER until 1941.

Gropius designed a number of houses in Massachusetts and on the East Coast, including his own house in Lincoln (1938). In 1963, he completed one of the most visible, controversial and iconic New York skyscrapers (in association with Emery Roth & Sons and Pietro Belluschi) - the Pan Am Building, now known as the MetLife Building.

GUARICHE, PIERRE 1926-1995
French furniture and lighting designer Pierre Guariche established his own design studio in 1951. Among his furniture designs were the Tonneau and Tulipe moulded plywood chairs (both 1953). His lamps and wall lights for Disderot offered a sense of sculptural playfulness allied with a delicacy of form and structure, and could be compared with the work of GINO SARFATTI and SERGE MOUILLE.

GUGELOT, HANS 1920-1965
Trained in Switzerland as an architect, Hans Gugelot worked with MAX BILL in the late 1940s and early 1950s, while also designing furniture for Wohnbedarf and Horgenglarus. In the 1950s he ran his own design studio and the design department at the Hochschule für Gestaltung, Ulm*. Gugelot designed products for Braun* from 1954 to 1965 and collaborated with DIETER RAMS on the design of the seminal Phonosuper SK4 record player and radio.

GUHL, WILHELM ('WILLY') 1915-2004
Swiss designer Willy Guhl invented a new kind of chair in 1954 with

his Loop (or 'Schlinge') seat. Made by Eternit, the chair was fabricated with a tensile loop of cement-fibre bond material, which combined a precise sculpted form with a raw industrial aesthetic. The chair was a forerunner of much contemporary outdoor furniture of rugged character, its heavy-duty nature making it ideal for gardens, terraces and pool sides.

GUNNLØGSSON, JAKOB HALLDOR 1918-1985
See p. 428.

GUSTAVSBERG POTTERY
See p. 186.

GWATHMEY, CHARLES 1938-2009
See p. 434.

HAERTLING, CHARLES 1928-1984
American architect Charles Haertling is best known for a series of futuristic, Space Age houses built in the 1960s. Haertling – who opened his architectural practice in Boulder, Colorado, in 1957 – favoured an organic, contextual approach and fluid, sinuous forms. His most famous house is the Brenton House in Boulder (1969) – an extraordinary amalgam of five rounded pods, each opening to a framed vista across a dramatic landscape. His work has been compared to the architecture of CHARLES DEATON and Antti Lovag*.

HAINES, WILLIAM ('BILLY') 1900-1973
A Hollywood actor turned interior designer, William Haines worked for a starry client list in the 1940s and '50s. He also designed many pieces of furniture, infused with sophisticated glamour. These include the Seniah chair (1949), Valentine sofa (1950) and Bel Air sofa (1951). Many of Haines's designs are still in production.

HARPER, CHARLEY 1922-2007
See p. 354.

HEAL & SONS
The furniture company Heal & Sons was first established in 1810 on Tottenham Court Road, London, where the company still trades today. Ambrose Heal designed many of the firm's pieces from the 1880s onwards in Arts & Crafts style. Heal's was an important and progressive presence during the 1950s and '60s. Within the mid-century context it is best known for its range of fabrics by LUCIENNE DAY and contemporaries

such as Robert Dodd and Hilda Durkin.

HEIN, PIET 1905-1996
Writer, poet, urban planner, mathematician, inventor, and product, lighting and furniture designer Piet Hein was a well-known Danish polymath. Among his best-known designs are the Ursa Major candelabra (1953), sculptural leather-seated steel bar stools for Fritz Hansen* (1971) and the Super Ellipse table (1968, Fritz Hansen), designed with Bruno Mathsson* and ARNE JACOBSEN.

HELVETICA
See MAX MIEDINGER, p. 366.

HENNINGSEN, POUL 1894-1967
See p. 136.

HERMAN MILLER
A major force in the evolution and promotion of mid-century furniture design, the Herman Miller company began life in 1923 when Herman Miller and his son-in-law Dirk Jan De Pree bought the Star Furniture Company in Zeeland, Michigan. Designer Gilbert Rohde encouraged De Pree to move away from traditional furniture-making and to embrace a modern approach and aesthetic, which the Herman Miller company began to do in the early 1940s.

In 1946, De Pree appointed GEORGE NELSON as design director and the company began working closely with key furniture and textile designers of the mid-century period, including Nelson himself, CHARLES & RAY EAMES, ISAMU NOGUCHI and ALEXANDER GIRARD. The company was at the forefront of innovations in materials such as plywood, as well as developing modular furniture systems and comprehensive office furnishings. Many key designs of the 1950s and '60s are still produced by Herman Miller. In Europe, many Herman Miller products are produced and marketed by Vitra* under a licensing agreement dating back to the mid-1950s.

HERNÁNDEZ, AGUSTÍN b. 1924
Mexican architect and designer Agustín Hernández is known for a striking group of houses and buildings built from the late 1960s onwards, fusing Mayan and modernist influences with Space Age and sci-fi elements. One of his most famous houses is his own Casa Hernández (1970) in Mexico City, which has the look of a concrete flying saucer landing upon a steep hillside.

GUHL, WILHELM A pair of fibrated concrete lounge chairs manufactured by Eternit, Switzerland, 1954.

HAINES, WILLIAM Desk in lacquered wood and stainless steel, c. 1952.

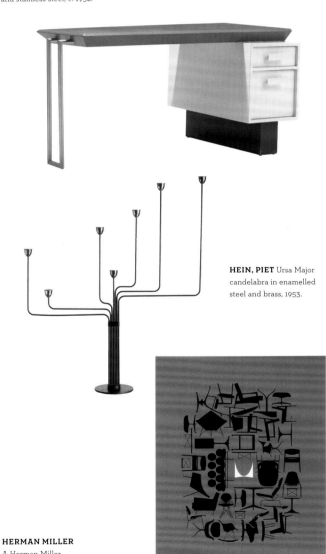

HEIN, PIET Ursa Major candelabra in enamelled steel and brass, 1953.

HERMAN MILLER A Herman Miller advertisement, designed by Don Ervin, 1961.

HICKS, DAVID 1929-1998
See p. 256.

HIQUILY, PHILIPPE 1925-2013
The work of French sculptor, artist and furniture-maker Philippe Hiquily has become highly collectable in recent years and has attracted a fresh following among designers and design aficionados. His furniture has a highly sculptural quality, generally featuring interlocking metallic elements. Pieces include his 1965 steel and glass-topped table for Edition Galerie Lacloche.

HOCHSCHULE FÜR GESTALTUNG, ULM
An influential but short-lived German design school founded in Ulm in 1953, the Hochschule für Gestaltung (HfG) was launched by OTL AICHER, MAX BILL (the first director of the school) and Aicher's wife, Inge Scholl. The modernist ethos of the school was influenced by Bauhaus* philosophy. Bill designed the school campus, which opened in 1955.

The HfG promoted inter-related studies – including semiotics and psychology – and a systematic/functional approach to design. Ulm professor Hans Gugelot* was one of a number of HfG tutors who forged close links with Braun* and designed products for the company. The school lost its local authority funding in 1968 and was closed.

HVIDT, PETER 1916-1986 & MØLGAARD-NIELSEN, ORLA 1907-1993
Danish designers Peter Hvidt and Orla Mølgaard-Nielsen both studied cabinet-making in Copenhagen and began working together in the mid-1940s. In 1944, they developed the Portex stacking chair and went on to design furniture for Fritz Hansen*, Søborg Møbelfabrik, France & Son and others. Their Fritz Hansen designs included the AX chair and table of 1947. Hvidt and Mølgaard-Nielsen's Model 316 dining chair (c. 1956) for Søborg Møbelfabrik has a pleasing organic and sculptural simplicity, with a teak frame and back-rest and a woven jute seat, that echoes the exquisitely crafted work of their contemporary, HANS WEGNER. Their Model 523 dining table (c. 1960) came in a set of six individual pieces that could be used singly or in a circular formation.

IITTALA
The Finnish glass manufacturer Iittala was founded in 1881 by Swedish glassblower Petter Magnus Abrahamsson and later merged with Karhula under the ownership of the Ahlström corporation. The company transformed itself into a leading player in the post-war period through collaborations with key designers such as KAJ FRANCK, TIMO SARPANEVA, Tapio Wirkkala* (chief designer from 1946), ALVAR AALTO and Aino Aalto*. Their work formed a golden age in Scandinavian glass-making and design.

INTERNATIONAL STYLE
The term 'International Style' was first used in the early 1930s and emerged from a seminal exhibition on the subject at the Museum of Modern Art in New York, curated by PHILIP JOHNSON and Russell Hitchcox. International Style referred to a grouping of deeply influential modernist architects and designers – including Le Corbusier* and followers of the Bauhaus* – whose work was increasingly transcultural and trans-atlantic, and placed a firm emphasis on geometrical purity, modern materials and functional order. The term was most intimately associated with the work of Walter Gropius* and LUDWIG MIES VAN DER ROHE.

International Style remained relevant in the post-war period, but did not appear to accommodate the regional modernist tendencies evolving in Scandinavia, Latin America and other parts of the world, nor the increasing emphasis on a more contextual approach advocated by many leading modernist architects. Ultimately, the term began to seem inadequate as a way of describing the multiplicity of approaches that developed under the broad umbrella of modernism and now is generally seen as referring to a particular period of design between the mid-1920s and the mid-1960s.

ISOKON
The innovative British furniture company Isokon was founded in London in 1935 by property developer and entrepreneur Jack Pritchard. Together with Wells Coates, Pritchard developed the Lawn Road apartment building (1934) in Hampstead – sometimes known as the Isokon building – before moving into furniture design in collaboration with Walter Gropius*.

Gropius became Isokon's first Controller of Design, but it was his Bauhaus* colleague, and fellow émigré, MARCEL BREUER who created many of Isokon's most famous designs – pieces that felt ahead of their time and, in many ways, anticipated the

HIQUILY, PHILIPPE A dining table in steel and glass, produced by Edition Galerie Lacloche, France, 1965.

HVIDT, PETER Model 523 set of six tables in circular formation, made in teak and brass by France & Son, c. 1960.

IITTALA Blue tumblers in pressed glass, designed by Aino Aalto, 1932.

ISOKON Nesting tables in beech plywood, made by Venesta for Isokon, 1936, designed by Marcel Breuer.

JALK, GRETE Nesting tables in teak plywood, produced by Poul Jeppesen, Denmark, 1963.

JEANNERET, PIERRE Lounge chair, c. 1955, and writing chair, c. 1960, from Chandigarh, in stained teak and cane.

JUHL, FINN Lounge chair in teak, oak and upholstery, produced by Søren Willadsens, Denmark, 1953.

mid-century aesthetic. They included the Isokon Long chair and dining table (1936), using plywood and timber laminates. Other designs include the Penguin Donkey bookcase, designed by Egon Riss in 1939 and updated by ERNEST RACE in 1963. Many pieces are still produced by Isokon Plus.

ISOLA, MAIJA 1927–2001
See MARIMEKKO, p. 266.

ISSIGONIS, ALEC 1906–1988
See p. 290.

JACOBSEN, ARNE 1902–1971
See p. 52.

JALK, GRETE 1920–2006
Danish designer Grete Jalk studied joinery and furniture design in Copenhagen before opening her own design studio in 1953. She designed furniture for Fritz Hansen*, France & Son, Johannes Hansen, Poul Jeppesen and other manufacturers. Her many pieces include her teak plywood nesting tables and lounge chair of 1963 for Poul Jeppesen; the chair, in particular, was an intricate and almost origami-like composition. Jalk also edited the *Mobilia* design journal for many years.

JEANNERET, PIERRE 1896–1967
Although somewhat overshadowed by the achievements and personality of his famous cousin and collaborator, Le Corbusier (Charles-Édouard Jeanneret)*, Pierre Jeanneret was an architect and furniture designer of distinction in his own right. He worked with his cousin on many key architectural projects and co-designed – with Le Corbusier and Charlotte Perriand* – a number of iconic furniture designs of the late 1920s, including the LC4/B306 chaise longue and Grand Confort club chair (both 1928). In the post-war period, however, Jeanneret furniture took on a more distinct and personal identity, including the Scissor chair of 1950 produced by Knoll*.

Throughout the 1950s Jeanneret designed an extraordinary – and highly sought after – range of chairs and other furniture for use in the many buildings designed by himself and his cousin for the highly ambitious Chandigarh development, India, where Jeanneret ultimately became chief architect. United by common elements and a shared aesthetic, this broad family of chairs, sofas and tables were originally created for Chandigarh's High Court, Punjab University and various administration buildings.

JENSEN, JACOB b. 1926
See p. 294.

JOHNSON, PHILIP 1906–2005
See p. 440.

JONES, A. QUINCY 1913–1979
American architect Archibald Quincy Jones built a series of modernist houses in California in the 1950s and '60s, characterized by open-plan living and a powerful relationship between interior and exterior space. Quincy Jones opened his own architectural office in 1945 and worked in Los Angeles, San Diego and Palm Springs. He designed houses for Joseph Eichler*'s tract developments and joined forces with Frederick Emmons from 1951 until 1969. One of their best-known private houses was built for actor Gary Cooper and his wife in Beverly Hills in 1955.

JONES, CHARLES HOLLIS b. 1945
An American furniture and lighting designer, Charles Hollis Jones is known for his use of Lucite and acrylic which lends his work a sense of 1920s glamour, spliced with a more contemporary feel. His work from the late 1960s and 1970s attracted celebrity and design industry clients, including Frank Sinatra and interior designer Arthur Elrod. Among his best-known pieces are the Waterfall series of benches, tables and chairs from the late 1960s and early 1970s, and the Edison table lamp of 1970.

JUHL, FINN 1912–1989
Danish architect and furniture designer Finn Juhl worked in both fields in the 1940s before setting up his own studio in 1945 and concentrating on furniture design. He worked with manufacturers such as Niels Vodder, France & Son and Baker, his pieces combining sinuous teak frames with rounded, sculpted cushion pads and upholstery, offering both ergonomic comfort and elegance. Pieces such as his Poet sofa (1941), NV-48 chair and Chieftain chair (both 1949) are inviting as well as aesthetically pleasing. Juhl also served as a senior tutor at the Fredericksberg Technical School, designed the interiors of the Trusteeship Council Chamber at the United Nations* building in New York, and designed ceramics and glassware.

KAGAN, VLADIMIR b. 1927
German-born designer Vladimir Kagan settled in the US at a young age and studied architecture at Columbia University. He began designing furniture and interiors in the late

KAGAN, VLADIMIR
Contour lounge chair in walnut and leather, manufactured by Kagan-Dreyfuss, USA, c. 1953.

KENMOCHI, ISAMU
Cedar-wood Kashiwado chair, 1961, produced by Tendo, Japan.

KJÆR, JACOB Lounge chair and ottoman in teak and leather, c. 1954.

KNOLL, FLORENCE
Model 122 cabinet designed by Florence Knoll for Knoll in birch, lacquered wood, Pandanus and leather, 1947.

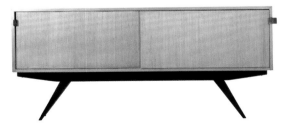

1940s and opened his first furniture store in New York in 1949. Private clients included Marilyn Monroe and Gary Cooper, while he also had a wide range of commercial clients. Many of Kagan's chair designs of the 1950s have a sculptural, sinuous and anthropomorphic quality, echoing the organic work of Italian counterparts such as CARLO MOLLINO and Carlo Graffi*. Kagan's sofas are fluid and curvaceous, and include the Floating Curve sofa of 1952 and Serpentine sofa of the early 1970s. Kagan pieces have become highly collectable.

KÅGE, WILHELM 1889-1960
See GUSTAVSBERG POTTERY, p. 186.

KAHN, LOUIS 1901-1974
Born in Estonia, architect Louis Kahn emigrated to America with his family at a young age and studied architecture at the University of Pennsylvania. He founded his own practice in Philadelphia in 1934. Many of his key projects date from the 1950s onwards. They include the Esherick House (1961) in Chestnut Hill, Philadelphia, as well as large-scale commissions that embody his ideas of 'poetic monumentality', such as the Yale University Art Gallery (1953) in New Haven, Connecticut; Salk Institute for Biological Studies (1965) in La Jolla, California; and Kimbell Art Museum in Fort Worth, Texas, completed in 1972.

KAPPE, RAY b. 1927
Californian architect Ray Kappe studied at the University of California and launched his own practice in the 1950s. Early projects included a series of timber houses, such as his own timber and concrete home in Pacific Palisades, completed in 1967. Kappe also worked in the field of prefabricated housing. He co-founded the Southern California Institute of Architecture in 1972.

KARTELL
Pioneering Italian furniture manufacturer Kartell was founded by engineer and chemist Giulio Castelli in Milan in 1949. The company explored the possibilities offered by new plastics and used them in the production of homeware in the 1950s, with many pieces designed by Gino Colombini*. Kartell expanded into furniture in the mid-1960s, with RICHARD SAPPER and MARCO ZANUSO designing one of the company's first chairs – the K 4999 children's chair of 1964. Kartell also worked with JOE COLOMBO, ACHILLE

CASTIGLIONI, VICO MAGISTRETTI and many other leading designers.

KENMOCHI, ISAMU 1912-1971
Japanese industrial designer Isamu Kenmochi is best known for his sculptural and inviting Rattan Round chair, Model T-3010, of 1965, made by Yamakawa Rattan. Kenmochi collaborated briefly with ISAMU NOGUCHI in the 1950s and developed a prototype chair with a bamboo seat and back and a steel frame. Other designs include his Tendo cedar chair of 1961.

KINNEIR, JOCK 1917-1994
See p. 360.

KJÆR, JACOB 1896-1957
Danish furniture designer and cabinet-maker Jacob Kjær trained in his father's workshop and in Paris and Berlin. Based in Copenhagen, he created many of his well known designs in the 1950s and these were originally produced by his own workshops. They include the UN chair, first developed in the late 1940s and later used in the United Nations* building in New York. Other designs include the B-48 armchair of 1950.

KJÆRHOLM, POUL 1929-1980
See p. 58.

KLINT, KAARE 1888-1954
See LE KLINT, p. 140.

KNOLL, FLORENCE b. 1917
& HANS 1914-1955
Hans Knoll, the son of a German furniture manufacturer, moved first to England and then to New York, where in 1938 he established the Hans G. Knoll Furniture Company. He began to work with JENS RISOM, who designed a number of pieces for the company, blended with imported designs.

In 1941, Knoll met Florence Schust, an architect who had trained at the Cranbrook Academy of Art* and with LUDWIG MIES VAN DER ROHE in Chicago before working, briefly, with MARCEL BREUER and Walter Gropius*. The pair began to develop the company, which became Knoll Associates in 1946, the year they married.

The Knoll collection expanded rapidly in the late 1940s and 1950s, with a number of Cranbrook graduates and connections – including EERO SAARINEN, HARRY BERTOIA and Ralph Rapson* – contributing designs. In 1948, the company also secured the rights to manufacture Mies van der Rohe's Barcelona collection.

Florence Knoll designed the company showrooms, guided the Knoll aesthetic – with the help of graphic designer HERBERT MATTER – and designed many key pieces of furniture. She saw these as part of a 'total design' approach to creating a cohesive, intelligently planned space, and was content for statement pieces by other designers in the Knoll stable to take the limelight, although many of her designs have since become classics in their own right. She was also the head of the Knoll Planning Unit – a planning and interior design department that realized the concept of total design. The unit was particularly active in the corporate sector, creating offices for companies such as IBM and pioneering the evolution of open-plan offices and system furniture.

After Hans Knoll's death in a car accident in 1955, Florence Knoll's position at the company became all-encompassing until she began to step back towards the end of the decade. By that time the company was already producing an extraordinary range of iconic furniture designs, including pieces by Saarinen, Bertoia, ISAMU NOGUCHI and many others. Florence Knoll retired from the company in 1965.

KOENIG, PIERRE 1925–2004
Born in San Francisco, Pierre Koenig studied architecture at the University of Southern California and designed and built his first house as a student (Koenig House 1, Glendale, California, 1950). He worked with Raphael Soriano* briefly before founding his own architectural practice. His houses – mostly steel-framed – promoted open-plan living and connections between indoor and outdoor living. He was also concerned with issues of sustainability and contextuality. Koenig was a leading light in the Case Study Program* and designed Case Study House #22 in Los Angeles (1960), also known as the Stahl House.

KOPPEL, HENNING 1918–1981
Danish silversmith and product designer Henning Koppel studied sculpture in Denmark and Paris, before moving to Sweden during World War II, where he designed for Orrefors* and Svenskt Tenn. After his return to Denmark he began working with Georg Jensen* – a highly productive collaboration that continued over the course of Koppel's career. His work for the company was highly sculptural, fluid,

sinuous and modern, and included pitchers, serving dishes, bowls and flatware. He also designed lighting, ceramics and watches.

KOSTA BODA
In 1946, Swedish glassworks Kosta and Boda merged and underwent a creative revival under the leadership of designer VICKE LINDSTRAND, who was artistic director until 1973. In 1989 the company merged again, with Orrefors*.

KRENCHEL, HERBERT b. 1922
Danish designer Herbert Krenchel is best known for his Krenit bowls, produced in delicate black ironware with vibrantly coloured enamelled interior surfaces. First produced in 1953, the bowls were highly popular in the 1950s and early '60s, and are now back in production.

KUKKAPURO, YRJÖ b. 1933
Finnish furniture designer Yrjö Kukkapuro founded his own design studio in Helsinki in 1959. He worked with fibreglass plastics in the early 1960s, creating the ergonomic and enveloping Karuselli ('Carousel') lounge chair and ottoman of 1964, made by Haimi. The fibreglass shell of the chair was coated with leather upholstery and anchored to a steel and aluminium support and swivel base. Kukkapuro developed a number of other fibreglass chairs in the 1960s, while his interest in ergonomics also fed into the design of his Fysio plywood office chair of 1978.

LA PIETRA, UGO b. 1938
Artist, architect, and furniture and lighting designer Ugo La Pietra is one of the multi-talented Italian polymath designers of the mid-century period. His geometric lighting designs of the late 1960s are particularly striking and include the Globo Tissurato lamp of 1966 and the Audiovisual table lamp of 1967, both for Zama Elettronica.

LANDBERG, NILS 1907–1991
Swedish glassware designer Nils Landberg studied in Sweden, Italy and France. He began working in engraved glass at Orrefors* and joined its design team in the mid-1930s. During the 1950s Landberg concentrated on a range of more abstract designs, often using elongated forms and tinted or layered glass, with inspiration drawn from the natural world.

LASDUN, DENYS 1914–2001
English architect Denys Lasdun worked with Berthold Lubetkin*

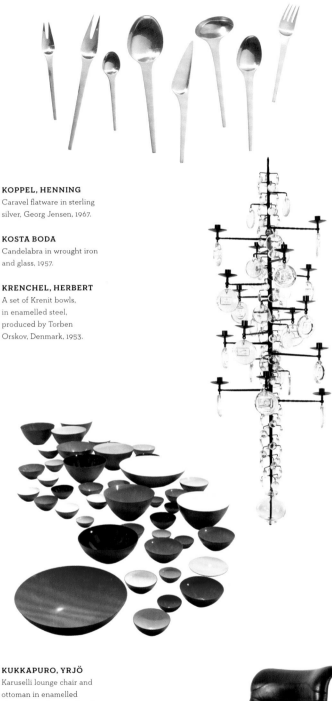

KOPPEL, HENNING
Caravel flatware in sterling silver, Georg Jensen, 1967.

KOSTA BODA
Candelabra in wrought iron and glass, 1957.

KRENCHEL, HERBERT
A set of Krenit bowls, in enamelled steel, produced by Torben Orskov, Denmark, 1953.

KUKKAPURO, YRJÖ
Karuselli lounge chair and ottoman in enamelled aluminium, chrome-plated steel and leather, produced by Haimi, Finland, 1964.

before co-founding his own practice. Tower housing projects in the late 1950s gave way to a series of respected educational buildings, including Fitzwilliam College, Cambridge (1963), and the principal buildings at the University of East Anglia in Norwich (1968). Lasdun's most famous project, begun in the late 1960s and completed in 1976, is the Royal National Theatre in London.

LAUTNER, JOHN 1911–1994
See p. 446.

LAVERNE, ERWINE 1909–2003
& ESTELLE 1915–1997
Husband-and-wife furniture designers and artists Erwine and Estelle Laverne both studied painting at the Art Students League in New York before founding their own design studio in 1938. Laverne Originals (later Laverne International) produced many of the couple's designs, plus pieces by a small coterie of other designers. Chief among the Lavernes' output is a sequence of chairs from the 1950s and early 1960s. These include the Invisible Group of 1957 in clear Perspex (the Daffodil, Jonquil and Champagne chairs among them), and the Lotus fibreglass chair of 1958. Experiments with both form and materials continued with their most famous design – the fibreglass Tulip armchair of 1960, where the back and armrests of the chair resemble sculpted petals.

LE CORBUSIER 1887–1965
Charles-Édouard Jeanneret, better known as Le Corbusier, was the most influential architect and architectural thinker of the 20th century. Also an artist, painter, muralist, writer and furniture designer, he was a pivotal figure within the evolution of modernism and International Style*.

Born in Switzerland, he moved to Paris in 1908 and began working with Auguste Perret. He launched his own practice in Switzerland but then relocated to Paris and adopted his *nom de plume* – an adapted version of his great-grandfather's name, meaning 'the raven'.

The Villa Savoye of 1931, in Poissy, France, became one of the seminal buildings of the modernist canon and – with its supporting pilotis, roof garden, open plan, horizontal strip windows and free façade – embodied Le Corbusier's famous 'five points of a new architecture'.

Other key buildings include the Chapel of Notre Dame du Haut at Ronchamp (1955) and the Dominican

monastery of Sainte Marie de la Tourette at Eveux-sur-Abresle (1960). There was also the epic commission to create the new city of Chandigarh in India during the 1950s – a project undertaken with his cousin, Pierre Jeanneret*, who collaborated on the design of many of Le Corbusier's buildings.

Pierre Jeanneret, together with Charlotte Perriand*, also collaborated on many of Le Corbusier's most famous furniture designs, which date from the 1920s, including the LC4/B306 chaise longue and Grand Confort club chair (both 1928).

LE KLINT
See p. 140.

LEACH, BERNARD 1887–1979
A highly influential British studio potter, Bernard Leach spent his early years in the Far East and Japan, where he later began working in ceramics. He set up his own pottery in St Ives in 1920 and was significantly influenced by Eastern pottery and ceramic techniques. He became well known from the 1940s onwards, after the publication of his *A Potter's Book*, and many respected studio potters served apprenticeships with him.

LENOR LARSEN, JACK b. 1927
See p. 262.

LINDBERG, STIG 1916–1982
See GUSTAVSBERG POTTERY, p. 186.

LINDSTRAND, VICKE 1904–1983
See p. 194.

LOEWY, RAYMOND 1893–1986
See p. 298.

LOUIS POULSEN
Danish lighting company Louis Poulsen began manufacturing electric appliances in 1918. A few years later the firm began a long and productive relationship with POUL HENNINGSEN. Louis Poulsen has also produced lights by ARNE JACOBSEN, VERNER PANTON, Henning Koppel* and others.

LOVAG, ANTTI b. 1920
Architect Antti Lovag worked with JEAN PROUVÉ before establishing his own practice in the south of France. He developed a unique form of futuristic organic architecture in the 1960s and '70s, partly influenced by his training as a naval architect. His most famous building is Pierre Cardin*'s Palais Bulles, which was begun in the early 1970s and finally completed in 1989.

LANDBERG, NILS Tulpan glass vase, manufactured by Orrefors, Sweden, 1961.

LAVERNE, ERWINE & ESTELLE Tulip chair in lacquered fibreglass and enamelled steel, Laverne International, 1960.

LOVAG, ANTTI Interior view of Palais Bulles, between Cannes and Nice, France, designed in the early 1970s.

LUNDIN, INGEBORG
Appel glass vase, made
by Orrefors, Sweden, 1957.

McCOBB, PAUL
Vanity table and chair in
enamelled steel, glass birch
and upholstery, produced
by Bryce Originals/
Furnwood, USA, 1953.

**MAGNUSSON-
GROSSMAN, GRETA**
Table lamp produced
by Ralph O. Smith, c. 1950,
in enamelled aluminium
and chrome-plated steel.

MALOOF, SAM Desk
in oak and walnut, c. 1960.

**MANGIAROTTI,
ANGELO** Dining table
in turned bronze and
rosewood, made by
the Bernini & Battaglia
foundry, Italy, 1959.

LUBETKIN, BERTHOLD 1901–1990
Born in Georgia, Berthold Lubetkin
studied in Berlin and Paris before
settling in the UK and co-founding
the Tecton architectural practice in
1932. He designed a series of
groundbreaking modernist buildings
in the late 1930s, including the
Highpoint buildings in Highgate,
London (1935 and 1938), before
concentrating on social housing in
the post-war period.

LUNDIN, INGEBORG 1921–1992
Swedish glassware designer Ingeborg
Lundin worked with Orrefors*
throughout the 1950s and '60s.
Key designs include her Timglas
('Hourglass') vases of 1953 and her
beautifully simple Appel ('Apple')
vase of 1957.

LUSTIG, ALVIN 1915–1955
American graphic and typeface
designer Alvin Lustig studied in
California and started working in book
design in Los Angeles before moving
to New York to take up a post on
Look magazine. He worked between
Los Angeles and New York from 1946
until the end of his life, which was cut
short by diabetes. Lustig also designed
interiors, textiles and furniture.

LYONS, ERIC 1912–1980
From 1936 to 1937 English architect
Eric Lyons worked for Walter Gropius*
(and Maxwell Fry) during the former
Bauhaus* director's brief period
in the UK before moving on to the
States. In 1948, Lyons co-founded
Span Developments, which went on
to build more than 2,000 homes in
the 1950s and '60s, spread across over
70 developments. These houses were
modernist in style but also placed
great emphasis on generating a sense
of community, with Span 'villages'
arranged around communal outdoor
space and shared landscape.

McCOBB, PAUL 1917–1969
American furniture designer Paul
McCobb studied painting in Boston.
He established his own design studio
in New York in 1945 and began
working as a consultant for Modernage
Furniture. His many furniture lines
of the 1950s included his Directional
collection for Custom Craft, the
Planner range made by Winchendon
Furniture and many pieces for Calvin
Furniture. McCobb's furniture was
well made and modern but also
affordable. As his success grew in the
mid-century period, he also designed
wallpapers, lighting, textiles and
household products.

MAGISTRETTI, VICO 1920–2006
See p. 146.

**MAGNUSSON-GROSSMAN,
GRETA** 1906–1999
Swedish-born lighting and furniture
designer Greta Magnusson studied
and worked in Stockholm before
marrying her American husband Billy
Grossman, then emigrating to the
States in 1940. Magnusson-Grossman
opened her own store in Los Angeles
selling her work and established a
Hollywood following. She produced
lighting and furniture designs for a
number of companies in the 1950s and
'60s, including a highly original range
of lighting for Barker Brothers and
Ralph O. Smith. Designs included the
Grasshopper floor lamp and Double
Cobra table lamp (both c. 1950);
double-headed lighting was a recurring
motif. Magnusson-Grossman also
designed a series of houses in Los
Angeles during the mid-century period.

MALOOF, SAM 1916–2009
American furniture designer and
woodworker Sam Maloof worked
from his Californian workshop at
Alta Loma and was a key practitioner
of studio furniture-making in the
post-war period. Industrial designer
Henry Dreyfuss* encouraged Maloof's
work in the early 1950s when he
commissioned him to produce pieces
for his own home. Maloof's work fused
Shaker and Scandinavian influences
but retained its own character. He
refused offers to design for factory
production but with the help of
assistants managed to produce as
many as three hundred pieces a year.

MANGIAROTTI, ANGELO
1921–2012
Italian architect, furniture and
product designer Angelo Mangiarotti
studied at the Politecnico di Milano
and worked in America during the
early 1950s. In 1955, he co-founded
an architectural practice with Bruno
Morassutti, then from 1960 onwards
established his own independent
design studio. A broad body of work
included furniture and product design,
as well as lighting. Among his best-
known furniture designs are his Eros
occasional table, made in marble by
Skipper (1971) – part of a significant
collection of marble pieces in a
modern style.

MARI, ENZO b. 1932
Italian furniture, product and lighting
designer Enzo Mari studied at the
Accademia di Belle Arti in Milan in
the 1950s before opening his own

MARI, ENZO A pair of chests in lacquered wood and leather, made by Poggi, Italy, c. 1970.

MARTENS, DINO Model 6801 cane vase, produced by Aureliano Toso, Italy, 1958.

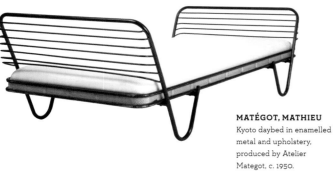

MATÉGOT, MATHIEU Kyoto daybed in enamelled metal and upholstery, produced by Atelier Matégot, c. 1950.

MATHSSON, BRUNO Maria folding table, manufactured by Firma Karl Mathsson, Sweden, 1967, in teak and beech.

MAURER, INGO Giant Light Bulb lamp in chrome-plated steel and glass, Ingo Maurer LLC, Germany, 1966.

design studio in the city. He began working with manufacturers such as Zanotta* and Driade, and developed a range of innovative plastic household products for Danese in the 1960s, including vases, pencil holders and desk calendars. His furniture designs of the 1970s included the Sof Sof chair of 1971 for Driade. Mari is also well known for his sophisticated jigsaw puzzles and his books on design.

MARIMEKKO
See p. 266.

MARKELIUS, SVEN 1889–1972
Swedish architect Sven Markelius was also a furniture and textile designer. Particularly active in the 1930s and post-war in the 1950s, he worked on projects including the Swedish Pavilion of the 1939 World's Fair in New York and was also involved with the planning committee for the United Nations* building. In the 1950s he designed a collection of geometric colourful textiles (with Astrid Sampe*) for Nordiska Kompaniet.

MARTENS, DINO 1894–1970
Venetian glassware designer Dino Martens studied painting and began working as a glass painter in Murano in the 1920s before moving into design. He was appointed artistic director of Aureliano Toso in 1939 and developed a range of original and experimental glassware during the 1950s, including his colourful Oriente series and a range of pieces using geometrical stripes of colour.

MATÉGOT, MATHIEU 1910–2001
Born in Hungary, furniture and interior designer Mathieu Matégot moved to France in 1931 and started his career as a set designer. From the late 1940s, after being held as a prisoner of war, he began designing furniture, focusing on the use of perforated sheet metal ('rigitulle') which could be bent and moulded to create seats, chairs and tables supported by a tubular steel framework. His pieces include the Nagasaki chair of 1952 and the Kobe chaise longue of 1955. He also designed textiles and tapestries in the late 1950s and 1960s.

MATHSSON, BRUNO 1907–1988
Swedish furniture designer Bruno Mathsson served an apprenticeship in his father Karl Mathsson's cabinet-making workshop and began experimenting with bentwood and laminate furniture in the 1930s. His pioneering furniture of the period – mostly bent birch frames with seats and backs using lattices of leather or canvas – was made in the family workshop. These pieces included the Gräshoppan ('Grasshopper') easy chair (1931) and the Eva chair and Pernilla lounge chair (both 1934). Their sculptural and organic character anticipated the mid-century soft modernist Scandinavian style.

During the 1950s Mathsson concentrated on architectural and interiors commissions, but returned to furniture design in the 1960s after taking over the leadership of the family company. Pieces from the 1960s include the Jetson office chair (1966), Maria folding table (1967) and Superellipsis (or 'Super Ellipse') table of 1964, designed with Piet Hein* and ARNE JACOBSEN and later manufactured by Fritz Hansen*.

MATTER, HERBERT 1907–1984
See p. 362.

MAURER, INGO b. 1932
German lighting designer Ingo Maurer originally studied graphic design and typography before moving to the States for an extended period during the early 1960s. He came to prominence in the '60s with his Pop-influenced Bulb table lamp – a bulb within a bulb. He established his own lighting design studio, Design M, in Munich in 1966. His work is well known for its playful abstraction.

MAY, CLIFF 1909–1989
Californian architect Cliff May was a leading exponent of what became known as the modern Californian ranch house. He built many bespoke homes and larger developments across southern California, with an emphasis on indoor/outdoor living and horizontal, open-plan living spaces. His outward-looking houses spliced ideas from traditional ranches and haciendas with modernist thinking.

MELLOR, DAVID 1930–2009
See p. 302.

MENDES DA ROCHA, PAULO b. 1928
See p. 452.

MIEDINGER, MAX 1910–1980
See p. 366.

MIES VAN DER ROHE, LUDWIG 1886–1969
See p. 458.

MOGENSEN, BØRGE 1914–1972
Danish furniture designer Børge Mogensen trained with Kaare Klint*

in Copenhagen and later worked as Klint's assistant. He established his own design practice in the early 1950s and developed a range of furniture – produced by companies such as Erhard Rasmussen, Fritz Hansen* and Fredericia Stolefabrik – that drew upon his interest in ergonomics, sustainability and traditional furniture forms as well as contemporary aesthetics.

Pieces such as the Model 1789 sofa (designed 1945) and Hunting chair (c. 1950) were reinterpretations of familiar designs, while other pieces combined comfort and organic textures with generous proportions and upholstery. The Spanish chair of c. 1958, with an oak frame and slung leather seat and back, recalls the work of Latin American contemporaries such as SERGIO RODRIGUES. Mogensen also experimented with plywood to great effect.

MOHOLY-NAGY, LÁSZLÓ
1895–1946
Hungarian-born artist, photographer, writer, film-maker and designer László Moholy-Nagy was a master at the Bauhaus* in the 1920s. He established a graphic design studio in Berlin in 1928, then moved to Amsterdam, London and finally the United States during the 1930s. He founded the New Bauhaus in Chicago in 1937, which soon became the Institute of Design, and ran the influential institution – itself influenced by Bauhaus philosophies – until his death in 1946. His successor was Serge Chermayeff*.

MOLLINO, CARLO 1905–1973
See p. 62.

MOLYVANN, VANN b. 1926
The leading Cambodian architect of the 1950s and '60s, Vann Molyvann was born in Ream and studied architecture in Paris. In 1956, he was appointed state architect by Prince Sihanouk and built a series of Cambodian landmark government buildings, as well as embassies abroad. One of his key projects was the National Sports Complex of 1962.

MOUILLE, SERGE 1922–1988
See p. 150.

MOURGUE, OLIVIER b. 1939
French furniture designer Olivier Mourgue studied design in Paris and Scandinavia. He established his own design studio in Paris in the mid-1960s and began designing furniture for Airborne, Prisunic and others. His

colourful, futuristic designs – such as the Model 8412 Djinn chaise longue for Airborne (1965) – used steel frames coated in foam upholstery held in place by elasticated fabrics. Mourgue furniture appeared in Stanley Kubrick's film *2001: A Space Odyssey* in 1968. With its Pop colours and informal, low-slung appeal, Mourgue's work is often compared with that of PIERRE PAULIN and VERNER PANTON.

MÜLLER-BROCKMANN, JOSEF
1914–1996
Swiss graphic designer and writer Josef Müller-Brockmann was a leading exponent of the Swiss Style* of graphic design and an advocate of a grid-based, systematic approach. His most famous poster designs were created in the 1950s for the Tonhalle concert hall in Zurich.

NAKASHIMA, GEORGE 1905–1990
See p. 66.

NATZLER, GERTRUD 1908–1971 & OTTO 1908–2007
See p. 198.

NELSON, GEORGE 1908–1986
See p. 72.

NEUTRA, RICHARD 1892–1970
See p. 464.

NIEMEYER, OSCAR 1907–2012
See p. 470.

NIZZOLI, MARCELLO 1887–1969
See p. 306.

NOGUCHI, ISAMU 1904–1988
See p. 154.

NOLL, ALEXANDRE 1890–1970
French sculptor, craftsman and furniture designer/maker Alexandre Noll started working with wood in the 1920s and continued working through the 1950s and '60s. Like his American contemporary Wharton Esherick*, Noll produced individual, hand-crafted pieces, working with a wide range of timbers and exploring the inherent qualities within each. Pieces range from hand-carved chairs to wooden pitchers, bowls, lights and abstract sculptures.

NOYES, ELIOT 1910–1977
American architect, product designer, design consultant and curator Eliot Noyes studied architecture at Harvard before working with MARCEL BREUER and Walter Gropius*. He became a curator at the Museum of Modern

MOGENSEN, BØRGE
A pair of Spanish chairs in oak and leather, produced by Fredericia Stolefabrik, Denmark, c. 1958.

MOURGUE, OLIVIER
Model 8412 Djinn chaise longue in enamelled steel and upholstery, Airborne International, France, 1965.

NOLL, ALEXANDRE
Carved sycamore pitcher, c. 1950.

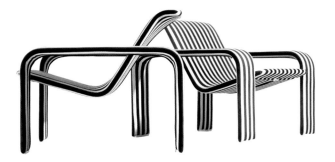

NOYES, ELIOT Telephone table in Formica, enamelled steel and chrome-plated steel, c. 1960.

NURMESNIEMI, ANTTI
Lounge chairs in chrome-plated steel, polyurethane foam and upholstery, produced by Vuokko, Finland, c. 1970.

Art in New York and later, in 1947, founded his own design studio in New Canaan, Connecticut. He worked for IBM as design director from 1956 until 1977 and designed the Selectric 1 typewriter (1961) and a number of other IBM products, as well as steering the graphic identity of the company in association with PAUL RAND. He also worked for a number of other corporations in the mid-century period, including Pan Am and Mobil.

NURMESNIEMI, ANTTI 1927-2003

Finnish product, interior, exhibition and furniture designer Antti Nurmesniemi designed everything from sauna stools to electricity pylons and ferry interiors during a long and highly productive career. From 1951 to 1956 he worked in the architectural office of Viljo Revell, designing interiors and furniture. One of his most famous designs of this period was the timber Sauna/Horseshoe stool of 1952, created for the Palace Hotel in Helsinki and manufactured by G. Soderstrom.

In 1956 Nurmesniemi founded his own design studio and a year later married textile designer Vuokko Nurmesniemi (née Eskolin). Product designs included lighting for Artek*, cookware, coffee pots and fluid lounge chairs and chaise longues produced by Vuokko.

NYLUND, GUNNAR 1904-1997

Scandinavian ceramicist Gunnar Nylund trained as an architect in Copenhagen and started his career in Denmark. Later he was a lead designer for the Swedish pottery Rörstrand and worked for the company during the 1950s.

OLSEN, HANS 1919-1992

Danish furniture designer Hans Olsen studied with Kaare Klint* in Copenhagen and founded his own design studio in 1953. His best-known design is his bent plywood Bikini chair of 1961, manufactured by Frem Røjle.

ORREFORS

Swedish glass manufacturer Orrefors began producing glass in the late 19th century. Designer VICKE LINDSTRAND began working with the company in 1928 and developed new glass-making techniques and designs. Other Orrefors designers of the 1950s and '60s included Ingeborg Lundin*, Nils Landberg* and Sven Palmqvist*. The company merged with Kosta Boda* in 1990.

PALMQVIST, SVEN 1906-1984

Swedish glassware designer Sven Palmqvist was intimately associated with Orrefors*, where he started working as a student in the 1920s and where he returned after studying in Paris, Italy and Germany. During the 1950s he pioneered a number of new glass-making techniques, including the Fuga series, whereby molten glass was shaped in a mould by a centrifuge method. Palmqvist's mosaic-effect Ravenna collection of the 1950s was also much admired.

PANTON, VERNER 1926-1998

See p. 78.

PARENT, CLAUDE b. 1923

French architect Claude Parent studied in Toulouse and at the École des Beaux-Arts in Paris before working in Le Corbusier*'s office in the 1950s. In 1963, he co-founded Architecture Principe and began promoting the 'fonction oblique', a design philosophy that argued in favour of fluid and sculpted architectural forms. Key buildings of the 1960s include Maison Drusch in Versailles and Maison Bordeux-Le Pecq in Normandy (both 1965) and the Church of Sainte-Bernadette-du-Banlay at Nevers (1966).

PARISI, ICO 1916-1996

Italian architect, film-maker, artist and furniture designer Ico Parisi also designed ceramics, lighting and glassware. He studied in Como and worked with architect Giuseppe Terragni. In the late 1940s he began working as an independent designer and collaborating with his wife, Luisa Parisi. He designed an extensive range of furniture in the 1950s and '60s, including pieces for MIM, Singer & Sons and Cassina*.

PAULIN, PIERRE 1927-2009

See p. 84.

PENTAGRAM

See KENNETH GRANGE, p. 286, and ALAN FLETCHER, p. 342.

PERRIAND, CHARLOTTE 1903-1999

French architect, interior architect and furniture designer Charlotte Perriand studied at the École de l'Union Centrale des Arts Décoratifs in Paris and graduated in 1925. Soon afterwards she joined Le Corbusier*'s architectural and design studio and collaborated with him – and his cousin Pierre Jeanneret* – on a number of iconic furniture designs of the inter-

NYLUND, GUNNAR
Vases and vessel in glazed stoneware, c. 1950, made by Rörstrand, Sweden.

OLSEN, HANS A pair of lounge chairs produced by Frem Røjle, Denmark, 1961, in laminated mahogany plywood and leather.

ORREFORS Ariel glass vase designed by Edvin Öhrström, 1950.

PALMQVIST, SVEN
Ravenna glass bowl, produced by Orrefors, Sweden, 1956.

PARISI, ICO Coffee table by Ico and Luisa Parisi, in walnut, walnut burl and brass, made by Singer & Sons, Italy, c. 1950.

PERRIAND, CHARLOTTE

Bloc cabinet in oak, enamelled steel, plastic and aluminium, Galerie Steph Simon, 1958.

PESCE, GAETANO UP4 settee, produced by C&B Italia, 1969, in stretch fabric over polyurethane foam.

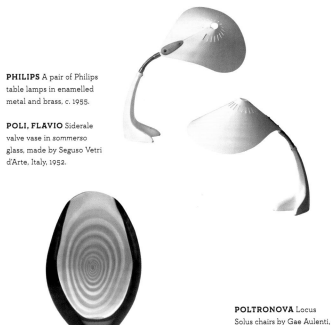

PHILIPS A pair of Philips table lamps in enamelled metal and brass, c. 1955.

POLI, FLAVIO Siderale valve vase in *sommerso* glass, made by Seguso Vetri d'Arte, Italy, 1952.

POLTRONOVA Locus Solus chairs by Gae Aulenti, in enamelled and tubular steel with upholstery, 1964.

war period, including the LC4/B306 chaise longue and the Grand Confort club chair (both 1928).

During the 1940s Perriand lived and worked in Japan and Vietnam before returning to France. In the 1950s she designed a number of key pieces manufactured by JEAN PROUVÉ's atelier and for the Steph Simon Gallery in Paris, as well as designing the interiors of a number of Alpine chalets in Méribel-les-Allues and the interiors of the French Tourist Office in London (with Ernö Goldfinger*, 1960). A number of Perriand's mid-century furniture pieces are both rare and highly collectable. They include a series of bookcases for the Maison du Brésil at the Cité Universitaire in Paris (c. 1959) and a bookshelf/storage unit/room divider for the Maison du Mexique in Paris (designed with Prouvé and Sonia Delaunay, 1953).

PESCE, GAETANO b. 1939

Born in La Spezia, architect and furniture designer Gaetano Pesce studied architecture and design in Venice. Based in Padua in the early 1960s, he later moved to Paris and then New York. His furniture designs include pieces for B&B Italia, Cassina*, Bernini and Vitra*. In 1969 Pesce designed his famous UP series of furniture for B&B Italia (then known as C&B Italia) – abstract and highly sculptural seating and ottoman designs in bright Pop colours, using stretch fabric coverings over moulded polyurethane. The pieces came vacuum-packed and expanded into the correct shape when unwrapped.

PHILIPS

Dutch electronics and lighting company Philips was founded in 1891 by Gerard Philips. In the 1950s architect Rein Veersema began designing many of the company's pioneering products of the period, including televisions, radios, hi-fi equipment and electric shavers. In 1963, the company developed the Compact Audio Cassette.

PIPER, JOHN 1903–1992

British painter, writer, stage designer, war artist, and fabric and stained glass designer John Piper began creating compositions in stained glass in 1953, beginning with the chapel at Oundle School. Other projects included stained glass windows for Eton College chapel and BASIL SPENCE's Coventry Cathedral (1959). Piper also designed windows for a series of churches in the Chilterns in the late 1960s and created a tapestry

for Chichester Cathedral (1966). His fabrics (including Heads, 1956) were produced by David Whitehead*.

PLATNER, WARREN 1919–2006
See p. 88.

POLI, FLAVIO 1900–1984

Italian glassware designer Flavio Poli began working in Murano, Venice, in the late 1920s. He is most intimately associated with the Seguso Vetri d'Arte glassworks, where he became artistic director and produced his key pieces of the 1950s, including a series of blown vases using stratas of colour and striped patterns.

POLLOCK, CHARLES 1930–2013

American product and furniture designer Charles Pollock worked in the office of GEORGE NELSON in the 1950s, where he began designing pieces for Herman Miller*. He founded his own design office in 1958, designing for Knoll* and Thonet*. Pollock's Knoll designs include the Model 657 sling chair (1960) and the highly successful Pollock chair (c. 1963).

POLTRONOVA

Italian furniture manufacturer Poltronova was founded in 1957. In the mid-century period the company established a strong reputation for experimental and avant-garde furniture by ETTORE SOTTSASS, Gae Aulenti*, Angelo Mangiarotti*, Massimo Vignelli*, Donato D'Urbino and others.

PONTI, GIO 1891–1979
See p. 92.

POP DESIGN

Influenced by the Pop Art movement and artists such as Andy Warhol and Roy Lichtenstein, Pop design of the 1960s was playful, colourful, youthful and vibrant, while borrowing themes and references from popular culture. Pop design became associated, in particular, with a new generation of plastic products and furniture developed in the 1960s, some of which had a disposable, ephemeral and sometimes kitsch character.

PORSCHE, FERDINAND ALEXANDER 1935–2012

German car and product designer Ferdinand Alexander Porsche was the grandson of the founder of the Porsche car company. Ferdinand Alexander studied at the Hochschule für Gestaltung, Ulm*, and began working at Porsche in 1958, where

PUCCI, EMILIO
Wall hanging for Braniff Airways, in printed silk jersey, c. 1965.

QUISTGAARD, JENS
Odin flatware in stainless steel, produced by Dansk, Denmark, 1962.

RAPSON, RALPH
Rapson rocking chair in birch and webbing, manufactured by Knoll, USA, 1945.

ROBSJOHN-GIBBINGS, T. H. Lounge chair and ottoman, Widdicomb, USA, c. 1950.

he designed the iconic 911 sports car (1963) as well as a number of other models. He also founded the Porsche Design Studio in 1972, concentrating on household and consumer products.

PORSET, CLARA 1932–1981
Although born in Cuba and educated in America (where Josef Albers* was a mentor), furniture and interior designer Clara Porset lived and worked in Mexico, and her work was influenced by the country's culture and traditions. Her designs include the Totonaca series of chairs and a 1950s collection produced by leading Mexican manufacturer IRGSA.

PRITCHARD, JACK 1899–1992
See Isokon.

PROUVÉ, JEAN 1901–1984
See p. 98.

PUCCI, EMILIO 1914–1992
Italian fashion and printed fabric designer Emilio Pucci is best known for his vibrant, colourful and playful patterns of the 1950s and particularly the 1960s, when his work chimed with the psychedelic aesthetic being explored by a number of designers and artists. Pucci designed uniforms for Braniff Airways in 1965, while ALEXANDER GIRARD worked on other elements of the company's corporate design identity.

QUANT, MARY b. 1934
English fashion designer Mary Quant opened her first store in London in 1955 and rose to prominence in the 1960s. She pioneered the development of the mini-skirt, naming the garment after the iconic motor car designed by ALEC ISSIGONIS. Other Quant staples of the 1960s included brightly coloured, patterned tights and hot pants. Her influence spread far beyond the fashion world.

QUISTGAARD, JENS 1919–2008
Danish furniture and product designer Jens Quistgaard studied sculpture and woodworking before serving an apprenticeship with silverware manufacturer Georg Jensen*. He co-founded his own manufacturing company, Dansk International, in 1954, with American partner Ted Nierenberg. Dansk produced many of Quistgaard's own designs, ranging from stools to ice buckets, cutlery and sculptural peppermills that looked like chess-set pieces crafted in teak. Much of Quistgaard's work was in wood or metal. He also designed

furniture for other manufacturers such as Richard Nissen.

RACE, ERNEST 1913–1964
See p. 102.

RAMS, DIETER b. 1932
See p. 308.

RAND, PAUL 1914–1996
See p. 368.

RAPSON, RALPH 1914–2008
American architect, academic and furniture designer Ralph Rapson studied at the Cranbrook Academy of Art*, where he met Florence Knoll*. In 1944, Knoll asked Rapson to design a collection of chairs and sofas, and these were released the following year. The line included the Rapson rocker, originally made in birch with a webbed cotton seat and back, but also upholstered in later versions.

Rapson taught architecture at the University of Minnesota for many years, becoming dean of the architectural school. He designed American embassies in Copenhagen and Stockholm (both 1954). Rapson and his wife also opened their own interiors and furniture store in Boston.

RICKARD, BRUCE 1929–2010
See p. 476.

RIE, LUCIE 1902–1995
See p. 202.

RISOM, JENS b. 1916
See p. 104.

ROBSJOHN-GIBBINGS, T. H.
1905–1976
English-born furniture and interior designer Terence Harold Robsjohn-Gibbings studied architecture in London before moving to the United States. He opened his own furniture showroom in New York in 1936 and also designed a series of houses for prestigious clients in New York and California. His work combined both modernist and classical influences and included a broad and successful collection for the Widdicomb Furniture Company designed between 1943 and 1956. In the 1960s he developed a new line of furniture with Greek manufacturer Saridis.

RODRIGUES, SERGIO b. 1927
See p. 106.

ROSENTHAL
German ceramics manufacturer Rosenthal was founded in the late 19th

century by Philip Rosenthal. In the mid-century period the company collaborated with a number of innovative designers, including Tapio Wirkkala*, Luigi Colani* and TIMO SARPANEVA.

ROYAL COPENHAGEN

Swedish porcelain, ceramics and homeware company Royal Copenhagen was founded in 1775. In the 1950s the company worked with AXEL SALTO, Magnus Stephenson, Gertrud Vasegaard and others.

ROYÈRE, JEAN 1902–1981
See p. 158.

RUDOLPH, PAUL 1918–1997
American architect Paul Rudolph studied at Harvard under Walter Gropius*. In the post-war period he based himself in Florida and built a number of pioneering modernist houses in the state, including the Milam House in Jacksonville (1962). He also served as dean of the architectural school at Yale University and designed the Yale Art and Architecture Building (1963). He designed a landmark penthouse apartment for himself on Beekman Place, New York, in the mid-1970s.

SAARINEN, EERO 1910–1961
See p. 108.

SAARINEN, ELIEL 1873–1950
Finnish architect, furniture designer and academic Eliel Saarinen worked in Finland for the first part of his career before emigrating to the United States in 1923, along with his wife Loja, a textile designer, and their children, EERO and Pipsan. In the 1930s, under the patronage of George Booth, he established the Cranbrook Academy of Art* in Bloomfield Hills, Michigan, designing a number of campus buildings and becoming the first president of the academy. The institution played a key role in helping to educate some of the most influential figures of mid-century modernist design, including CHARLES & RAY EAMES and HARRY BERTOIA.

SABATTINI, LINO b. 1925
Italian metalware and cutlery designer Lino Sabattini taught himself design and founded his own metalworking studio in Milan in 1955. He also took up a post as design director of Parisian manufacturer Christofle Orfèvrerie. In addition, Sabattini designed ceramics and glassware.

SALTO, AXEL 1889–1961
See p. 206.

SAMPE, ASTRID 1909–2002
Swedish textile designer Astrid Sampe trained in Stockholm and London. In 1937, she was appointed head of textiles for the Swedish department store Nordiska Kompaniet – a post she held until the early 1970s. She experimented with geometric, contemporary patterns but was also influenced by folk art and traditional motifs. She designed textiles for a number of other companies, including Knoll*.

SAPPER, RICHARD b. 1932
See p. 312.

SARFATTI, GINO 1912–1984
See p. 162.

SARPANEVA, TIMO 1926–2006
See p. 210.

SAVIGNAC, RAYMOND 1907–2002
French graphic and poster designer Raymond Savignac was a protégé of the legendary Art Deco poster artist A. M. Cassandre in the 1930s. Savignac rose to prominence in the late 1940s and 1950s with a series of advertising posters that were colourful, joyful, simple, accessible and full of artistry, delight and humour. His clients included Air France, Monsavon soap, Perrier and Bic.

SCARPA, CARLO 1906–1978
Italian architect and designer Carlo Scarpa studied architecture in Venice and founded his own architectural and design practice in 1927. He designed the Olivetti showroom in Venice (1958) and a number of museum projects, while his houses included the influential Villa Ottolenghi in Verona (1978). Scarpa also designed furniture for Cassina*, Bernini and Gavina, and glassware and lighting for Venini.

SCARPA, TOBIA b. 1935
& AFRA b. 1937
The son of architect Carlo Scarpa*, Tobia Scarpa, along with his wife Afra, studied at the Istituto Universitario di Architettura in Venice. In the late 1950s – like Carlo Scarpa before them – they began designing glassware for Venini. Their furniture of the 1960s includes the Bastiano sofa for Gavina (1960) and Soriana lounge chairs for Cassina* (1970). Their architectural and interiors projects include factories for Benetton and B&B Italia, as well as showrooms and residences. They also designed lighting for Flos*.

SCHULTZ, RICHARD b. 1926
American furniture designer and sculptor Richard Schultz began his

ROSENTHAL Porcelain vases and vessels, c. 1975.

RUDOLPH, PAUL Custom desk by Paul Rudolph and Ralph Twitchell, in Douglas fir, steel, glass and aluminium, c. 1948.

SAARINEN, ELIEL Candelabrum in nickel-plated brass, produced by Cray, USA, 1947, designed by Eliel Saarinen and Robert F. Swanson.

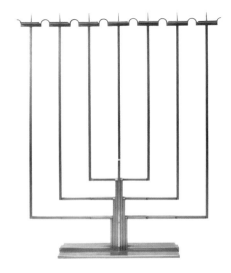

career working with Knoll* in the early 1950s, collaborating initially with HARRY BERTOIA. He went on to design the Petal range of tables for Knoll in 1960, with timber petals arranged upon an aluminium support and spoke wheel base. This was followed by the Leisure collection of 1966 – a range of hard-wearing but stylish outdoor furniture with aluminium frames and nylon mesh seating that was first intended for the hotel market but has since become a favourite for pool sides and terraces. Knoll reissued the Schultz classics in 2012.

SCOTT TALLON WALKER
Irish architectural practice Scott Tallon Walker was founded in 1960 by Michael Scott, Ronald Tallon and Robin Walker. Their modernist buildings include Knockanure Church in County Kerry (1964) and the extraordinary glass and steel Goulding House (1972), cantilevered out over the River Dargle in Enniskerry, County Wicklow.

SEA RANCH
Founded in the mid-1960s on the coastline of Sonoma County, California, the Sea Ranch community combines organic contextuality and a soft modernist aesthetic, as well as a deep-rooted sense of respect for landscape and nature. Early and seminal buildings on the site – which set the 'Sea Ranch Style' – were designed by MLTW Architects and Joseph Esherick, whose own house at Sea Ranch, the Esherick Hedgerow House, was completed in 1966. His uncle was furniture maker and sculptor Wharton Esherick*.

SEIDLER, HARRY 1923–2006
See p. 482.

SEIFERT, RICHARD 1910–2001
British architect Richard Seifert graduated from the Bartlett School of Architecture in 1933 and became well known for his dramatic modernist towers of the 1960s, including London's Centre Point (1964). Seifert's practice built around five hundred office buildings in London, including the NatWest Tower (1981).

SHULMAN, JULIUS 1910–2009
The most influential architectural photographer of the mid-century period, Julius Shulman created images that have come to define the modernist aesthetic of the 1950s and '60s, and Californian modernism in particular. Shulman began taking pictures in the 1930s and became RICHARD NEUTRA's photographer of choice.

He worked for John Entenza*'s *Arts & Architecture* magazine and took a landmark series of pictures of Pierre Koenig*'s Case Study House #22, the Stahl House. He also documented the work of Raphael Soriano* and commissioned a house from Soriano, which was completed in 1950.

SKIDMORE, OWINGS & MERRILL
American architectural practice Skidmore Owings & Merrill (SOM) was founded in Chicago in the late 1930s by Louis Skidmore, Nathaniel Owings and John Merrill, and has grown to become a global practice. SOM pioneered the evolution of high-rise buildings in the mid-century period, when landmark projects included Manhattan House (1951) and Lever House (1952) in New York, and Sears Tower (1973) in Chicago. Notable SOM architects have included ARTHUR WITTHOEFFT and Gordon Bunshaft*.

SMITHSON, ALISON 1928–1993 & PETER 1923–2003
See p. 488.

SONY
Japanese electronics company Sony was founded in Tokyo in 1946 by Masaru Ibuka and Akio Morita, who started working with radios and tape recorders. The company began manufacturing transistors in 1954 and introduced the first transistorized radio in Japan – the TR-55 – a year later. The 1950s were a period of rapid innovation for Sony, with the TR-63 pocket radio launched in 1957 and the TV8-301 transistorized and portable television released in 1959 – the first compact television ever to be produced. Sony remained at the forefront of the miniaturization movement in the 1960s and '70s, and introduced the Walkman in 1979.

SORIANO, RAPHAEL 1904–1988
American architect Raphael Soriano worked with RICHARD NEUTRA in the early 1930s and completed his first residential commission under his own name in 1936. In post-war California, he designed a series of innovative, steel-framed, modernist houses – including a home for Julius Shulman* (1950) – and participated in John Entenza's Case Study Program* with the design for a house in Pacific Palisades. In the mid-1950s, Soriano also developed designs for tract developer Joseph Eichler*.

SOTTSASS, ETTORE 1917–2007
See p. 314.

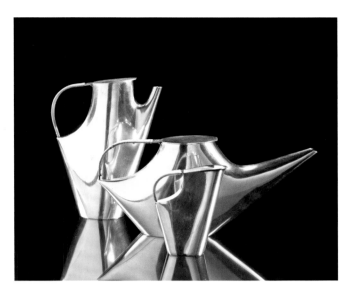

SABATTINI, LINO Model M464 Como tea set, produced by Christofle, Italy, 1956, in silverplate.

SCARPA, TOBIA Soriana sofa in chrome-plated steel and leather, manufactured by Cassina, Italy, 1970.

SCHULTZ, RICHARD Petal dining table in redwood, enamelled steel and aluminium, manufactured by Knoll, USA, 1960.

STOLLER, EZRA
Gelatin silver print, 1958, of the Seagram Building, designed by Ludwig Mies van der Rohe and Philip Johnson.

STRENGELL, MARIANNE Hand-woven rug in dyed wool and mixed fibres, c. 1950.

SPAN HOUSING
See Eric Lyons.

SPENCE, BASIL 1907–1976
See p. 492.

STILL, NANNY 1926–2009
Finnish glass and ceramics designer Nanny Still began working with the Riihimäen Lasi Oy/Riihimaki glass manufacturers in 1949 and continued working with them until 1976. She also designed for Normark, Val-Saint Lambert, Heinrich Porzellan, Hackman, Rosenthal* and others.

STIRLING, JAMES 1926–1992
British architect James Stirling was both highly influential and controversial. He founded his first practice in 1956 with James Gowan and then established a second practice in the 1960s, in which Michael Wilford became a partner. Projects of the 1950s and '60s included the Department of Engineering building at the University of Leicester (1963) and the History Faculty library at the University of Cambridge (1968). Commissions of the 1970s took Stirling onto an international stage and he was awarded the Pritzker Prize in 1981.

STOLLER, EZRA 1915–2004
Like Julius Shulman*, photographer Ezra Stoller documented the evolution of mid-century modernist architecture in evocative style. He photographed work by Frank Lloyd Wright*, LUDWIG MIES VAN DER ROHE, ALVAR AALTO and many other mid-century icons.

STONE, EDWARD DURELL
1902–1978
American architect Edward Durell Stone first captured attention for his role on the design team of Radio City Music Hall in the early 1930s and opened his own practice shortly after its completion. During the 1930s he developed a modernist architectural approach, with a strong European influence, but in the post-war period he began to develop a warmer, more complex and sometimes more playful interpretation of modernist thinking, with an infusion of subtle Beaux-Arts, vernacular and neo-classical influences. Key projects of the 1950s and '60s include the US embassy in New Delhi, India (1954), and the Kennedy Center for the Performing Arts in Washington, DC (1962).

STRAUB, MARIANNE 1909–1994
Swiss-born textile designer and weaver Marianne Straub settled in

Britain in the 1930s. From 1937 to 1950 she designed for Helios, and then for Warner & Sons fabrics throughout the 1950s and '60s. She also designed the Surrey pattern for the Festival of Britain* of 1951.

STRENGELL, MARIANNE
1909–1998
Finnish textile designer Marianne Strengell emigrated to the United States in 1937 to teach at the Cranbrook Academy of Art*, where she became head of the textile department. In the late 1940s and 1950s she designed textiles for Knoll* and also for use as car upholstery.

SUPERSTUDIO
A short-lived but highly influential collective of avant-garde Italian architects and designers, Superstudio was founded in Florence in 1966 by Adolfo Natalini and Cristiano Toraldo di Francia and disbanded in 1978. Key designs of the late 1960s and early 1970s include their Gherpe lights for Poltronova* (1967) and the Quaderna table for Zanotta* (1971).

SVENSKT TENN
See JOSEF FRANK, p. 246.

SWISS STYLE
A term applied to a specific typographical and graphic design movement prevalent in the 1930s to 1950s, the Swiss Style – or International Typographic Style – was characterized by clean, clear, sans serif typefaces and an ordered, rational and often grid-based approach, as well as the use of techniques such as photomontage. Key masters include MAX BILL, Jan Tschichold and ADRIAN FRUTIGER. The influence of the Swiss school was felt internationally in the mid-century period.

TAKAHAMA, KAZUHIDE
1930–2010
Japanese designer Kazuhide Takahama studied architecture in Tokyo before moving to Italy in 1954, where he began working for Gavina. He designed seating and storage ranges for Gavina through the 1950s and '60s, including the ESA modular seating system using hexagonal units of polyurethane foam. In 1965, he designed his Suzanne seating system for Knoll*. He also designed lighting for Sirrah and others.

TANGE, KENZO 1913–2005
Japanese architect and designer Kenzo Tange studied architecture at the University of Tokyo and was

SUPERSTUDIO Olook hanging lamp in chrome-plated steel, fibreglass and plastic, produced by Poltronova, Italy, 1968.

TAKAHAMA, KAZUHIDE
A pair of Gaza chairs in chrome-plated steel and upholstery, produced by Simon International for Gavina, Italy, c. 1969.

TANGE, KENZO Bench in Keyaki wood, Japan, c. 1960.

THONET S-Stuhl Model 275 beech plywood chair, designed by Verner Panton, 1956, produced by A. Sommer for Thonet.

influenced by both traditional Japanese architecture and the work of Le Corbusier*. He founded his own practice in 1946 and completed the Hiroshima Peace Memorial Museum in 1955. His Yoyogi National Gymnasium of 1964 was designed for the Tokyo Olympics. By the 1970s Tange was working internationally. He won the Pritzker Prize in 1987.

TAPIOVAARA, ILMARI 1914–1999
Finnish furniture and product designer Ilmari Tapiovaara began his career in the 1930s in the London office of Artek*. He then briefly worked in the Paris office of Le Corbusier*, before serving as the art director of the Finnish furniture company Asko.

In the post-war period, Tapiovaara's work became more ambitious and he began to look abroad, as well as continuing his collaborations with Scandinavian manufacturers. He was particularly fascinated with the idea of developing an affordable, well designed chair and created the Domus birch plywood stacking chair in 1946 for the Domus Academy in Helsinki. This was initially produced in Finland, but in the 1950s it was produced by Knoll* as the Model 140 series. Tapiovaara also designed a Domus lounge chair with a tall, sculpted back.

He established his own design studio in Helsinki in 1950 and began broadening his portfolio. Pieces included his Pirkka lounge chair, made by Laukaan Puu, and his Mademoiselle lounge chair (both 1956). He also designed for Thonet* and Wilhelm Schauman, and he worked in the States for a time in the early 1950s (including a period spent in the office of LUDWIG MIES VAN DER ROHE). Other projects included aircraft interiors for Finnair and the design of other products, such as cutlery, hi-fi equipment, lighting, textiles and glassware.

TEAGUE, WALTER DORWIN
1883–1960
American industrial, furniture, lighting, graphic and product designer Walter Dorwin Teague was a pioneer of streamlined design, reaching the height of his career in the 1930s. He applied his talents to a broad range of products, from cameras to desk lights, and paved the way for a younger generation of multi-faceted industrial designers who came to the fore in the post-war period. His clients of the 1950s included Boeing, Polaroid and UPS.

TENREIRO, JOAQUIM 1906–1992
See p. 112.

THOMPSON, BRADBURY 1911–1995
American graphic designer, typographer and art director Bradbury Thompson worked as art director of *Mademoiselle* magazine in the late 1940s and 1950s. Key projects included designing the influential design industry publication *Westvaco Inspirations*, the typographically influential *Washburn College Bible* and a series of postage stamps for the US Postal Service.

THONET
Austrian furniture company Thonet was founded by Michael Thonet and his sons in Vienna in 1849 and specialized in steam-bent wooden furniture, which was soon produced in high volumes and at affordable prices. In 1929, a sister company – Thonet Frères – began producing tubular steel furniture by LUDWIG MIES VAN DER ROHE, MARCEL BREUER and others. In the mid-century period the company continued to innovate, working with designers such as VERNER PANTON and PIERRE PAULIN.

TOTAL DESIGN
See WIM CROUWEL, p. 340.

TUBBS, RALPH 1912–1996
An architect and writer, Ralph Tubbs was one of the principal figures behind the Festival of Britain* of 1951. He designed the Dome of Discovery – a vast flying saucer of a building that formed one of the most important structures at the Festival site on London's South Bank. The Dome was 365 feet (111 m) in diameter, with an aluminium-clad roof and a pioneering prefabricated aluminium and steel frame resting on concrete foundations and buttresses. The interior was dominated by a series of discovery zones devoted to themes such as the polar regions, the sky and outer space.

Around eight million people visited the Festival but the Dome was torn down just eleven months later and sold for scrap metal, along with many other associated buildings.

Tubbs had trained at the Architectural Association before starting work with the modernist architect Ernö Goldfinger*. He wrote two best-selling architecture books during the war years. The Dome cemented his reputation as an architect, and other key buildings included Baden-Powell House in London for the Scout Association

(1956). The Dome, like the Festival itself, is still regarded as a high point for British mid-century design.

TYNELL, PAAVO 1890-1973
Finnish designer Paavo Tynell founded his lighting company, Taito, in 1918. The company produced many of Tynell's own designs in the 1940s and '50s, which were exported to the States from 1948 onwards. His chandeliers, in particular, were infused with sophisticated glamour and a playful, original quality.

ULM SCHOOL
See Hochschule für Gestaltung, Ulm.

UNITED NATIONS HEADQUARTERS
A highly resonant and symbolic architectural as well as political/diplomatic statement, the UN building in New York was one of the great collaborative design projects of the mid-century period. Completed in 1952 on a site funded by the Rockefeller family, the final design by OSCAR NIEMEYER and Le Corbusier* was selected by a multinational planning team. Many other artists and designers contributed to the interiors of the complex.

UTILITY FURNITURE
The term 'Utility furniture' was given to simply made and unadorned furniture produced in Britain between 1941 and 1951 under the country's war-time and post-war rationing programme. In an effort to control the use of valuable raw materials, Utility furniture was limited in availability and largely restricted to households that had suffered bomb damage or to newly married couples. The production and design of Utility furniture was closely monitored by an advisory board.

UTZON, JØRN 1918-2008
The son of a naval designer, Danish architect Jørn Utzon studied at Copenhagen's Royal Academy of Fine Arts and worked with ALVAR AALTO before establishing his own practice in 1945. In 1957, Utzon won the competition to design the Sydney Opera House – a project only completed in 1973. Among other projects, he designed a number of superlative private houses, including Can Lis, his own house on the island of Majorca, completed in 1972.

VENINI, PAOLO 1895-1959
See p. 214.

VENTURI, ROBERT b. 1925
American architect, furniture designer, writer and theorist Robert Venturi studied at Princeton University and worked with EERO SAARINEN and Louis Kahn* before co-founding his own practice in 1960, ultimately known as Venturi, Scott Brown & Associates. His work fused a multiplicity of influences within a 'less is a bore' approach. One of his first completed buildings – the Vanna Venturi House in Philadelphia, designed for his mother and finished in 1964 – also proved to be one of his most influential. He was awarded the Pritzker Prize in 1991.

VIGNELLI, MASSIMO b. 1931
Polymath Italian-born designer Massimo Vignelli worked in graphic design, corporate identity, product and industrial design, interiors and glassware. He studied architecture at the Politecnico di Milano and also studied in Venice, then began designing glassware for Venini in the early 1950s. In 1965, he co-founded the Milanese design studio Unimark and also established an office in New York, which in 1971 became Vignelli Associates, with Vignelli working in collaboration with his wife, Lella.

A diverse portfolio of projects in the 1960s and early 1970s included signage for the New York subway system, corporate identity and logo design for Knoll* from 1966 onwards, as well as work for American Airlines and Ford. Vignelli also designed lighting and furniture, including pieces for Poltronova* and Casigliani.

VITRA
German furniture manufacturer Vitra was founded by Willi Fehlbaum in 1950 and secured a European licensing agreement with Herman Miller*, producing ranges by CHARLES & RAY EAMES, GEORGE NELSON and others. Independently, Vitra also developed its own collections and worked closely with designers such as VERNER PANTON, developing the Panton chair of 1967. The company expanded both its range and factory campus under the guidance of the founder's son, Rolf Fehlbaum, from 1977 onwards.

VOLTHER, POUL 1923-2001
Danish furniture designer Poul Volther's most famous design is his Corona chair of 1961, produced by Eric Jørgensen. With a steel frame and a series of elliptical seat and back pads upholstered in leather or fabric, the name suggests the dynamic idea of the phased stages of an eclipse.

TYNELL, PAAVO
Brass chandelier, c. 1955, produced by Taito, Finland.

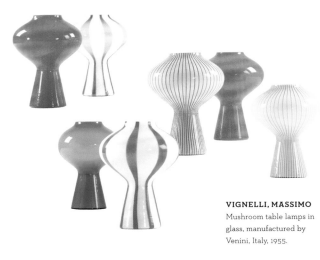

VIGNELLI, MASSIMO
Mushroom table lamps in glass, manufactured by Venini, Italy, 1955.

VOLTHER, POUL
Corona chair in chrome-plated steel and vinyl, produced by Erik Jørgensen, Denmark, 1964.

WAGENFELD, WILHELM
1900-1990
German product, industrial and lighting designer Wilhelm Wagenfeld studied in Bremen, Hanau and at the Bauhaus*. Many of his most famous designs date from the 1930s, but he remained active in the 1950s and established the Wagenfeld Workshop in Stuttgart in 1954. In the post-war period he designed lighting, cutlery, tableware and other pieces for WMF, Peill and Putzler, Braun* and others. He also designed glassware and ceramics.

WANSCHER, OLE 1903-1985
Danish furniture designer Ole Wanscher studied with Kaare Klint* and immersed himself in furniture history, drawing lessons and inspiration from a wide spectrum of historical designs from around the world. He also stressed the importance of craftsmanship within his work, along with the integrity of materials. In the 1940s and '50s he designed for a number of producers, including Fritz Hansen*, Cado and A.J. Iversen Snedkermester. Among his most enticing designs are his Colonial armchair of 1949 for Poul Jeppesen and his rosewood and leather rocking chair of 1951 for France & Son.

WEGNER, HANS 1914-2007
See p. 114.

WELCH, ROBERT 1929-2000
British silversmith and product designer Robert Welch began training as a painter before moving into silversmithing, including a period at the Royal College of Art in the early 1950s. Welch, who was influenced by Scandinavian design, established his own workshop in 1955 and designed for Old Hall Tableware, Prinz, Lauffer and other manufacturers. Other products included clocks and lighting. He opened his first eponymous store in 1969 selling Welch cutlery, cookware and other designs. His company continues today under the guidance of his children.

WIINBLAD, BJØRN 1918-2006
Danish ceramicist and furniture, textile and lighting designer Bjørn Wiinblad began to design for the Nymølle pottery in 1946 and founded his own design studio in 1952. He designed dinnerware, candlesticks and other ceramic pieces for Rosenthal*, and was also known for his whimsical, folk-inspired ceramic figurines. Wiinblad applied ceramics to other product genres,

such as tables with earthenware tops and lighting with pottery bases. He also worked as a theatre designer and illustrator.

WILLIAMS, E. STEWART
1909-2005
Together with contemporaries such as Albert Frey* and William Cody, architect Ernest Stewart Williams helped give shape and voice to Palm Springs in the 1950s and '60s, making it the epicentre of sophisticated desert modernism as well as a haven for the Hollywood elite. He worked with RAYMOND LOEWY and designed ships for the US Navy before joining the family architectural practice in Palm Springs. His most famous houses include Twin Palms for Frank Sinatra (1947), the Edris House (1954) and the Kenaston House (1957). Stewart Williams also designed the Palm Springs Desert Museum (1976).

WIRKKALA, TAPIO 1915-1985
Finnish glassware and furniture designer Tapio Wirkkala studied sculpture in Helsinki. He started designing glassware for Iittala* in 1946 and continued working with the company until his death. His pieces included vases, lighting pendants and more sculptural art objects, such as his Iceberg vase of 1951 and his abstract, ice-inspired Inari bowl of 1967.

Wirkkala also designed ceramics for Rosenthal* and, again, many of these pieces exhibit highly sculptural abstraction, including his Pollo vases of 1970 and the Aphrodite vase of 1973. In addition, Wirkkala designed furniture, including his birch and ply Nikke chair of 1958 for Asko. His Leaf platters for Soinne et Kni (1951) – using laminated birch in sinuous striped swirls – became design icons in themselves. Wirkkala also worked briefly for RAYMOND LOEWY in the mid-1950s and applied his unique sense of artistry to many other products, including cutlery and silverware.

WITTHOEFFT, ARTHUR b. 1919
See p. 496.

WORMLEY, EDWARD 1907-1995
See p. 120.

WRIGHT, FRANK LLOYD 1867-1959
One of the most influential architects of the 20th century, Frank Lloyd Wright began his career working with Louis Sullivan in Chicago in 1887 and opened his own practice six years later. Over the coming years Wright

WAGENFELD, WILHELM Prototype table lamp in enamelled and chrome-plated steel, produced by WMF, Germany, c. 1953.

WANSCHER, OLE Beech bed produced by Fritz Hansen, c. 1945.

WIINBLAD, BJØRN Candelabra in porcelain, made by Rosenthal, c. 1975.

WIRKKALA, TAPIO Leaf dish in laminated birch and teak plywood, produced by Soinne et Kni, Finland, c. 1951.

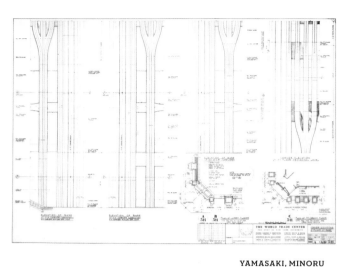

YAMASAKI, MINORU
Corner elevations and plans at base for the North Tower of the World Trade Center, New York, 1967.

YANAGI, SORI A pair of Butterfly stools, in rosewood and brass, manufactured by Tendo, Japan, 1954.

ZALSZUPIN, JORGE
Sofa in rosewood ply, leather and aluminium, c. 1965.

ZANOTTA Primate chair, designed by Achille Castiglioni, in chrome-plated steel and leather, 1970.

established himself as one of the most original voices in American architecture, pioneering a uniquely American style – although influenced by Arts & Crafts traditions and Japanese architecture – that placed a particular emphasis on an organic and contextual approach.

Key Wright projects include the Robie House of 1909, the Hollyhock House of 1920 and his masterpiece, Fallingwater, in Bear Run, Pennsylvania, completed in 1939. Wright continued working in the post-war period, with a prolific portfolio of houses and other projects across the 1940s and '50s. A second masterpiece, the Solomon R. Guggenheim Museum in New York, was begun in 1943 and completed in 1959 – the year of Wright's death.

WRIGHT, RUSSEL 1904–1976
See p. 220.

YAMASAKI, MINORU 1912–1986
American architect Minoru Yamasaki is best known for his design of the Twin Towers of the World Trade Center in New York, begun in 1966 and completed in 1972. Born in Seattle to Japanese-American parents, Yamasaki founded his own architectural practice in New York in 1949. Other key projects include the Pacific Science Center in Seattle, built for the World's Fair of 1962.

YANAGI, SORI 1915–2011
Japanese furniture designer Sori Yanagi studied architecture in Tokyo and worked briefly with Charlotte Perriand* when she established an office in Japan in the 1940s. Yanagi established his own design studio in 1952. His most famous design is his beautifully crafted plywood Butterfly stool of 1954, made by Tendo.

ZALSZUPIN, JORGE b. 1922
Polish-born furniture designer Jorge Zalszupin studied architecture in Romania before emigrating to Brazil in 1950. Settling in São Paulo, he founded L'Atelier in 1955, producing his own designs, mostly in wood. These included a distinctive series of ribbed-back rosewood/jacaranda sofas, supported by steel frames or aluminium rods, from the 1960s. Other Zalszupin pieces were manufactured by Chalesko.

ZANOTTA
Italian furniture manufacturer Zanotta was founded by Aurelio Zanotta in 1954 in Milan. The company embraced avant-garde and experimental design and worked with leading Italian designers of the post-war era, including ACHILLE & PIER GIACOMO CASTIGLIONI, JOE COLOMBO, MARCO ZANUSO, ETTORE SOTTSASS and De Pas, D'Urbino & Lomazzi*.

ZANUSO, MARCO 1916–2001
See p. 312.

ZAPF, HERMANN b. 1918
Influential German typographer Hermann Zapf designed the Palatino (1950) and Optima (1955) typefaces for the Stempel type foundry. Through his writing and teaching – as well as his typefaces – he helped to shape the evolution of mid-century graphic design.

ZEISEL, EVA 1906–2011
Hungarian-born ceramicist Eva Zeisel studied and served an apprenticeship in Budapest, as well as setting up her first workshop in the city. She spent time living and working in the Soviet Union before emigrating to America in 1938. She was given a solo exhibition at the Museum of Modern Art in 1946. In 1952, she designed her famous Classic Century dinnerware for the Hall China Company in crisp white earthenware. She also designed for Bay Ridge, Red Wing Pottery, Charles Seliger and Sears Roebuck, and taught at the Pratt Institute. Zeisel stepped back from designing for mass production in the mid-1960s.

CONTRIBUTORS' BIOGRAPHIES

ALBERTO BASSI focuses his studies on the history and criticism of design. He is associate professor at IUAV University of Venice. He also collaborates with specialist magazines such as *Casabella*, *Auto&Design* and *Il giornale dell'architettura*, and with the newspaper *Il Sole 24 ore*. His publications include *Le macchine volanti di Corradino D'Ascanio* (with M. Mulazzani); *Antonio Citterio: Industrial Design*; *Design anonimo in Italia: Oggetti comuni e progetto incognito*; and *Design: Progettare gli oggetti quotidiani*.

MICHAEL BOYD is a California-based furniture, landscape, interior and architectural designer, whose design and restoration work has been featured in books and magazines internationally. In 2012 he created PLANEfurniture, which has been accessioned into the permanent collections of SFMOMA, Palm Springs Museum of Art and the UCSB Gebhard Architecture & Design Collection. He is principal of BoydDesign, a consultancy for the restoration of modernist architecture and collection of modern design. Boyd curated and designed the installation for the design section of the travelling exhibition, 'Birth of the Cool: California Art, Design, and Culture at Midcentury'. He has restored historical architecture by many of the modernist masters, including Oscar Niemeyer, Paul Rudolph. Richard Neutra, Craig Ellwood, John Lautner, R. M. Schindler and A. Quincy Jones. He regularly advises museums and institutions on modern architecture and design.

SOPHIE CHURCHER is a specialist in vintage posters at Christie's in London. She joined Christie's in 2005, having graduating from the University of Sussex with a BA in Art History and upon completion of an art foundation, specializing in printmaking. She became a specialist in 2007 and is now Head of Sale for the bi-annual Vintage Posters auctions. She was appointed Associate Director in 2012. She has valued and catalogued many large public and private collections internationally, including the Wagon-Lits poster archive in Paris. In 2012, she worked closely with the London Transport Museum, resulting in the landmark auction, 'Posters with a Purpose: The London Transport Museum Sale'. In 2013, she organized the sale of 'Graphic Masterworks: A Century of Design',

the most important private collection of avant-garde posters to come to auction. Together with her colleague, Nicolette Tomkinson, she has ensured that Christie's poster department is the international market leader in the field.

MATT GIBBERD comes from a family of architects, and his grandfather – Sir Frederick Gibberd – was one of the modern movement's most influential figures. His father only ever gave him one piece of careers advice: 'Do anything you like, as long as it's not architecture'. Gibberd has indulged his passion for buildings in every way possible without actually designing them. In 2004, he co-founded The Modern House, the UK's foremost estate agency for architect-designed property. He has also written on architecture for many magazines and newspapers, including *The World of Interiors* and *The Sunday Telegraph*.

ALUN GRAVES is a Senior Curator in the Sculpture, Metalwork, Ceramics and Glass Department of the Victoria and Albert Museum in London. He has responsibility for the collections of 20th-century and contemporary ceramics, and has published frequently in this field, as well as on sculpture and historic tiles. He was a member of the project team in the redevelopment of the V&A's Ceramics Galleries, opened in 2009 and 2010.

JUDITH GURA is on the faculty of The New York School of Interior Design, where she heads the Design History and Theory programme and is consultant on lectures and public programmes. Her published works include *Design After Modernism: Furniture and Interiors, 1970–2010*; *New York Interior Design, 1935–1985*; *Sourcebook of Scandinavian Furniture: Designs for the 21st Century*; *Guide to Period Styles for Interiors*; *Harvey Probber: Modernist Furniture, Artworks and Design*; and *Edward Wormley: The Other Face of Modernism*. A graduate of Cornell University, she has a Master's degree in History of Design and the Decorative Arts from the Bard Graduate Center. She has also taught at Pratt Institute and FIT, and has worked on design exhibitions at the Brooklyn Museum, Whitney Museum and National Museum of Women in the Arts. She is a contributing editor for *Art+Auction*, and a frequent lecturer and panellist.

DANIEL HEATH is an independent wallpaper, textile and surface designer known for his nostalgic, hand-drawn illustrations of animals and motifs. Since graduating from the Royal College of Art in 2007 he has completed a number of high-profile commissions for both domestic and commercial interior projects. Most recently he has worked in collaboration with London-based architects Retrouvius on a number of projects using a combination of sustainable materials, contemporary material treatments and traditional craft processes. Alongside running his London-based studio, he also teaches and lectures in a range of institutions.

STEVEN HELLER is the co-chair of the MFA Design: Designer as Author & Entrepreneur programme at the School of Visual Arts in New York. He is the author or editor of over 150 books on design and popular culture, and the recipient of the 2011 Smithsonian National Design Award.

KLAUS KLEMP is Head of Exhibitions and Curator of Design at the Museum of Applied Art in Frankfurt and Professor of the History of Design at the Hochschule Rhein-Main, Wiesbaden. He has written several books on design, architecture and art, and curated numerous exhibitions, including 'Less and More: The Design Ethos of Dieter Rams', 'Fragile: Russian Table Culture from the 18th to 20th Century' and 'Korea Power: Design and Identity'.

JOY McCALL joined Christie's in 2003, after having been a specialist at another London auction house from 1997. Initially with responsibility for British Decorative Arts at Christie's, in 2008 she was named Head of 20th Century Decorative Art & Design in London and saw a gesso panel, 'The White Rose and The Red Rose' by Margaret Macdonald Mackintosh, realize a record price of £1.7m. McCall was subsequently made a director and, besides leading the 20th Century Decorative Art & Design sales in London, handles the bi-annual specialist Lalique sales in South Kensington. McCall has acted as a consulting editor for the *Miller's Art Nouveau and Art Deco Price Guide* and the *Miller's Glass Price Guide*, and played an important role in the compilation of the *Miller's Glass*

Antique Checklist. She has a degree in the History of Art with Ancient History from the University of Leicester and holds a Master's degree from the University of Sussex, where she studied British Art History and Critical Theory.

SUE PRICHARD is Curator of Modern and Contemporary Textiles at the Victoria and Albert Museum in London. She has curated a number of contemporary textile displays at the V&A, including 'Recent Acquisitions 1992-2002: A Decade of Collecting Textiles', 'Concealed-Discovered-Revealed: New Work by Sue Lawty' and 'Penelope's Thread: Contemporary Tapestry from the Permanent Collection'. She was the curator of 'Quilts 1700-2010' held at the V&A and lead curator of 'Quilts 1700-1945' (Queensland Art Gallery, Brisbane). She has written several publications, including *The Fifties: V&A Pattern*, was editor of *Quilts 1700-2010: Hidden Histories, Untold Stories*, and collaborated with the Henry Moore Foundation on *Henry Moore Textiles*, for which she wrote the introductory essay. Research interests include the 1950s, the domestic interior, and feminist art and literature.

JANA SCHOLZE is Curator of Contemporary Furniture and Product Design at the Victoria and Albert Museum in London. She has worked on major exhibitions, including 'Cold War Modern: Design 1945-1970'. Her expertise and passion for contemporary design practice have been recognized internationally and she is regularly asked to lecture, publish, teach and critique. Special interests are modern and contemporary design, its discourse and exhibition theory, all subjects on which she has published, including the monograph *Medium Ausstellung*.

RICHARD WRIGHT is the founder and president of Wright auction house in Chicago. Since its first sale in 2000, the company has grown to be the defining auction house in the field of modern design. Richard Wright has over two decades of experience in handling and documenting 20th-century works. He has published several books and monographs in addition to nearly 100 award-winning auction catalogues on the subject. He has also lectured widely on the history and market of modern design.

FURNITURE

1   Quoted at www.harrybertoia.org.
2   Quoted at www.arne-jacobsen.com.
3   Quoted in *Scandinavian Design* by Charlotte and Peter Fiell, Taschen, 2005.
4   Quoted in Pierre Paulin's obituary by Pierre Perrone in *The Independent*, 6 August 2009.
5   Quoted at www.knoll.com.
6   Quoted in Gio Ponti entry, Design Museum: designmuseum.org.
7   Interview with the author.
8   Interview with the author.
9   Quoted in *Eero Saarinen* by Jayne Merkel, Phaidon, 2005.
10 Quoted at www.collectdunbar.com/discover_edward.html.

LIGHTING

1   Charlotte and Peter Fiell (eds), *1000 Lights: 1960 to Present*, Vol. 2, Taschen, 2005, p. 80.
2   Quoted by the Isamu Noguchi Museum.

GLASS AND CERAMICS

1   Martin Eidelberg, *Eva Zeisel: Designer for Industry*, Musée des Arts Décoratifs de Montréal, 1984, pp. 32-33.
2   Lucie Young, *Eva Zeisel*, Chronicle Books, 2003, p. 40.
3   Bernd Fritz, 'New impulses at Rosenthal: Loewy's designs for chinaware', in Angela Schönberger (ed.), *Raymond Loewy: Pioneer of Industrial Design*, Prestel, 1990, pp. 140-41.
4   Dora Billington, 'The New Look in British Pottery', *The Studio*, No. 742, January 1955, p. 18.
5   Tanya Harrod, *The Crafts in Britain in the 20th Century*, Yale University Press, 1999, pp. 214 and 257.
6   Edmund de Waal, *The Guardian*, 25 May 2012.
7   Russel Wright, *Good Design is For Everyone*, Manitoga/Russel Wright Design Center/Universe, 2001.

TEXTILES

1   Already in the late 19th century William Morris had championed the unification of the arts and crafts. His ethos that good design should be accessible to all was taken up by the Deutsche Werkstätten and the Wiener Werkstätte.
2   The decade after the cessation of hostilities witnessed the establishment of a number of high-quality British art and design courses, including the Central School of Arts and Crafts, led by the influential Dora Batty, and the Royal College of Art, which Robin Darwin reinvented along the lines of the Bauhaus school.
3   In 1950, John Murray, Director of Furnishing Fabric for David Whitehead, published an article in the journal *Design* entitled 'The Cheap need not be Cheap and Nasty'. See *The Ambassador*, Issue 11, 1953, p. 13, and S. Prichard, 'British Textile Design: The Quest for a New Aesthetic' in A. Feldman (ed.), *Henry Moore Textiles*, Lund Humphries, 2008.
4   Silk screen-printing originated from the Japanese technique of stencilling and had been developed in both America and Europe in the late 19th and early 20th centuries. Screen-printing, like hand block-printing in the 19th century, offered artists and designers scope for experimentation. Mechanized rotary screen-printing allowed prices to be reduced but more importantly led to a dramatic increase in production volume.
5   Utility regulations permitted a restricted palette of five colours, with small pattern repeats. The success of the new modern furnishing fabrics, in bright vivid colourways, owed much to the development of hard-wearing and colour-fast fabrics such as nylon and terylene in Britain and Orlon and Dynel in the USA.
6   V. Mendes, *Ascher: Fabric – Art – Fashion*, V&A Publishing, 1987, p. 55.
7   The artists were not asked to create textile designs but rather paintings which would serve as inspiration and could be adapted. As outlined by Hans Juda: 'The fact that some of the commissioned artists are not acquainted with the difficulties and techniques of textiles can paradoxically become an asset. This ignorance, almost in the nature of a random element, leads to an adventurous approach which may create difficulties for the converter, but at the same time can be a spark for an unexpected and even startling design' ('Paintings into Textiles' exhibition catalogue, ICA, October 1953).
8   *The Ambassador*, 1953, No. 11. In the editorial to the edition, Juda stated: 'Little but good can come from a closer association between the Arts and textiles. The sketches and paintings we commissioned were calculated to stimulate everyone concerned – the designer, the manufacturer, the converter – and provide a *starting point* from which to develop saleable goods.'
9   David Whitehead Fabrics pioneered mechanized screen-printing for home furnishings, creating a number of artist-designed textiles that were truly affordable and accessible to the public at large.
10 See L. Jackson, *20th Century Pattern Design*, Mitchell Beazley, 2002, pp. 146-48.
11 Robin and Lucienne Day writing in the Preface to Lesley Jackson's *Robin and Lucienne Day: Pioneers of Contemporary Design*, Mitchell Beazley, 2001.
12 Quoted in Herman Miller promotional literature.
13 David Hicks, *Style & Design*, Viking, 1987.
14 Interview with Jack Lenor Larsen and Pierre Paulin by Laurie Manfra, *American Craft*, April-May 2008.
15 Jack Lenor Larsen, writing in *Crafting Modernism: Midcentury American Art and Design*, Abrams/Museum of Art & Design, 2012.
16 Interview with Patricia Malarcher, reproduced at www.longhouse.org.

PRODUCT AND INDUSTRIAL DESIGN

1   See John Harwood, *The Redesign of Design: Multinational Corporations, Computers and Design Logic, 1945-1976*, Columbia, 2006.
2   Noyes designed IBM's Education Centre (1956-58) and a Research and Development Laboratory (1956-59), both of which served as models for laboratories around the globe.
3   Neuhart et al., *Eames Design: The Work of the Office of Charles and Ray Eames*, Harry N. Abrams, 1989, p. 223.
4   John Harwood, 'Imagining the Computer: Eliot Noyes, the Eames and the IBM Pavilion', in David Crowley and Jane Pavitt (eds) *Cold War Modern: Design 1945-1970*, 2008, p. 192.
5   Crowley and Pavitt, *ibid.*, 2008, p. 19.
6   See René Spitz, *HfG Ulm: The View Behind the Foreground. The Political History of the Ulm School of Design 1953-1968*, Edition Axel Menges, 2002. The HfG was located in the American Occupation Zone and had to submit its curriculum for approval. In 1953, it received substantial funding from the US High Commission under John J. McCloy.
7   See David Crowley, 'Thaw Modern: Design in Eastern Europe after 1956', in Crowley and Pavitt, *op. cit.*, 2008, pp. 128-51.
8   Nixon cited in 'The Two Worlds: A Day-Long Debate', *New York Times*, 25 July 1959, p. 1.
9   During the war, most radios in Japan had the shortwave unit disconnected to enable listening to enemy propaganda; the demand for international news was even greater.
10 P. Kunkel, *Digital Dreams: The Work of the Sony Design Center*, Universe Publishing, 1999, p. 13.
11 *Ibid.*, p. 14.
12 See Crowley and Pavitt, *op. cit.*, p. 66, and particularly footnote 13 referencing a conversation between Pavitt and Sottsass in 2005.
13 Theodor Heuss – Managing Director and board member of the Werkbund from 1918 to 1933 – became the first Federal President of West Germany (1949-59).
14 Hans Schwippert, 'A Werkbund letter', in *Work and Time, H. 3*, 1952, quoted by Hans Wichmann, 1998, pp. 49 and 51. Schwippert studied architecture in Hanover, Darmstadt and Stuttgart. He had contact with Paul Schmitthenner, Erich Mendelsohn, Ludwig Mies van der Rohe and Rudolf Schwarz, and was therefore closely associated with German pre-war modernism. From 1946 he began to reorganize the teaching at the Art Academy Düsseldorf and it became an important institution under his presidency, which lasted until 1966.
15 See 'Transculturation: Forms of Life after the Dissolution of Cultures', in *Information Philosophy*, 1992, Issue 2, pp. 5-20.
16 See Günter Höhne, in Erika Penti and Bebo Sher, *Classics of GDR Design*, Schwarzkopf & Schwarzkopf, 2001, p. 218.
17 *Ibid.*, p. 86.
18 In *Der Spiegel*, No. 43, 1951, pp. 30-32.
19 Quoted by Barbara Möller, in 'The GDR paid by the square centimetre', *Hamburger Abendblatt*, 28 July 2003.
20 Kenneth Grange writing in *Living by Design*, by the Partners of Pentagram, Lund Humphries, 1979.
21 Interview with Hilary Rose, *The Times Magazine*, 17 January 2004.
22 Kenneth Grange writing in *British Design from 1948: Innovation in the Modern Age*, Christopher Breward & Ghislaine Wood (eds), V&A Publishing, 2012.
23 Dieter Rams, quoted in the Design Museum exhibition 'Less and More', London, November 2009.
24 *Ibid.*

SELECT BIBLIOGRAPHY

GRAPHICS AND POSTERS

1 Paul Rand, writing in *Design, Form and Chaos*, Yale University Press, 1993.
2 Interview with the author.
3 G. O. Austen, 'AOA', *Graphis* magazine, 1947, p. 118, quoted in Charles Rosner, *Air France: Graphis*, Amstutz & Herdeg, 1957, No. 71, Vol. 13.
4 Anthony Scott and Oliver Green, *British Aviation Posters: Art, Design and Flight*, Surrey, 2012, p. 103.
5 Charles Rosner, *Recent Air Travel Publicity: Graphis*, Amstutz & Herdeg, 1957, Vol. 9, 1953.
6 *Ibid.*, p. 258.
7 Ashley Havinden, 1964, in a supplement from *The Times*.
8 Saul Bass, quoted in *Saul Bass: A Life in Film & Design* by Jennifer Bass & Pat Kirkham, Laurence King, 2011.
9 Wim Crouwel, interviewed by Tony Brook in *Wim Crouwel: A Graphic Odyssey*, Unit Editions, 2011.
10 Alan Fletcher, quoted in an interview with Rick Poynor, *Eye* magazine, Issue 83, Winter 1991.
11 Adrian Frutiger, quoted on the Linotype website.
12 Charley Harper, letter to a Mr Hannah, reproduced at www.charleyharperprints.com.
13 *Ibid.*
14 Margaret Calvert, quoted in an interview with Elizabeth Hilliard Selka, *The Telegraph*, 19 April 2012.
15 Paul Rand, in a Yale exhibition catalogue, quoted by the American Institute of Graphic Arts website.
16 Paul Rand, quoted in Steven Heller, *Paul Rand*, Phaidon, 1999.
17 *Ibid.*

HOUSES AND INTERIORS

1 Lina Bo Bardi, writing in *Lina Bo Bardi*, Instituto Lina Bo e P. M. Bardi/ Edizioni Charta, 1994.
2 *Ibid.*
3 Antonio Bonet, quoted by Luis Ridao in 'To The Letter', *World of Interiors*, August 2010.
4 Charles Deaton, quoted in Philip Jodidio, *Architecture Now!* 3, Taschen, 2003.
5 Interview with the author.
6 *Ibid.*
7 Interview with the author.
8 *Ibid.*
9 Dr Edith Farnsworth, quoted by Maritz Vandenberg in *The Farnsworth House*, Phaidon, 2003.
10 *Ibid.*
11 Interview with the author.
12 Interview with the author.

ARCHITECTURE AND INTERIORS

Andreoli, Elisabetta, & Adrian Forty, *Brazil's Modern Architecture*, Phaidon, 2004
Artigas, Rosa (ed.), *Paulo Mendes da Rocha: Projects 1957-2007*, Rizzoli, 2007
Bassi, Alberto (with L. Castagno), *Giuseppe Pagano Designer*, Laterza, 1994
Bo Bardi, Lina, *Lina Bo Bardi*, Instituto Lina Bo e P. M. Bardi/Edizioni Charta, 1994
Bradbury, Dominic, & Richard Powers, *The Iconic House: Architectural Masterworks Since 1900*, Thames & Hudson, 2009
——, *The Iconic Interior: 1900 to the Present*, Thames & Hudson, 2012
Campbell-Lange, Barbara-Ann, *John Lautner*, Taschen, 2005
Carley, Rachel, *Litchfield: The Making of a New England Town*, Litchfield Historical Society, 2011
Cobbers, Arnt, *Marcel Breuer*, Taschen, 2007
Cohen, Jean-Louis, *Le Corbusier*, Taschen, 2006
Coquelle, Aline, *Palm Springs Style*, Assouline, 2005
Cygelman, Adèle, *Palm Springs Modern*, Rizzoli, 1999
De Anda Alanís, Enrique X., *Felix Candela*, Taschen, 2008
Driller, Joachim, *Breuer Houses*, Phaidon, 2000
Droste, Magdalena, *Bauhaus*, Taschen, 2011
Edwards, Brian, *Basil Spence: 1907-1976*, Rutland Press, 1995
Faber, Tobias, *New Danish Architecture*, Architectural Press, 1968
Frampton, Kenneth, & Philip Drew, *Harry Seidler: Four Decades of Architecture*, Thames & Hudson, 1992
Gagliardi, Juliana, *Móvel Brasileiro Moderno*, FGV Projetos/Aeroplano Editora, 2012
Gordon, Alastair, *Beach Houses: Andrew Geller*, Princeton Architectural Press, 2003
——, *Weekend Utopia: Modern Living in the Hamptons*, Princeton Architectural Press, 2001
Hess, Alan, *The Architecture of John Lautner*, Thames & Hudson, 1999
——, *Oscar Niemeyer Houses*, Rizzoli, 2006
Heuvel, Dirk van den, & Max Risselda (eds), *Alison & Peter Smithson: From the House of the Future to a House of Today*, 010 Publishers, 2004
Hines, Thomas S., *Richard Neutra and the Search for Modern Architecture*, Rizzoli, 2005

Jackson, Lesley, *Contemporary: Architecture & Interiors of the 1950s*, Phaidon, 1994
Jackson, Neil, *Craig Ellwood*, Laurence King, 2002
——, *Pierre Koenig*, Taschen, 2007
Johnson, Philip, & Hilary Lewis, *The Architecture of Philip Johnson*, Bulfinch, 2002
Khan, Hasan-Uddin, *International Style: Modernist Architecture from 1925 to 1965*, Taschen, 2011
Koenig, Gloria, *Albert Frey*, Taschen, 2008
Kries, Mateo, et al (eds), *Le Corbusier: The Art of Architecture*, Vitra Design Museum, 2007
Laaksonen, Esa, & Ásdis Ólafsdóttir (eds), *Alvar Aalto Architect, Volume 20: Maison Louis Carré 1956-63*, Alvar Aalto Foundation, 2008
Lahti, Louna, *Alvar Aalto*, Taschen, 2004
Lahti, Markku, *Alvar Aalto Houses*, Rakennustieto, 2005
Lamprecht, Barbara, *Richard Neutra*, Taschen, 2006
Long, Philip, & Jane Thomas (eds), *Basil Spence: Architect*, National Galleries of Scotland, 2008
Lupfer, Gilbert, & Paul Sigel, *Walter Gropius*, Taschen, 2006
McCartney, Karen, *50/60/70: Iconic Australian Houses*, Murdoch Books, 2007
McCoy, Esther, *Craig Ellwood: Architecture*, Alfieri, 1968
Massey, Anne, *Interior Design of the 20th Century*, Thames & Hudson, 1990
Merkel, Jayne, *Eero Saarinen*, Phaidon, 2005
Montaner, Josep Ma., & Maria Isabel Villac, *Mendes da Rocha*, Gustavo Gili, 1996
Niemeyer, Oscar, *The Curves of Time: The Memoirs of Oscar Niemeyer*, Phaidon, 2000
Oliveira, Olivia de, *Subtle Substances: The Architecture of Lina Bo Bardi*, Gustavo Gili, 2006
Pfeiffer, Bruce Broosk, *Frank Lloyd Wright*, Taschen, 2006
Postiglione, Gennaro, et al (eds), *One Hundred Houses for One Hundred Architects*, Taschen, 2004
Rosa, Joseph, *Louis I. Kahn*, Taschen, 2006
Serraino, Pierluigi, *Eero Saarinen*, Taschen, 2006
Sharp, Dennis, *Harry Seidler: Selected & Current Works*, Images Publishing, 1997
Smith, Elizabeth A. T., *Case Study Houses*, Taschen, 2006

Steele, James, *Eames House*, Phaidon, 2002
Vacchini, Livio, et al, *Craig Ellwood: 15 Houses*, Gustavo Gili, 1999
Vandenberg, Maritz, *Farnsworth House*, Phaidon, 2003
Webb, Michael, *Modernist Paradise*, Rizzoli, 2007
Whitney, David, & Jeffrey Kipnis (eds), *Philip Johnson: The Glass House*, Pantheon Books, 1993
Williamson, Leslie, *Handcrafted Modern*, Rizzoli, 2010
Zanco, Federica (ed.), *Luis Barragán: The Quiet Revolution*, Skira/Barragán Foundation/Vitra Design Museum, 2001
Zimmerman, Claire, *Mies van der Rohe*, Taschen, 2006

DESIGN

Aynsley, Jeremy, *Designing Modern Germany*, Reaktion Books, 2009
Breward, Christopher, & Ghislaine Wood (eds), *British Design from 1948: Innovation in the Modern Age*, V&A Publishing, 2012
Byars, Mel, *The Design Encyclopedia*, Laurence King, 2004
Dormer, Peter, *Design Since 1945*, Thames & Hudson, 1993
Eidelberg, Martin (ed.), *Design 1935-1965: What Modern Was*, Abrams/Le Musée des Arts Décoratifs de Montréal, 1991
Falino, Jeannine (ed.), *Crafting Modernism: Midcentury American Art & Design*, Abrams/Museum of Arts & Design, 2012
Fiell, Charlotte & Peter, *Design of the 20th Century*, Taschen, 1999
——, *Masterpieces of British Design*, Goodman Fiell Publishing, 2012
——, *Plastic Dreams: Synthetic Visions in Design*, Fiell Publishing, 2009
——, *Scandinavian Design*, Taschen, 2005
——, *Tools for Living: A Sourcebook of Iconic Designs for the Home*, Fiell Publishing, 2010
Godau, Marion, & Bernd Polster (eds), *Design Directory: Germany*, Pavilion, 2000
Jackson, Lesley, *The Sixties: Decade of Design Revolution*, Phaidon, 1998
Julier, Guy, *Design Since 1900*, Thames & Hudson, 1993
McDermott, Catherine, *20th Century Design*, Carlton Books, 1999
Miller, Judith, *Miller's 20th Century Design*, Miller's/Mitchell Beazley, 2009
Neumann, Claudia (ed.), *Design Directory: Italy*, Pavilion, 1999
Polster, Bernd (ed.), *Design Directory: Scandinavia*, Pavilion, 1999

—, et al, *The A-Z of Modern Design*, Merrell, 2009

Wright, Russel, *Good Design Is For Everyone*, Manitoga/Russel Wright Design Center/Universe, 2001

FURNITURE

Berry, John R., *Herman Miller: The Purpose of Design*, Rizzoli, 2009

Ferrari, Fulvio, & Napoleone, *The Furniture of Carlo Mollino*, Phaidon, 2010

Fiell, Charlotte & Peter, *1000 Chairs*, Taschen, 2005

Gura, Judith, *Design After Modernism: Furniture and Interiors, 1970–2010*, W. W. Norton, 2012

—, *Guide to Period Styles*, Harry N. Abrams, 2005

—, *Scandinavian Furniture: A Sourcebook of Classic Designs for the 21st Century*, Thames & Hudson, 2007

Jackson, Lesley, *Robin & Lucienne Day: Pioneers in Modern Design*, Mitchell Beazley, 2001

Koenig, Gloria, *Charles & Ray Eames*, Taschen, 2005

Lutz, Brian, *Knoll: A Modernist Universe*, Rizzoli, 2010

Peters, Nils, *Jean Prouvé*, Taschen, 2006

Roccella, Graziella, *Gio Ponti*, Taschen, 2009

GLASS AND CERAMICS

Birks, Tony, *Hans Coper*, William Collins & Sons, 1983

Harrod, Tanya, *The Crafts in Britain in the 20th Century*, Yale University Press, 1999

Houston, John (ed.), *Lucie Rie*, Crafts Council, 1981

Jackson, Lesley, *20th Century Factory Glass*, Mitchell Beazley, 2000

Waal, Edmund de, *20th Century Ceramics*, Thames & Hudson, 2003

—, *The Pot Book*, Phaidon, 2011

Watson, Oliver, *Studio Pottery*, Phaidon, 1993

GRAPHICS AND POSTERS

Anthony, Scott, & Oliver Green, *British Aviation Posters: Art, Design and Flight*, Lund Humphries, 2012

Bass, Jennifer, & Pat Kirkham, *Saul Bass: A Life in Art & Design*, Laurence King, 2011

Bos, Ben & Elly (eds), *Graphic Design Since 1950*, Thames & Hudson, 2007

Brook, Tony, & Adrian Shaughnessy (eds), *Wim Crouwel: A Graphic Odyssey*, Unit Editions, 2011

Eskilson, Stephen K., *Graphic Design: A History*, Laurence King, 2012

Garfield, Simon, *Just My Type*, Profile Books, 2010

Gorb, Peter (ed.), *Living by Design: Pentagram*, Lund Humphries, 1978

Heller, Steven, *Paul Rand*, Phaidon, 1999

—, & Gail Anderson, *New Modernist Type*, Thames & Hudson, 2012

—, & Véronique Vienne, *100 Ideas That Changed Graphic Design*, Laurence King, 2012

Hollis, Richard, *Graphic Design: A Concise History*, Thames & Hudson, 1994

Livingstone, Alan & Isabella, *Graphic Design & Designers*, Thames & Hudson, 1992

Oldham, Todd, *Charley Harper: An Illustrated Life*, AMMO Books, 2009

Rosner, Charles, *Air France*, Graphis, Herdeg/Amstutz, 1957 No. 71, Vol. 13

—, *Recent Air Travel Publicity*, Graphis, Herdeg/Amstutz, Vol. 9, 1953

LIGHTING

Bassi, Alberto, *Italian Lighting Design: 1945–2000*, Phaidon, 2004

Fiell, Charlotte & Peter (eds), *1000 Lights: 1879–1959*, Taschen, 2005

—, *1000 Lights: 1960–Present*, Taschen, 2005

PRODUCT AND INDUSTRIAL DESIGN

Bayley, Stephen, *Sony Design*, The Conran Foundation, 1982

Betts, Paul, *The Authority of Everyday Objects: A Cultural History of West German Industrial Design*, Berkeley, 2004

Crowley, David, & Jane Pavitt (eds), *Cold War Modern: Design 1945–1970*, V&A Publishing, 2008

Fiell, Charlotte & Peter, *Industrial Design A–Z*, Taschen, 2000

Harwood, John, 'Imagining the Computer: Eliot Noyes, the Eames and the IBM Pavilion', in, Crowley, David, & Jane Pavitt (eds), *Cold War Modern: Design 1945–1970, op. cit.*, pp. 192–97

Jatzke-Wigand, Hartmut, & Jo Klatt, 'Design+Design Zero: Wie das Braun-Design entstand', in *Independent Magazine for Design Collectors*, Hamburg, December 2011

Klatt, Jo, & Günter Staeffler, *Braun+Design Collection: 40 Jahre Braun Design 1955–1995*, Hamburg, 1995

Kries, Mateo, & Alexander von Vegesack (eds), *Joe Colombo*, Vitra Design Museum, 2005

Kunkel, Paul, *Digital Dreams: The Work of the Sony Design Center*, Universe Publishing, 1999

La Pietra, Ugo, *Gio Ponti*, Rizzoli, 2009

Neuhart, John, Marilyn Neuhart & Ray Eames, *Eames Design: The Work of the Office of Charles and Ray Eames*, Harry N. Abrams, 1989

Phaidon Design Classics: Volume Two, Phaidon, 2006

Raizman, David, *History of Modern Design*, Laurence King, 2010

Shannon, Claude, & Warren Weaver, *The Mathematical Theory of Communication*, University of Illinois, 1963

Sparke, Penny, *A Century of Car Design*, Mitchell Beazley, 2002

— (ed.), *Design Directory: Great Britain*, Pavilion, 2001

Spitz, René, *HfG Ulm: The View Behind the Foreground. The Political History of the Ulm School of Design 1953–1968*, Edition Axel Menges, 2002

Stile Olivetti: Geschichte und Formen einer italienischen Industrie, exh. cat., Museum für Kunst und Gewerbe Hamburg, 1962

Ueki-Polet, Keiko, & Klaus Klemp (eds), *Less Is More: The Design Ethos of Dieter Rams*, Gestalten, 2009

TEXTILES

Aav, Marianne (ed.), *Marimekko: Fabrics, Fashion, Architecture*, Bard Graduate Center/Yale University Press, 2003

Berthoud, Roger, *The Life of Henry Moore*, Giles de la Mare, 2003

Boydell, Christine, *Horrockses Fashions: Off-the-Peg Style in the '40s and '50s*, V&A Publishing, 2010

Breward, Christopher, & Claire Wilcox (eds), *The Ambassador Magazine: Promoting Post-War British Textiles and Fashion*, V&A Publishing, 2012

—, & Ghislaine Wood (eds), *British Design from 1948: Innovation in the Modern Age*, V&A Publishing, 2012

Brunet, Geneviève, *The Wallpaper Book*, Thames & Hudson, 2012

Buckley, Cheryl, *Designing the 'Detergent Age': Design in the 1950s and '60s*, Reaktion Books, 2007

Cumming, Elizabeth (ed.), *The Art of Modern Tapestry: Dovecot Studios Since 1912*, Lund Humphries, 2012

Evans, Paul, & Peter Doyle, *The 1940s Home*, Shire Publications, 2011

Feldman, Anita (ed), *Henry Moore Textiles*, Lund Humphries, 2008

Fogg, Marnie, *1950s Fashion Print*, Batsford, 2010

Girard, Alexander, & Todd Oldham, *Alexander Girard*, AMMO Books, 2012

Hicks, Ashley, *David Hicks: A Life of Design*, Rizzoli, 2009

Hicks, David, *Living With Design*, Weidenfeld & Nicolson, 1979

—, *Style & Design*, Viking, 1987

Ikoku, Ngozi, *The Victoria & Albert Museum's Textile Collection: British Textile Design from 1940 to the Present*, V&A Publications, 1999

Jackson, Lesley, *20th Century Pattern Design: Textile and Wallpaper Pioneers*, Mitchell Beazley, 2002

—, *Alastair Morton and Edinburgh Weavers: Visionary Textiles and Modern Art*, V&A Publishing, 2012

—, *Robin & Lucienne Day: Pioneers of Contemporary Design*, Mitchell Beazley, rev. ed. 2011

—, *Shirley Craven and Hull Traders: Revolutionary Fabrics and Furniture 1957–1980*, ACC Editions, 2009

Larsen, Jack Lenor, *Fabric for Interiors: A Guide for Architects, Designers & Consumers*, Van Nostrand Reinhold Company, 1976

Leighton, Sophie, *The 1950s Home*, Shire Publications, 2011

MacDonald, Sally, & Julia Porter, *Putting On the Style: Setting Up Home in the 1950s*, Geffrye Museum/Christie's, London, 1990

Mendes, Valerie D., *Ascher: Fabric – Art – Fashion*, V&A Publishing, 1987

Peat, Alan, *David Whitehead Ltd: Artist-Designed Textiles, 1952–1969*, Oldham Leisure Services, 1993

Prichard, Sue, 'Dodging and Weaving: The Dovecot Studios', in *Selvedge*, Issue 11, pp. 62–64

—, *V&A Pattern: The Fifties*, V&A Publishing, 2009

Rayner, Geoffrey, Richard Chamberlain & Annamarie Stapleton, *Artists' Textiles in Britain, 1945–1970*, Antique Collectors' Club, 1999

PICTURE CREDITS

All photographs are from Wright, wright20.com, unless otherwise stated. All photographs in the 'Houses and Interiors' section are © Richard Powers unless otherwise stated.

a = above; b = below; c = centre; l = left; r = right

pp. 1 Le Klint, Odense; 2 Photo Todd Oldham. © Charley Harper Art Studio; 6 © Bettmann/Corbis; 7 © PoodlesRock/Corbis; 8a Private collection/DaTo Images/Bridgeman Art Library; 9a Private collection; 9b © Bettmann/Corbis; 10bl Courtesy Modernity, Stockholm; 10br Private collection; 11 Photo Slim Aarons/Hulton Archive/Getty Images; 12-13 Victoria & Albert Museum, London; 16 Courtesy Estate of Marvin Koner; 17a Courtesy Knoll, New York; 17bl Courtesy Modernity, Stockholm; 22 Private collection; 23a, 23b, 24c, 24b, 25 Courtesy Modernity, Stockholm; 40, 41, 43al V&A Images/Alamy; 102 Courtesy Race Furniture; 103a Courtesy twentytwentyone London, www.twentytwentyone.com; 126b © Bettmann/Corbis; 140-145 Le Klint, Odense; 146, 147 Courtesy Artemide. Studio Magistretti Archive – Vico Magistretti Studio Museum Foundation; 148a, 148bl, 148br Courtesy Oluce. Studio Magistretti Archive – Vico Magistretti Studio Museum Foundation; 149a, 149ar, 149b Courtesy Artemide. Studio Magistretti Archive – Vico Magistretti Studio Museum Foundation; 166 Courtesy Iittala; 168 © H. Armstrong Roberts/ClassicStock/Corbis; 169 Courtesy Modernity, Stockholm; 172 Photo Christie's Images Limited 2014; 175ar, 175b Photo Courtesy Richard Dennis Publications; 176a Courtesy Rosenthal, Germany; 176b Dr and Mrs Yvonne Mayer. Crafts Study Centre, University for the Creative Arts, Farnham, Surrey; 177 Courtesy Portmeirion Group; 180b, 181 Crafts Study Centre, University for the Creative Arts, Farnham, Surrey; 182, 183 Courtesy Iittala; 184 Photo Bukowskis Auctions; 185a, 185bl Courtesy Iittala; 189al, 189b Courtesy Modernity, Stockholm; 203 Dr and Mrs Yvonne Mayer. Crafts Study Centre, University for the Creative Arts, Farnham, Surrey; 205a Estate of the Artist, Byron Slater Photography; 205c University of East Anglia, Norfolk/Lady Sainsbury Collection/Bridgeman Art Library. © Lucie Rie; 205b Dr and Mrs Yvonne Mayer. Crafts Study Centre, University for the Creative Arts, Farnham, Surrey; 220-21 Courtesy Steubenville, Oneida and Bauer Pottery; 224, 241a, 242-43, 245c, 245b Centre for Advanced Textiles, Glasgow; 226 Estate of David Hicks; 227al Courtesy Ascher Studio Inc., www.aschersquares.com; 227r Courtesy

Sanderson; 229l Victoria & Albert Museum, London; 229r Victoria & Albert Museum, London/Bridgeman Art Library; 230 Courtesy Svenskt Tenn, Stockholm; 231 Courtesy Sanderson; 232a, 232c, 232b Courtesy Ascher Studio Inc., www.aschersquares.com; 233l Reproduced Courtesy of Harris Museum and Art Gallery, Preston. Photo Norwyn Ltd (PRSMG: 2003.81)/Bridgeman Art Library; 233r Collection of Jill A. Wiltse and H. Kirk Brown III, Denver; 234a Courtesy David Whitehead Ltd; 234b Courtesy Heal's; 235a Courtesy Ascher Studio Inc., www.aschersquares.com; 235c Courtesy David Whitehead Ltd; 235b Design Council Slide Collection; 236-39 Courtesy Signature Prints, Sydney; 241b, 244a, 244b, 245a Collection of Jill A. Wiltse and H. Kirk Brown III, Denver; 246-49 Courtesy Svenskt Tenn, Stockholm; 250-54, 255a Girard Studio, LLC, Maharam under licence; images courtesy of Maharam; 256-61 Estate of David Hicks; 262, 263a, 264b Minneapolis Institute of Arts, MN/Gift of Cowtan & Tout, Inc./Bridgeman Art Library; 266-69 Copyright Marimekko; 270, 272a Courtesy Bang & Olufsen; 272b Photo Bernard Hoffman/Time & Life Pictures/Getty Images; 273 Courtesy Vitsœ; 275 © Charles E. Rotkin/Corbis; 276 Photo Robert Lerner. LOOK Magazine Photograph Collection, Library of Congress, Prints & Photographs Division, Washington, D. C. (LC-L901A-59-8225-2); 277a Olivetti Corporation; 277b Sony Corporation; 279 Simon Clay, Courtesy National Motor Museum, Beaulieu; 281a Courtesy Uhrenfabrik Junghans GmbH & Co. KG; 281b Braun GmbH, Kronberg; 282a Private collection; 282b © Interfoto/Alamy; 284 Piaggio Archive; 285a Private collection; 285b Piaggio Archive; 286 British Rail; 287 National Railway Museum/Science & Society Picture Library – All Rights Reserved; 288a, 288b Victoria & Albert Museum, London; 289 Kodak; 290 Haynes Publishing; 291 British Motor Industry Heritage Trust; 292a, 292b, 293 National Motor Museum, Beaulieu; 294-97 Courtesy Bang & Olufsen; 298 © PoodlesRock/Corbis; 300, 301 Private collection; 302, 303a, 303b, 304a David Mellor Design; 304bl David Mellor Design/Design Council; 304br, 305a, 305b David Mellor Design; 306 Courtesy Spazio 900, Milan www.spazio900.net; 307al Olivetti Corporation; 307ar © Marc Tielemans/Alamy; 307b © The Art Archive/Alamy; 308, 309l Copyright Braun GmbH, Kronberg; 309r © Interfoto/Alamy; 310 © nagelstock.com/Alamy; 311a Courtesy Vitsœ; 311b Copyright Braun GmbH, Kronberg; 312, 313a, 313c Brionvega; 318 © ERCO; 320 © Gary Leonard/Corbis; 321l Courtesy Ian McLaren; 321r Private collection; 321b Blue Note Records;

322 Alvin Lustig Archive (alvinlustig.org); 323 Hearst Publishers; 324 IBM; 325 Courtesy Seymour Chwast; 326 Poster collection. Museum für Gestaltung, Zürich; 327 Film sequence, United Artists; 329, 330l Photo Christie's Images Limited 2014; 330r Photo Christie's Images Limited 2014. © Estate of Abram Games; 331 Photo Christie's Images Limited 2014; 332l United Airlines; 332r Bell; 333ar Columbia/The Kobal Collection/Saul Bass; 333bl Film sequence, Columbia; 334 British Film Institute Poster; 335 Columbia/The Kobal Collection/Saul Bass; 336l, 336r Uhrenfabrik Junghans GmbH & Co. KG; 337 © ERCO; 338, 339 Photos akg-images. Copyright IOC (International Olympic Committee); 340 Courtesy Wim Crouwel. Collection Stedelijk Museum, Amsterdam; 341a Courtesy Wim Crouwel; 341b Courtesy Wim Crouwel. Collection Stedelijk Museum Amsterdam; 342 Courtesy Alan Fletcher; 343a Courtesy Alan Fletcher. Penguin Special: *The Jazz Scene*, by Francis Newton (Penguin Books, 1961). Cover reproduced with permission from Penguin Books; 343bl Courtesy Alan Fletcher. Penguin Reference books: *A Dictionary of Electronics* (Penguin Books, 1973). Cover reproduced with permission from Penguin Books; 343rb, 343rc, 344al, 344ar Courtesy Pentagram/Alan Fletcher; 344bl, 344br Courtesy Alan Fletcher; 345 Courtesy Pentagram/Alan Fletcher; 347a, 347bl, 347br, 348a, 348b Adrian Frutiger; 350 Photo The National Archives/SSPL/Getty Images; 351 Estate of Abram Games; 352l © Estate of Abram Games; 352r Estate of Abram Games; 353 IWM via Getty Images. Estate of Abram Games; 354-59 Photos Todd Oldham. © Charley Harper Art Studio; 360 Design Council Slide Collection; 361l Margaret Calvert & Jock Kinneir; 361r © NRM/Pictorial Collection/Science & Society Picture Library – All rights reserved; 362a New Haven Railroad; 362-63 Photo Felix Wiedler. Permission courtesy of Alex Matter; 363 Permission courtesy of Alex Matter; 364, 365 Courtesy Knoll, New York; 366, 367 Max Miedinger; 368a Paul Rand Archives. Yale University Library, New Haven, Connecticut; 368l IBM; 368br abc network; 369-73 Paul Rand Archives. Yale University Library, New Haven, Connecticut; 374-75 Victoria & Albert Museum, London; 381 © J. Paul Getty Trust. Used with permission. Julius Shulman Photography Archive, Research Library at the Getty Research Institute, Los Angeles (2004.R.10); 382 © The Modern House; 383b © Morley von Sternberg; 386 Photo courtesy Michael Boyd. © Scott Frances; 502-03 Victoria & Albert Museum, London; 511a © AirTeamImages.com; 512cb Courtesy Ercol; 516b Courtesy Hermann Miller, New York; 517cb Courtesy Iittala.

ACKNOWLEDGMENTS

The author would like to express his gratitude to all those who have contributed, in one way or another, to the evolution and production of this book. They include the contributing essayists, many of whom provided additional advice and assistance that was much appreciated. Sincere thanks are also due to the owners and guardians of the houses featured in this book for their support and their permission to photograph their homes.

Particular thanks are due to Richard Wright at Wright20 auction house (www.wright20.com) in Chicago, along with his colleague Jennifer Mahanay, for their assistance and support in collating many of the images of furniture, glass, ceramics and other products that appear in the book. Thanks also to those many designers, manufacturers and producers who have assisted us by supplying additional images and material.

Particular thanks are also owed to the following: Richard Powers and Danielle Miller, Gordon Wise and Richard Pike at Curtis Brown, Ashley Hicks, Martha McNaughton at Fritz Hansen, John Pardey, Carlos Junqueira at Espasso, and Faith, Florence, Cecily and Noah Bradbury.

Gratitude and appreciation are also due to Karolina Prymaka and to all at Thames & Hudson, particularly Lucas Dietrich, Adélia Sabatini, Jenny Wilson, Maria Ranauro and Paul Hammond. This book would have been an impossible task without their much-valued work and support.